SHAKESPEARE AN[
OF RICH[

Shakespeare and the Remains of Richard III explores how recollections and traces of the reign of Richard III survived a century and more to influence the world and work of William Shakespeare. In *Richard III*, Shakespeare depicts an era that had only recently passed beyond the horizon of living memory. The years between Shakespeare's birth in 1564 and the composition of the play in the early 1590s would have seen the deaths of the last witnesses to Richard's reign. Yet even after the extinction of memory, traces of the Yorkist era abounded in Elizabethan England—traces in the forms of material artefacts and buildings, popular traditions, textual records, and administrative and religious institutions and practices. Other traces had notoriously disappeared, not least the bodies of the princes reputedly murdered in the Tower, and the King's own body, which remained lost until its apparent rediscovery in the summer of 2012. *Shakespeare and the Remains of Richard III* charts the often complex careers of these pieces of the past over the course of a century framed on one side by the historical reign of Richard III (1483-85) and on the other by Shakespeare's play. Drawing on recent work in fields including archaeology, memory studies, and material biography, this book offers a fresh approach to the cultural history of the Tudor era, as well as a fundamentally new interpretation of the wellsprings and preoccupations of *Richard III*. The final emphasis is not only on what Shakespeare *does with* the traces of Richard's reign but also on what those traces *do through* Shakespeare—the play, in spite of its own pessimistic assumptions about history, has become the medium whereby certain fragments and remains of a long-lost world live on into the present day.

Shakespeare and the Remains of Richard III

PHILIP SCHWYZER

OXFORD
UNIVERSITY PRESS

OXFORD
UNIVERSITY PRESS

Great Clarendon Street, Oxford, OX2 6DP,
United Kingdom

Oxford University Press is a department of the University of Oxford.
It furthers the University's objective of excellence in research, scholarship,
and education by publishing worldwide. Oxford is a registered trade mark of
Oxford University Press in the UK and in certain other countries

First published 2013
First published in paperback 2015

Published in the United States of America by Oxford University Press
198 Madison Avenue, New York, NY 10016, United States of America

British Library Cataloguing in Publication Data
Data available

Library of Congress Cataloging in Publication Data
Data available

ISBN 978–0–19–967610–1 (Hbk.)
ISBN 978–0–19–872803–0 (Pbk.)

Links to third party websites are provided by Oxford in good faith and
for information only. Oxford disclaims any responsibility for the materials
contained in any third party website referenced in this work.

For my mother
Alison Moore Schwyzer

Acknowledgements

I must express my gratitude, first of all, for the extraordinarily dynamic and generous community of colleagues and graduate students at the University of Exeter whose encouragement and conversation have inspired me at every stage of this long project. In particular, I wish to thank Pascale Aebischer, Samir al-Jasim, Jen Barnes, Paul Bryant-Quinn, Karen Edwards, Henry French, Briony Frost, Marion Gibson, Sarah Hamilton, Johanna Harris, David Harvey, Eddie Jones, Elliot Kendall, Tim Kendall, Nick McDowell, Rachel McGregor, Gerald Maclean, Andrew McRae, Ayesha Mukherjee, Ed Paleit, Victoria Sparey, Jane Whittle, Nicola Whyte, Margaret Yoon, and Zhiyan Zhang. I am no less grateful for the support and guidance I have received from colleagues in Britain and the United States, including Stephen Greenblatt, Steven Gunn, Andrew Hadfield, Tom Healy, John Kerrigan, Jeffrey Knapp, Paulina Kewes, Willy Maley, Stewart Mottram, Ethan Shagan, Alex Walsham, and Richard Wilson. For advice on archaeological matters I am particularly grateful to Howard Williams and Estella Weiss-Krejci. My guide to many aspects of Ricardian lore has been John Ashdown-Hill. In the last months of writing I received a wonderful intellectual boost from a workshop on periodization and multitemporality at Freie Universität Berlin, where the participants included Anke Bernau, Andrew Johnston, David Matthews, Cathy Shrank, and Greg Walker.

Much of the research for this project was enabled by a generous Research Fellowship from the Leverhulme Trust, as well as by two periods of study leave granted by the University of Exeter. I owe a debt of thanks to both of these institutions. I am additionally grateful to the librarians, archivists, and keepers of collections at a range of institutions and organizations, including the Society of Antiquaries, the College of Arms, the Richard III Society, and the Worshipful Company of Wax Chandlers.

A version of Chapter 2 has been previously published as "Lees and Moonshine: Remembering Richard III, 1485–1635," *Renaissance Quarterly* 63 (2010). A version of Chapter 3 has been previously published as "Trophies, Traces, Relics and Props: The Untimely Objects of *Richard III*," *Shakespeare Quarterly* 63 (2012). I am grateful to both journals for permission to republish these pieces in different form here.

This book is dedicated to my mother, Alison Schwyzer, who has never yet turned down a conversation about Richard III.

No words are sufficient to acknowledge my debt to Naomi Howell. Every page bears the mark of our conversations and of her inspiration. This book is truly hers as much as mine.

Contents

List of Illustrations

Reference Notes

Except where noted, all references to Shakespeare's plays and poems are to *The Norton Shakespeare*, ed. Stephen Greenblatt, Walter Cohen, Jean E. Howard, and Katherine Eisaman Maus, second edition (New York: W. W. Norton, 2008). References to Q and F are to the first Quarto (1597) and first Folio (1623) texts of *Richard III*. In all original-spelling quotations, u/v and i/j have been modernized.

The following abbreviations are used in the footnotes:

Andre, *Historia*	Bernard Andre, *Historia regis Henrici septimi*, in *Memorials of King Henry the Seventh*, ed. J. Gairdner (London: Rolls Series, 1858)
Fabyan	Robert Fabyan, *The New Chronicles of England and France* (London, 1516)
GCL	*The Great Chronicle of London*, ed. A. H. Thomas and I. D. Thornley (London: George Thomas, 1938)
Hall	Edward Hall, *The Union of the Two Noble and Illustre Fameles of Lancastre & Yorke* (London, 1548)
Hanham, *Richard III*	Alison Hanham, *Richard III and His Early Historians, 1483–1535* (Oxford: Clarendon Press, 1975)
Holinshed	Raphael Holinshed, *Chronicles*, 3 volumes (London, 1587)
Mancini, *Usurpation*	Dominic Mancini, *The Usurpation of Richard III*, trans. C. A. J. Armstrong (Oxford: Clarendon Press, 1969)
More, *History*	Thomas More, *The History of King Richard III,* ed. R. S. Sylvester, Volume 2 of *The Complete Works of St. Thomas More* (New Haven, CT: Yale University Press, 1963)
Stow, *Survey*	John Stow, *A Survey of London: Reprinted from the Text of 1603,* ed. C. L. Kingsford (Oxford: Clarendon Press, 2000)
Vergil, *Three Books*	Polydore Vergil, *Three Books of Polydore Vergil's English History, comprising the reigns of Henry VI, Edward IV, and Richard III,* ed. Sir Henry Ellis (London: Camden Society, 1844)

Introduction

On a summer morning late in the fifteenth century, a battle was fought in a marshy field in Leicestershire, not far from the town of Market Bosworth. By the early afternoon more than 1,000 men lay dead upon the plain, including the King of England, whose naked and broken body was strapped to a horse's rump and borne in triumph into Leicester. It was the end of the two-year reign of Richard III—the end, too, of a quarter century of Yorkist dominance, and of more than three centuries in which England had been ruled by scions of the House of Plantagenet. Bosworth Field signalled not only the fall of one dynastic regime and the rise of another, but (later observers would insist) the end of an age of civil war and the dawn of an era of peace and prosperity. It even marked (still later writers would attest) the end of the Middle Ages and the dawn of the English Renaissance. A lot of things ended, or were supposed to have ended, with the life of Richard III.

From the afternoon of 22 August 1485 the England of Richard III was a lost world, accessible only in the traces of itself it had contrived to preserve or accidentally left behind. To begin with, of course, these traces were largely continuous with the material and cultural environment inhabited by Henry VII and his subjects. Well into what we have learned to call the Tudor period, most of the buildings people lived in, most of the clothes they wore, and most of the books they read either dated from Richard's reign or had passed through it. Although Henry's first Parliament made a point of abrogating all of Richard's acts, foundations, and charters, in practice many of the institutions he created or fostered survived and continued to evolve. More importantly for most English men and women, the fundamental patterns of religious worship and communal life had barely altered at all. Personal memories of the preceding era remained plentiful and vivid, even if relatively few people were willing or able to record their recollections in ways that have come down to us. From an early Tudor perspective there was little reason to regard the immediate past as a foreign country.

As time went by, the surviving traces of the reign of Richard III became an identifiable and ever-dwindling assemblage. Swords and spoons bent or succumbed to rust, garments wore through or fell irretrievably out of fashion. People died. By the midpoint of the sixteenth century, almost every man and woman capable of remembering the era before Bosworth had gone, though in some cases—we cannot tell how many—they transmitted

Fig. I.1. Portrait of Richard III, early sixteenth century. By permission of the Society of Antiquaries of London.

their recollections to children or grandchildren. The continual, gradual attrition of memories, objects, and practices associated with the world of Richard III was punctuated by a few grand extinctions, the greatest of which came as a consequence of the English Reformation. As a cultural revolution that affected almost every aspect of English life, from formal and informal rites of remembrance to the status of a variety of objects, the Reformation inevitably put an end to many vestiges of an era already fifty years in the past. Nonetheless, even a hundred years after the death of Richard III the physical and cultural landscape was still littered with traces of his world—traces in the form of inherited memories and household articles, established institutions and popular practices, texts, and tombs. These traces formed part of the environment into which William Shakespeare was born and in which he lived and wrote.

Shakespeare was an Elizabethan through and through—one of a generation who came of age towards the end of the sixteenth century without ever having known another monarch, let alone another religious or dynastic order. We are habituated to imagining Shakespeare against an Elizabethan (or Jacobean) background, and studies which seek to set his work in historical context (the dominant movement in Shakespeare criticism for the past thirty years) almost invariably read his plays alongside other texts, artworks, objects, or events produced in the same era. Illustrated editions of Shakespeare's collected works and museum exhibitions based on his career centre heavily on portraits, books, and artefacts created in the reigns of Elizabeth and James. Some of these images have now attained iconic status, partly through their association with Shakespeare (though the playwright himself may never have laid eyes on them).[1] Too often, we succumb to the assumption that the material and visual world inhabited by the playwright was composed mainly of objects and images dating from his own lifetime. Yet a moment's thought should be sufficient to expose this assumption as patently false. Even today, when the increase in the average human life-span has been matched by a decline in the use-life of many objects, few of us inhabit such a relentlessly contemporary world as the one we imagine for Shakespeare. The stuff of Elizabethan life was not made up exclusively, or even primarily, of Elizabethan stuff.

Shakespeare lived and wrote in a world shot through with shards of the late-medieval, pre-Tudor past. What does this mean for his plays, and what, in particular, does it mean for *Richard III*? When we talk about the "sources" of Shakespeare's history plays, we are generally talking about texts, and in particular about the great sixteenth-century chronicles of Holinshed and Hall. There is no doubt that Shakespeare did rely upon the chronicles in writing *Richard III*, possibly to an even greater degree than in others of his history plays. Yet however crucial their influence and

---

[1] The recent British Museum exhibition "Shakespeare: Staging the World" (July–November 2012) is a case in point. From Wenceslaus Hollar's panorama of London (1647) to the "Sieve Portrait" of Queen Elizabeth (1583), and Isaac Oliver's portrait of Edward Herbert as a melancholy lover (*c*.1613–14), the exhibition succeeded in gathering under one roof a remarkable number of images and objects familiar to students of Shakespeare (and especially users of collected works such as the *Norton* or the *Riverside*) as illustrations of his world. Yet the large majority of the items on display were manufactured, painted, or printed in or after the lifetime of the playwright. The exhibition also featured some objects associated with medieval monarchs such as Henry V and Richard III (including the Chiddingly Boar and the Bosworth Crucifix, both pictured in this book), as well as a sampling of Catholic church plate, yet the implicit presentation of these things as relics of a lost world only enhanced the impression that objects and images made before the Reformation formed a vanishingly small part of Shakespeare's environment. See the exhibition catalogue: Jonathan Bate and Dora Thornton, *Shakespeare: Staging the World* (London: British Museum Press, 2012).

importance, textual histories were not the only cultural technology capable
of bridging the gulf between the 1480s and the early 1590s.[2] The sources
available to the playwright also included popular songs and sayings, major
buildings, minor heirlooms, and even ways of navigating the streets of
the Bishopsgate neighbourhood where Shakespeare and Richard of
Gloucester lived side by side (in space if not in time). The marks left on the
dramatic text by this wider panoply of sources are not always accessible to
modern scholarship (we cannot, by definition, demonstrate Shakespeare's
reliance on an otherwise unrecorded oral tradition). Yet even beyond those
passages which can be shown to incorporate a specific object, phrase, or
bodily practice passed down from the late fifteenth century, the multiple
points of contact between Richard's world and Shakespeare's are registered
in *Richard III*'s dense and tangled temporality. This is a play that from the
beginning—indeed, from its opening word—pulls the rug from under the
ordinary distinction between "then" and "now."

The relationship between Shakespeare's play and the historical Richard III has been explored in various ways before. Both the
late-fifteenth-century monarch and the late-sixteenth-century dramatic
text are objects of intense and enduring fascination, and it has long
been all but impossible to think of one without thinking of the other.
Yet the story has generally been told from a perspective that implicitly
casts either the king or the playwright as protagonist. On the one hand,
there are historical studies demonstrating how Shakespeare colluded
(wittingly or unwittingly) in the Tudor demonization of a not-ungift-
ed fifteenth-century monarch.[3] On the other, there are literary studies
demonstrating how Shakespeare transformed the dense and often drab
material of chronicle into powerful drama.[4] Looking at the period from
one perspective or the other, it is difficult to avoid couching the evidence
within a wider narrative of redemption or decline. (The English Reformation, which falls almost precisely midway between the monarch and
the play, can give powerful encouragement to either of these storylines.)

This is not a book about Richard III; it offers no new interpretation of his reign, and adopts no position on such vexed questions as his

[2] *Richard III* was probably written at some point in 1592, though if the play was not
ready for performance before plague closed the public theatres in June of that year, it would
not have been performed in London before 1593. See James Siemon's discussion of the date
in Shakespeare, *King Richard III*, ed. Siemon (London: Methuen, 2009), 44–51.

[3] On the depiction of Richard III in Tudor histories, see Hanham, *Richard III*. On
Shakespeare's perpetuation of the "black legend," see David Hipshon, *Richard III* (London:
Routledge, 2011), 208–17; Paul Murray Kendall, *Richard the Third* (New York: W. W.
Norton, 1996), 496–506.

[4] Dominique Goy-Blanquet, *Shakespeare's Early History Plays: From Chronicle to Stage*
(Oxford: Oxford University Press, 2003).

involvement in the disappearance of the Princes in the Tower. Nor is it—though it contains a good deal of attention to the Shakespearean text—a book about *Richard III*. It is a book about everything in between. Its chief protagonists are the left-over remnants and traces of the years 1483–85 that made the journey into the sixteenth century, though not always to its end. In examining the fate of these objects and traditions, I am less concerned with what they can tell us about either the monarch or the dramatist than with their shifting fortunes and significance in specific historical and cultural moments. In the chapters that follow, my chief aim has been to observe how the present turns into the past (generally at nothing resembling a steady rate), and to explore how the past negotiates a place for itself in the present. Ultimately, this book aspires to make us think more deeply about what it means to set and see a work of art within its historical context.

Shakespeare and the Remains of Richard III emerges from and aims to contribute to a number of relatively recent conversations that have, in different ways, challenged long-established boundaries imposed by academic disciplines and conventional historical periods. Recent scholarship has grown increasingly impatient with the artificial (though not entirely arbitrary) division between late medieval and early modern literatures and histories—a division that has too often impeded recognition of the manifest continuities between the culture and politics of the late fifteenth century and those of the sixteenth.[5] A related development in English studies has been an increased attention to Shakespeare's engagements with the medieval, both as the historical other and as an aspect of his own world.[6] A more radical alternative to periodization is found in some recent books that challenge the basic tendency to read cultural artefacts in light of their moment of origin, arguing instead for an untimely, multitemporal,

---

[5] James Simpson, *Reform and Cultural Revolution: 1350–1547* (Oxford: Oxford University Press, 2004); Gordon McMullan and David Matthews (eds.), *Reading the Medieval in Early Modern England* (Cambridge: Cambridge University Press, 2007); Jennifer Summit and David Wallace (eds.), *Medieval/Renaissance: After Periodization* (Special Issue), *Journal of Medieval and Early Modern Studies* 37.3 (2007). C. S. L. Davies has recently argued against the longstanding habit of hailing 1485 as a decisive break, proposing that for most of the sixteenth century English subjects had little sense of living in a "Tudor era" distinct from the preceding period; see Davies, "Tudor: What's in a Name?" *History* 97 (2012), 24–42. For a broader critique of periodization, see Kathleen Davies, *Periodization and Sovereignty: How Ideas of Feudalism and Secularization Govern the Politics of Time* (Philadelphia: University of Pennsylvania Press, 2008).

[6] Helen Cooper, *Shakespeare and the Medieval World* (London: Methuen Drama, 2010); Curtis Perry and John Watkins (eds.), *Shakespeare and the Middle Ages* (Oxford: Oxford University Press, 2009); Sarah Beckwith and James Simpson (eds.), *Premodern Shakespeare* (Special Issue), *Journal of Medieval and Early Modern Studies* 40.1 (2010).

or anachronic understanding of the artwork or the text.[7] Finally, my work aims to enter into dialogue with a number of excellent studies of Shakespeare's *Richard III* which have explored the play's deeply self-conscious relation to the historical past.[8]

The question remains: why Richard III? Why not Richard II, Henry V, or indeed King John? Colleagues and friends with whom I have discussed my research have sometimes assumed that I wrote with the aim of absolving Richard from the calumnies that Shakespeare—and a host of other Tudor writers—had foisted upon him. In fact, my reasons for focusing on the afterlife of the period 1483–85 are more pragmatic. Firstly, the period lies on the very threshold of the Tudor era. Secondly, it is very brief (Richard reigned for a shorter time than any crowned English monarch since 1066). The combination of these factors allows for the theoretical possibility of identifying a significant proportion of the surviving or recorded traces of this period and of charting their fortunes across the subsequent century. To undertake a comparable survey with respect to King John, who ruled for almost twenty years and died three and half centuries before Shakespeare was born, would be a task of inconceivable complexity. To do it with the remains of Richard III may still be impossible, but it is at least conceivable. In the cases of some kinds of trace (for example, institutions which received their charters from Richard III, or bodies of Plantagenets who died between 1483 and 1485), I have been able to undertake a fairly complete survey. In the case of others (such as family traditions and domestic objects associated with Richard III), I have been able to identify and explore only a small proportion of those which must once have existed, yet I believe my samplings are reasonably representative of the surviving evidence.

The five core chapters of this book explore the afterlives of different kinds of objects or phenomena across the period between Richard's death and Shakespeare's play (and, in most cases, a little way beyond). Chapter 1 is concerned with remains of the most literal sort, examining the shifting meanings and traditions associated with the bodies of Richard III and his nephews. In different ways, I argue, these missing bodies took on an

[7] Jonathan Gil Harris, *Untimely Matter in the Time of Shakespeare* (Philadelphia: University of Pennsylvania Press, 2008); Alexander Nagel and Christopher S. Wood, *Anachronic Renaissance* (New York: Zone Books, 2010).

[8] See, especially, Brian Walsh, *Shakespeare, the Queen's Men, and the Elizabethan Performance of History* (Cambridge: Cambridge University Press, 2009); Stephen Marche, "Mocking Dead Bones: Historical Memory and the Theater of the Dead in Richard III," *Comparative Drama* 37 (2003), 37–57; Linda Charnes, *Notorious Identity: Materializing the Subject in Shakespeare* (Cambridge, MA: Harvard University Press, 1993). These studies have tended to emphasize the specifically theatrical/performative nature of the play's engagement with the past—a perception I would not contest, though it is less central to my arguments in this book.

enhanced significance after the Reformation, as they became bound up with a nation's struggles to strike a new bargain with its dead. Chapter 2 deals with memories of Richard III and his reign, charting the transmission of memory from one generation to the other and the persistent split between memorial and historical discourses, which endured long after the death of anyone with personal recollections of the fifteenth century. Chapter 3 turns back to the material world of domestic articles and personal possessions, exploring the survival and sometimes the destruction of objects associated with Richard III (including his bed, his dagger, and his prayer book), culminating with their re-emergence as symbolically charged theatrical properties in Shakespeare's play. In Chapter 4 the focus is on sixteenth-century institutions and practices marked in one way or another by Richard's reign. The range of traces explored here is particularly broad, encompassing established institutions like the College of Arms, the built environment of sixteenth-century London, and the uncodified practices of everyday life. Chapter 5 turns to the representation of Richard and his contemporaries in poems, songs, and plays, from the strikingly reticent and gnomic verses composed shortly after Bosworth to the veritable flood of poetic laments and historical tragedies that characterized the Elizabethan era. The concluding chapter, "Now," focuses on *Richard III*, arguing that the play's extraordinary temporal effects are the product of Shakespeare's imaginative and practical engagement with the traces of Richard's reign surviving in his world.

The attentive reader will note an obvious omission from this catalogue of traces: that of the various Tudor histories and chronicles dealing with Richard III. Historical writers such as John Rous, Bernard Andre, Robert Fabyan, Polydore Vergil, Edward Hall, and, above all, Thomas More make frequent appearances in the pages that follow, but I make no attempt to assess their works on their own terms, nor to map out the complex relationship between their histories. Fortunately, this aspect of Richard's posthumous legacy has been well-explored over the years by a range of scholars, especially as regards the sources, composition, and subsequent influence of More's *History of Richard III*.[9] In keeping with this book's studied agnosticism regarding the "real" Richard III, I have avoided passing judgement

---

[9] Hanham, *Richard III*; Hanham, "Honing a History: Thomas More's Revisions of his *Richard III*," *Review of English Studies* 59 (2008), 197–218; David Womersley, *Divinity and State* (Oxford: Oxford University Press, 2010), 40–56; Daniel Kinney, "The Tyrant Being Slain: Afterlives of More's *History of King Richard III*," in *English Renaissance Prose: History, Language and Politics*, ed. Neil Rhodes (Tempe, AZ: Medieval & Renaissance Texts & Studies, 1997), 35–56; Elizabeth Story Donno, "Thomas More and Richard III," *Renaissance Quarterly* 35 (1982), 401–47; A. R. Myers, "Richard III and the Historical Tradition." *History* 53 (1968), 181–202; George Bosworth Churchill, *Richard III up to Shakespeare* (Berlin: Mayer and Muller, 1900).

on the reliability or motives of one historian or another. My focus is rather on the way they tell their stories and the kinds of evidence they employ (or wish to be seen to employ). Where there are points of controversy regarding the relationship between texts, the discussion or the footnotes will generally make my position clear.

One matter relating to the chronicle tradition should be clarified in this Introduction, as it affects my citational practices throughout the book. The English text of More's *History of Richard III* (*c.*1515) exists in two distinct versions: one printed by Richard Grafton in his editions of the chronicles of John Hardyng (1543) and Edward Hall (1548), and one printed by William Rastell in 1557. (There are also multiple versions of the parallel Latin text.) Although it has been suggested that the Hardyng/Hall version of the *History* represents More's final draft, David Womersley has argued convincingly that this version incorporates Grafton's post-Reformation emendations (with consequences I consider further in Chapters 1 and 5).[10] Therefore, where I am concerned with what More wrote, I quote from R. S. Sylvester's Yale edition of the *History*, which follows Rastell. Where I am concerned with what Shakespeare read, or with how More's work was adapted to suit a post-Reformation providentialist perspective, I quote from Hall.

From the start, I knew that it would take me a good deal longer to finish this book than it took Shakespeare to finish *Richard III*. In the event, the writing of it has lasted twice as long as the historical Richard's reign. Over that period of time, the past has disconcertingly failed to stand still. When I began my research in 2007, key questions surrounding the end of Richard's life and reign remained shrouded in doubt and mystery. The location of the "Bosworth" battlefield was disputed between several locales, most of them lying within a few miles of Ambion Hill. The fate of Richard's own body was unknown, as it had been since the dissolution of the Greyfriars Priory in the 1530s, giving rise to a remarkable variety of traditions and conjectures (detailed in Chapter 1). Yet even as I began work, the Bosworth Battlefield Survey was underway, leading in 2009–10 to the probable identification of the field, including the boggy patch known as Fenn Hole, where the King himself is likely to have fallen.[11] Amongst the revelations of the survey was the remarkable amount of heavy shot found on the field. A battle traditionally associated with the last charge of English chivalry turned out to have heralded the rise of a

---

[10] See Hanham, "Honing a History"; Womersley, *Divinity and State*, 40–56.
[11] Glenn Foard and Anne Curry, *Bosworth 1485: A Battlefield Rediscovered* (Oxford: Oxbow Books, 2013).

new mode of warfare. (Here we might speak of the past being shot through with fragments of the future.)

In September 2012, archaeologists made a still more surprising discovery beneath a car park in Leicester. From a roughly cut grave in what had been the choir of the dissolved Greyfriars Priory emerged a skeleton with a pronounced spinal curvature and evidence of massive trauma to the skull. At a press conference in February 2013, a team of archaeologists, geneticists, and historians confirmed what had been suspected from the first, that the remains were indeed those of Richard III. Few archaeological discoveries since the days of Schliemann have garnered such extraordinary international attention. The old debate over Richard's true character and possible crimes has been revived with unprecedented vigour; there has been much public discussion, and some parliamentary wrangling over how and where the body should be reinterred, with Leicester Cathedral, York Minster, and Westminster Abbey the leading candidates. Some enthusiasts have called for a burial with full royal honours, whilst others have questioned whether an Anglican funeral service would be appropriate for a king who lived and died a Catholic.[12] The discussions have mostly been conducted with good humour, yet their implications and potential consequences extend well beyond the final resting place of a single skeleton. Not for the first time, Richard III has thrust his way into debates over the shape and meaning of national history, the legitimacy and future of the English monarchy, and the longstanding divisions between north and south. It might seem absurd to attribute any kind of contemporary agency to these unhappy bones, whose condition bears stark witness to a final and fatal defeat. Yet they illustrate a phenomenon that is far from unusual. The time we call the present harbours active remnants of many prior eras, including the late medieval world of Richard III. If these remnants generally fail to provoke the same wonder and excitement as the Greyfriars skeleton, that is only because they have never been out of view. Such pieces of the past define our temporality as much as they disrupt it. Richard III has not ceased to be our contemporary.

---

[12] The initial results of the Greyfriars excavation, led by Richard Buckley, were made public at a press conference at the University of Leicester on 12 September 2012. An illuminating review of the ensuing coverage and debates is Anthony Faiola, "Unverified remains dig up twisted legacy of Richard III," *Washington Post*, 24 November 2012, 1. The results of carbon dating, osteo-archaeological analysis, and DNA testing, leading to the conclusion that the remains were beyond reasonable doubt those of Richard III, were announced in a press conference at the University of Leicester on 4 February 2013. At that time, the decision that his body should be reinterred at Leicester Cathedral was also confirmed.

1

"Where is Plantagenet?"

"Where is Bohun? Where is Mowbray? Where is Mortimer? Nay, which is more, and most of all, where is Plantagenet? They are entombed in the urns and sepulchres of mortality."[1]

Chief Justice Ranulph Crewe, 1625

King Henry VI died in the Tower of London on the night of 21 May 1471, a little more than a fortnight after Edward IV's decisive victory at Tewkesbury. Although a contemporary Yorkist account claimed that Henry died "of pure displeasure, and melencoly" following the death of his son and the defeat of his cause, few have ever doubted that his end was a violent one.[2] One chronicler writing near the end of Edward's reign states guardedly that Richard Duke of Gloucester was present at the Tower with "many other" at the time of Henry's death; later writers, less reticent, would assert that Richard personally slew him with a dagger.[3] The royal corpse was displayed on the following day at St Paul's, and a day later at Blackfriars priory. In both places it is said to have bled afresh, an inescapable indication of the king's violent end. From Blackfriars the king was conveyed up river for burial at Chertsey Abbey, which soon became a site of pilgrimage as the cult of the saintly king grew rapidly in popularity. Then, in 1484, Richard III made the surprising decision to have Henry's body exhumed and translated to Windsor, there to be reinterred alongside his arch-rival, Edward IV. According to John Rous, the king's body was largely uncorrupted, though the face appeared sunken, and the "holy body was very

---

[1] Quoted in John Campbell, *The Lives of the Chief Justices of England* (London: John Murray, 1849), 1:374.

[2] *Historie of the Arrivall of Edward IV*, ed. John Bruce (London: Camden Society, 1838), 38.

[3] John Warkworth, *A Chronicle of the First Thirteen Years of the Reign of King Edward the Fourth* (London: Camden Society, 1839), 21. The attribution of authorship to Warkworth is considered uncertain. The *Great Chronicle of London* and Fabyan's chronicle are the first English histories to blame Richard for actually committing the murder. Philippe de Commynes makes the same accusation in his *Memoires*. The dagger itself became a relic in the cult of Henry VI; see Chapter 3.

pleasantly scented, and certainly not from spices, since he was buried by his enemies and butchers."[4] Whatever remained of Henry VI—probably rather less than Rous wished to believe—was taken to pieces for burial at Windsor. Excavation of Henry's unmarked grave in 1911 revealed a small wooden box containing "a decayed mass of human bones, lying in no definite order."[5] Missing were the bones of the right arm, but in their place was found the humerus of a small pig—the mark, perhaps, of the Boar?

"Enter the corpse of Henry VI. . ." (1.2.0). Beginning with this stage direction, the second scene of *Richard III* incorporates various elements of Henry VI's weird posthumous history, but—like the bones in the chest—in no definite order. It would be impossible to specify just when the action is supposed to be taking place. The widowed Anne declares that she is escorting the body of her father-in-law from St Paul's to Chertsey, which would seem to point very precisely to 23 May 1471, whilst Richard's reference to the battle of Tewkesbury "some three months since" (1.2.227) would indicate the late summer of the same year; yet the scene takes place in the context of Clarence's imprisonment in the Tower (1477) and the worsening health of Edward IV (who fell ill just ten days before his death in 1483). Anne pointedly laments Henry's "untimely fall" (1.2.4), and indeed his body is the piece of untimely matter around which the scene's discrepant chronologies seem to cluster.[6] "Poor key-cold figure of a holy king,/Pale ashes of the house of Lancaster,/Thou bloodless remnant of that royal blood" (1.2.5–8): Anne's words to the corpse figure it variously as a stone effigy, a cremated remnant, and a desiccated husk, thereby highlighting its extreme existential and apparently temporal distance from the living Henry. Yet in Richard's presence blood flows from those "cold and empty veins where no blood dwells" (1.2.59). The miracle which in Shakespeare's sources testifies in a general way to violent death here becomes the means of identifying the specific murderer. In a far stronger sense than the chronicle accounts of Hall or Holinshed would suggest, the bleeding of the corpse serves as a reference to—even a re-enactment

---

[4] *Historia Johannis Rossi Warwicensis de Regibus Anglie*, translated in Hanham, *Richard III*, 123.

[5] W. H. St John Hope, "The discovery of the remains of King Henry VI in St George's chapel, Windsor Castle," *Archaeologia* 62 (1910/11): 535. The bones lay in a decayed wooden box within a leaden chest within the disintegrated remains of a wooden coffin; it was concluded the corpse had been dismembered for placement in the box, following exhumation from an earthen burial.

[6] I take the phrase from Jonathan Gil Harris, *Untimely Matter in the Time of Shakespeare* (Philadelphia: University of Pennsylvania Press, 2009). See also Anthony Purdy's discussion of how the uncorrupted corpse can function as a "mnemotope" with the "power to abolish temporal distance, to make the past present"; Purdy, "The Bog Body as Mnemotope: Nationalist Archaeologies in Heaney and Tournier," *Style* 36 (2002): 93–110.

of—the moment and manner of Henry's death in the Tower. Yet in spite of the active resistance of the corpse, Richard succeeds not only in wooing Anne, but in taking charge of the body.

As he bids farewell to Anne, the supposedly penitent Gloucester promises to see the king's body "solemnly interred/at Chertsey monast'ry" and to "wet his grave with my repentant tears" (1.2.201–3). As soon as Anne is gone, however, he alters both his tone and his itinerary.

> RICHARD: Sirs, take up the corpse.
> SERVANT: Towards Chertsey, noble lord?
> RICHARD: No, to Whitefriars. There attend my coming. (1.2.211–12)[7]

The redirection of Henry's corpse to Whitefriars—presumably the Carmelite abbey in the Fleet—is Shakespeare's innovation. What he knew from Holinshed's *Chronicles* was that the body of the king was carried from St Paul's "to the Blackfriers, and bled there likewise: and on the next daie after, it was conveied in a boat, without priest or clerke, torch or taper, singing or saieng, unto the monasterie of Chertseie . . . "[8] Shakespeare's reworking of this material involved not only the substitution of Whitefriars for Blackfriars, but the alteration of a stop en route into an alternative destination. Richard is quite clearly redirecting the corpse, not simply explicating its route. Though the motive for the redirection is unclear (remaining so even if, as in some editions, "white friers" is emended to Blackfriars), Richard conveys the sense that he has pulled off a notable coup.[9] "No, to Whitefriars." In performance the half-line may be delivered distractedly or with deliberate sarcasm, even with a triumphant cackle, creating a moment of no little mystery and considerable dramatic force.

The brief passage in which the body of the king is redirected to Whitefriars telescopes a complex and protracted set of negotiations, lasting over almost fifteen years, between the living Richard and the dead Henry VI.

---

[7] Although *Oxford Shakespeare* and *Norton Shakespeare* emend the place-name to Blackfriars, both Q and F have "Whitefriars" here.

[8] Holinshed, 690.

[9] Critics and editors have offered a range of explanations for the redirection of the corpse. Janis Lull suggests that "The detail here, apparently invented by Shakespeare, shows Richard's peremptory habits. He contradicts, evidently just for the sake of contradiction, what he told Anne he would do"; William Shakespeare, *Richard III*, ed. Janis Lull (Cambridge: Cambridge University Press, 1999), 70. For Alexander Leggatt, the obscurity of motivation is the point: "we wonder what he is up to and we may entertain dark suspicions. But . . . we never know"; Leggatt, *Shakespeare's Political Drama: The History Plays and the Roman Plays* (London: Routledge, 1988), 35–6. In Stephen Marche's view, the motive for the redirection "is immaterial to the story and never explained . . . the point is that Richard, through his theatrics, has managed to wrest control over the corpse. By shaping the story, he has literally altered the resting place of the dead"; Marche, "Mocking Dead Bones: Historical Memory and the Theater of the Dead in *Richard III*," *Comparative Drama* 37 (2003): 42.

In particular, the scene collapses two distinct historical moments in which Richard sought to assert direct authority over the body of the dead king. The first of these is the king's murder in the Tower on 21 May 1471—a moment which Henry's body relives (or redies?) through its bleeding in Richard's presence. The second is that in which the body of the king was directed away from Chertsey (where it had rested for thirteen years) to a new destination (not Whitefriars but Windsor). At both of these key moments—and at points between them—the relationship between Richard and the dead king's body is charged with mystery and ambiguity. Did Richard wield the dagger in person? What exactly did Henry's posthumous bleeding signify? Out of what combination of motives did Richard as king have Henry's body moved—to control Henry's posthumous cult, to profit from it, to seek absolution, or even to claim Henry as an alternative ancestor (as Henry V had done with his reinterment of Richard II at Westminster Abbey)?[10] Did the burial of Henry beside the man who almost certainly ordered his death suggest a posthumous, subterranean union of the red rose with the white? What can be deduced from the removal of the dead king's right arm—smuggled away by a relic-hunter, or hewn off like the limb of a traitor? And how did a pig's leg become mixed with the remains?[11]

[10] In translating the body of his predecessor, Richard has been described as "courting popularity and perhaps absolution"; Thomas S. Freeman, "'Ut Verus Christi Sequester': John Blacman and the Cult of Henry VI," in *The Fifteenth Century V: "Of Mice and Men": Image, Belief and Regulation in Late Medieval England*, ed. Linda Clark (Woodbridge: Boydell Press, 2005), 129. As Estella Weiss-Krejci observes in relation to Habsburg and Babenberg burials of the medieval and post-medieval eras, "bodies of murdered, executed and excommunicated individuals have been used by survivors for political purposes and therefore were exhumed and reburied in pompous ceremonies." "Unusual Life, Unusual Death and the Fate of the Corpse: A Case Study from Dynastic Europe," in *Deviant Burial in the Archaeological Record*, ed. Eileen M. Murphy (Oxford: Oxbow Books, 2008), 186.

[11] Given that Henry VI apparently had an earthen burial at Chertsey, bones other than his own may have been gathered up accidentally with his at the point of translation. This would make it a similar case to the Babenberg burials at Melk, where a sarcophagus containing the remains of fifteen members of the dynasty was found also to hold the humeri of wild and domestic pigs, along with other animal bones. See Friederike Spitzenberger, "Die Tierknochen aus der Babenbergergruft der Melker Stiftskirche," *Annalen des Naturhistorischen Museums Wien* 78 (1974): 481–3. (I am grateful to Estella Weiss-Krejci for this reference.) Yet it is quite possible that the pig bone was added intentionally, either as an insult, or as a substitute for the arm stolen as a relic. Though an informed eye would presumably not mistake the humerus of a small pig for a human bone, Chaucer's Pardoner is said to practice just this sort of deceit: "He hadde a croys of latoun ful of stones,/And in a glas he hadde pigges bones./But with thise relikes . . ."; *Riverside Chaucer*, ed. L. D. Benson, (Oxford: Oxford University Press, 1988), General Prologue, 699–701. In 1536 Hugh Latimer preached a sermon denouncing the worship of "pig's bones" as holy relics. Peter Marshall, "Forgery and Miracles in the Reign of Henry VIII," *Past and Present* 178 (2003), 52.

From Henry's death in 1471 to Richard's death in 1485, the two men were engaged in a kind of dance (a genuine *danse macabre*) in which the dead body was much more than a puppet in the living man's arms. If it is true that Richard mostly led the dance, determining where the cadaver went and how it was treated, Henry's body retained and arguably enhanced its own agency, through its tell-tale bleeding, its signifying, and its power to attract worshipers. Twice in Richard's reign, those who vowed pilgrimages to Henry's shrine were cured of scrofula—a saintly miracle which was also an assertion of continuing regal authority on Henry's part, since scrofula, or the King's Evil, was traditionally healed by the touch of the rightful king.[12]

Richard's long negotiations with the remains of Henry VI, and Shakespeare's drastically abbreviated depiction of their relationship, bear witness to a world in which bodies have agency. In the play, and perhaps above all in this scene, Shakespeare's Richard is determined to pit his sheer will against the multifarious power of the body (of Henry's to testify against him, of his own to repulse, of Anne's to be repulsed by him). When Anne is gone and Henry dispatched to Whitefriars, he celebrates his victory as of one of mind over matter, or rather of his sheer nullity over corporeal fact. "To take her in her heart's extremest hate,/With curses in her mouth, tears in her eyes,/The bleeding witness of my hatred by . . . And yet to win her, all the world to nothing?" (1.2.219–25)[13] Yet at the same time the play—not least through the person of Richard himself—represents the body as historical actor, as agent and determining force. As he explains unequivocally in the first scene, it is by his monstrous, unassimilable body that Richard is first of all "determinèd to prove a villain" (1.1.30).[14]

Shakespeare's Richard is at once all body and no-body, standing for the power of the body in its stubbornly irreducible corporeality to shape history, yet somehow also signifying a triumph over the body, the reduc-

---

[12] The parents of nine-year-old Agnes Freeman were said to have rejected advice to take their daughter before Richard, preferring to vow pilgrimage to Henry's tomb at Windsor, which vow was itself sufficient to work the child's cure. John W. McKenna, "Piety and Propaganda: The Cult of Henry VI," in *Chaucer and Middle English Studies in Honor of Rossell Hope Robbins*, ed. B. Rowland (Kent, OH: Kent State University Press, 1974), 75. Writing in the reign of Elizabeth, the imprisoned Catholic Nicholas Harpsfield celebrated Henry's miracles of justice as confirmations of his ongoing royal authority. "When I think of these wonders, I seem to see him again on his royal throne, no less powerful than of old or less desirous of administering justice than when he was vested with his royal power"; *Historia Anglicana ecclesiastica*, translated and quoted in Francis Aidan Gasquet, *The Religious Life of King Henry VI* (London: G. Bell, 1923), 69–70.

[13] See the subtle discussion of this line in Ken Jackson, "'All the World to Nothing': Badiou, Zizek and Pauline Subjectivity in *Richard III*," *Shakespeare* 1 (2005): 29–52.

[14] On Richard's determination, see Linda Charnes, *Notorious Identity: Materializing the Subject in Shakespeare* (Cambridge, MA: Harvard University Press, 1993), 62–3.

tion of all that worldly physicality to "nothing." If this is a paradox, it is a paradox borne out of what in Shakespeare's time was a notorious fact. The bodies that had shaped the history of the late fifteenth century, the bodies which in various ways might have been expected to provide an ongoing link to that history, had simply disappeared. "Where is Plantagenet?" asked Chief Justice Ranulph Crewe in a famous flight of legal oratory in 1625.[15] The question may have been rhetorical in any case, but as far as the last Plantagenets were concerned, no definite answer would have been possible. The body of Richard III, as well as those of his nephews Edward V and Richard Duke of York, had long since passed beyond the reach of human knowledge, though not by any means beyond the scope of curious speculation.

   This chapter surveys the evolving discourse surrounding the lost bodies of the last Plantagenets over the course of two centuries. In a period in which the relationship between the living and the dead was opened up for drastic renegotiation, it is perhaps not surprising that these three late-medieval bodies became the site of proliferating and conflicting meanings, in spite or indeed because of their notorious unlocatability. Long after his death, the body of Richard III retained its signifying power and capacity to challenge Tudor orthodoxies, taking part in emerging debates over matters of royal authority and national identity, the nature of tyranny, the claims of the dead, and the limits of humanity. As for the Princes in the Tower, the apparently insoluble question of what had become of their bodies would come to resonate powerfully with the larger plight of a society which, following the Reformation, seemed to have lost its links with its dead and with its past.

1.1 "LIKE A DOG": THE REMAINS OF RICHARD III

In the brief period of his Protectorship and reign, Richard III could not escape giving a good deal of thought to the disposal of royal remains. In addition to the burial of both his queen, Anne, and his sole legitimate child, Edward of Middleham (the former in Westminster, the latter, possibly, in the parish church of Sheriff Hutton, North Yorkshire),[16] the years 1483–85 saw

---

[15]   See fn. 1 in this chapter.
[16]   Anne was buried at the cost of £42 12s in Westminster Abbey, south of the high altar in an unmarked place. Richard presumably intended to devise a monument for Anne, and indeed for himself, but in both cases his plans came to nothing. Only tradition and guess-work link the unrecorded burial place of Edward of Middleham with the worn effigy of a crowned child at Sheriff Hutton. See Mark Duffy, *Royal Tombs of Medieval England* (Stroud: Tempus, 2003), 260–5.

the interment of as many as three of his royal predecessors: Henry VI, Edward IV, and (probably) Edward V. The first, as already noted, was translated with dignity from Chertsey to Windsor, though without being granted a monument. The last, as will be seen later in this chapter, was variously rumoured to lie hidden in the Tower of London or in the darkest depths of the Thames estuary. But it was Edward IV whose funeral rites and interment conformed most fully to the conventions of royal burial, and whose sending off provided the model which Richard himself must have hoped to emulate.

When Edward died in 1483, more than sixty years had passed since the last interment of an anointed and reigning king; few of the living would have possessed any secure memory of how the thing was done.[17] The old ordinance for "the observaunce at the deth and buryall of a annoynted king" was recopied for the occasion, its language a model of frankness and clarity which to modern ears may seem to verge on irreverence:

> laie him on a faire burde, covered with clothe of gold, his one hand upon his bely and a septur in the other hand, and on his face a kerchief, and so shewid to his nobles by the space of ii dayes and more, if the weder will it suffre. And when he may not goodly lenger endur take hym away and bowell hym and then eftsones bame hym.[18]

If there is nothing ornate or elaborate in the prose of the ordinance, the same cannot be said for the ritual it describes. The embalmed body was wrapped in layers of linen and velvet tied with cords of silk, the outermost layer being of cloth of gold, before being placed in its coffin. For seven days it then lay in the king's private chapel in Westminster, whilst requiem masses were sung, and members of the royal household watched beside it. Edward's body was then solemnly conveyed to Westminster Abbey and thence in slow procession to his place of burial at Windsor, accompanied by an "ymage" or "personage like to the similitude of the king, in habet royall, crowned with the crown oon his hede, holding in the one hand a septur and in the other

---

[17]   The closest thing to a royal funeral subsequent to that of Henry V had been the reburial of Richard, Duke of York (d. 1460) at Fotheringhay in 1476. Although he was never crowned, Yorkist ideology held that Richard had been the true king of England; at Fotheringhay, his hearse was surmounted by an effigy and the figure of an angel bearing a golden crown, making explicit his kingship in right if not in fact. See P. W. Hammond, Anne F. Sutton & Livia Visser-Fuchs, "The Reburial of Richard, Duke of York, July 21–30, 1476," *Ricardian* 10 (1994–96): 122–65. For an overview of English royal funerary practices in the period, see Ralph Griffiths, "Succession and the Royal Dead in Later Medieval England," in *Making and Breaking the Rules: Succession in Medieval Europe, c. 1000—c. 1600/Établir et abolir les normes: la succession dans l'Europe médiévale, vers 1000—vers 1600*, ed. Frédérique Lachaud and Michael Penman (Turnhout: Brepols), 97–109.
[18]   College of Arms MS I.7, in Anne F. Sutton and Livia Visser-Fuchs with R. A. Griffiths, *The Royal Funerals of the House of York at Windsor* (Bury St Edmunds: Richard III Society, 2005), 33.

hand a ball of silver and gilt with a cross pate."[19] This temporary mul-
tiplication of images or "bodies" of the king was a normal part of royal
funeral observances, giving visible form to the legal doctrine that a reigning monarch possessed two bodies, the undying "body politic" and the
mortal "body natural."[20] Following the burial, where the late king's servi-
tors signified the end of their loyalty by breaking their staves and casting
them into the open grave, the body politic was supposed to pass to the
successor, whilst the body natural moldered in the ground.[21]

Poems lamenting the death of Edward IV focus to a striking extent on his
natural body. This, after all, was the part of him which was understood to have
died; one would hardly presume to mourn his kingliness which, in theory,
had been transmitted intact to his successor. And Edward's body had always
attracted unusual attention. One elegy, perhaps by a former servitor, recalls
vividly how the king rejoiced in physical exertion: "Rydyng a hontyng, hym-
silff to sporte and playe . . . Hit was a wordle [*sic*] to se hym ride aboute."[22] The
elegist can hardly accept that the body of the king is gone from the world, every
part of which contrives to recall him, and gesture deceptively to his presence:

> Me thynkith ever this kyng sholde not be gon,
> I see his lordis, I see his knyghtis all;
> I see his plasis made of lyme and ston;
> I see his servauntes sittyng in the hall,
> And walkyng among them his marchall.
> Whate sholde I say? he was here yesterday!
> All men of Englond ar bounde for hym to pray.[23]

[19] *The Royal Funerals of the House of York at Windsor*, 36.
[20] In the funeral rite, as Ernst Kantorowicz remarks, "the king's body seemingly doubled: the two bodies, unquestionably united in the living king, were visibly segregated in the king's demise"; Ernst H. Kantorowicz, *The King's Two Bodies: A Study in Medieval Political Theology* (Princeton: Princeton University Press, 1957), 423; see also Griffiths, "Succession and the Royal Dead," 103–4.
[21] In the instructions for his tomb provided in his will, Edward IV seemed determined to forestall the sundering of body politic from body natural by having them depicted in tandem on his monument. He willed that his remains should be "buried lowe in the grownde," sur-mounted by a "figure of Dethe," a sculpted cadaver surrounded by the king's armorial bear-ings; over this was to be raised a tomb chest, topped by "an Image for oure figure we wil bee of silver and gilte or at the lest coopre and gilt" (quoted in Sutton et. al., *Royal Funerals of the House of York*, 96). Such double monuments, featuring both a lifelike effigy and a representa-tion of the decaying corpse, or transi, were not unknown in fifteenth-century England, and were particularly favoured by high-ranking clergymen. Yet a royal transi tomb such as Edward devised would have constituted a deeply ambivalent image, with its insistent juxtaposition of the regal figure with the representation of decay threatening to imply the dissolution of the body politic itself. The tomb was never completed as willed. See Paul Binski, *Medieval Death: Ritual and Representation* (Ithaca: Cornell University Press, 1996), 151.
[22] "King Edward the iiiith" (John Rylands University Library MS Eng. 113), in Sutton, et. al., *Royal Funerals of the House of York*, 86.
[23] "King Edward the iiiith," 87.

Astonished at his absence from palace and hall, the elegist asks again and again after Edward's whereabouts: "Wher is this Prynce that conquered his right . . . Wher is he nowe, that man of noble men. . . ?"[24] Such questions, examples of the conventional *ubi sunt* formula, point to a loss that can only be made good in the next world. Yet they are nonetheless capable of a quite literal and earthly answer. The elegist's professed uncertainty about the location of Edward's soul or self reflects an absolute certainty about the location of his physical remains. As the dead king himself is made to declare in another poem of the same date, "I ly now in mold" and "*nunc in Wynsore yn pulvere dormio*" [now at Windsor I sleep in dust].[25] In the case of Edward's successors, Edward V and Richard III, there would be no such abiding certainty as to the body's location.

Of the fate of Richard's remains in the hours and days immediately following his death there is little room to doubt. Shortly after Bosworth, the victor issued a proclamation whereby "the king ascertaineth you that Richard duke of Gloucester, late called King Richard, was slain at a place called Sandeford, within the shire of Leicester, and brought dead off the field unto the town of Leicester, and there was laid openly, that every man might see and look upon him."[26] The public display of the royal corpse was a well-established practice, intended to obtain general assent that the king was indeed dead. In Richard's case, it effectively ensured that there would be no rumours of his escape and survival. But the display of Richard's body differed from that of Edward IV, or even the murdered Henry VI, in the apparent determination to humiliate the deceased.[27] Richard's naked, mangled body needed no recourse to miraculous bleeding to testify to the manner of his death. *The Great Chronicle of London* would recall that

> as gloriously as he by the mornyng departid ffrom that Toun, So as Inreverently was he that afftyr noune, browght Into that toun, ffor his body Dyspoylid to the skyn, and nougth beyng lefft abouth hym, soo much as wold covyr his pryvy membyr he was trussyd behynd a pursevaunt callid Norrey as an hogg or an othyr vyle beest, and soo all to besprung with myyr & fflylth

[24] "King Edward the iiiith," 86.
[25] "Lament of the Soul of Edward IV," in Sutton, et al., *Royal Funerals of the House of York*, 83–4. On the inherent tension in the *ubi sunt* tradition between the awareness of the body rotting in the earth and the hoped-for harbour of the soul in heaven, see Katherine H. Terrell, "Rethinking the 'Corse in clot': Cleanness, Filth, and Bodily Decay in *Pearl*," *Studies in Philology* 105 (2008): 429–47.
[26] Hanham, *Richard III*, 59.
[27] Analysis of the bones unearthed at Greyfriars in 2012 indicated that the corpse had sustained posthumous "humiliation injuries" to parts of the body including the pelvis, suggesting that the dead man had been stabbed through the buttocks.

was browgth to a chirch In leycetyr ffor all men to wondyr uppon, and there lastly Inreverently buried.[28]

Richard's body was displayed for two days in the College of St Mary in the Newark, an old burial place of the Earls and Dukes of Lancaster, as if it was thought that even the dead might wish to feast their eyes on his abjection.

The exhibition of the dead king's torn and naked body had an impact on collective memory, well beyond those who might actually have witnessed the spectacle. References to the display of the naked corpse would become a staple of the ballad tradition. *Bosworth Feilde* (probably composed before 1495) reports how

> they brought King Richard thither with might
> as naked as he borne might bee.
> & in Newarke Laid was hee,
> that many a one might looke on him.[29]

Likewise, the alliterative Flodden poem *Scotish Feilde*, which devotes no more than ten lines to its recollection of Richard, lays special stress on his posthumous treatment:

> Thus was he dongen to death with many derffe strokes,
> And cast him on a Capull [horse], and carryed him to Liester,
> & Naked into Newarke.[30]

The theme of Richard's posthumous humiliation looms surprisingly large in the Tudor popular tradition, larger indeed than that of his reputed deformity. For most English people before Shakespeare's play, mention of the body of the Richard III would bring to mind not the image of a halting hunchback, but that of a naked corpse on a horse's rump. Somewhere in the background of Shakespeare's Richard's repeated references to himself as naked—"thus I clothe my naked villainy" (1.3.334); "I lay it [my bosom] naked to the deadly stroke" (1.2.165)—is the memory of a battered and disrobed body displayed in triumph and contempt.

---

[28] *GCL*, 238. In a letter of March 1, 1486 to Ferdinand and Isabella of Aragon and Castile, Diego de Valera reported that the victorious Henry had "ordered the dead king to be placed in a little hermitage near the place of battle, and had him covered from the waist downward with a black rag of poor quality, ordering him to be exposed there three days to the universal gaze." Translated in Pamela Tudor-Craig, *Richard III* (Ipswich: The Boydell Press, 1973), 67–8.

[29] *Bosworth Feilde*, in *Bishop Percy's Folio Manuscript: Ballads and Romances*, ed. John W. Hales (London: N. Trübner, 1868), 3.258–9, ll. 643–6.

[30] *Scotish Feilde*, in *Scotish Feilde and Flodden Feilde: Two Flodden Poems*, ed. Ian F. Baird (New York: Garland, 1982), 2, ll. 33–5. "Newarke" here refers to Leicester's liberty of the Newarke, not to the town of Newark, as Baird surmises.

Henry VII presumably intended the display of Richard's corpse to serve as an emblem of his crimes and the fate of tyrants generally. The brutal exercise, which provoked some unease even among chroniclers generally supportive of Henry, had the effect of forging an overwhelming association between the idea of the king and the image of that degraded, utterly defeated body.[31] For a time, it would prove all but impossible to think of one without thinking of the other. Yet, as an emblem, the naked corpse is inevitably multivalent, and far from securely in the victor's control. On the one hand, the mangled, undignified body could serve to sum up—or reveal—the twisted and dishonourable nature of Richard's practices in life. Yet an image calculated to provoke abhorrence and contempt also had the potential to evoke pity—above all perhaps in the fifteenth century, the great age of affective piety, when the contemplation of a naked or semi-naked corpse covered in wounds lay near the heart of Christian spiritual practice. A text like *Bosworth Feilde* seems to gesture towards these Christ-like parallels with its description of the dead Richard "naked as he [was] borne," recalling the iconographic parallelism of the infant Jesus and the crucified Christ, both frequently imagined as naked. Even if no one in the late fifteenth century could think of Richard without thinking of his brutalized naked corpse, it by no means follows that responses to that spectacle—whether seen or imagined—were unambiguous or uncontested.

In York in 1491, several citizens were called before the Mayor and his council over a dispute bearing on Richard's character, his physical appearance, and the disposal of his body. By one account, John Payntor had begun the quarrel by stating that the recently assassinated earl of Northumberland (*d*.1489) "was a traytor and bytrayed Kyng Richard."[32] The schoolmaster William Burton, being "distempide awther wt aill or wyn," had retorted that Richard was "an ypocrite, a crochebake, & was beried in a dike like a dogge." Payntor gave Burton the lie and attempted to strike him "with a litill rod," adding that "the Kynge's good grace hath beried hym like a noble gentilman." Burton's "unfyttyng langage" regarding Richard, with its specific reference to dikes and dogs, was recalled by several witnesses. The Prior of Bolton assured the council that no one present had spoken treason, though he recalled Burton saying of Richard that "he luffede hym

---

[31] The author of the second continuation of the Crowland Chronicle remarks that the corpse was treated with "insufficient humanity (a rope being placed around the neck)"; *The Crowland Chronicle Continuations: 1459–1486*, ed. Nicholas Pronay and John Cox (London: Richard III and Yorkist History Trust, 1986), 183.

[32] Robert Davies, ed, *Extracts from the municipal records of the city of York, during the reigns of Edward iv. Edward v. and Richard iii* (London: J. B. Nichols, 1843), 220.

never and was beired in a dike. John Payntor saide hit maid little mat[ter] nowther of his luff not his . . . and as for his beriall, hit pleside the Kynge's grace to bery him in a worshipfull place."[33] The Mayor charged both parties to keep the peace, and pursued the matter no further.

Burton's intemperate denunciation of Richard is indicative of how thoroughly memories of the late king had become associated with his body and its posthumous humiliation. His association of the fate of Richard's corpse with his having been a "crochebake" (the earliest recorded reference to this deformity) is particularly suggestive, almost as if Burton were reading the brokenness of the dead body back onto the living form.[34] Likewise, the schoolmaster uses what he knows regarding Richard's death to draw conclusions about the subsequent fate of his remains. It seems swiftly to have become a byword that Richard met his death like a "dog killed in a dyke"; the phrase, which occurs in a poem written shortly after Bosworth by the Welsh bard Dafydd Llwyd of Mathafarn, finds a close echo in Burton's assertion that Richard "was beried in a dike like a dogge," but with the reference transferred from his death to his interment.[35]

If what had happened to Richard's body in the days immediately following his death was a matter of public notoriety, its fate from then on was surprisingly unclear. John Payntor was determined to believe that Henry VII had "beried hym like a noble gentilman," which at the very least implies in holy ground, but he could not name the place. Even the court historian Bernard Andre, who made a point of emphasizing Henry's concern to see Richard buried with due reverence, was forced to leave a blank in his manuscript where the location ought to have been specified.[36] Some supposed

---

[33] Davies, ed, *Extracts*, 224, 221, 222, 221, 223, 224.

[34] Possibly writing before Bosworth, the bard Robin Ddu derided Richard as "Un eiddil gorff, yn Iuddew" ("a feeble-bodied Jew"), but without reference to a specific deformity. See Gruffydd Aled Williams, "The Bardic Road to Bosworth," *Transactions of the Honourable Society of Cymmrodorion* (1986): 20. Analysis of the bones unearthed in Leicester in 2012 indicates that Richard III suffered from adolescent-onset scoliosis, leading one shoulder to be higher than another (as noted by John Rous), but he did not have a hunched or "crouch" back.

[35] "Y ci a las yn y clawdd": *Gwaith Dafydd Llwyd o Fathafarn,* ed. W. Leslie Richards (Cardiff: University of Wales Press, 1964), 70 (my translation). For a full English translation of the poem see Andrew Breeze, "A Welsh Poem of 1485 on Richard III," *Ricardian* 18 (2008): 46–53. The idea that Richard died in a ditch is some way from the valiant last charge described by Polydore Vergil among others. However, Jean Molinet (*c*.1490) has a similar account, in which, interestingly, the act is attributed to a Welshman: "His horse leapt into a marsh from which it could not retrieve itself. One of the Welshmen then came after him, and struck him dead with a halberd . . . And so he who miserably killed numerous people, ended his days iniquitously and filthily in the dirt and mire." Translated in Michael John Bennett, *The Battle of Bosworth* (Stroud: Alan Sutton, 1985), 161.

[36] "Imprimis ipsius Richardi regis in * * * cum omnimoda reverentia sepeliendum sentio." Andre, *Historia,* 34.

that Richard had been interred where he lay on show in the Newark, but St Mary's status as a Lancastrian mausoleum, the very thing that made it appropriate as a site of ironic display, ruled it out as a final resting place for the last Yorkist king. John Rous recorded that Richard "at last was buried in the choir of the Friars Minor [i.e. Franciscans, or Greyfriars] at Leicester."[37] Early sixteenth-century historians confirm the location:

> the body of king Rycherd nakyd of all clothing, and layd uppon an horse bake with the armes and legges hanginge downe on both sydes, was browght to thabbay of monks Franciscanes at Leycester, a myserable spectacle in good sooth, but not unwoorthy for the mans lyfe, and ther was buryed two days after without any pompe or solemne funerall.[38]

The lack of reverence with which Richard was laid to rest is noted by several chroniclers; Hall makes the ironic observation that Richard received "no lesse funeral pompe and solempnitie" than the nephews he had unnaturally murdered.[39] It is not clear whether these phrases connote overt insult, or merely the absence of due ceremony in the burial—if indeed there is a definite distinction between these. Burial in the choir was generally perceived as a mark of reverence, and this was the position in the church interior most sought after by high-ranking laity.[40] Yet the excavation of the Greyfriars site in 2012 revealed that Richard's body had been interred in a roughly-cut grave too small for his stature, leaving the head propped above the body. He did not receive the close wrapping in lead favoured by royalty in the period; rather, his naked form appears to have been interred without a coffin or even a simple shroud. The skeleton lay in a peculiar position with the wrists joined over the lower abdomen, suggesting that they may have been bound together.[41] With or without reverence, Richard was clearly buried in haste.

There was apparently no initial provision for a tomb. In 1491, when Burton and Payntor had their quarrel, Richard's body probably lay beneath a bare slab—not in a ditch to be sure, but not exactly in a manner befitting a noble gentleman, much less a king. Then, some ten years after Bosworth, a flurry of activity around the site of Richard's burial leaves its mark in official records. In the mid-1490s alabasterer Walter Hylton was apparently offered

---

[37] *Historia Johannis Rossi*, in Hanham, *Richard III*, 123–4.

[38] Vergil, *Three Books*, 226. Fabyan reports the same (ccxxx^r).

[39] Hall, Richard III, lix^r. *GCL* records that Richard was "Irreverently buried" (238), and Fabyan that he was "with little reverence buried" (ccxxx^v).

[40] Roberta Gilchrist and Barry Sloane, *Requiem: The Medieval Monastic Cemetery in Britain* (London: Museum of London Archaeological Service, 2005), 57, 108.

[41] The shape of the grave and the position of the body within it were described by Richard Buckley and Jo Appleby in a press conference at the University of Leicester on 4 February 2013.

£50 to construct a fitting monument; in 1495, one James Keyley was paid
£10 1s for his work on "King Rich. Tombe." Whether Keyley was working
with Hilton or had succeeded in underbidding him is unclear, but it would
appear that some sort of monument including a representation of the king
was in place before the end of the century.[42] Although no contemporary
description survives, Holinshed—writing when the tomb was no longer to
be seen—records that "K. Henrie the seventh caused a toome to be, made
and set up over the place where he was buried, in the church of the graie
friers at Leicester, with a picture of alabaster representing his person." The
"picture" was probably not a three-dimensional effigy but merely a figure
incised on the alabaster slab.[43]

Conscious of the parallel with Richard's own reinterment of a fallen
royal enemy, Holinshed describes Henry as

> dooing that honour to his enimie, upon a princelie regard and pitifull zeale,
> which king Richard (mooved of an hypocriticall shew of counterfeit pitie)
> did to king Henrie the sixt, whom he had first cruellie murthered, and after
> in the second yeare of his usurped reigne, caused his corps to be remooved
> from Chertseie unto Windsore, and there solemnlie interred.[44]

Leaving aside the chronicler's tendentious gloss on the two kings' respec-
tive motives, it is clear that the cases are not directly comparable; there
was no posthumous cult of Saint Richard III for Henry VII to contend
with. Henry had probably simply come to the conclusion that he could
not let this particular sleeping dog lie. To define his own place in national
and dynastic history, he had to define Richard's. Had his predecessor been
a genuine king, albeit a tyrant, or a mere pretender? What exactly did it
mean for him to have been, as the statutes of the new regime typically
styled him, "king in dede but not in right"?[45] Had Richard usurped the
throne—and if so, from what rightful claimant? On the answers to these
questions rested Henry's own claim. His place in history must be constructed, quite literally, over Richard's dead body.

---

[42] On the construction, description, and destruction of Richard's tomb, see David Baldwin, "King Richard's Grave in Leicester," *Transactions of the Leicester Archaeological and Historical Society*, 60 (1986): 21–4; John Ashdown-Hill, *The Last Days of Richard III* (Stroud:
The History Press, 2010), 97–109.
[43] Holinshed, 761. The Leicestershire antiquary William Burton, who may or may not
have had a source of information other than Holinshed, described Richard's tomb as "a
faire Alablaster Monument, with his picture cut out, and made thereon"; *The Description of
Leicestershire* (London, 1622), 163.
[44] Holinshed, 761.
[45] See A. F. Pollard, "Tudor Gleanings I.—The 'de facto' Act of Henry VII," *Bulletin of the
Institute of Historical Research* 7 (1929): 1–12. As Pollard observes, Yorkist Parliaments had
used the same phrase with reference to Henry VI.

Somewhere in close proximity to the new tomb in Greyfriars was fixed the official epitaph of Richard III, a Latin poem of sixteen largely uncomplimentary lines. The epitaph may have appeared on the monument itself or on a scroll or plaque hung nearby. Whatever form it took, the original has long since been lost, along with the tomb itself. The text survives in two sixteenth-century manuscript copies, and in two seventeenth-century printed versions which differ in several key readings. The transparent purpose of the epitaph is to settle Richard's place in history, and in particular the relationship of his reign to that of Henry VII. Yet with its ambiguous phrasing and intriguingly unstable text, it raises more questions than it answers.

Richard's epitaph was first recorded by the herald Thomas Wriothesley (*d*.1534), who had served both of Henry VII's sons as a pursuivant before becoming Garter King of Arms in 1505. A leading figure for several decades in the College of Arms (Richard III's creation, as discussed in Chapter 4), Wriothesley kept extensive records including sketches of funeral monuments.[46] Whether he ever visited Richard's resting place is unclear, though the text's apparent errors and deletions could lead the reader to infer that he was working from a difficult inscription in metal or stone. Wriothesley's transcription was in turn copied with some amendments by a younger herald, Thomas Hawley (*d*.1557), whose text was printed in the late seventeenth century by yet another herald, Francis Sandford:[47]

> Hic ego, quem vario tellus sub marmore claudit
> Tertius a multa voce Ricardus eram
> Nam patris tutor patrius pro iure nepotis
> dirupta tenui regna Britanna, fide
> Sexaginta dies binis duntaxat ademptis
> Estatesque tuli non mea sceptra duas.
> Fortiter in bello merito desertus ab Anglis,
> Rex Henrici, tibi, septime, succubui.
> At sumptu, pius ipse, tuo, sic ossa decoras
> Non regem facis regis honore coli.

---

[46] The *Oxford Dictionary of National Biography* notes of Wriothesley: "his collections are an essential link between the heraldry of the middle ages and that of the later College of Arms, while his drawings of monuments anticipate the work of later Tudor heralds."

[47] Francis Sandford, *A Genealogical History of the Kings of England* (London, 1677), 410. The manuscript transcriptions of Wriothesley (BL Add MS 45131, fol. 10ᵛ) and Hawley (College of Arms MS I 3, fol. 4) are printed with facsimiles in John Ashdown-Hill, "The Epitaph of King Richard III," *Ricardian* 18 (2008): 41–4. The version of the epitaph printed here follows Sandford in its corrections and expansions of the text in the sixteenth-century manuscript versions, except on the few occasions where Sandford gives altered wording under the apparent influence of the different version of the epitaph printed in George Buck's *History of Richard III*, discussed below.

Quatuor exceptis jam tantum, quinque bis annis,
Acta trecenta quidem, lustra salutis erant.
Anteque Septembris undena luce kalendas,
Redideram rubrae debita iura Rosae.
At mea, quisquis eris, propter commissa precare,
Sit minor ut precibus pena fienda tuis.

I, here, whom the earth encloses under various coloured marble,
Was by many called Richard III.
As Protector of the country, on behalf of a nephew's inherited right,
I held the British kingdoms by broken faith.
For just sixty days less two,
And two summers, I wielded sceptres that were not mine.
Fighting bravely in war, deservedly deserted by the English,
I succumbed to you, King Henry VII.
But you yourself, piously, at your expense, thus honour my bones
And cause a non-king to be revered with the honour of a king,
When in twice five years less four
Three hundred five-year periods of our salvation have passed.
And eleven days before the Kalends of September
I surrendered to the red rose the right it was owed.
Whoever you are, pray for my offences,
That my punishment may be lessened by your prayers.[48]

The rather arcane equation in lines 11–12 appears to result in the date 1494, which would accord with the construction of the tomb in Greyfriars (the honouring of Richard's bones proclaimed in lines 9–10).[49] Yet the reference to a day eleven days before the start of September, which at first seems to add further specificity to the date above, clearly refers rather to Bosworth (22 August 1485). The intended effect may be to elide the space of ten years between Richard's death and the construction of his tomb—years in which his body had lain first in shameful view, and then in shameful obscurity.

The text of the epitaph as reported by Wriothesley and subsequent heralds is strongly negative in its account of Richard's reign and legitimacy, to the point of declaring him not only a usurper of the throne but a non-king. Yet this is not the only surviving version of Richard's epitaph. In his *History of King Richard III* (c.1619), which sought to exculpate the king from many of the crimes imputed to him under the Tudors, George Buck presented an alternative text derived, he declared, from "the copy in a recorded manu-script book, chained to a table in a chamber in the Guildhall of London."[50] Although Buck's text concurs in accusing Richard of faithlessness and in affirming the outcome of Bosworth as just, it differs from what we can term the Heralds' Version in several key respects. In line 2, Buck has *justa* instead of *multa*, giving the reading "justly called Richard III"; line 7 has *certans* (con-tending) in place of *merito* (deservedly), emphasizing Richard's valour and removing the suggestion that his followers did well to desert him; in the ref-erence to sceptres, *tunc* (then) replaces *non*, so that Richard's right to them is not denied; likewise, *non regem*, a non-king, becomes *regem olimque*, a former king; and rather than yielding the red rose the right it was owed (*debita iura*), Buck's text has the red rose receiving merely the right it sought or desired (*iura petita*). In each case, what is at stake in the differences between the two versions of the epitaph is not Richard's essential character, but the compara-tively technical question of whether or not he was a legitimate monarch.

Which version of the epitaph is more likely to be faithful to the lost original? Buck's text is admittedly much later in date, its source is conveni-ently lost, and Buck, who acknowledged having emended the epitaph's "faults and corruptions," had a pro-Ricardian axe to grind.[51] Yet the inter-nal evidence is more ambiguous. In two cases, the discrepant word is, in the Herald's Version, the simple negation "non." The line beginning "non regem" in the Heralds' Version does not scan, while the equivalent line in Buck beginning "Regem olimque" does.[52] If it was Buck who altered the

---

[50] George Buck, *The History of King Richard III*, ed. Arthur Noel Kincaid (Glouces-ter: Alan Sutton, 1979), 217–18. An English translation of Buck's version of the epitaph appears in John Hackett, *Select and remarkable epitaphs on illustrious and other persons . . . with translations of such as are in Latin* (London, 1757), vol. 2, 92–3.

> I who am laid beneath this Marble Stone,
> Richard the Third, possess'd the British Throne.
> My Country's Guardian in my Nephew's claim,
> By Trust betray'd I to the Kingdom came.
> Two Years and sixty Days, save two, I reign'd;
> And bravely strove in Fight; but, unsustain'd
> My English left me in the luckless Field,
> Where I to Henry's Arms was forced to yield.
> Yet at his Cost my Corse this Tomb obtains,
> Who piously interr'd me, and ordains
> That Regal Honours wait a King's Remains.
> Th' Year thirteen Hundred was and eighty four,
> The twenty-first of August, when its Pow'r
> And all its Rights I did to the red Rose restore.
> Reader, whoe'er thou art, thy Pray'rs bestow,
> T'attone my Crimes, and ease my Pains below.

[51] Buck, *History of King Richard III*, 217.
[52] For this reason, perhaps, Sandford here follows Buck rather than his manuscript source.

epitaph, he seems also to have improved both its lexicon and its prosody. If, on the other hand, the doctoring took place in the other direction, the case looks rather more straightforward; there is nothing easier than to excise a word and replace it with "non." It is at least possible, then, that the Heralds' Version is the one that has been tampered with, perhaps by Wriothesley, who was both punctilious in matters of title and instinctively loyal to the Tudor claim. The faithful herald may have failed to grasp that, in the political context of the 1490s, the legitimacy of the new regime was better safeguarded by accepting the legality of Richard's reign than by rejecting it. As John Ashdown-Hill has observed, denying that Richard had been a true king risked playing into the hands of Yorkist pretenders like Perkin Warbeck, who stood for the right of Edward IV's direct heirs. Burying the Yorkist claim was best achieved with belated funeral honours to the last Yorkist king, Richard III.[53]

The poem's larger goal is to put not only Richard but the past in its place: whatever the rights and wrongs of the pre-Tudor period, it seems to say, none of that matters any more. This is clear above all in the epitaph's studied use of national nomenclature. Richard is described as having ruled not over England but over the British kingdoms (*regna Britanna*). The phrase chimes with early Tudor royal iconography; Henry VII and certain of his followers were keen to press a British vision of his reign, even to the extent of proposing that he had restored the rule of the ancient British kings, after a millennium of Anglo-Saxon misrule. The court historian Bernard Andre identified Richard's reign as the culmination of the era of "Anglorum saevitia," the savagery of the English.[54] (Andre is indeed a plausible candidate for the authorship of the epitaph.) Richard is cast here as the possessor of the British throne, but at Bosworth his following is identified specifically with the English—the battle is thus framed as an ethnic confrontation, between Richard's faithless Englishmen on the one hand and Henry's victorious British (i.e., Breton and Welsh) forces on the other. The triumph of Britishness over Englishness consigns Richard's reign to a bygone epoch. In this sense, his burial place is England's too.

For some forty years after the construction of the tomb, Richard's remains lay peacefully in the choir of the Greyfriars beneath his alabaster effigy. We can be sure that tens of thousands of masses were said within a few feet of where he lay; we cannot know what prayers were said for him.

---

[53] Ashdown-Hill argues that even the most hostile readings are "far less hostile to him than might have been expected, given its period of composition" ("Epitaph of King Richard III," 39–40).

[54] Andre, *Historia*, 10. On the Tudor claim to descent from Cadwaladr, last king of the Britons, see Philip Schwyzer, *Literature, Nationalism and Memory in Early Modern England and Wales* (Cambridge: Cambridge University Press, 2004), 13–48.

In addition to the friars and their servants, occasional visiting dignitaries and perhaps even some curious tourists may have been permitted to view his small monument. There is little to indicate what the local inhabitants thought of the royal burial in their midst, not at least until the eve of the Reformation. In November 1530, the disgraced and ailing Cardinal Wolsey arrived in Leicester, en route to London to face charges of treason. Reaching the Augustinian Abbey of St Mary, known as Leicester Abbey, he told the abbot "I am come hither to leave my bones among you."[55] A week later, the ambassador Chapuys wrote to his master Charles V, "The cardinal of York died on St Andrew's Day, at a place where king Richard was killed. They are both buried in the same church, which the people call The Tyrants' Sepulchre."[56]

Although the two men were in fact buried in different churches, several miles apart—a fact that would have been inescapably obvious to the people of Leicester—Chapuys is unlikely to have been alone in perceiving significant parallels between the king and the cardinal. By 1530, Richard's reputation as the paradigmatic domestic tyrant was already well-established, with the historians Robert Fabyan, Thomas More and Polydore Vergil having all explicitly accused him of tyranny.[57] This reputation allows for the buried wit of the remark quoted by Chapuys, which creates a metonymic association between Richard and Wolsey through their supposedly common sepulchre. The man buried in Richard's tomb was a tyrant: hence, Wolsey was a tyrant. But to play with terms and tombs in this fashion could be a dangerous game. Henry VIII had already made clear his intention to appropriate the lavish sarcophagus of black porphyry which Wolsey had prepared for himself.[58] Symbolically stepping into the cardinal's tomb just as Wolsey stepped into Richard's, Henry too might be

---

[55] George Cavendish, *The Life of Cardinal Wolsey*, ed. Samuel W. Singer (London: Harding and Lepard, 1827), 380.

[56] London, December 4, 1530. *Letters and Papers, Foreign and Domestic, Henry VIII, Volume 4: 1524–1530* (1875), 3054.

[57] Vergil affirms that Richard "thowght of nothing but tyranny and crueltie," and plotted to "convert the regall authoritye into tyranny" (*Three Books*, 180, 182). More describes the murder of the princes as "traytorous tiranny" and identifies Richard as "the tiraunt" (More, *History*, 86, 90). Fabyan judges that Richard "rulyd most . . . by rygour and tyranye" (Ccxxx'). Though the Crowland writer does not accuse Richard himself of tyranny, he condemns his northern liegemen for tyrannizing over the south of England.

[58] See Nigel Llewellyn, "The Royal Body: Monuments to the Dead, For the Living," in *The Renaissance Body: The Human Figure in English Culture, c. 1540–1660*, ed. Lucy Gent and Nigel Llewellyn (London: Reaktion, 1990), 232–6; Alfred Higgins, "On the Work of Florentine Sculptors in England in the Early Part of the Sixteenth Century, with special reference to the tombs of Cardinal Wolsey and King Henry VIII," *Archaeological Journal* 51 (1894): 120–2. In the event, Henry did not receive burial in Wolsey's tomb; the coveted sarcophagus can be found today in the crypt of St Paul's Cathedral, where it shelters the remains of Lord Nelson.

said to occupy "the Tyrant's Sepulchre." In 1530, to be sure, the king was only beginning to attract the accusations of tyranny that would lead to his reputation as "the greatest tyrant that ever was in England," on a par with Nero, Domitian, and Richard III.[59]

The life of the Leicester Greyfriars, a monastic community founded at the dawn of the thirteenth century, came to an end on November 10, 1538, when the last warden, William Gyllys, surrendered his house to the royal commissioners. Leicester Abbey, where Wolsey lay, had fallen a month earlier. The meagre furnishings of a house whose reported annual net income came no higher than £1 2s would not have taken long to strip and sell off.[60] No contemporary record survives detailing the fate of Richard's tomb. Certainly, Greyfriars had no reason to expect special treatment on account of housing a royal grave. Various other monasteries had pleaded for a special dispensation on the basis of their royal dead; yet King Stephen's tomb at Faversham and Henry I's at Reading, not to mention King Arthur's at Glastonbury, were swept away together with the monastic churches which had sheltered them for centuries.[61] As the Elizabethan vicar Michael Sherbrook lamented, "Kings' . . . tombs were regarded no more than the tombs of all other inferior persons: for to what end should they stand, when the Church over them was not spared for their cause?"[62] If any note of regret was sounded, it came from one of the few surviving representatives of the house of York, Richard's niece, the Countess of Salisbury. Interrogated on charges of treason a few days after Greyfriars fell, the sixty-five year old Margaret admitted to grieving at the fall of "the houses where her ancestors lay."[63]

Within a short while, the remains of Greyfriars had disappeared almost entirely, with some of the timber and masonry going to the repair of the nearby St Martin's church (now Leicester Cathedral).[64] The topographer

[59] Greg Walker, *Writing under Tyranny: English Literature and the Henrician Reformation* (Oxford: Oxford University Press, 2005), 6–7. In 1536, Reginald Pole warned Henry that he might meet the fate of Richard III, finding few friends one day; *Letters and Papers, Foreign and Domestic, Henry VIII, Volume 10: January–June 1536* (1887), 405–6.

[60] W. G. Hoskins, *A History of the County of Leicestershire, Volume 2* (1954), 33.

[61] Philip Lindley, *Tomb Destruction and Scholarship: Medieval Monuments in Early Modern England* (Donington: Shaun Tyas, 2007), 16.

[62] Michael Sherbrook, "The Fall of Religious Houses," in *Tudor Treatises*, ed. A. G. Dickens, YAS Rec. Ser. 125 (Wakefield: Yorkshire Archaeological Society, 1959), 124.

[63] *Letters and Papers, Foreign and Domestic, Henry VIII, Volume 13 Part 2: August–December 1538* (1893), 327. Margaret's interrogation took place 12–13 November. The Countess's parents, George Duke of Clarence and Isabel Neville, were buried at Tewkesbury Abbey, whose church survived the dissolution, being converted to a parish church in 1539; their tombs are intact to this day.

[64] Charles James Billson, *Medieval Leicester* (Leicester: Backus, 1920), 78. That Leicester Cathedral is partly composed of masonry from the dissolved Greyfriars makes the decision that Richard's recently discovered remains should be reinterred there peculiarly fitting.

John Leland, whose itinerary brought him through Leicester in the early 1540s, writes of the house and its funeral monuments in the past tense: "The Gray-Freres of Leircester stode at the ende of the hospital of Mr Wigeston. Simon Mountefort, as I lernid, was founder there: and there was byried King Richard 3 and a knight caullid Mutton, sumtyme Mayre of Leyrcester."[65] Leland usually notes those occasions when he saw a tomb or monument with his own eyes (as he did at the Leicester Blackfriars, whose church was still standing); it seems apparent that in this case he did not. Even the limited information he was able to gather was inaccurate. The priory was not in fact established by Simon de Montfort, and Sir William Moton or Mutton (*d*.1362), whose body had indeed lain in the church with Richard's, never served as Mayor. Memories had faded swiftly in post-dissolution Leicester. Leland seems to have heard nothing as to what became of Richard's tomb, or his remains.

For more than seventy years following the fall of Greyfriars, no definite rumour of Richard's final fate comes down to us. There is an intriguing reference in the poetic complaint of Shore's Wife which Thomas Churchyard contributed to the *Mirror for Magistrates* (1563). Churchyard has the wronged mistress of Edward IV curse Richard's body both living and dead: "I aske of God a vengeance on thy bones,/Thy stinkinge corps corrupts the ayre I know."[66] The description of Richard's body as unburied is striking in the context of a complaint by a dead woman who has drawn attention to the position of her own body "low in earth"; although the reference may be to the initial public display of Richard's corpse, it is just possible that it reflects a tradition regarding the fate of his remains after the dissolution of Greyfriars. This would accord with the first explicit account of what happened to Richard, which is found no earlier than 1610–11 in John Speed's *History of Great Britain*. Speed's story is sensational, and has maintained a hold on the popular imagination ever since, though the historian himself expresses skepticism about the "report":

> his Tombe . . . at the suppression of that Monastery was pulled downe, and utterly defaced; since when his grave overgrowne with nettles and weedes, is very obscure and not to be found. Onely the stone chest wherin his corpes lay, is now made a drinking trough for horses at a common Inne, and retaineth the onely memory of this Monarches greatnesse. His body also (as tradition hath

---

[65] *The Itinerary of John Leland in or about the Years 1535–1543*, ed. Lucy Toulmin Smith, Volume 1 (London: G. Bell, 1907), 15. "The tomb which Leland noticed was in all probability that of Sir William Moton, of Peckleton, Knight, who, according to Burton, was buried at the church of the Grey Friars in Leicester in the year 1362"; Billson, *Medieval Leicester*, 78.

[66] *The Mirror for Magistrates*, ed. Lily B. Campbell (Cambridge: Cambridge University Press, 1938), 384, ll. 323–4.

delivered) was borne out of the City, and contemptuously bestowed under the end of *Bow-Bridge,* which giveth passage over a branch of *Stowre* upon the west side of the Towne. Upon this Bridge (the like report runneth) stood a stone of some height, against which King *Richard,* as hee passed toward *Bosworth,* by chance strucke his spur, and against the same stone as he was brought backe, hanging by the horse side, his head was dashed and broken, as a wise woman (forsooth) had foretold, who, before *Richards* going to battell, being asked of his successe, said, that where his spurre strucke, his head should be broken; but of these things, as is the report, so let be the credite.[67]

For four centuries, down to the discovery of a battered human skeleton in the excavation of Greyfriars in 2012, Speed's story has been the most commonly repeated and widely known account of the ultimate fate of Richard's remains. The tale is not altogether implausible. There is no doubt that many dead bodies were cast out of their graves in the dissolution. The seventeenth-century antiquary John Weever lamented the mixture of coarseness, cupidity, haste and zeal which, for a short while, made the most abominable actions seem almost routine: "the foulest and most inhumane action of those times, was the violation of Funerall Monuments. Marbles which covered the dead were digged up, and put to other uses . . . Tombes hackt and hewne a peeces . . . dead carcases, for gaine of their stone or leaden coffins, cast out of their graves. . . ."[68] Weever is undoubtedly accurate in suggesting that, for the most part, the mistreatment of corpses was a byproduct of the violence directed, for one reason or another, at their tombs: "for greedinesse of the brasse, or for that they were thought to bee Antichristian."[69] Tombs could be dismantled and sold off; bodies, having no re-use value, were cast out as so much garbage. In just a handful of reported cases, reformers directed their violence specifically against dead bodies. According to a widely circulated report, the bones of Thomas Becket were placed on trial, burnt and scattered to the winds.[70] In this case, at least, we cannot escape the sense of real vindictiveness being directed towards the individual corpse. Officially, however, the sole justification for abusing human remains was to combat superstition and demonstrate the lack of efficacy of so-called relics.[71] Needless to say, no one had ever been inclined to venerate the relics of Richard III.

[67] John Speed, *The History of Great Britaine* (London, 1611), 725.
[68] John Weever, *Ancient Funerall Monuments* (London, 1631), 51.
[69] Weever, *Ancient Funerall Monuments,* 51.
[70] On the uncertain evidence for this deed, see Thomas F. Mayer, "Becket's Bones Burnt! Cardinal Pole and the Invention and Dissemination of an Atrocity," in *Martyrs and Martyrdom in England, c.1400–1700,* ed. Thomas S. Freeman and Thomas F. Mayer (Woodbridge: Boydell, 2007), 126–43.
[71] At St Swithin's shrine in Winchester, 1538, Thomas Wriothesley (nephew of the herald who had recorded Richard's epitaph) wrote to the king of his intention "to sweep away all the

Richard had been no saint, but he had been a king, and the body of a king had its own charismatic aura. In 1538, some older citizens of Leicester would still have remembered the remarkable day in 1485 when two kings entered the city together, one in triumph, the other slung over a horse's rump. Speed's account of the matter draws a link between the passage of Richard's body over Bow Bridge before and after Bosworth, and his supposed return to the same spot 53 years later. In the report that he was "borne out of the city" following the dissolution of Greyfriars, there is a hint of a mock royal progress. To repeat the story of Richard's corpse being dumped in the River Soar was to let the mind dwell on the idea of handling a royal body in a radically transgressive manner. Simply to imagine and describe the action would not fail to convey a subversive frisson, a whiff of dangerous excitement.

The tale had undoubtedly been in circulation for some time before it was recorded in Speed's *History*. Speed himself refers to the story both as a "tradition" and as a "report"—the former term suggesting a matter of oral history within a community, the latter the testimony, probably written, of a single individual. Perhaps the "report" was a letter from a correspondent on the content of collective memory in Leicestershire. The story was clearly sufficiently well-known and accepted in the city for the sarcophagus which had reputedly housed Richard's remains to be a familiar sight at a local inn. That the story was old does not, of course, mean that it was true. Elements of the tradition clearly predate the dissolution itself, seeming like refractions of the original events of 1485, when Richard's body was indeed paraded through the streets, perhaps suffering some climactic humiliation at Bow Bridge, and was said to have been tossed away like rubbish ("beried in a dike"). There are hints of yet more ancient folk-memories as well, linking the local river with the body of a king. According to the medieval historian Geoffrey of Monmouth, no less a personage than King Lear had been laid to rest in an underground chamber beneath the river Soar.[72] Urban memory and legend thus provided ample material out of which to mould the story of Richard's reburial in the river in the 1530s.

rotten bones that be called relics; which we may not omit lest it should be thought we came more for the treasure than for avoiding of the abomination of idolatry." *Letters and Papers, Foreign and Domestic, Henry VIII, Volume 13 Part 2: August–December 1538* (1893), 155.

[72] Geoffrey of Monmouth, *The History of the Kings of Britain*, trans. Lewis Thorpe (London: Penguin, 1966), 86. Geoffrey also describes the drowning of various figures from British antiquity in the rivers Severn and Humber, rivers that will mark Britain's internal borders. In these cases as in that of Lear, Geoffrey seems to draw a link between fluvial interment and the division of Britain.

The early seventeenth century saw a sharp rise of interest in Richard's burial place. For Richard Corbett, the tyrant's grave, unlocatable as it was, ranked among the chief attractions of the county town:

> Is not th' usurping *Richard* buryed here,
> That King of hate, and therefore slave of feare;
> Drag'd from the fatall field *Bosworth,* where hee
> Lost life, and what he liv'd for, Cruelty?
> Search, finde his name, but there is none; O Kings
> Remember whence your Powre, and vastnesse springs:
> If not as *Richard* now, so may you bee,
> Who hath no Tombe, but Scorne and Memorie.[73]

Corbett shows no awareness of the tradition regarding Richard's last watery tomb. He believes rather that Richard's remains still lie somewhere within the city precincts, in an unmarked grave—unmarked owing not to the dissolution of the priory but to Richard's misdeeds. Richard's tomblessness in Corbett's account serves as a sharp lesson to would-be tyrants. Yet his information is inaccurate, for it seems by 1612 there were not one but two competing monuments to be seen in Leicester. An empty sarcophagus thought to be Richard's was serving as a horse trough at an inn, as Speed attests. And a more dignified memorial could be viewed in the garden of a prominent local citizen, according to the report of Christopher Wren (father of the architect):

> The wicked and tyrannical Prince King Richard III. being slain at Bosworth, his Body was begged by the nuns at Leicester, and buried in their Chapel there; at the Dissolution whereof, the Place of his Burial happened to fall into the Bounds of a Citizen's Garden, which being (after) purchased by Mr Robert Herrick (some Time Mayor of Leicester) was by him covered with a handsome Stone Pillar, three Foot high, with this Inscription, "Here lies the Body of Richard III, some Time King of England." This he shewed me (Chr. Wren) walking in the Garden, *Anno* 1612.[74]

---

[73] Richard Corbett, *Certain Elegant Poems* (London, 1647), 4. Corbett draws a parallel with Wolsey's interment. "And though from his owne store *Wolsey* might have/A Palace, or a Colledge for his grave;/Yet here he lyes interr'd, as if that all/Of him to be remembred were his fall:/Nothing but earth to earth, nor pompous weight/Upon him but a pebble, or a quayte" (4). John Weever, too, seems to have believed Richard was still buried somewhere in Leicester, remarking at one point in *Ancient Funerall Monuments,* "But here enough of King *Richard,* untill I come to Leicester, and there to the place of his buriall" (522). Unfortunately, Weever's great antiquarian survey of tombs and monuments never arrives at Leicester.
[74] Christopher Wren, *Parentalia: or, Memoirs of the Family of the Wrens* (London, 1750), 144. A version of the anecdote with only minor differences occurs amongst "A Collection of Divers Curious Historical Pieces" in Francis Peck, *Memoirs of the Life and Actions of Oliver Cromwell* (London, 1740), 85. Herrick's garden was clearly not the wasteland "overgrown with nettles and weeds" described by Speed. Speed's map of the city of Leicester suggests that he may have been mistaken as to the site of the Franciscan priory; the map puts Greyfriars on what was in fact the location of the Blackfriars. See Ashdown-Hill, *Last Days of Richard III,* 108–9, pl. 28.

The two monuments would seem to be mutually exclusive—one testifying to Richard's absence, the other proclaiming his continuing presence. While there is no further record of Mr Herrick's pillar, the trough would survive as a tourist attraction for well over a century. In 1654 John Evelyn described Leicester in his diary as "famous for the tomb of the tyrant, Richard the Third, which is now converted to a cistern, at which (I think) cattle drink."[75] In 1698 Celia Fiennes was disappointed not to see the stone on Bow Bridge against which Richard had struck both his heel and his head (it had been removed), but she did see what was left of the coffin, "which was cut out in exact form for his body to lye in, that remains to be seen at the Grey-hound in Leaster but is partly broken."[76] The coffin was still on display in the early eighteenth century, in increasingly fragmented form. When William Hutton, the historian of Bosworth, went in search of it in 1758, he was told that it had finally been "destroyed about the latter end of the reign of George I, and some of the pieces placed as steps in a cellar, at the same inn where it had served as a trough."[77]

Somehow, the very absence of Richard's body made him paradoxically present in Leicester, centuries after his death. Lacking a tomb, he lacked a vehicle to conduct him safely into the past. Part of the function of the tomb or grave is to help us to forget the dead body, both by concealing it and by providing a visible and material substitute for it, a surrogate social self. Tombs both cover and cover for the dead. An empty sarcophagus, on the other hand, brings home the fact of the body by testifying to its loss, a loss which is always felt as recent because the body is out of its proper place. "Whate sholde I say? he was here yesterday!" The disappearance of the body from its container recalls and tropes the disappearance of the person from the world through death: a missing corpse thus literalizes the *ubi sunt* motif in a way that undermines its conventional otherworldly resolutions. The paradoxical power of the empty tomb to make the absent present may also explain why the coffin-trough survived so long in the public imagination, even becoming—with faint echoes of another empty sepulchre—an object of curious pilgrimage.

[75] *The Diary of John Evelyn, Volume 1* (London: Routledge/Thoemmes Press, 1996), 87.

[76] Celia Fiennes, *The Journeys of Celia Fiennes*, ed. John Hillaby (London: Macdonald, 1983), 192.

[77] William Hutton, *The Battle of Bosworth Field*, second edition with additions by J. Nichols (London: Nichols, 1813), 143; see also 223. By the early eighteenth century the trough was associated with the White Horse Inn rather than Fiennes's Greyhound. There is nothing to link the coffin displayed in the seventeenth and eighteenth centuries with the fifteenth-century stone coffin now on display at the Bosworth visitor's centre; nor is there anything to link either coffin with Richard III. See also Ashdown-Hill, *The Last Days of Richard III*, 93.

What traditions or rumours might have reached Shakespeare's ears regarding the ultimate fate of Richard's body? *Richard III* offers little definite evidence on the question. In a suggestive passage near the end of the play, Richmond exhorts his followers against "The wretched, bloody, and usurping boar,/That . . . makes his trough/In your inbowelled bosoms" (5.2.7–10). The image of the trough can be read as both reproducing and transfiguring that of the coffin-cum-trough at the Greyhound Inn. One is an empty case whose interior replicates the form of a human body; the other, a human body transformed into an empty case. The passage hints at a kind of poetic justice: the boar, who has turned the bodies of others into hollow troughs, will suffer a version of the same fate. Yet intriguing as the parallel is, there is little else in the play to indicate that Shakespeare paid much heed to the story of Richard's exhumation and deposition in the Soar, or indeed to any tradition regarding the fate of his remains. The play is undoubtedly preoccupied to a remarkable extent with the theme of watery burial, but this is more likely to spring from a tradition involving the Princes in the Tower, as will be seen in the next section of this chapter.

If anything, the play seems intent on drawing our attention away from the question of what final fate awaits Richard's body. Unlike *Richard II* and *King John,* both of which also conclude with the death of the eponymous monarch, and unlike all but a handful of Shakespeare's tragedies, *Richard III* ends without any mention of burial arrangements for its central character.[78] In the final scene, the victorious Richmond inquires "what men of name are slain on either side" (5.8.12) and, being informed, orders his followers to "inter their bodies as become their births" (5.8.15). This command comes only fifteen lines after Richard's death, and, depending on the staging, his corpse may still be lying at the victor's feet. Yet there is no stated provision for Richard's body. If the omission seems unusual in the context of Shakespeare's other works, it is still more remarkable in the context of this play, in which Richard's material body has been represented as almost an actor in itself, a key agent in the unfolding of the tragedy. Richard's body determined his villainy. And now: all the world to nothing! Perhaps the body's final act of defiance lies in its refusal to provide a forwarding address, to answer the *ubi sunt.*

The play draws our attention away from the fate of Richard's corpse in part to concentrate its focus on the manner of his end. This much is clear: he dies like a dog. The canine quality of his departure is signalled well

[78] Among Shakespeare's tragedies, *Titus Andronicus, Romeo and Juliet, Julius Caesar, Hamlet, Antony and Cleopatra, Coriolanus,* and *Timon of Athens* all devote their final moments to specifying funerary arrangements for the central character or characters. Only *King Lear, Macbeth,* and *Othello* do not.

in advance. Margaret, who repeatedly refers to Richard as a dog, a hell-hound, and a cur, prays before her final exit "That I may live and say, 'The dog is dead'" (4.3.78). Immediately following Richard's death, Richmond enters with thanks to God for answering that prayer: "The day is ours, the bloody dog is dead" (5.8.1). As we have already seen, Richmond's spiteful phrase dates back to the very era of Bosworth (something that can be demonstrated with regard to very few lines in the play). Within months of Richard's death, Dafydd Llwyd was expressing his contempt for the "dog killed in a dyke"; in York not long after, bibulous William Burton proclaimed that Richard "was beried in a dike like a dogge." If Shakespeare is unlikely to have known of either Burton's or Llwyd's use of the phrase, he certainly did know the passage in Thomas More's *History of King Richard III* which describes the abuse of Richard's corpse: "slain in the fielde, hacked and hewed of his enemies handes, haryed on horsebacke dead, his here in despite torn and togged lyke a cur dogge."[79]

For all his animus against Richard, did More recognize that the doggishness of his death and posthumous maltreatment might redound as much to the discredit of the victors as of the vanquished? Very probably he did; earlier chroniclers, no less ill-disposed to Richard, had admitted qualms over the "insufficient humanity" displayed towards his corpse. Shakespeare's adaptation of More's phrase, whereby the historian's observation becomes the victor's crow, heightens the ambiguity. There is something uncomfortable, even alarming about Richmond's choice of words, as if in the moment of triumph his mask had slipped and the face of the vengeful Margaret had peeped out from behind that of God's self-proclaimed captain. For modern productions of the play seeking ways to suggest that the new regime will be no more gracious than the old, the line that speaks of the bloody dog (coupled with the Hitlerian outburst that follows, "What traitor hears me and says not amen?") provides the likeliest grounding for such an interpretation.

"Like a dog." The bitter jibe applied to Richard in the days and years after his defeat has echoed dismally down the centuries. We hear it again in the dehumanizing death of Kafka's Joseph K., stripped and butchered by nonchalant functionaries ("'Like a dog!' he said; it was as if the shame of it must outlive him").[80] The techniques of twenty-first century interrogators confirm that reduction of the human to dog-like status remains the

---

[79] More, *History*, 87.
[80] Franz Kafka, *The Trial*, trans. Willa and Edwin Muir (New York: Schocken Books, 1992), 229.

very index of abjection.[81] Yet if the phrase "like a dog" points us forward from the early modern era to all-too-contemporary failures of humanity, it can also lead us back to classical discourses of justice and ethics. As Thomas More perhaps remembered, the phrase occurs in Book 5 of Plato's *Republic*, precisely in reference to the violation of the corpses of enemies killed in war. Here, however, it is not the dead but their abusers who are compared to dogs. Socrates, who seeks to prove that "we must abstain from spoiling the dead or hindering their burial," asks Glaucon the question:

> "is there not illiberality and avarice in robbing a corpse, and also a degree of meanness and womanishness in making an enemy of the dead body when the real enemy has flown away and left only his fighting gear behind him,—is not this rather like a dog who cannot get at his assailant, quarrelling with the stones which strike him instead?"
>
> "Very like a dog," he said.[82]

1.2 "THE BONES OF THE CHILDREN COULD NEVER BE FOUND": THE MYSTERY OF THE PRINCES

"Where is Plantagenet?" That urgent, insoluble question predates the disappearance of Richard III's remains, and indeed his death. From the early summer of 1483 to the present day, few missing persons have excited more speculation and controversy than Richard's nephews, Edward V and Richard Duke of York. Edward, aged 12, was lodged in the Tower of London by the middle of May, his nine-year-old brother Richard joining him there on 16 June when their mother was prevailed upon to relinquish him from sanctuary in Westminster Abbey. Initially, according to the *Great Chronicle of London*, "the children of King Edward were seen shooting and playing in the garden of the Tower at sundry times."[83] The Protector and his council clearly thought it wise to demonstrate to the populace that the boys were alive and well. Yet, as the Italian visitor to London Dominic

---

[81] A former commander of US detention facilities in Iraq and Guantanamo Bay instructed subordinates "to treat the prisoners like dogs"; at the notorious Abu Ghraib prison, detainees were humiliated by being forced to walk on all fours and bark. For these examples, and for an interrogation of US tactics against the moral compass provided by Kafka, see Alex Danchev, "Like a Dog: Humiliation and Shame in the War on Terror," *Alternatives: Global, Local, Political* 31 (2006): 259–83.

[82] Plato, *The Republic*, Book V, in *Plato's Dialogues*, trans. Benjamin Jowett, third edition (Oxford: Clarendon Press, 1892), 3.166.

[83] *GCL*, 234.

Mancini recorded, sightings of the princes became less frequent after the fall of their chief defender, the Lord Hastings. "[Edward] and his brother were withdrawn into the inner apartments of the Tower proper, and day by day began to be seen more rarely behind the bars and windows, till at length they ceased to appear altogether."[84]

The slow yet inexorable withdrawal of the princes from the field of the visible looks very much like a tactic designed to prefigure and normalize the idea of their deaths. No one quite knew when the princes had last been seen; no one could say just when the nagging fears as to their fate had given way a dull certainty. When Mancini left England at the time of Richard's coronation, rumours of the death of Edward V were already current: "I have seen many men burst forth into tears and lamentations when mention was made of him after his removal from men's sight; and already there was a suspicion that he had been done away with."[85] Yet six months later Mancini had received no confirmation as to the princes' fate. Neither under Richard nor under Henry VII (for whom their death was at least equally convenient) were the bodies of the princes produced in evidence of their demise, nor was any official account given of how they had met their end, nor of the fate of their remains. Well into the 1490s, rumours circulated that at least young Richard had escaped—a belief exploited to the full by the Yorkist Pretender Perkin Warbeck.

Early chroniclers of Richard's reign were determined to affirm one fact above all about the princes—that they had died at their uncle's behest shortly after his usurpation of the throne. John Rous states that Richard "killed [Edward V] together with his brother," some three months after receiving him with kisses.[86] But the earliest chroniclers provide little information or even guesswork as to how the boys met their deaths, or about the subsequent fate of their bodies. Rous remarks cryptically that "it was afterwards known to very few by what manner of death they had suffered," a phrase perhaps intended to imply that the chronicler himself knows more than he can reveal.[87] The Crowland chronicler ascribes their death to "some unknown manner of violent destruction"; Polydore Vergil is confident in ascribing the bloody deed to Sir James Tyrrell, but acknowledges "with what kinde of death these sely chyldren wer executyd yt is not certainely known."[88] The earliest specific account of how the children met their deaths is that of the Spanish diplomat Diego de Valera, writing in 1486, who states that Richard had the princes poisoned, though he rather spoils his credibility by claiming

---

[84] Mancini, *Usurpation*, 93.   [85] Mancini, *Usurpation*, 93.
[86] Rous, *Historia*, in Hanham, *Richard III*, 121.
[87] Rous, *Historia*, in Hanham, *Richard III*, 120.
[88] *Crowland Chronicle Continuations,* ed. Pronay and Cox, 163; Vergil, *Three Books*, 188.

the crime took place in the reign of their father, Edward IV, said to have been fighting in the north at the time.[89]

The first English text to speculate on how the murder was committed is the *Great Chronicle of London*, completed *c*.1512: "of theyr dethis maner was many oppynons, ffor some said they were murderid atwene ii ffethyr beddis, some said they were drownyd in malvesy, and some said they were stykkid with a veny-mous pocion."[90] In years to come, the mysterious murder of the children would become the subject of increasingly elaborate and detailed narratives. Thomas More, writing in the mid-1510s, described how, under Tyrrell's direction,

> Miles Forest and John Dighton, about midnight (the sely children lying in their beddes) came into the chamber, and sodainly lapped them up among the clothes so be wrapped them and entangled them keping down by force the fetherbed and pillowes hard unto their mouthes, that within a while smored and stifled, theyr breath failing, thei gave up to god their innocent soules into the joys of heaven, leaving to the tormentors their bodyes dead in the bed.[91]

More's account, with its unprecedented wealth of circumstantial detail, would become the standard version of how the princes met their deaths, though later writers would embroider upon it to enhance both the pity and the horror of the scene. In his *Pastyme of People* (1529), More's brother-in-law John Rastell includes a ghastly vignette in which the younger prince momentarily escapes the murderer's clutches and huddles naked beneath the bedstead, only to be hauled out and butchered. Rastell then goes on to provide a second and entirely different version of the crime, in which both princes are persuaded by a cry of treason to hide themselves in a chest, which is then buried under a stair-case in the Tower, leaving them to suffocate. Both accounts invite the reader to imagine and identify with the princes' protracted pain and terror (something glossed over in More, where the princes make a swift transition from sleep to heavenly joys)—and perhaps to identify also with the killers, through whose eyes the reader witnesses the victims' last moments. Rastell's distinctively nasty account stands at the origins of a tradition that culminates in John Everett Millais' 1878 portrait (Fig. 1.1), which comes very near to gloating over the princes' helpless fear.

Alongside a sometimes salacious curiosity as to the means by which the princes were dispatched, the reign of Henry VIII saw the development of a new and keen interest in their place of burial. This, again, was a matter on which the early chroniclers could provide no certain information. There was, however, a general assumption that the boys who had disappeared

[89] Diego de Valera, letter to to Isabella and Ferdinand of Castile and Aragon, March 1, 1486, translated in Tudor-Craig, *Richard III*, 68.
[90] *GCL*, 236–7.   [91] More, *History*, 85.

Fig. 1.1. Sir John Everett Millais, "The Princes Edward and Richard in the Tower," oil on canvas, 1878. Courtesy of the Bridgeman Art Library.

within the confines of the Tower had never come out of it, alive or dead. In statute books such as Robert Pynson's *Magna Carta cum statutis* (1508), Edward's date of death is summarily recorded as 22 June 1483, and his place of burial as the Tower.[92] A short verse chronicle of the kings of England since William the Conqueror printed in 1530 likewise states of Edward that he "was never crowned/Yet he reigned as it is expowned/Two monthes and xviii dayes gone/And than buryed at the towre of London."[93] Yet around this time, an unknown hand copying information from this or a similar chronicle into the table of years in an old cartulary made a surprising departure from established certainties: "Obitus Edwardi v^ti xxij° mens Junij regnavit ii menses et viij° dies set non coronatus fuit occisus et nemo s[c]it ubi sepultus." ("Edward V died on 22 June, he reigned two months

and eight days but was not crowned, nobody knows where he is buried.")[94]
In some minds, at least, the site of the princes' burial had been transformed
from an uncomplicated assumption into a matter of intriguing doubt.

Once again, Thomas More's account lies at the root of subsequent
speculation. In his version, immediately after the deed the killers "laide
their bodies naked out uppon the bed, and fetched sir James to see them.
Which upon the sight of them, caused those murtherers to burye them
at the stayre foote, metely depe in the grounde under a great heape
of stones."[95] More then has Tyrrell ride in haste to bring the news to
Richard, who knights him on the spot. This would seem to mark the
conclusion of the sorry episode, with innocence extinguished and villainy (temporarily) rewarded. But More will not let the matter—or the
princes—rest there.

> But he [Richard] allowed not as I have heard, the burying in so vile a cor-
> ner, saying that he woulde have them buried in a better place, because thei
> wer a kinges sonnes. Loe the honourable corage of a kynge. Wherupon thei
> say that a prieste of syr Robert Brakenbury toke up the bodyes again, and
> secretely entered them in such place, as by the occasion of his deathe, whiche
> onely knew it could never synce come to light.[96]

More thus introduces what will be a staple of further speculation, the idea
that the princes were initially buried under the stairs (where Rastell will have
them buried alive), and then moved to another location. The cause of the second
move is Richard, with his characteristically priggish principles on the matter of
royal burial. The site of the subsequent burial is unknown, but given that the
task is entrusted to a priest of the Tower, and that "better place" presumably
means consecrated ground, we might infer a site associated with the Chapel of St
Peter ad Vincula, where prisoners executed in the Tower—eventually to include
Thomas More himself—were typically interred.[97] There is no implication in
More's account that the bodies were removed from the confines of the Tower.

More asserts that Tyrrell and Dighton confessed to the crime under
examination in 1502, "but whither the bodies were removed thei could
nothing tel."[98] If true, this would suggest at least some degree of official
interest in the location of the corpses. There is, however, no evidence of a

---

[94] C. F. Richmond, "The Death of Edward V," *Northern History* 25 (1989): 278. For the
likely source of this information, see Gunn, "Early Tudor Dates." Lodowick Lloyd, *The First
Part of the Dial of Days* (London, 1590), gives the date of Edward's death as 24 May, which
would cast the political maneuverings of June 1483 in a very different light.
[95] More, *History*, 85.   [96] More, *History*, 86.
[97] Thomas More, John Fisher, Anne Boleyn, Katherine Howard, and Jane Grey were all
buried in the chancel of St Peter ad Vincula; their headless bodies were exhumed and transferred to the chapel crypt in the nineteenth century.
[98] More, *History*, 86.

search being made for the bodies at any point in the reign of Henry VII. It may have been More's own history which first prompted some curious individual to scour the Tower for the princes' remains. If so, nothing was discovered. As Rastell reports in 1529, "the bones of the sayd children could never be founde buryed nother in the Towre nor in nother place."[99] To the puzzle of the missing bodies, Rastell presents a new and remarkable solution. Enclosed in a chest, the bodies were loaded by an intimate of Richard's on board a ship bound for Flanders: "& whan the shyppe was in the blacke Depes this man threwe bothe those dede bodyes so closed in the cheste over the hatches into the see." To be submerged in the aptly-named Black Deeps at the mouth of the Thames estuary was, needless to say, to be lost beyond all hope of recovery.

The question of what had happened to the princes became still murkier when More's history appeared in print for the first time in the 1540s. In Richard Grafton's editions of the chronicles of John Hardyng (1543) and Edward Hall (1548), details apparently drawn from Rastell's *Pastyme* are inserted somewhat awkwardly into More's narrative. Having described how Brakenbury's priest reburied the bodies in an undisclosed location, the text continues:

> some say that Kyng Rycharde caused the priest to take them up and close them in lead and put them in a coffyne full of holes hoked at the endes with ii hokes of yron, and so to cast them into a place called the Blacke depes at the Themes mouth, so that they should never rise up nor be sene agayne. This was the very trueth unknowen by reason that the sayd priest died so shortly and disclosed it never to any person that would utter it.[100]

Here, the "better place" of burial stipulated by the king becomes a grim joke indeed. There is no hint how the priest's unrevealed and irrecoverable secret became available to the historian. As the passage piles circumstantial detail upon detail, only to conclude that the truth never became known, the cumulative effect is one of perhaps intentional absurdity.[101]

Although the passage savours of More's habitual irony, it also seems to speak to the preoccupations and anxieties of a post-Reformation England More never lived to see. The unequivocally sinister role of the priest, the inversion of holiness—his "better place" being a black pit—smack of the satire levelled by Protestant reformers at corrupt and ruthless Catholic clergy. At the same time, and more ambivalently, the story of the boys

---

[99] John Rastell, *The Pastyme of People* (London, 1529), F6ᵛ.

[100] Hall, Edward V, xxviiᵛ–xxviiiʳ.

[101] Alison Hanham, in the course of her reading of More's *History* as a satirical drama, suggests that this passage must have been written either by More himself or by someone with "the same impish sense of humour"; Hanham, *Richard III*, 212.

encased in lead and enclosed in an iron coffin full of holes carries echoes of medieval saints' lives. The *Golden Legend* of Jacobus de Voragine includes numerous tales of bodies cast into the sea by persecuting tyrants, only to be miraculously recovered: St Bartholomew, whose corpse floated "in a tombe of lede" from India to the shores of Sicily; St Vincent, cast in the sea with a millstone around his neck but arriving back on dry land sooner than the ship that carried him; St Clement, bound to an anchor and drowned, only for the prayers of his disciples to cause the sea to part and reveal his resting place.[102] First printed in England by William Caxton in 1483, the year of the princes' disappearance and probable death, and reprinted regularly into the 1520s, the *Golden Legend* would have been part of the mental furniture of a great many readers of Hall and Hardyng. They would have registered both the familiar outlines of the story, and the startling disparity in its conclusion, with no consoling miracle. This is a dark fable for a disenchanted age: there could hardly be a more telling measure of how profoundly and rapidly the world had changed.

The story of the Black Deeps certainly stuck in the mind of one early reader of the chronicle, Thomas Stanley, Bishop of Sodor and Man, who at some point before his death in the 1560s was inspired to record these verses on the fate of the princes' remains:

> In Londons Toure in one plase or anoder
> Interryd lay Kyng Edward and his Broder,
> Who by there wicked Eme were guyltles sleyne,
> And basely beryd, yet tooke up ageyne
> And cast into the blacke deepes at Tems mouth.
> Now whether wreckt, or tost from North to South,
> Their reliques are, it recks not; ther soules rest
> In Hev'n amangst Gods children ever blest.[103]

Like Bishop Stanley's longer work, *The Stanley Poem* (a rollicking verse history of his own family, discussed in Chapter 5), this brief poem works to transform the matter of chronicles into a kind of folklore. Recast as the nameless "wicked eme," Richard III seems more a figure of fable than a real fifteenth-century king. Yet whilst the verses read almost like a rhyme for children, they resonate with concerns which were deep and widespread among adults in the immediate post-Reformation era. The description

---

[102] Jacobus de Voragine, *Legenda aurea sanctorum* (London, 1483), cclxx^v, cxxii^r, ccclxxxii^v. "Hokes of yron" also recur frequently in the *Golden Legend*, though as instruments of torture rather than being attached to coffins. There is also, because of the age and innocence of the victims, resonance with the story of Little St. Hugh of Lincoln, and indeed with the boy in Chaucer's *Prioress's Tale*, whose bodies hidden in wells or privies by their Jewish murderers are brought miraculously to light.

[103] Weever, *Ancient Funerall Monuments*, 521.

of the princes' remains as "reliques" serves as a reminder of the host of saints whose shrines had been dissolved in the 1530s, their once-honoured bones disposed of ignobly or scattered on the winds. The bodies of several kings, as has been seen, had also vanished without trace, whilst the remains of less exalted ancestors had disappeared *en masse*, either in the dissolution of the monasteries or in the subsequent dissolution of chantries and charnel houses under Edward VI. The poem's affirmation that, wherever the princes' bodies are, their souls are in heaven, now reads like a response to anxiety not only about Edward IV's sons but about the many missing saints, kings, and commoners whose tombs could no longer be visited, whose bodies lay who knows where. More than a whimsical meditation on an old murder, Bishop Stanley's poem can be read as a lightly coded response to a somber contemporary concern.

Down to the end of the sixteenth century, the unlocatability of the princes was both a notorious fact and a potentially poignant emblem of the limits of historical knowledge. The impossibility of finding Edward V and his brother seems to become matter for a dark joke in *The Mirror for Magistrates* (1563), when William Baldwin excuses their absence from his volume of verse biographies. "Have you theyr tragedy? No surely (quoth I) The Lord Vaulx undertooke to penne it, but what he hath done therein I am not certayne, & therfore I let it passe til I knowe farder."[104] Like the priest who died without revealing the location of the bodies, Lord Vaux (1510–1556) had been dead for several years when the *Mirror* was printed; the lost poem on the princes naturally never appeared.[105] The notoriety of the princes' unknown resting place receives ironic attention again in *The True Tragedy of Richard III*, where the murderer Miles Forrest reports, "I have conveyd them to the staires foote among a heape of stones, and anon ile carry them where they shall be no more found againe, nor all the cronicles shall nere make mention what shall become of them."[106] (Earlier in the same play, Richard himself drops a casual hint to what many supposed to be their real end, describing them as potential "food for fishes."[107])

---

[104] *Mirror for Magistrates*, 297.
[105] This is one of a number of temporal slippages in the text of *The Seconde Parte of the Mirror for Magistrates*, discussed further in Chapter 5.
[106] *The True Tragedie of Richard the Third* (London, 1594), F1ᵛ.
[107] In the passage quoted, in which he contemplates the goal of disposing of the princes, Richard weirdly conflates means of causing their deaths and means of disposing of the bodies. "Why, what are the babes but a puffe of/Gun-pouder? A marke for the soldiers, food for fishes,/Or lining for beds, devices enough to make them away" (*True Tragedie*, B4ʳ). Where the received account has the boys murdered with bed clothes and then, possibly, fed to the fishes, the line raises the grotesque idea that the murderers might conceal the bodies by turning them into blankets.

In the 1590s the murder in the Tower was represented or vividly reported on the stage in at least three distinct versions: *The True Tragedy*, Shakespeare's *Richard III*, and Heywood's *Second Part of Edward IV*. (Shakespeare's play differs from the others in declining to show the deed itself.) Probably as a result of these performances, the association of the Tower with the death and disappearance of the princes became still more firmly fixed in the popular imagination. As Kristen Deiter has shown, by the beginning of the seventeenth century the tale of the murder of the princes was a memorable highlight of the Tower tour undertaken by many foreign and domestic visitors.[108] What was still lacking, of course, was a tomb or burial place which might be displayed as the culmination of the tour. But that problem would be resolved in the seventeenth century—not just once, but several times over.[109]

In his *History of King Richard III* (c. 1619), Sir George Buck reported the curious recent discovery of "certain bones, like to the bones of a child, found lately in a high and desolate turret in the Tower." Some, he acknowledged, took these for the bones of Edward V:

> But others are of the opinion that this was the carcase and bones of an ape which was kept in the Tower and that in his old age he either chose that place to die in, or else had clambered up thither, according to the light and idle manner of those wanton animals, and after, being desirous to go down, and looking downward, and seeing the way to be very steep and deep and the precipice to be very terrible to behold he durst not adventure to descend, but for fear he stayed and starved there. Although this ape was soon missed and being sought for, yet he could not be found, by reason that that turret being reckoned but as a wast and damned place for the height and uneasy access thereunto; nobody in many years went up to it.[110]

It is a strange and a haunting anecdote. There are elements here of a bland and conventional moral allegory—the "light and . . . wanton" ways of the creature leading to folly, despair, death and damnation. Yet something in the vivid imagining of the ape's plight makes it hard to forget that Buck was himself now on the very precipice of madness and death. He left off work on the *History* in 1619; in 1622 he was declared insane, dying later in the same year.

---

[108] Kristen Deiter, *The Tower of London in English Renaissance Drama: Icon of Opposition* (London: Routledge, 2008), 73–7. The development of a narrative associating the murder of the princes with the "Bloody Tower" is discussed further in Chapter 4.

[109] The three "discoveries" discussed here are considered in more detail, with extensive quotation from the primary sources, in Helen Maurer, "Bones in the Tower: A Discussion of Time, Place and Circumstance" [Parts 1 and 2], Ricardian 8 (1990): 474–93; *Ricardian* 9 (1991): 2–22.

[110] Buck, *History of King Richard III*, 140.

Buck would hardly have invented the story of the bones in the Tower; it is only because the rumoured discovery was seen by some as firm evidence of foul play that he as Richard's defender felt required to provide an alternative explanation. The earliest published reference to the discovery of what might be royal bones in the Tower is found in 1622, in Ralph Brooke's *Catalogue and Succession of the Kings . . . of England*. Brooke declares that Richard Duke of York "was (with his brother Prince Edward) murdered in the Tower of London; which place ever since hath been mured up, and not known untill of late, when as their dead carcases were there found, under a heape of stones and rubbish."[111] Even in this sparse report it is clear that the details differ in important respects from Buck's story. The bones are described as sealed off and buried under rubble, not lying loose in a desolate tower, and the remains are those of two children, not one. We could almost be dealing with a separate discovery.

Twenty-five years later we encounter yet another tale of bodies discovered in the Tower—a version which may or may not share a common source with Brooke's brief account, but which is impossible to square with Buck's.

> August ye 17th 1647. Mr Johnson a Counsellor sonne of Sr Robert Johnson affirmed to mee and others when in Company that when ye Lo. Grey of Wilton and Sir Walter Raleigh were prisoners in ye Tower, the wall of ye passage to ye King's Lodgings then sounding hollow, was taken downe and at ye place marked A was found a little roome about 7 or 8 fo. square, wherein there stood a Table and uppon it ye bones of two children supposed of 6 or 8 yeeres of age, which by ye aforesaid noble and all present were credibly believed to bee ye carcasses of Edward ye 5th and his brother the then Duke of York. This gent was also an eyewitnesse at ye opening of it, with Mr Palmer and Mr Henry Cogan, officers of ye minte and others with whom having since discoursed hereof they affirmed ye same and yt they saw the skeletons. J. Webb.[112]

---

[111] *A Catalogue and Succession of the Kings, Princes, Dukes, Marquesses, Earles, and Viscounts of this Realme of England* (London, 1622), 33. This is the second edition of Brooke's catalogue. In the 1619 edition the same passage reads ". . . the Tower of London; which place ever since is called, The bloody Tower . . ." (¶¶¶[r]). In another place, the 1619 edition states of Richard of York that "his place of buriall was never knowne certainly to this day" (267); this passage is left unchanged in 1622, though it is now contradicted by information elsewhere in the edition.

[112] Printed in Lawrence E. Tanner and William Wright, "Recent Investigations Regarding the Fate of the Princes in the Tower," *Archaeologia* 84 (1935): 26. The copy of More is said to have been in the possession of Miss Gwladys E. Daniel; its current location is apparently unknown. Mr. Johnson is unknown, but Henry Cogan, Comptroller of the Mint, and Andrew Palmer, Assay Master, are both named in a listing of

The story above was recorded by the architect John Webb in a flyleaf of his copy of More's history of Richard III. Webb was intimately familiar with the layout of the Tower, and he accompanied his sketch with a plan of the King's Lodgings. It is not clear whether the date at the head of the note refers to the conversation with Mr. Johnson or, more probably, the date of writing, when Webb had been able to confirm Johnson's story in conversations with two officers of the mint. Whichever it is, the date contributes a contemporary resonance to the narrative; in August 1647, in the interim between the first and second civil wars, Charles I lay under house arrest (he would escape, briefly and disastrously, three months later). Webb was an ardent royalist; in the past he had spied for his king and smuggled money to him, for which he was briefly jailed. Recording notes on the fate of Edward V in his copy of More (published in 1641 under the title *The historie of the pitifull life, and unfortunate death of Edward the Fifth, and the then Duke of Yorke, his brother*), Webb was looking back to the last time a reigning monarch had been imprisoned—and to the outcome of that event.

Webb would have read in More how the bodies of the princes were first laid naked on a bed, then buried under the stairs, and finally shifted to another, undisclosed location. His anecdote fixes their bodies, paradoxically, in the initial tableau, laid out for display just as More described—albeit on a table rather than a bed. A later version of the same remarkable discovery, published by the French author Louis Aubery du Maurier in 1680, corrects this detail, describing how the boys were found "upon a bed . . . with two halters around their necks." Though Aubery differs from Webb in other respects, dating the discovery to the reign of Elizabeth rather than James, there can be little doubt that their stories spring from a common source, probably belonging to the first years of the seventeenth century. But Aubery is also in a position to record a fresh development. Though the bodies had been walled up after their initial discovery by order of the queen (who was unwilling to "revive the memory of such an execrable deed"), the chamber had recently been entered again with a different result: "the King of England, out of compassion that these two princes were deprived of burial, or from other reasons that I am ignorant of, has resolved to erect a Mausoleum, and have them transported to Westminster Abbey where the tombs of the Kings are."

In fact, the event Aubery refers to did not involve the bodies supposedly first revealed earlier in the century, but yet another (the third?) distinct discovery of bones believed to be those of the princes. This took place on 17 July 1674, as labourers were removing a set of stairs on the exte-

Fees and Diets of the Officers and Ministers of the Mint dated July 6, 1649; *Journal of the House of Commons: Volume 6: 1648–1651* (1802), 252.

rior of the White Tower, leading from the King's Lodgings to the royal chapel. Some ten feet below ground they hit upon a decayed wooden chest containing the skeletal remains of two children. The event was described by two witnesses, the herald John Gibbon (Bluemantle Pursuivant) and the royal surgeon John Knight. Writing in his copy of Brooke's *Catalogue and Succession* (the 1622 edition, with its earlier and obviously incompatible account of the same discovery), Gibbon described the unforgettable moment: "I my selfe handled ye Bones Especially ye Kings Skull."[113] The herald does not explain to what purpose he lingered over the skull he took for Edward V's, but there is little need to wonder. How often is it given to a man to cradle in his hands the cranium of a king? One thinks inevitably of the graveyard scene in *Hamlet*, but here the roles are reversed: the motley servitor holds the skull of his prince.

Not everyone was moved by the same instinctive reverence as Bluemantle. The smaller of the two skulls "was Broken in ye digging," and it seems that the bones had been cast aside with the rest of the debris of the excavation before their significance was guessed.[114] Knight reports that the laborers were then ordered "to sift the rubbish, and by that means preserved all the Bones."[115] The fate of these relics in the four years following their discovery is somewhat shadowy. By 1678, when they were finally deposited in Westminster Abbey in a monument designed by Sir Christopher Wren (Fig. 1.2), many of the bones were missing, and those that remained had somehow become mixed with a range of animal bones including "those of fish, duck, chicken, rabbit, sheep, pig and ox."[116] It is difficult not to think of Richard III's other supposed royal victim, Henry VI, laid to rest with a pig's leg at Windsor.

In 1933 the Westminster urn was opened and the bones examined by Lawrence Tanner of the Society of Antiquaries and William Wright, a Professor of Medicine. The results of their investigations, published in the journal *Archaeologia*, have remained controversial to this day. Wright concluded that the bones were those of closely related males—the younger between nine and eleven, the elder not yet thirteen. If these estimates are accurate, and if the skeletons are indeed those of the princes, it would seem

---

[113] Quoted in Maurer, "Bones in the Tower" [Part 2]. The copy of Brooke's *Catalogue* with Gibbon's notes remains in the library of the College of Arms.
[114] Quoted in Maurer, "Bones in the Tower" [Part 2].
[115] Sandford, *A Genealogical History of the Kings of England*, 404. Sandford here quotes the testimony of John Knight, "a Gentleman, an eye-witness, and principally concerned in the whole scrutiny" (402).
[116] Tanner and Wright, "Recent Investigations," 20. On the political context of the 1678 inurnment, see Maurer's suggestion that, on the eve of the exclusion crisis, the bones served as "touching symbols of the evils of deposition and thwarted succession."

Fig. 1.2. Christopher Wren, Monument of Edward V and Richard, Duke of York. © Dean and Chapter of Westminster.

to demonstrate that the boys met their deaths early in the reign of their uncle. But Wright's methods, driven by an undisguised determination to confirm the account of Thomas More, have been challenged on many fronts. No part of his report seems more dubious than the claim that a stain on the larger skull's lower jaw, "of a distinctly blood-red colour," was residue of the blood that had suffused the prince's face when suffocated under a pillow, as described by Thomas More.[117] Such a suggestion finds little support in modern forensic science. But Wright made no attempt to offer scientific backing for his hypothesis regarding the facial stains. Instead, he found the evidence he needed in the most authoritative source of all: the plays of William Shakespeare. In *Henry VI Part 2*, Wright observed, the

---

[117] Tanner and Wright, "Recent Investigations," 18.

face of the suffocated Humphrey Duke of Gloucester is described as being "black and full of blood."[118] Rather than accusing Wright of malpractice, we might read this as the doctor's wry acknowledgement that the debate over the Princes in the Tower could by no means be extricated from an historical vision of the fifteenth century derived ultimately from Shakespeare. He concludes his triumphant demonstration that the skeletons are indeed those of Edward and Richard with an invocation of divine justice: "while the bones of Richard III have long since disappeared, trampled into common clay, those of the princes freed from all undignified associations rest secure, in the company of those of their mighty ancestors, at the very heart of the national shrine."[119]

Whether or not the remains held at Westminster are indeed those of Edward and Richard, it is clear that Wright's findings are derived as much from his reading of Shakespeare and More as from the skeletal materials themselves. Indeed, it is tempting to say that these bones—and all the rest discovered in the Tower in the course of the seventeenth century—are in a real sense the products of reading. As we have seen, Webb recorded his account in the flyleaf of More's history, and his story places the princes— with a somewhat irrational fidelity to the source—in precisely the tableau in which More has them laid out initially. Similarly, the bones discovered in 1674 were found when "digging down the Stairs . . . about ten foot in the ground"—a location and a phrasing that match up precisely with where More has Dighton and Forrest leave the bodies, "at the stayre foote, metely depe in the grounde."[120] This again is not unproblematic, in that according to More the Tower chaplain subsequently moved the bodies to a different location altogether. Yet the proximity of the bones to the royal chapel perhaps suggests the "better place" to which they were supposed to have been translated; and indeed, the earliest printed account of the 1674 discovery insists that they were found in "the very place where it seems that poor Priest buried them, who afterwards dyed for his Piety."[121]

The several discoveries reported in the seventeenth century, each one according in a different respect with More's seminal account, resemble a series of snapshots from the scene of the crime. They present us with a strange case in which representation seems to precede reality, and writing somehow calls matter into being. The skeletons which so gratifyingly came to light—again and again—in the seventeenth century did so in response

---

[118] Tanner and Wright, "Recent Investigations," 19. See Shakespeare, *2 Henry VI*, 3.2.168.
[119] Tanner and Wright, "Recent Investigations," 20.
[120] Sandford, *A Genealogical History of the Kings of England*, 402; More, *History of King Richard III*, 85.
[121] Winston Churchill, *Divi Britannici* (London, 1675), 278.

to expectations and desires provoked by an early-sixteenth-century text. These "discoveries" recall a phenomenon in Jorge Luis Borges' imaginary world of Tlön, where mental conceptions influence material reality to the extent that "the duplication of lost objects is not infrequent. Two persons look for a pencil; the first finds it and says nothing; the second finds a second pencil, no less real, but closer to his expectations."[122] In Tlön, such "secondary objects," known as *hrönir*, can take the form not only of pencils but of human remains. Borges describes how a group of students, encouraged to go digging for a non-existent tomb, "unearthed—or produced—a gold mask, an archaic sword, two or three clay urns and the moldy and mutilated torso of a king whose chest bore an inscription which it has not yet been possible to decipher."[123] In this parable, as in the seventeenth-century Tower, not only the newly born but the long dead are the fruits of human desire.

In the sixteenth century the bodies of the princes had served as emblems of the irrecoverable past; in the seventeenth, their significance shifted so as to stand for a past that was lost but might yet be (must now be) recovered. The remains of Richard III followed a markedly similar cultural trajectory. From the dissolution of the Greyfriars to the end of the sixteenth century, his resting place, like that of the princes, was unknown—though the fate of the uncle's body excited nothing like the curiosity associated with his nephews. The years after 1600, however, witnessed a flurry of activity around the remains of the last Plantagenets. Just as the princes were reportedly discovered in three separate locations in the Tower, Richard's body—though still undisclosed—became associated in the 1610s with three distinct sites around Leicester: the bed of the river Soar, the monument in Mr. Herrick's garden, and the empty sarcophagus at the Greyhound Inn. This conspicuous new concern with location and marking in relation to both the king and the princes clearly owes something to receding memories of the Reformation, and to the rise of the antiquarian impulse; somewhere too in the mingled causes of this phenomenon lurks the influence of Shakespeare's *Richard III*.

Like *The True Tragedy of Richard III*, and like other later Tudor texts, Shakespeare's play draws pointed attention to the mystery surrounding the princes' bodies and place of burial. Tyrrell reports Forrest's description of the sleeping princes as if they were already a funeral monument, "girdling one another/Within their alabaster innocent arms" (4.3.10–11). The play thus grants the princes the tomb denied them by history—a

---

[122] Jorge Luis Borges, "Tlön, Uqbar, Orbis Tertius," in *Labyrinths*, ed. and trans. Donald A. Yates and James E. Irby (New York: New Directions, 1964), 13.
[123] Borges, "Tlön, Uqbar, Orbis Tertius," 14.

white alabaster effigy to match their uncle's—but only in the improbable poetry of one murderer quoting another. As to their final resting place, Shakespeare heightens the mystery by leaving even Richard in the dark:

> RICHARD: But didst thou see them dead?
> TYRREL: I did, my lord.
> RICHARD: And buried, gentle Tyrrell?
> TYRREL: The chaplain of the Tower hath buried them;
>   But where, to say the truth, I do not know.[124] (4.3.27–30)

It is not only Richard who seeks in vain to know the resting place of the princes. The vengeful Margaret taunts Elizabeth with a string of *ubi sunts*: "Where is thy husband now? Where be thy brothers? Where are thy two sons?" (4.4.92–93) Face to face with their killer, Elizabeth addresses the same question to Richard: "Tell me, thou villain slave, where are my children?" (4.4.144) Neither Margaret nor Elizabeth, we must suppose, is seeking a literal answer. Their questions are rhetorical, a way of figuring the princes' absence from the world (one only asks "where" about that which is not here). Yet, as I have suggested, bodies which are literally lost complicate the workings of the *ubi sunt* motif, lending the rhetorical question an uncommon and unruly urgency. Elizabeth can not separate the idea of her sons' deaths from that of their bodies lying somewhere in the ground. When Richard calls her reasoning too shallow and quick, she responds "O no, my reasons are too deep and dead—/Too deep and dead, poor infants, in their graves" (4.4.293–4). Later, they are the "two tender playfellows for dust—/Thy broken faith hath made the prey for worms" (4.4.316–17). The Duchess of York too harps on inhumation, calling to witness "England's lawful earth/Unlawfully made drunk with innocents' blood" (4.4.29–30). Only Richard holds out the possibility that the princes are not yet buried, their resting place not yet determined, and this in a particularly grotesque turn whereby he seems to equate their bodies with his own semen: "in your daughter's womb I bury them,/Where, in that nest of spicery, they will breed,/Selves of themselves . . . " (4.4.354–56). Richard speaks as if, in killing the princes, he has also in some sense consumed them, assimilating them into his own dynastic person. As far as the body politic of Edward V is concerned, this is arguably true enough; in terms of the legal theory, the body that was Edward's is now Richard's. Hence, perhaps, his annoyed bafflement that these wailing women should continue to harp on the string of *ubi sunt*.

---

[124] In Q, not only the location but the manner of the princes' burial is made a matter of doubt, the line reading "But how or in what place I do not know."

Elizabeth's repeated references to her sons' resting place as "deep" convey faint echoes of Hall's story of the heavy chest sunk in the Black Deeps. So, too, does the curse which the princes' ghosts pronounce against their murderer on the eve of battle: "Let us be lead within thy bosom, Richard,/ And weigh thee down to ruin, shame, and death" (5.5.101–2). Beyond these vague allusions, there is no specific reference in the play to the tradition that the princes were disposed of by burial at sea. Yet it can hardly be accidental that images of sea-burial—of drowning, of being lost in deep waters, and of the ocean bed—occur so frequently in this play.[125] Even in the preceding history, Henry VI compares Richard to "the sea,/ Whose envious gulf did swallow up his [Prince Edward's] life" (*3 Henry VI*, 5.6.24–25). In *Richard III*, Richard takes up the theme in his opening soliloquy, declaring "all the clouds that loured upon our house/In the deep bosom of the ocean buried" (1.1.3–4). Almost reflexively, he calls up the same image when new clouds appear on the horizon: told that "Richmond is on the seas," he snaps "There let him sink, and be the seas on him" (4.4.393–94). Nor is the imagery of watery burial confined to Richard alone. Buckingham describes England as "almost shouldered in the swallowing gulf/Of dark forgetfulness and deep oblivion" (3.7.128–29). When the sorrowing Elizabeth longs "to drown the world" in her "plenteous tears" (2.2.69), her brother counsels her rather to "Drown desperate sorrow in dead Edward's grave" (2.2.89.11). Later Elizabeth imagines that she might "Like a poor barque of sails and tackling reft,/Rush all to pieces" in a "bay of death" (4.4.221.12–14).

The most sustained and remarkable passage concerning sea burial in the play (and perhaps, at least prior to Ariel's song in *The Tempest*, in English literature) is the dream which the imprisoned Clarence describes to his warder in the Tower.

> Methoughts that I had broken from the Tower,
> And was embarked to cross to Burgundy,
> And in my company my brother Gloucester
> Who from my cabin tempted me to walk
> Upon the hatches; there we looked toward England,
> And cited up a thousand heavy times
> During the wars of York and Lancaster
> That had befall'n us. As we paced along
> Upon the giddy footing of the hatches,

[125] The play inaugurates a theme that would haunt Shakespeare throughout his career, from *Richard III* and *Henry V* to *Pericles* and *The Tempest*; see Steve Mentz, *At the Bottom of Shakespeare's Ocean* (London: Continuum, 2009); and Philip Schwyzer, *Archaeologies of English Renaissance Literature* (Oxford: Oxford University Press, 2007), 1, 121.

> Methought that Gloucester stumbled, and in falling
> Struck me—that thought to stay him—overboard
> Into the tumbling billows of the main. (1.4.9–20)

Thus Clarence finds himself, with other obstacles to his brother's advancement, in the deep bosom of the ocean buried. There is a dark prophetic quality to the dream: later in the same scene, Clarence will indeed be fatally submerged (in a butt of malmsey) by Richard's hired assassins. Yet the details of Clarence's dream seem to refer to something more than his personal fate. His journey over and then under the sea precisely matches the trajectory of the princes' corpses in the tale first told by Rastell. Like the boys in the fatal chest, Clarence exits the Tower surreptitiously to board a ship bound for Flanders (incorporated, in the period in which the play is set, within the Duchy of Burgundy). The ship is perhaps just passing out of the Thames estuary when Clarence, looking back towards England, is thrown overboard. What follows in his dream is a gorgeous yet nightmarish vision of the Black Deeps.

> O Lord! Methought what pain it was to drown,
> What dreadful noise of waters in mine ears,
> What sights of ugly death within mine eyes.
> Methoughts I saw a thousand fearful wrecks,
> Ten thousand men that fishes gnawed upon,
> Wedges of gold, great ouches, heaps of pearl,
> Inestimable stones, unvalued jewels,
> All scattered in the bottom of the sea.
> Some lay in dead men's skulls; and in those holes
> Where eyes did once inhabit, there were crept—
> As 'twere in scorn of eyes—reflecting gems,
> Which wooed the slimy bottom of the deep
> And mocked the dead bones that lay scattered by. (1.4.21–33)

Here, as elsewhere in the play and indeed throughout Shakespeare's works, the ocean bed is a world apart, the site and figure of irrecoverable loss. As Steve Mentz has reminded us, "the deep sea's floor [was] as unreachable to early modern Europeans as the moon"—for the living, at any rate.[126] A bourn from which no traveler might return, the seabed in Shakespeare is associated with death, and yet more disquietingly with the nullification of the human perspective, including its ways of measuring virtue and worth. Lying beyond the possibility of recovery or use, the jewels in the slimy deep are literally without value. In a sense, a jewel on the seabed is no jewel at all. A prince on the seabed is no prince.

---

[126] Mentz, *At the Bottom of Shakespeare's Ocean*, xiii. The seabed of which Clarence dreams is clearly much deeper than the "full fathom five" of Alonso's body in *The Tempest,* which, as Mentz points out, means just thirty feet below the surface.

Clarence's vision of the seabed can be read as a particularly dark vision of the historical process, and more specifically of the relationship—or lack of relationship—between the living and the dead. As such it is also implicitly a reflection on the capacities of historical drama. Indeed, critics have repeatedly turned to Clarence's dream for an understanding of what Shakespeare thinks he is doing with the dead in this play.[127] Interpreted as an expression of where the past lies in relation to ourselves— in the ocean's bosom, totally divorced from and irrecoverable by the present—the dream would seem to cast sharp doubt on the oft-proclaimed project of the Elizabethan history play, which was precisely to revive the past, or at least to keep its value on the market. How could any play hope to raise the dead from the bottom of the Black Deeps? Yet such a pessimistic reading of Clarence's dream risks ignoring the way it stages the seabed itself as an edifying spectacle. Arguably, the ocean floor in this scene represents not the repository from which the dead are raised to the historical stage, but the stage itself. The entranced and helpless Clarence is spectator (and auditor) at an uncannily lively morality play, in which the lifeless players woo and mock their audience, as well as one another.

The gems that twinkle on the seabed "mock the dead bones" not only by casting scorn upon them, but also by impersonating or doubling them (capturing their reflections), and above all by deceiving the senses of the spectator, causing the dead to appear almost alive. Such "mockery" can be read as a kind of performance, comparable to what living actors do, not least when called upon to stand in for those who are dead and gone (a point Shakespeare would return to in *Henry V*, where the audience is instructed to mind "true things by what their mock'ries be" [4.0.53]).[128] Clarence's dream thus points us to an understanding of what goes on in

---

[127] As Nicholas Brooke observes, "the shining brilliance set in dead men's skulls on the slimy bottom seems to me too perfect an image of the play to be set aside"; "Reflecting Gems and Dead Bones: Tragedy Versus History in *Richard III*," *Critical Quarterly* 7 (1965): 123–34. For Stephen Marche, in contrast to the description of Alonso's sea-change in *The Tempest*, "There is no comfort in Clarence's dream . . . The bottom of the sea, where the dead are, is not a place of hidden beauty; it is the repository where what is good and beautiful is obscured from the light of day. That obscurity is not waiting to be uncovered as in *The Tempest*. The lost are unimaginably removed there" (Marche, "Mocking Dead Bones," 39). Clarence's dream is also central to Brian Walsh's recent reading of the play, though his discussion focuses primarily on the shipboard conversation and the subsequent entry into Hell, rather than the scene of drowning; see Walsh, *Shakespeare, the Queen's Men, and the Elizabethan Performance of History* (Cambridge: Cambridge University Press, 2009), 139–78.

[128] Shakespeare's Macbeth, too, responds to the spectacle of a dead man raised before his eyes by calling it a "mock'ry" (3.4.106). *Richard III* contains several uses of "mock" to delineate relationships between the living and the dead, from Margaret's description of Elizabeth as "a mother only mock'd with two sweet babes" (4.4.87) to Buckingham inviting the ghosts of his victims to "mock my destruction" (5.1.9).

history plays that is both more plausible and somewhat subtler than the hyperbolic claim that the dead can be brought to life again on stage. This understanding begins with the recognition that we have no access to the past save through what survives of it in the present: flotsam and jetsam, broken remnants, bones and stones. The dramatist's aim is not to leap beyond that which survives in order to revivify the lost past, but rather to assemble these scattered traces into spectacles capable of wooing, mocking, and bewitching the eye. A play such as *Richard III* is fashioned out of the same materials as those witnessed by Clarence on the seabed; no play of the period adheres more closely to the available historical sources, yet none brings history more firmly under the rule of art. From Rastell and Hall's story of the sinking of the princes, I would argue, Shakespeare drew not only the recurrent motif of burial at sea, but a new way of thinking about how the stage can present history, and make it present. His *Richard III* does not simply *refer* to the Black Deeps. It takes place there.

2

Lees and Moonshine

Memory and Oral Tradition

The memorie of King Richard was so strong, that it lay like Lees in the bottome of mens hearts; and if the Vessell was but stirred, it would come up.

—Francis Bacon (1561–1626)

Wyat why art thou such a foole, thou servest for moonshine in the water, a beggarly fugitive; forsake him, and become mine . . .

—Richard III to Sir Henry Wyatt, in the commonplace book of
Thomas Scott (*c*.1566–1635)

In the scene immediately following that in which the murder of the princes in the Tower is reported, Shakespeare's Richard III urges their grieving mother to put the past behind her: "in the Lethe of thy angry soul/ . . . drown the sad remembrance of those wrongs,/Which thou supposest I have done to thee" (4.4.237–39). The association of the past with watery burial is, as we have seen, typical of this play. Richard's choice of words seems particularly unfortunate in its dramatic context, perhaps only serving to remind Elizabeth of her sons' rumoured resting place in the "Black Deeps" of the Thames estuary. Defying Richard's invitation to drown remembrance in favor of "the time to come" (4.4.318), the widowed Queen asserts that the future too is a realm of memory:

> The children live, whose fathers thou hast slaughtered—
> Ungoverned youth, to wail it in their age.
> The parents live, whose children thou hast butchered—
> Old barren plants, to wail it with their age.
> Swear not by time to come, for that thou hast
> Misused ere used, by times ill-used o'erpast. (4.4.322–27)[1]

---

[1] On the troubled temporality of this passage, see Mark Robson, "Shakespeare's Words of the Future: Promising Richard III," *Textual Practice* 19 (2005): 25–7.

When characters in Shakespeare's plays start talking about the future, they are more often than not talking about what his audience called the present. We might think of Henry V's "Crispin's Day" oration, with its promise of performative commemoration in times to come, or of the conspirators in *Julius Caesar* foreseeing their deed being "acted over/In states unborn and accents yet unknown" (3.1.113–14). But is it plausible that early audiences would have identified Elizabeth's traumatized "time to come" with their own time, late in the reign of a different and largely happier Elizabeth? It is more or less out of the question that anyone with personal memories of Richard's reign could have survived to see his deeds re-enacted on Shakespeare's stage in the early 1590s. Yet Richard III maintained a life in orally transmitted memory—distinct from and sometimes at odds with his image in written history—down to the end of the sixteenth century, and even beyond. This chapter will explore the culture of memory out of which the play emerged in the last decade of the sixteenth century—and over which it would exert a remarkable reciprocal influence in the decades that followed.

2.1 "FOR YET SHE LIVETH": PERSONAL MEMORIES, 1485–1572

From the afternoon of 22 August 1485, Richard III lived only in memory. For the remainder of the fifteenth century, some memory of his reign, and with it most probably some conception formed in that period of the king's character, was the common possession of every adult English man and woman. Yet, in part because they were so ubiquitous, very few of these memories are preserved in the textual record, nor is it easy to guess at their coloring or content. Although the first generation of historians to record the brief reign of Richard III—the anonymous Crowland chronicler, Dominic Mancini, John Rous, and Robert Fabyan—inevitably relied both on their own memories and those of informants, they had no stake in presenting events as matters of personal memory. Appeals to the remembrance of the chronicler were preserved mainly for wonders, where a claim to eye-witness knowledge was appropriate. Thus, Rous states that he himself saw the elephant displayed in London under Edward IV;[2] none of his bitterly defamatory account of Richard's reign is verified by comparable appeals to personal memory, either his own or that of others.

---

[2] *Historia Johannis Rossi Warwicensis de Regibus Anglie*, translated in Hanham, *Richard III*, 118.

For centuries we have been familiar with the idea that the early Tudors subjected Richard III to a campaign of posthumous character assassination, "forging the most atrocious calumnies to blacken [the house of York's] memories and invalidate their just claim."[3] Although the case of Rous, who hastily reversed his glowing judgement of Richard after Bosworth, provides an obvious example of such propaganda, there is little evidence from Henry VII's reign of a concerted effort to remold popular memories of Richard. Instead, the whole period was to some extent buried in oblivion. Rather than dwelling on the demerits of the defeated regime, early Tudor historians and panegyrists tended to proceed as if the reigns of Edward IV and Richard III were merely a hiatus or interregnum, with the accession of Henry marking the resumption of continuity, either with the previous Lancastrian dynasts or—more radically—with the Welsh–British monarchs of early Christian Britain.[4]

The city of York, always a stronghold of Yorkist and Ricardian sentiment, offers an example of how it was possible to remember the late king and forget him as well. York had greeted the news of Richard's defeat and death with "grete hevynesse."[5] Two months after Bosworth, city records could still to refer to "the most famous prince of blessed memory, King Richard, late deceased."[6] How did the city fathers tally this enduring attachment to Richard's memory with their necessary allegiance to his conqueror? They seem to have done so by letting the two monarchs inhabit two distinct temporalities. When Henry entered the city in 1486 he was greeted by a pageant featuring the city's ancient British founder, Ebraucus, who rejoiced that "by cource of liniall succession/Myne heires this my Citie shuld have in possession."[7] Next the king was presented with all six previous English monarchs who had borne the name of Henry, and who now yielded the sceptre to their namesake. "Their primordiall princes of this principalitie/Haith preparate your reame the viith by succession."[8] Presenting the king with three complimentary versions of his lineage (British,

[3] Horace Walpole, *Historic Doubts on the Life and Reign of King Richard III* (London: J. Dodsley, 1768), 17.

[4] Thus Henry's historian Bernard Andre, endorsing the Tudor claim to continuity with ancient Welsh rulers, summed up the eight centuries between the deaths of Cadwaladr (682) and Richard III with the phrase "Anglorum saevitia intercalatum est"; Bernard Andre, *Historia*, 10. See Philip Schwyzer, *Literature, Nationalism, and Memory in Early Modern England and Wales* (Cambridge: Cambridge University Press, 2004), 13–31.

[5] Robert Davies, ed., *Extracts from the Municipal Records of the City of York* (London: J. B. Nichols & Son, 1843), 218.

[6] Angelo Raine, ed. *York Civic Records, volume 1* (Leeds: Yorkshire Archaeological Society, 1939), 126.

[7] Alexandra F. Johnston and Margaret Rogerson, eds, *Records of Early English Drama: York* (Toronto: University of Toronto Press, 1979), 1.140.

[8] Johnston and Rogerson, 1.141.

Lancastrian, and that of his Christian name), the pageants stressed Henry's seamless continuity with the past whilst effectively eliding a quarter century of Yorkist rule.[9] For the city of York there were thus two pasts, that of public (or national) history, in which its loyalty to Henry's line was beyond dispute, and that of private (or civic) memory, in which Richard remained an object of "blessed" and nostalgic recollection.

The veil drawn over the recent past is evident in the remarkable vagueness of early memories of Bosworth Field. Bernard Andre, in his 1502 biography of Henry VII, declines to describe the battle, preferring to leave a blank page:

> I have heard something of the battle by oral report, but the eye is a safer judge than the ear in such a matter. Therefore, I pass over the date, the place, and the order of the battle, rather than assert anything rashly; for as I have said before, I lack clear sight. And so until I obtain more knowledge of this debatable field, I leave both it and this page blank.[10]

Andre's privileging of the eye over the ear—first-hand experience over second-hand knowledge—plays on the fact that he himself was blind. Generalizing from his own sightlessness, Andre comes close to suggesting that personal memory is incommunicable; since he cannot possibly become a retrospective witness to the battle, there is apparently no way for his page to be filled. No doubt his reluctance to record the accounts he had heard of the battle owes as much to political prudence as to epistemological anxiety. As James Siemon observes, such reticence was the rule, given that "the battle was at once a dynastic watershed and also a potential source of reproach for the survivors (and their families)."[11] The dubious role played by the Earl of Northumberland was especially delicate territory, both before and after the Earl's assassination in 1489.

There were exceptions to the rule of silence. Sir Ralph Bigod (*d.*1515), once carver to Richard and subsequently to Lady Margaret Beaufort, made no secret of his unfailing loyalty to his former master, enthralling listeners

---

[9] There are two accounts of the pageants—one being the plan drawn up in advance, the other a record of the event by a member of Henry's retinue (Johnston and Rogerson, 1.137–52). Only the former mentions the six Henries; the latter mentions instead a tableaux of ships "tokenyng the kinges landing at Milforde havyn" (1.148). The discrepancy could indicate that the organizers were prevailed upon at the last minute to include some reference to the defeat of Richard III; or simply that the witness was determined to perceive such a reference, whether intended or not. On the politics of the York pageants, see also Sydney Anglo, *Spectacle, Pageantry, and Early Tudor Policy* (London: Oxford University Press, 1969); C. E. McGee, "Politics and Platitudes: Sources of Civic Pageantry, 1486," *Renaissance Studies* 3 (1989): 29–34.

[10] Andre, *Historia*, 32; translation in Hanham, *Richard III*, 53.

[11] James R. Siemon, "Reconstructing the Past: History, Historicism, Histories," in *A Companion to English Renaissance Literature and Culture*, ed. Michael Hattaway (Oxford: Blackwell, 2002), 667.

with his recollections of the king's last hours.[12] Henry Tudor's mother commended Bigod's adherence to his former master, noting in it not sedition but rather steadfast loyalty. Undoubtedly many privately shared his sentiments, especially in Richard's northern heartlands. As we have seen, in 1491, York's Mayor and Council heard with sympathy the case of John Payntor, who had called the late Earl of Northumberland "a traytor [who] bytrayed Kyng Richard" and attempted to strike William Burton when the latter likened Richard to a dead dog.[13]

As the dispute between Burton and Payntor indicates, recollections of Richard could be controversial, but they were also underground, caught in the historical record only by mischance. Writing in the seventeenth century, Francis Bacon would use a remarkable image for the submerged memory of Richard in the north in Henry's reign:

> the people upon a sudaine grew into great mutinie, and saide openly, that they had endured of late yeares a thousand miseries . . . This (no doubt) proceeded not simply of any present necessitie, but much by reason of the old humour of those Countries, where the memorie of King Richard was so strong, that it lay like Lees in the bottome of mens hearts; and if the Vessell was but stirred, it would come up.[14]

Adherents of the venerable "Baconian" theory have drawn attention to the poetic conclusion of this passage as supplying evidence for Bacon's authorship of Shakespeare's plays.[15] What seems more probable is that Bacon was unconsciously influenced by *Richard III*'s repeated images of watery burial. Yet the difference between Shakespeare's bodies "scattered in the bottom of the sea" and "lees in the bottome of mens hearts" is that the latter does not suggest loss beyond all hope of recovery. Far from it—the sediment in wine is always prone to "come up," and does so not as a discrete object, a relic of the lost past, but by being reintegrated in the solution, part of the wine itself. It is thus a remarkably effective and unsettling figure for the capacity of the past to become present.[16]

Richard's memory would not lie undisturbed forever. If collective memory is so much vinous sediment, societies seem to make a habit of stirring

---

[12] Bigod's recollections would be recorded by Henry Parker, Lord Morley, discussed below.

[13] Davies, *Extracts*, 220–221.

[14] Francis Bacon, *The historie of the raigne of King Henry the Seventh* (London, 1622), 67.

[15] Eg, Edwin Reed, *Brief for Plaintiff: Bacon vs. Shakespeare* (New York: De Vinne Press, 1892), 38.

[16] The merging of temporalities is heightened in the second (1627) edition of Bacon's *History*, where the phrase is altered from "lay like Lees" to "lies like Lees." The weird use of the present tense seems to suggest that even in the Caroline era the memory of King Richard retained its latent power (a suggestion not quite as absurd as it may appear, as will be seen).

the vessel at regular intervals. Social psychologists point to a tendency on the part of both individuals and groups to revisit the past at intervals of 20–30 years, confronting traumatic or transformative events and evaluating them in a fresh light.[17] In modern Europe and America, such cycles of memory correlate with the creation of monuments and historical films, for instance. These cyclical phases are considered to signify both the achievement of psychological distance from the past, and the pragmatic fact that most of the chief political actors will have left the public stage, through death or otherwise. Every 25 years or so it becomes both possible and necessary to reopen the doors of memory locked in the last generation.[18]

The great monument to emerge from the first cycle of social memory thirty years after Bosworth is indisputably Thomas More's *History of Richard III*, composed in the mid-1510s.[19] More was five when Richard came to the throne, seven when he died. The eldest son of a prominent London family, he may well have been witness to some of the public events he describes. However, he makes no claim to rely on personal recollection, but rather on the memories of a range of witnesses, almost all of whom go unnamed.[20] It is often assumed that his chief informant was Cardinal Morton, in whose household More spent his early teens. Be that as it may, there would have been no shortage of living Londoners with relevant memories of the 1480s, and it seems likely that a good many were glad to share their recollections under condition of anonymity. More frequently attributes rumours—e.g., of Richard's role in the deaths of Henry VI and Clarence—to what "menne constantly say" or "wise menne . . . weene," occasionally pausing to wonder "whither

---

[17] See James W. Pennebaker and Becky L. Banasik, "On the Creation and Maintenance of Collective Memories"; and Juanjo Igartua and Dario Paez, "Art and Remembering Traumatic Collective Events: The Case of the Spanish Civil War," in Pennebaker *et al.*, eds, *Collective Memory of Political Events: Social Psychological Perspectives* (Mahwah, NJ: Lawrence Erlbaum Associates, 1997), 3–19, 79–102.

[18] It might be questioned whether this model could apply to collective memory in the early modern era, when the average life-span was considerably shorter than it is today. Yet the distance between generations was roughly similar to what it has been in most modern European societies in the modern era.

[19] The new openness to memory in the 1510s should not be exaggerated. Although a brief period saw the completion of three major accounts of Richard's reign—More's *History*, Polydore Vergil's *Anglica Historia* (1513), and *The Great Chronicle of London* (1512)—all would remain in manuscript for decades to come (centuries, in the case of the *Great Chronicle*). Fabyan's *New Chronicles* may have been completed as early as 1504, but saw print only in 1516, three years after the author's death. Fabyan's crisp comment that some at Bosworth "stode hovynge aferre of tyll they sawe to which partye the victory fell" (ccxxx) indicates the need for circumspection even a generation on.

[20] On More's use of oral testimony, see Brian Walsh, *Shakespeare, the Queen's Men, and the Elizabethan Performance of History* (Cambridge: Cambridge University Press, 2009), 140–1.

menne of hatred reporte above the trouthe."[21] On a small handful of occasions, he appeals to the personal memories of his informants.

The first of these passages occurs early in the text, on the very night of King Edward's death: "one Mystlebrooke longe ere mornynge, came in great haste to the house of one Pottyer dwellyng in reddecrosse strete without crepulgate." Beating on the door, he was let in swiftly and revealed the news of the king's death. "By my trouthe manne," Potter replied, "then wyll my mayster the Duke of Gloucester bee kynge" (9). A private conversation between two persons of no historical significance who do not reappear in the narrative, this story does not belong to public history. It is a memory, vivid in circumstantial detail, recounted to Sir John More (*c.*1451–1530) by one who overheard the exchange, and by Sir John to his son, Thomas.[22] It seems plausible that in late-fifteenth-century London, everyone remembered where they were when they heard King Edward was dead. Such recollections are known today as "flashbulb memories"— highly detailed memories in which a personal situation becomes saturated with the significance of a devastating public event.[23]

More is particularly apt to cite the memories of informants when describing the physical characteristics and mannerisms of his long-dead subjects. The vivid portrait of Richard after the murder of the princes— eyes whirling about, "his hand ever on his dager," his sleep "troubled wyth fearful dreames"—is ascribed to what "I have heard by credible report of such as wer secrete with his chamberers" (87). Witnesses to Richard's coronation could still recall the Duke of Buckingham's self-betraying reaction: "I have heard of som that said thei saw it, that the duke at such time as the crown was first set upon the protectors hed, his eye could not abide the sight thereof, but wried hys hed an other way" (90). In passages like these, More is effectively recording two events at once: a moment in the 1480s when a Richard or a Buckingham did something with their bodies, and a moment decades later when those who still remembered those bodies chose to speak. The apparently tautological phrase "I have heard of som that said they saw it" (rather than the more streamlined "I have heard of some that saw it," or the yet briefer "Some say they saw") seems designed to capture the moment of transmission, now itself part of the past, from both points of view. The witnesses, it seems, were concerned not only to

---

[21] More, *History*, 8, 7.
[22] More attributes this anecdote explicitly to his father in the Latin version of the text; in the English version it is described simply as "credible informacion."
[23] See Olivier Luminet and Antonietta Curci, *Flashbulb Memories: New Issues and New Perspectives*, (Hove: Psychology Press, 2009); Pennebaker and Banasik, "On the Creation and Maintenance of Collective Memories."

say what they saw but to say *they* saw it; likewise, More himself is concerned to convey not only what his informants said, but that *he heard*.[24]

More's most extended and melancholy meditation on memory as a historical source comes in his portrait of Shore's wife, onetime mistress of Edward IV. "Proper she was & faire: nothing in her body that you would have changed, but if you would have wished her somewhat higher. Thus say thei that knew her in her youthe" (55). Mistress Shore's youthful beauty enters the text marked out as memory, the oral witnesses to her bygone fairness elbowing their way into the passage alongside her. More seems uncertain how to relate the remembered fact of Mistress Shore's beauty to the larger themes of his history, or even to the elderly woman who still dwells in London.

> Albeit some that now se her (for yet she liveth) deme her never to have ben wel visaged. Whose jugement semeth me somwhat like, as though men should gesse the bewty of one longe before departed, by her scalpe taken out of the charnel house: for now is she old lene, withered & dried up, nothing left but ryvilde skin & hard bone. And yet being even such: whoso wel advise her visage, might gesse & devise which partes how filled, wold make it a faire face. (55–56)

Here the historian plays the forensic archaeologist, clinically reconstructing a mental picture of Shore's vanished beauty. Yet he can do so only with the aid of resources—her aged but living face, the memories supplied by his informants—which are themselves on the point of disappearance. Memory can put flesh on dry bones; yet memory is akin with flesh, and no less mortal. Already, Shore's wife herself can barely recall her bygone days of luxury.[25] When she and those who remember her are together in the charnel house, the beauty which can still be summoned from the brink of non-existence will be gone indeed. (Significantly, More refers not to the grave, where bodily integrity is preserved, but to the charnel, site of the indiscriminate mixing of remains, where individual identity is annihilated.) What is entirely lacking from this passage is the confidence that written words might have the power to preserve the

---

[24] More's phrase draws attention to how the transmission of memory in the early modern period typically involves a transition from a visual to an aural archive, a point also emphasized by Andre, above. By contrast, visual media such as family photographs are usually considered central to the creation of modern "postmemories"; see Marianne Hirsch, *Family Frames: Photography, Narrative, and Postmemory* (Cambridge, MA: Harvard University Press, 1997).

[25] "But she, who was once famous herself, has now outlived her friends and all her acquaintances, and with the years, as it were, she has passed into another age. Even her own recollection of her former luxury has been almost defaced by her long-continued sufferings . . ." (232).

memory of beauty. The sentiment that would come as second nature to a generation of Elizabethan poets is as distant from More's imaginative world as the modern science of facial reconstruction.

Over the course of the sixteenth century, as More's *History* was incorporated into a succession of chronicles, the beauty of Shore's wife would continue to be marked out as a matter of living memory, even as this forced the chronicler into contortions of verbal tense. The passage in Hall's chronicle begins as if those who remembered her beauty were still in position to give oral testimony, before awkwardly historicizing the whole account: "This saye they that knewe her in her youthe, soem sayed and judged that she had bene well favoured, and some judged the contrary . . . & this judgement was in the tyme of kyng Henry the eyght, in the .xviii. yere of whose reigne she dyed, when she had nothyng but a reveled skynne and bone."[26] Holinshed's chronicle likewise preserves the present tense for "Thus saie they that knew hir in hir youth," only adding beside the phrase "for yet she liveth" the marginal note "Meanyng when the storie was written."[27] In each case the memory of Shore's wife is preserved at the point of oral transmission, a personal reminiscence stalled forever on the threshold of recorded history.

From the 1510s, a definite historical vision of Richard's reign—one characterized by ruthless violence and rank hypocrisy, presided over by a morally and physically misshapen tyrant—took shape and gathered weight in manuscript histories and printed chronicles. Given the absence of documentary evidence for some of Richard's more notorious crimes, notably the murder of the children in the Tower and the disposal of their bodies, chroniclers habitually cited oral tradition or "report": "some said they were murderid atwene ii ffethyr beddis, some said they were drownyd in malvesy, and some said they were stykkid with a venymous pocion."[28] While there can be no doubt that historians such as Polydore Vergil (*c.*1470–1555) relied to a significant extent on "history surviving in oral form," it is equally probable that the Richard of textual history began from a very early point to influence oral traditions and even private memories of Richard's reign.[29]

Yet the pressure of textual history on living memory would not have been experienced solely or universally as a pressure to conform. With the emergence of an official version comes the possibility of consciously

---

[26] Hall, Edward V, fol. xvi[r]; the passage occurs first in Hardyng's *Chronicle* (London, 1543), fol. lxi[r].

[27] Holinshed, 724.   [28] *GCL*, 236–7.

[29] Denys Hay, *Polydore Vergil: Renaissance Historian and Man of Letters* (Oxford: Clarendon Press, 1952), 95; Hanham, *Richard III*, 116.

dissenting oral traditions.[30] For some, the awareness that their private recollections conflicted with or disproved the public version of events may have lent additional urgency to preserving the memory and passing it on. As a young man in London, John Stow (*b*.1525/26) spoke with "old and grave men who had often seen King Richard, and . . . affirmed that he was not deformed, but of person and bodily shape comely enough."[31] Both parties surely experienced a certain thrill in sharing recollections which ran against the grain of official history. At the same time, the young Stow must have been keenly aware that the time for the transmission of such memories was rapidly running out. Turning ten years old around the fiftieth anniversary of Bosworth, he would have had access to a good number of men and women whose memories stretched back so far. Even in 1545, we can imagine Stow seeking out septuagenarians who had been teenagers in Richard's reign. But as the century nears its midpoint, the numbers tell their own remorseless story.

The *Oxford Dictionary of National Biography* includes some 189 individuals born between the years 1460 and 1480. Of these, 76, or 40% were still alive in 1540—that is, they had lived at least into their sixties. This figure is rather higher than one would expect to find in a survey of the general population; by its nature, the *ODNB* selects for individuals who enjoyed successful adult careers. By 1545, however, the number of survivors has dropped to 41, or 21%. In 1550 we find 23 individuals still living, while in 1555 there are only eight, 4% of the original cohort having reached the age of 75 above. Between 1540 and 1555, 90% of surviving witnesses to the pre-Tudor era passed away. The drop-off among their less illustrious contemporaries would have been no less steep, and possibly steeper.

At least one instance can be found of an individual born in or before 1480 surviving to transmit memories of Richard's reign seventy years later, in the reign of Mary—though the memories in question are not quite first-hand, and undoubtedly colored by Tudor propaganda. Henry Parker, Baron Morley, the translator of Petrarch and Seneca, died in 1556; born between 1476 and 1480, he would certainly have had some memories of Bosworth and its aftermath, for his father had been Richard's stand-ard-bearer. Morley had subsequently grown up in the court of Margaret Beaufort, mother of the reigning Henry VII, and there he had known Sir Ralph Bigod, whose unwavering loyalty to Richard was tolerated and even encouraged by the Countess. Two years before his death, Morley described

[30] See, for example, Alison Shell, *Oral Culture and Catholicism in Early Modern England* (Cambridge: Cambridge University Press, 2007).
[31] Sir George Buck, *The History of Richard III (1619)*, ed. A. N. Kincaid (Gloucester: Alan Sutton, 1979), 129.

in a treatise on the Eucharist presented to Queen Mary how he had often heard Bigod speak of the confusion that reigned in Richard's camp on the morning of the battle. Mass could not be celebrated, for "when his chappelyns had one thing ready, evermore they wanted another; when they had wyne they lacked breade, and ever one thing was myssing. In the meane season King Henry comyng on apace, King Rychard was constrayned to go to the battayle."[32] The story as Richard's faithful follower seems to have told it is not sinister in tone, and indeed is tinged with comedy. Morley, however, draws a hard moral. "[G]od wolde not that same day, that he shulde se the blyssed sacrament of the Aulter, nor heare the holy masse, for his horrible offence comytted against his brothers children."[33] Morley may have been old enough to remember Richard's reign, yet his image of a damnable monster is the product of Tudor discourse, and is deployed in the service of a mid-Tudor debate over the nature and holiness of the Eucharist. This would be far from the last time that memories of Richard III became bound up with Reformation controversies.

Morley was conscious that few individuals in England had memories stretching back as far as his own. Of those who had served the old Countess of Richmond, he wrote in 1554, "I think there is unethe syxe men and women alyve at this present day."[34] Even fewer could remember Richard III. Of the 189 individuals in the *ODNB* who might have told tales of those distant days, only one was still alive in 1564, when Shakespeare was born. This was William Paulet, the earl of Winchester, who died in 1572 (Fig. 2.1). Probably born around 1474, Paulet would have been 97 or 98 at death. Contemporaries held him to be still older, dating his birth to 1465, which would make his age at death at least 106.[35]

In his parable "The Witness," Borges imagines the death of the last man to remember Anglo-Saxon England before the coming of Christianity: "With him will die, and never return, the last immediate images of these pagan rites; the world will be a little poorer when this Saxon has died . . . In time there was a day that extinguished the last eyes to see Christ; the battle of Junín and the love of Helen died with the death of a man. What will die

---

[32] Henry Parker, Lord Morley, "Account of Miracles Performed by the Holy Eucharist"(1554), BL Add. MS 12060, 19ᵛ–20ʳ. On Morley's recollections of "Bygoff," [Bigod], see Retha M. Warnicke, "Sir Ralph Bigod: A Loyal Servant to King Richard III," *The Ricardian* 6 (1984): 299–301; "Lord Morley's Statements about Richard III," *Albion* 15 (1983): 173–8.

[33] Parker, "Account of Miracles," 20ʳ. Morley also associates Richard's defeat with divine providence in a treatise on the psalms, where he numbers Henry VII's triumph over the "tyrant kynge Rycharde" among examples of God's providence. Henry Parker, Lord Morley, *The exposition and declaration of the Psalme, Deus ultionum Dominus* (London, 1539), A5ᵛ.

[34] Parker, "Account of Miracles," 20ᵛ.

[35] On Paulet's life dates, see D. M. Loades, *The Life and Career of William Paulet* (Aldershot: Ashgate, 2008), 5–7.

Fig. 2.1. Sir William Paulet, first Marquess of Winchester, oil on oak panel, after 1551. By permission of the Society of the Antiquaries of London.

with me when I die, what pathetic or fragile form will the world lose?"[36] So we may ask, what memories and mental images of a vanished England were lost forever when William Paulet closed his eyes? In search of a clue to Paulet's experience, we might turn to a memorial poem that appeared some months after his death. Rowland Broughton's *Briefe discourse of the lyfe and death of . . . Sir William Pawlet* relates how "he a subject dutifull/ five Kynges and Queenes dyd serve," from Henry VII, under whom he was made a justice of the peace, to Elizabeth, whose Lord Treasurer he was.[37] Yet while detailing his steady rise and unwavering integrity in office, the poem is reticent on the subject of Paulet's personal experience and recollections. Indeed, Broughton commends "Forgetfullnes" as one of his chief virtues, along with Prudence and Obedience.[38] A careful step, a ready bow,

---

[36] Jorge Luis Borges, *Labyrinths*, trans. Donald Yates and James Irby (New York: New Directions, 1964), 243.

[37] Rowland Broughton, *A briefe discourse of the lyfe and death of . . . Sir William Pawlet* (London, 1572), B8ʳ.

[38] Broughton, *Briefe discourse,* B3ᵛ.

and a weak memory—these are the virtues of a political survivor in an era marked by so many changes of regime and religion. Although the poem avers that Paulet died "In perfect state of memorie," the impression is that Paulet's memory was perfect in the sense of a blank canvas or a cloudless sky, unsullied by any recollection whatsoever.[39] And so England bade farewell to one who may well have been the last man to remember Richard III.

2.2 "CERTAINTY OF THINGS WHICH THEY DID NOT SEE": ACTIVE MEMORY, 1564–1605

Shakespeare's biographers find it hard to resist imagining scenes he might have witnessed, people he might have met, especially in his all-but-undocumented youth. Yet even by the liberal standards of the genre, an encounter between a seven-year-old William and the centenarian Paulet stretches the bounds of conjecture. It is possible that the immediate Stratford neighborhood afforded a handful of ancient people whose births predated the Tudor era. Shakespeare's environment and interests may not have been so very different from those of John Aubrey who, in Wiltshire in the 1630s and 1640s, "did ever love to converse with old men, as living histories."[40] Or perhaps Shakespeare received memories of that distant time at second- or third-hand—memories not the less vivid for that and perhaps more so. M. C. Bradbrook speculates on whether Shakespeare's great-great-grandfather (named in the family's grant of arms as having done "valiant service" under Henry VII) had fought at Bosworth, and whether this had become a matter of family legend.[41]

Whatever the demography of Warwickshire in the 1560s and 1570s, by the time Shakespeare began writing for the London stage the last surviving witnesses to the reign of Richard III had almost certainly passed away. Composed in the early 1590s, his *Richard III* occupies a distinctive historical moment in relation to its subject—a period after the extinction of living memory, but still within the horizon of what is variously termed "active" or "communicative memory," the period of 90–120 years in which memories may be transmitted over three or four generations,

---

[39] Broughton, *Briefe discourse,* C1ʳ.

[40] John Aubrey, *Brief Lives,* ed. Richard Barber (Woodbridge: Boydell Press, 1982), 11. Aubrey's informants, not all of them men, included Goodwife Dew, who died in 1649 at the reputed age of 103, and who could recall incidents from the reign of Edward VI; Aubrey, *The Natural History of Wiltshire,* ed. John Britton (London: Wiltshire Topographical Society, 1847), 69.

[41] M. C. Bradbrook, *Shakespeare: The Poet in His World* (London: Weidenfeld & Nicolson, 1978), 58. On the mysterious "grandfather" of the grant of arms, see Chapter 4 of this book.

whilst retaining at least some of the vividness and immediacy of personal recollection. Such memories, Jan Assmann writes, rely "not just on actual experiences but also on the direct communications of others. This is the past that accompanies us because it belongs to us and because there is a living, communicative need to keep it alive in the present."[42] Here, modern and medieval understandings of generational memory are in harmony. For the twelfth-century writer Walter Map, the 100-year period within the scope of active memory constituted modernity, or "our times":

> by our times I mean this modern period, the course of these last hundred years, at the end of which we now are, and of all of whose notable events the memory is fresh and clear enough; for there are still some centenarians alive, and there are very many sons who possess, by the narration of their fathers and grandfathers, the certainty of things which they did not see.[43]

Like Map, early modern English men and women believed that communicated memories afforded them "the certainty of things which they did not see." Such recollections carried social authority and, at least in some circumstances, a degree of legal weight. The legal scholar John Cowell claimed that to prove the endurance of a custom over a hundred years, "it is enough . . . if two or more can depose, that they heard their fathers say, that it was a custome all their time, and that their fathers heard their fathers also say, that it was likewise a custome in their time."[44] In 1628, a Wiltshire man testifying in a dispute over forest rights drew evidence not only from his own memory but "before his tyme and tyme out of minde, as he has credibly heard by the relacion of [his] father who well knewe the same beinge aged one hundred yeares or thereabouts att the tyme of his

---

[42] Jan Assmann, *Religion and Cultural Memory: Ten Studies*, trans. Rodney Livingstone (Stanford: Stanford University Press, 2006), 24. Whereas Assmann defines the scope of communicative memory as 80–100 years, Elisabeth van Houts assigns to active memory the longer scope of 90–120 years (*Memory and Gender in Medieval Europe, 900–1200* [Toronto: University of Toronto Press, 1999], 6–7). Experience seems to bear out the longer period. My own earliest "memory" of this kind derives from my grandmother's recollection of seeing the aviator Lincoln Beachey crash into San Francisco Bay at the 1915 World's Fair. She witnessed the fatal crash when she was four years old, and passed the story on to me when I was not much older; for me it is and will remain a "personal" memory. Should I reach the age of retirement (in or around 2035), this vivid recollection will have survived 120 years. The memory may by then have lost any vestige of the social utility which Assmann associates with communicative memory. Yet, as this footnote itself seems to testify, memories often survive by assuming an unanticipated relevance to emerging concerns.

[43] Walter Map, *De Nugis Curialium/Courtier's Trifles*, ed. and trans. M. R. James, rev. C. N. L. Brooke and R. A. B. Mynors (Oxford: Clarendon Press, 1983), 123–35 (Dist.i, c.30). Map's assumption of a purely masculine line of memorial transmission is revealing and, as the case of Jane Wyatt discussed in this chapter indicates, very open to challenge.

[44] John Cowell, *The Interpreter* (London, 1607), V4ʳ. A civil lawyer, Cowell here describes what he may regard as the laxer standards of the common law.

death."[45] Elizabethan and Jacobean inherited memories stretched back as far as the Wars of the Roses. In turn-of-the-century Gloucestershire, John Smyth of Nibley "often heard many old men and weomen . . . born in the time of king Henry the seaventh . . . relate the reports of their parents kinsfolks and neighbours" who had witnessed the battle of Nibley Green in 1469. As late as 1603, an old man of the neighborhood could give a full account of the skirmish "as if the same had been but yesterday," and with a mass of particular detail "not possible almost by such plaine Country people to be fained."[46]

What kind of memories of Richard III's reign were still in circulation at the close of the sixteenth century? To what extent did the Richard of memory differ from or have the power to challenge the Richard of history, as received through chronicle, ballad, and (increasingly) drama? It is very difficult to know, not least because any memories which have been preserved are themselves inevitably mediated by textuality. We cannot know, for instance, if some features of Shakespeare's play with no clear source in the chronicles derive from memories retailed to him by those who heard them from their grandparents; if so, they have undergone a seachange, losing the hallmarks of orally transmitted memory.[47] Nonetheless, we can be certain that century-old recollections of Richard were passed on in the late Elizabethan period, from a second generation to a third or from a third to a fourth or fifth. Some of these stories were eventually written down in the seventeenth century, without entirely shedding the marks of personal memory. I want to examine three such memories, the first of which we have already glanced at.

John Stow in his *Chronicles of England* had followed Thomas More's description of Richard III's deformities—"little of stature, yll featured of limmes, crooke

---

[45] Quoted in Adam Fox, *Oral and Literate Culture in England, 1500–1700* (Oxford: Oxford University Press, 2000), 276.

[46] John Smyth, *The Lives of the Berkeleys, Vol. 2*, ed. John MacLean (Gloucester, Bristol and Gloucestershire Archaeological Society, 1883), 114–15.

[47] An intriguing possible example of a memory embedded in the play is Richard's naming of his favorite horse as "White Surrey" (5.4.43)—a name unattested in the play's known sources (see Shakespeare, *Richard III*, ed. John Jowett [Oxford: Oxford University Press, 2000], 336n.43). Richard's biographer Paul Murray Kendall reported that the name occurred in a list of the king's horses in a register of the royal secretariat. This would strongly suggest the possibility of oral transmission—and, indeed, the name of a favoured horse is the kind of detail likely to linger in folk memory over a long period. Unfortunately, the name White Surrey does not in fact occur in the relevant place (f4) of Harleian MS 433. Kendall's statement would thus appear to be another case of a "memory" with its real origins in Shakespeare. Cf. Kendall, *Richard III* (New York: W. W. Norton, 1996), 571n.1; *British Library Harleian Manuscript 433*, ed. Rosemary Horrox and P. W. Hammond (Gloucester: Richard III Society, 1979).

backed, his left shoulder much hygher than his right"—without demur.[48] Was it caution that prevented him from recording in print the memories of those long-dead witnesses who had told him otherwise? Though Stow was unwilling to publish these recollections, he in his own old age was glad to pass them on to a younger man. It was probably in the 1590s, perhaps even in a conversation prompted by Shakespeare's play, that Stow told George Buck the story he would later record in his provocatively revisionist *History of King Richard III*:

> [S]ome say peremptorily that he was not deformed. One of these is the honest John Stow, who . . . by all his search could not find any not[es of such] deformities in the person of king Richard, albeit he had made great inquisition to know the certainty thereof, as he himself told me. And further, he said he had spoken with old and grave men who had often seen King Richard, and that they affirmed that he was not deformed, but of person and bodily shape comely enough, but they said that he was very low of stature.[49]

Buck completed his manuscript history in 1619, two decades or more after the conversation in which Stow recalled words spoken by old men half a century before. The manuscript would not be printed until 1646, a quarter century after Buck's own death.

The second example consists in the remarkable recollections of Sir Henry Wyatt's imprisonment under Richard, as recorded in the commonplace book of his great-great-grandson, Thomas Scott, in the 1610s. Scott had heard the stories from his grandmother, Jane Wyatt, wife of Sir Thomas Wyatt the Younger; she had apparently received them directly from her husband's grandfather, Sir Henry. "[I]t was his own relation unto them, from whom I had it," as Scott takes care to specify.[50] Jane Wyatt lived at least forty years after her husband's execution for rebellion under Mary; it could have been in the 1580s or 1590s that she passed on her memories to her grandson. To be sure, some of her recollections are of the sort denigrated by contemporaries as "old wive's tales," though this is not

---

[48] John Stow, *The Chronicles of England from Brute unto this Present Yeare of Christ* (London, 1580), 755. The note in the margin points the reader to "The description of Richard III," perhaps drawing attention to the passage as a set-piece. Stow adds no details of his own regarding Richard's deformity, though his account of Richard's reign is lurid enough in other respects.

[49] Buck, *History of Richard III*, 129.

[50] "Some passages taken out of an old manuscript written by Thomas Scott of Egreston," BL Add MS 62135, n.d., f. 465ᵛ. Scott's use of "them" could indicate more than one source for the memories he records, but no other member of the family seems to provide a direct link with Henry Wyatt, and his grandmother is the only source Scott specifies (467ʳ). Jane Haute married Thomas Wyatt the Younger in 1537, some months after the death of Sir Henry in November 1536, but had presumably been introduced to her prospective grandfather-in-law.

necessarily a reflection on their veracity.[51] It is not unlikely that Sir Henry, starving in a Scottish prison, was glad to dine on pigeons brought him by a friendly cat (many of us have received similar services, albeit probably with less gratitude). Less plausible on the whole is Scott's account of Sir Henry's face-to-face encounter with Richard, who came to tempt him after his torture: "Wyat why art thou such a foole, thou servest for moonshine in the water, a beggarly fugitive; forsake him [Henry Tudor], and become mine, who can reward thee, and I sweare unto thee, will."[52] Sir Henry responds with an assertion of feudal loyalty worthy of Sir Ralph Bigod:

> S[ir] if I had first chosen you for my master, thus faithfull would I have been to you, if you should have needed it, but the Earle, poor and unhappy, tho he be, is my Master, and no discouragement or allurement shall ever drive or draw me from him, by Gods grace; att this the Tyrant stood amazed and turning to the Lords that stood about him, brake out into these words; oh how much more happy is that runaway Rogue in his extreame calamitie, than I, in my greatest seeming prosperitie—hee hath a freind whom hee may trust in his misery, I in this appearing happiness, am unhappy onely through the want of this happiness, is there any of you all that will thus stick unto me, that is not already ready to leave mee.[53]

Part of this story at least was passed on by Sir Henry himself. His son, the poet Sir Thomas Wyatt, knew it, referring in a letter to his own son to "the tirant that could find in his hart to see him [Sir Henry] rakkid."[54] Yet the language attributed to Richard is distinctive, suggesting the subsequent influence of Shakespeare's play. Scott's Richard is not merely the heartless tyrant of tradition, but a wry skeptic who delights in mocking the beautiful ideal—and crystallizes his derision in delightful images. "Thou servest for moonshine in the water"— though the phrase never occurs in *Richard III*, it is almost a distillation of the play's two most potent motifs, namely water as a signifier of inaccessibility ("in the deep bosom of the ocean buried" [1.1.4]), and the insistent language of shadows and reflections ("to spy my shadow in the sun/And descant on mine own deformity" [1.1.26–27]; "Shine out, fair sun, till I have bought a glass,/That I may see my shadow as

---

[51] On women as curators of memory, see Fox, *Oral and Literate Culture,* 173–212; Houts, *Memory and Gender in Medieval Europe*; Henk Dragstra, "'Before woomen were Readers': How John Aubrey Wrote Female Oral History," in *Oral Traditions and Gender in Early Modern Literary Texts*, ed. Mary Ellen Lamb and Karen Bamford (Aldershot: Ashgate, 2008), 41–53.

[52] Scott, "Some passages," 467ᵛ.   [53] Ibid., 467ᵛ.

[54] Sir Thomas Wyatt to his son, April 15, 1537: Letter no. 1; in Patricia Thomson, *Sir Thomas Wyatt and his Background* (Stanford: Stanford University Press, 1964), 3.

I pass" [1.2.249–50]).[55] Likewise, when Scott's Richard slides into self-pity, he echoes both the characteristic suspicion of Shakespeare's king ("Ay, ay, thou wouldst be gone to join with Richmond./But I'll not trust thee" [4.4.421–22]) and his despair on the eve of battle ("There is no creature loves me,/And if I die no soul will pity me" [5.5.154–55]).

The memories recorded by Buck and Scott survived some 130 years in the memory stream—that is, they had their sole existence in people's heads, with at least two instances of transmission from one head to another—before entering the textual record. Quite different factors are likely to account for the survival of these two traditions. The memory that Richard's body was "comely enough" was worth storing up and passing on precisely because it contradicted orthodox opinion and written history. This was a memory that could look after itself, so long as it could seek out individuals like Stow and Buck for whom storing up and sharing such subversive information was a source of intellectual and interpersonal enjoyment. The story of Wyatt's torture, by contrast, was not preserved for what it said about Richard, but for what it said about Sir Henry and his descendants. This was a family story, and the story of a political family. The specific route of transmission Scott chooses to emphasize, from his great-great-grandfather to his grandmother to himself, highlights three generations that found themselves in direct and potentially fatal conflict with royal power. Sir Henry had suffered the rack for defying the king; Jane Wyatt's husband died on the block for rebellion against Mary; Thomas Scott, political radical and godly controversialist, was embarking on a career of increasingly pronounced opposition to royal policy.[56] Where one memory (Stow/Buck) owes its transmission to its intrinsic political significance, another (Wyatt/Scott) takes on a contingent political significance with respect to the chain of transmission. Yet, in their different ways, both memories thematize and celebrate resistance to authority, be it textual or monarchical.

A third example of a memory recorded for the first time in the early seventeenth century bears resemblances to both of these, in that it supplies

---

[55] In the play, moonshine and watery burial are united in the widowed Queen's wish "That I, being governed by the wat'ry moon,/May send forth plenteous tears to drown the world" (2.2.69–70). On some level, Scott's "moonshine in the water" also alludes to the tale-type of the fool who dives for the moon in the water thinking it is cheese, a version of which occurs in *A Hundred Merry Tales* (see Katharine M. Briggs, *A Dictionary of British Folk-Tales in the English Language, Part A: Folk Narratives* [London: Routledge & Kegan Paul, 1970] 1:109, 169–70). But what Richard seems to be mocking in Scott's anecdote is not so much Wyatt's active pursuit of the inaccessible—diving for cheese—as his stubborn fidelity to the cheese-ideal in the face of its inaccessibility.

[56] On Scott's Protestant patriotism and identification with the Wyatt Rebellion, see Cesare Cuttica, "Thomas Scott of Canterbury (1566–1635): Patriot, Civic Radical, Puritan," *History of European Ideas* 34 (2008): 475–89.

information lacking from the historical record, whilst testifying to the endurance and character of the community of transmission. In his *Description of Leicestershire* (1622), William Burton (1575–1645) attempts to do what Bernard Andre could or would not do, that is, fix the location of the battle of Bosworth. Burton does not rely on written records, but on archaeological evidence (arrowheads in particular) and local memory: "by relation of the inhabitants, who have many occurences and passages yet fresh in memory, by reason: that some persons thereabout which saw the battle fought, were living within lesse then 40 yeares; of which persons, my selfe have seene some, and have heard of their discourses, though related by the second-hand."[57] Whatever is puzzling in this sentence becomes clear with reference to the significant dates. Writing in the early 1620s, Burton claims some witnesses were still alive less than 40 years ago, which would indicate the early 1580s. Perhaps there were indeed centenarians in the Bosworth area who had seen the battle as children. Born in 1575, Burton could thus have "seene" some of these individuals, as he says. He would not have been in a position to question them closely about their memories before their deaths, however, and thus it is that he received their memories second-hand—probably from their children or grandchildren—in the 1590s, when he began his research in county history.

Like Buck and Scott, Burton specifies a precise chain of transmission between the original witnesses and himself. In each case, only a single intermediary is required to link the fifteenth-century witness with the seventeenth-century writer. All three, moreover, draw attention to their own place in the chain: "as he himself told me"; "it was his own relation unto them, from whom I had it"; "my selfe have seene some, and have heard of their discourses." Each formulation carries echoes of Thomas More, writing a full century earlier: "I have heard of som that said thei saw it." For these Jacobean writers, as for More, detailing the chain of transmission and their own place within it serves not only to verify the story, but to lay claim to a privileged relationship with it, a relationship we must recognize as a species of memory. Memory is fundamentally distinct from history in that it is the past that in some sense belongs to us.[58] Yet, writing in the second and third decades of the seventeenth century, Buck, Scott and Burton are surely at

---

[57] William Burton, *The Description of Leicestershire* (London, 1622), 47.
[58] Katharine Hodgkin and Susannah Radstone. "Introduction: Contested Pasts," in *Memory, History, Nation: Contested Pasts*, ed. Hodgkin and Radstone, (Piscataway, NJ: Transaction, 2005), 1–21; Marianne Hirsch, "The Generation of Postmemory," *Poetics Today* 29 (2008): 108–11. For a robust critique of any attempt to lay claim to a past other than that which we ourselves experienced, see Walter Benn Michaels, "'You who never was there': Slavery and the New Historicism, Deconstruction and the Holocaust," *Narrative* 4 (1996): 1–16.

the outermost limit of communicative or active memory—a circumstance both reflected in the decision to write, and sealed in the act of writing.[59]

Each of the memories discussed above was transmitted by word of mouth fairly late in Elizabeth's reign, before being written down under James. It cannot have been many years before or after Shakespeare's composition of *Richard III* that Stow passed his secret on to Buck, that Jane Wyatt trained her grandson in family lore, or that Burton collected oral histories from the folk of Bosworth. Shakespeare must have been well aware that memories of Richard's reign remained in circulation in his day; and it seems he was no less inclined than we may be to doubt their reliability. This indeed is the satirical nub of the scene in which the prattling Duke of York calls to mind certain second-hand recollections of Richard's own infancy:

> YORK: Marry, they say my uncle grew so fast
>   That he could gnaw a crust at two hours old.
>   'Twas full two years ere I could get a tooth.
>   Grannam, this would have been a biting jest.
> DUCHESS OF YORK: I pray thee, pretty York, who told thee this?
> YORK: Grannam, his nurse.
> DUCHESS OF YORK: His nurse? Why, she was dead ere thou wast born.
> YORK: If 'twere not she, I cannot tell who told me. (2.4.27–34)

This is one of several passages in the play that force the question of how, if at all, we can know the past we did not ourselves experience. As the Scrivener's soliloquy casts doubt on written records, and Prince Edward's naive faith in truths that "live from age to age" (3.1.76) raises problems with oral tradition, the prattling of little York points up how soon transmitted "memories" lose touch with their origins.

---

[59] Although oral traditions can survive over a far longer period than those traced here, where they do not retain the sense of personal connection they cannot meaningfully be described as memories. A tale involving Bosworth recorded later in the seventeenth century by John Aubrey, in some ways similar to Burton's relation, points up the contrast: "In one of the great Fields at Warminster in Wiltshire, in the Harvest, at the very time of the Fight at Bosworth Field, between King Richard III, and Henry VII, there was one of the Parish took two Sheaves, crying (with some intervals) Now for Richard, Now for Henry: at last, lets fall the Sheaf that did represent Richard; and cryed, Now for King Henry, Richard is slain: This Action did agree with the very Time, Day and Hour. When I was a School-boy, I have heard this confidently delivered by Tradition, by some Old Men of our Country"; Aubrey, *Miscellanies upon the Following Subjects* (London, 1696), 88. Born in 1626, Aubrey could conceivably have spoken in the 1630s with octogenarians who had heard the story as children from those who actually witnessed it. Yet, unlike Burton or Buck, Aubrey is not concerned to trace each step in the chain of transmission. Similarly, he records as "a tradition" the story told to him in 1648 by a man of eighty, that Richard III was born at Fasterne near Wootton Bassett; there is no attempt to fill in the 116-year gap between Richard's birth and that of the witness; Aubrey, *Natural History of Wiltshire*, 76.

ory, would soon exert an unparalleled influence over memories of Richard III.
We have seen how it may have intruded into Scott's story of his great-great-
grandfather's ordeal. And even as Burton was writing up his research into the
location of Bosworth field, local traditions were becoming harder and harder
to sort from Shakespeare's version of the battle. This is the point of the passage
in Richard Corbett's "Iter Boreale" (*c.*1621) in which an innkeeper, "full of
Ale, and History" gives the poet and his party a tour of Bosworth field, at the
climax of his narrative confusing history with Shakespeare's play:

> Upon this Hill they met; why, he could tell
> The Inch where Richmond stood, where Richard fell;
> Besides what of his knowledge he could say,
> Hee had Authentique notice from the Play;
> Which I might guesse by's mustring up the Ghosts,
> And policies not incident to hosts:
> But chiefly by that one perspicuous thing,
> Where he mistooke a Player for a King,
> For when he would have said, King Richard dy'd,
> And call'd a Horse, a Horse, he Burbage cry'd.[60]

2.3 "THE HANDSOMEST MAN IN THE ROOM": REMEMBERING RICHARD, 1604–35

The foregoing discussion has been grounded in the assumption that for
the adult Shakespeare and his contemporaries, Richard's reign had passed
beyond the horizon of living memory. This is almost certainly the case.
Yet would those living in the late sixteenth and early seventeenth centuries
have agreed with the suggestion that no-one alive could remember Richard III? Here the answer is much less certain. The period saw the rise of
a fascination with—almost a cult of—extraordinary longevity.[61] William
Paulet's reputed attainment of 106 years would be surpassed in the early
seventeenth century by others who were said to have lived twice the allot-
ted three score years and ten, and even more. The most celebrated centenarians of the era, Katherine Fitzgerald, Countess of Desmond (*d.*1604)
and Thomas Parr (*d.*1635), were both said, like Paulet, to have been born

---

[60] Richard Corbett, *Certain Elegant Poems* (London, 1647), 11–12.
[61] See Laslett, "The Bewildering History of the History of Longevity," in *Validation of Exceptional Longevity*, ed. Bernard Jeune and James W. Vaupel (Odense: Odense University Press,
1999), 23–40; Lynn Botelho, ed., *The History of Old Age in England, Volume 1: The Cultural Conception of Old Age in the Seventeenth Century* (London: Pickering & Chatto, 2008), 193–219.

in the reign of Edward IV. It is almost as if the steady prolongation of reported life-spans over this period were being driven by a need to believe that someone yet living—or only just deceased—could still remember England before the dawn of the Tudor era.[62]

"I my selfe knew the old Countesse of Desmond of Inchiquin in Munster, who lived in the yeare 1589 and many yeares since, who was married in Edward the fourths time, and held her Joynture from all the Earles of Desmond since then."[63] Sir Walter Ralegh did not attempt to estimate the Countess's age at death; the date of her nuptials was sufficient indication of her extraordinary lifespan. Writing only slightly later than Ralegh, Fynes Moryson and Francis Bacon would specify her age at death as 140, adding the curious detail that she grew a third set of teeth late in life.[64] Other colorful rumours soon circled round her, including Robert Sidney's tale that she died following a fall from a nut tree.[65] No early source refers to what memories the Countess might have stored up in the course of her long pilgrimage. 150 years later, however, Horace Walpole would make a startling claim: "the old Countess of Desmond, who had danced with Richard, declared that he was the handsomest man in the room except his brother Edward, and was very well made."[66]

However unlikely Walpole's tale, he was not guilty of outright fabrication. The tradition of the Countess's dance with Richard was passed down orally within Anglo-Irish families of his acquaintance, and he heard the story from at least two sources. A correspondent provided him with a somewhat flawed genealogy of transmission which purported to demonstrate that the memory had been passed down from the Countess herself with only two intermediaries.[67] If there is every reason to doubt that Katherine Fitzgerald

---

[62] Writing after the Restoration, Edward Leigh cites the longevity of Parr and adds in the margin "He as well as the Countess of *Desmond* (so much spoken of for her great age) is said to have lived in the Raign of *Edward* the fourth" (212)—as if that were the true mark of agedness, in any era; see Leigh, *Choice Observations of all the Kings of England from the Saxons to the Death of King Charles the First* (London, 1661), 221.

[63] Walter Ralegh, *The History of the World* (London, 1614), 78.

[64] Fynes Moryson, *An Itinerary* (London, 1617), Part 3, 43. Bacon, 1627, 194; 1638, 188. There were rumors of the Countess's survival to an even greater age. Richard Steele (1622–1692) says she "died within our memories, being, as it is credibly affirmed, an 184 years old"; *A Discourse Concerning Old Age* (London, 1688), 17.

[65] Robert Sidney's Table-Book, quoted in "The Old Countess of Desmond," *The Dublin Review* 51 (1862): 51.

[66] Walpole, *Historic Doubts*, 102.

[67] A Mr. Meyrick informed Walpole that he had heard the story from his wife's grandfather, Lord St John of Battersea (d. 1742), who had heard it from his father, who had heard it from the Countess herself. Lord St John's father cannot have heard the story from the Countess, as he was born some twenty years after her death. Meyrick's account does nonetheless hint that the tradition was in circulation by the mid-1600s. The correspondence is quoted and the claims investigated in "The Old Countess of Desmond," 56–9.

had really danced with Richard III, there is some reason to believe that the tale of her having done so was in circulation not long after her death.

The tradition may even hold a grain of truth. Though the Countess's actual date of birth was probably later than 1500, her husband was some fifty years her senior, and could well have laid eyes on Richard III, if not danced with him.[68] Yet it is equally possible that the story of the dance had its origins in the seventeenth century, on the model of John Stow's report regarding Richard's appearance. It conveys essentially the same point, whilst supplying more vivid circumstantial detail, and repackaged as a personal rather than second-hand memory. It seems significant that Stow himself died in 1605, a year after the Countess, and precisely 120 years after Bosworth—the outer limit, as Elizabeth van Houts suggests, of active memory. Perhaps the anecdote in which the Countess of Desmond is thematized as the last living witness to the world of Richard III came into being as a way of registering the passage of that world beyond any form of recollection.

Did the death of the Countess of Desmond then mark the final passage of the reign of Richard III beyond human memory? Not quite. 1635 saw the arrival in London, with no little fanfare, of old Tom Parr of Hereford-shire, who was said to have been born in 1483, in the last months of the reign of Edward IV (Fig. 2.2). He was thus 152 years old. Among a clutch of publications celebrating Parr's unparalleled longevity was John Taylor's *The Old, Old, Very Old Man*, issued twice while its subject was yet alive and again after his death (Parr died after just six weeks in the city). Taylor draws attention to the many monarchs Parr had supposedly outlived:

> This Thomas Parr hath liv'd th' expired Raigne
> Of ten great Kings and Queenes, th' eleventh now sways
> The Scepter, (blest by th' ancient of all days.)
> Hee hath surviv'd the Edwards, fourth and fift;
> And the third Richard, who made many a shift
> To place the Crowne on his Ambitious head;
> The seventh & eighth brave Henries both are dead,
> Sixt Edward, Mary, Phillip, Elsabeth,
> And blest remembred James . . .[69]

Of the rulers listed here, none had a shorter reign than Richard III, yet none looms larger in this catalogue. Where no other monarch is granted even a full

---

[68] Her husband was Thomas Fitzgerald, 11th Earl of Desmond (1454–1534). See John Gough Nichols, "The Old Countess of Desmond," *N&Q* vol. s3-I, 16 (1862): 302.

[69] John Taylor, *The old, old, very old man: or, The age and long life of Thomas Par . . . Where-unto is added a postscript, shewing the many remarkable accidents that hapned in the life of this old man* (London, 1635), B2ᵛ.

Fig. 2.2. Engraving of Thomas Parr, 1635. © National Portrait Gallery, London.

pentameter line, Richard's two years on the throne earn him two. It is as if Richard's reign, finished before Parr was three years old, were nonetheless the chief historical event in the old man's life, at least until the accession of Charles I.

Fascinated by what such an old man might be able to remember, Taylor goes on to speculate, oddly and delightfully, on what unfathomable depths of time might reside in his inherited memory, if his father, grandfather, and great-grandfather had all lived equally long lives:[70]

> Had their lives threds so long a length been spun,
> They (by succession) might from Sire to Son

---

[70] Taylor may well have been inspired by M. P.'s ballad *The Wandring Jews Chronicle*, first printed in 1634. The Jew of the ballad claims to have been fifteen years old at the time of the Norman Conquest, and to recall the reign of every monarch since. Richard III figures

Have been unwritten Chronicles, and by
Tradition shew Times mutabillity.
Then Parr might say he heard his Father well,
Say that his Grand-sire heard his Father tell
The death of famous Edward the Confessor,
(Harrold) and William Conq'rour his successor . . .[71]

Richard and his contemporaries again feature prominently in this much-expanded catalogue of rulers:

Then of fourth Edward, and faire Mistrisse Shore,
King Edwards Concubine Lord Hastings (—)
Then how fift Edward, murthered with a trick
Of the third Richard; and then how that Dick
Was by seventh Henrie slaine at Bosworth field . . .[72]

Yet in spite of Taylor's obvious pleasure in speculating on what the very old man *might* remember, he comes to the disappointing conclusion that Parr remembers nothing at all—nothing, that is, that could be of interest to either historians or general readers.

Thus had Parr had good breeding, (without reading)
Hee from his sire, and Grand sires sire proceeding,
By word of mouth might tell most famous things
Done in the Raigns of all those Queens and Kings.
But hee in Husbandry hath bin brought up,
And nere did taste the Helliconian cup,
He nere knew History, nor in mind did keepe
Ought, but the price of Corne, Hay, Kine, or Sheep.[73]

In his keenness to align himself with an elite and orthodox vision of history—wherein the famous deeds of kings and queens are what matter, not fluctuations in the price of agricultural commodities—Taylor skirts over the fact that the memories of aged farmers regarding "the price of Corne, Hay, Kine, or Sheep" could carry legal authority, and political significance. In 1552, when older people might indeed have remembered commodity prices in the reign of Richard III, an

prominently in this exceedingly brief chronicle. In addition to having been present when Richard murdered Henry VI, and at his persecution of Jane Shore, the Jew asserts "I was at Bosworthfield/Well armed there with spear and shield,/meaning to try my force:/Where Richard losing life and Crown/Was naked born to Leicester Town/upon a Colliers horse" (single sheet). See Henk Dragstra, "The Politics of Holiness: Royalty for the Masses in *The Wandring Jews Chronicle*," in *Transforming Holiness: Representations of Holiness in English and American Literary Texts*, ed. Irene Visser, Helen Wilcox (Leuven: Peeters, 2006), 61–80.
[71] Taylor, *Old, old, very old man*, C3ʳ.   [72] Taylor, *Old, old, very old man*, C3ᵛ C4ʳ.
[73] Taylor, *Old, old, very old man*, C4ʳ.

attempted rising in Berkshire had called for "the prices of victualles to be brought lower agayne as they were in King Rychardes time."[74] The memories of the aged could be dull, as Taylor suggests, but they could also be dangerous.[75]

An anonymous broadside, *The Three Wonders of the Age* (1636), contributes more details regarding Parr's memories of commodity prices, probably based on the old man's actual conversation: "he did call to mind that in the fourteenth yeare of his age, mault was sold for twelve pence the quarter, and 17 at the dearest."[76] The broadside also attributes to him other, more disturbing memories of the reign of Edward IV. "This Thomas Parre, did remember, as our History Record, in King Edward the 4th his reign, one Margaret Davy for poysoning of eleven persons, and one Richard Rose a cooke, for poysoning of sixteene, were at severall times boyled to death in Smith-field." The historical information, drawn from Stow's chronicle, is sadly accurate, except that the executions did not take place under Edward IV, but in 1532 and 1542 respectively. Only for a relatively short period under Henry VIII was boiling alive the punishment for poisoning. It is possible that the author chose these "memories" for Parr more or less at random. Yet it is also possible, if "old Parr" was indeed near a century old, that his childhood imagination had been scarred by tales of such grisly punishments. It is little wonder that Taylor shied away from the matter of Parr's personal memory, if his talk embraced not only the price of malt, but the brutality of kings. By the same token, the prominence of the murderous Richard III in Taylor's catalogue of rulers may reflect the fact that Parr's recollections of the exercise of royal power were disturbingly dark.

In a second edition of his pamphlet, Taylor appended a survey of the chief events Parr was supposed to have lived through: "The changes of Manners,

---

[74] *Calendar of Patent Rolls*, Edward VI, IV.343. See Andy Wood, *The 1549 Rebellions and the Making of Early Modern England* (Cambridge: Cambridge University Press, 2007), 82. Similarly, the demands in Kett's rebellion in 1549 had included the reduction of rents to the levels they were "in the first year of the reign of King Henry VII."

[75] Taylor's dismissal of Parr's memory also reflects skepticism about the value of oral testimony: "distrust of aged memories grew during the sixteenth and seventeenth centuries, as records of the past proliferated and became more widely available"; Daniel Woolf, *The Social Circulation of the Past: English Historical Culture 1500–1730* (Oxford: Oxford University Press, 2003), 279–80.

[76] *The Three Wonders of the Age* (London, 1636), broadside. At no point in the fifteenth or sixteenth century were malt prices so low. Yet, rather remarkably, in 1497 (when Parr was supposedly 14) the price stood at 2s 9½d—among the lowest points in the fifteenth century and never to be matched again. Prices were much higher in the 1540s, a more plausible decade for Parr's teenage years, but still lower than they would ever be again. The 1630s, when Parr came to London, saw exceptional highs in malt prices. See J. E. Thorold Rogers, *A History of Agricultural Prices in England* (Oxford: Clarendon Press, 1866–87), 3.287, 3.292, 5.260.

the variations of Customes, the mutability of times, the shiftings of Fashions, the alterations of Religions, the diversities of Sexts, and the intermixtures of Accidents which hath hapned since the Birth of this old Thomas Parr . . ."[77] Beginning with the rising of Lambert Simnel "in the sixt yeare of his Age," the postscript serves as a sort of prosthetic historical memory for the amnesiac old man. As Taylor turns to the religious turmoil of the sixteenth century, Parr emerges as a humbler version of the grand survivor William Paulet, excelling in prudence, obedience, and forgetfulness:

> All which time, Thomas Parr hath not been troubled in mind for either the building or throwing downe of Abbyes, and Religious Houses; nor did hee ever murmur at the manner of Prayers, let them be Latin or English, hee held it safest to be of the Religion of the King or Queene that were in being; for he knew that hee came raw into the world, and accounted it no point of Wisedom to be broyled out of it: His name was never questioned for affirming or denying the Kings Supremacie: He hath known the time when men were so mad as to kneele down and pray before a Blocke, a Stock, a Stone, a Picture, or a Relique of a Hee or Shee Saint departed; and he liv'd in a time when mad men would not bow their knee at the name of Jesus . . ."[78]

Such bland indifference to religious controversy reflects prudence, and perhaps a natural inclination for the mellow middle way of Anglicanism. Taylor's old man comes across as an instinctive moderate, wryly observing without actively resisting the madness of Catholics and Puritans alike. Yet in the midst of this passage we find again the horrifying image of being "broyled" by royal command—as if nothing had left a more enduring mark on Parr's long memory than the very real possibility of being cooked alive.

Thomas Parr was not 152 years old when he died. Nonetheless, he must have harboured memories of a world very different from anything the young could recall or perhaps even imagine. It is conceivable that Parr was born before the dissolution of the monasteries; and it is altogether likely that he remembered several drastic shifts in patterns of worship, before the Elizabethan settlement. Such memories could be uncomfortable, even dangerous, both for their bearers and for those who might form the next link in the chain of transmission. Hence the insistence, from Paulet to Parr, that the chiefest virtue of the extraordinarily long-lived was forgetfulness.[79]

---

[77] Taylor, *Old, old, very old man*, B2ᵛ.   [78] Taylor, *Old, old, very old man*, D3ʳ⁻ᵛ.
[79] On memories of Catholicism see Alison Shell, *Oral Culture*, 276–7; Eamon Duffy, "Bare Ruined Choirs: Remembering Catholicism in Shakespeare's England," in *Theatre and Religion: Lancastrian Shakespeare*, ed. Richard Dutton, Alison Findlay and Richard Wilson (Manchester: Manchester University Press, 2003), 40–57. The anxious combination of admiration for extreme longevity with hostility to recollection of the religious

The case of Thomas Parr—a man whose childhood recollections of England under Henry VIII were interpreted by himself and others as memories of the late fifteenth century—is a particularly overt and literal example of a more widespread displacement of memory.[80] The different world at the edge of recollection was not the Catholic England of 1530, but the misty medieval realm of 1480. The epochal break between one era and another was not confessional but dynastic. The brutal violence lurking like a nightmare at the back of collective memory was not associated with the Reformation but with the Wars of the Roses and, above all, Richard III. We see this displacement in the broadside's crude backdating of executions for poisoning, but also in the memoirs of Thomas Scott, for whom his ancestor's torture under Richard became a way of addressing and interpreting his grandfather's execution under Mary.

It would be needlessly reductive to suggest that memories involving Richard III were merely coded references to the Reformation and the way of life supplanted by it. Yet, from a relatively early point, it is clear that a relationship developed between Richard and the Reformation as objects of memory. Why these two chronologically distinct phenomena should become intertwined can be explained in part with reference to the unfolding of memory cycles. As we have seen, for a variety of reasons societies tend to revisit events 20–30 years after their occurrence; the first cycle of collective memory is associated with the construction of narratives, memorials, authoritative accounts. The second cycle, 50–60 years after the event, differs in its commemorative priorities; as the last witnesses near the ends of their lives, anxieties center on the transmission of personal memory.[81] Finally, we may detect yet another cycle at the outer limit of what Walter Map called "our times," that is, 100–120 years. At this point the original

past is very clear in another old-age pamphlet belonging to the early seventeenth century. In praise of a 108-year-old Morris dancer, it is said: "Such an olde Mad cappe deserves better to bee the stuffing of a Cronicle, then Charing Crosse does for loosing his rotten head, which (through age being wind-shaken) fell off, and was trod upon in contempt" (*Old Meg of Hereford-shire, for a Mayd-Marian* [London, 1609], C2ᵛ.) The point being that the old dancer is living in the present—not lingering on as a relic of a past best-forgotten.

[80] For readings of the Reformation as an historical trauma whose psychological consequences may be traced in Elizabethan and Jacobean literature, see Thomas P. Anderson, *Performing Early Modern Trauma from Shakespeare to Milton* (Aldershot: Ashgate, 2006), 19–56, 125–168; Katharine Goodland, *Female Mourning in Medieval and Renaissance English Drama* (Aldershot: Ashgate, 2005), 173–82.

[81] This second cycle can also witness what Stephen Greenblatt calls the "fifty-year effect," a time in the wake of the great, charismatic ideological struggle in which the revolutionary generation that made the decisive break with the past is all dying out and the survivors hear only hypocrisy in the sermons and look back with longing at the world they have lost"; Greenblatt, *Hamlet in Purgatory* (Princeton: Princeton University Press, 2000), 258.

event is passing beyond communicable memory into the comparatively inert "past," a transition sometimes marked by last-ditch memorial activity.

Fifty years after Richard III came to the throne, Henry VIII was excommunicated; the dissolution of the monasteries began fifty-one years after Bosworth. A key cycle in the collective memory of Richard's reign thus coincided with the most tumultuous years of the Reformation. Memories of the distant past were passed on or withheld in the context of massive change in the present.[82] For those living through this time of transformation, the era immediately preceding the accession of the Tudors was readily available as a symbol of the world they had lost. Fifty years on, the last (100-year) cycle of Ricardian memory coincided with the second cycle of Reformation memory. At a time when a handful of survivors with clear recollections of Catholic practice were attempting, often in secret, to pass on their memories, we find a resurgence of interest in Richard's reign, not least on the stage.[83] Finally, a century on from the Reformation, when the events of the 1530s were themselves slipping beyond the grasp of active memory, we meet the impossible notion that memories of Richard III might still survive, in the head of Old Tom Parr.

How does *Richard III* respond to or reflect the imbrication of memory cycles? No play of Shakespeare's is so thoroughly saturated in the sanctimonious and sometimes savage vocabulary of reform.[84] Powerful echoes of Reformation controversies can be detected in Richard's apparent war against memory, his determination to cut the ties between the present and the past so that the future may be his. Like a Protestant polemicist heaping scorn on Purgatory, Richard insists there can be no commerce between the dead and the living. "God take King Edward to his mercy/And leave the world for me to bustle in" (1.1.151–52); "I'll turn yon fellow in his grave,/And then return lamenting to my love" (1.2.247–48); "Harp not on that string, madam. That is past" (4.4.295).

---

[82] On the impact of the Reformation on both personal and social memory, see Alexandra Walsham, "History, Memory, and the English Reformation," *The Historical Journal* 55 (2012): 899–938.

[83] Public dramas about Richard III and private memoirs of Catholicism are among the most typical literary productions of the 1590s. Richard's reign was staged at least thrice in the decade, in the anonymous *True Tragedy of Richard III* (c.1589–91), Shakespeare's *Richard III* (c.1592), and Heywood's *2 Edward IV* (c. 1599), not to mention Richard's prominent role in Shakespeare's *3 Henry VI* (c.1591); all four plays were in print before 1600. See Chapter 5; see also Kristen Deiter, *The Tower of London in English Renaissance Drama* (London: Routledge, 2008), 74–7. The same years saw the composition of such recusant memoirs as Roger Martin's recollections of Long Melford (c.1590) and the *Rites of Durham* (1593). See Duffy, "Bare Ruined Choirs."

[84] See Hugh Richmond, "*Richard III* and the Reformation," *JEGP* 83 (1984): 509–21.

To the extent that the play presents Richard as an implicitly Protestant foe of Catholic rites of memory, it can be read as a fantasized reversal of the Reformation, with mourning women and righteous ghosts combining to dispatch the heartless innovator who sought to silence them.[85] Yet while *Richard III* is deeply invested in Reformation debates, its dramatic conflicts do not always map neatly onto confessional controversies. Richard, the proclaimed enemy of remembrance, is also the play's chief memorialist of better times gone by. It is he who instructs the upstart Woodvilles: "Let me put in your minds, if you forget,/What you have been ere this, and what you are;/Withal, what I have been, and what I am" (1.3.131–33). Richard (and in this, if in nothing else, he resembles the historical king) repeatedly summons up nostalgia for a past marked by chivalry and hierarchy, as opposed to the debased present. His first soliloquy contrasts "Now" (1.1.1) with a better, simpler era of manly violence; his final speech to his troops likewise recalls a past of English military prowess, when "our fathers . . . in record" (5.6.63–65) defeated the Bretons on their own soil. As the play broods over old debates, the king alternates between Protestant-inflected amnesia and Catholic-inflected nostalgia for the old social order. In his contempt for the cult of the dead, Richard indeed sounds like an Edwardian reformer; yet in his nostalgia for a lost organic community, he sounds like an Elizabethan recusant.

Richard III is the fruit of the conjunction of two cycles of memory. To say that the play is conscious of its late-Elizabethan historical moment is in large part to say that it is conscious of what is happening in the realm of memory and recollection. It is conscious of what old John Stow is telling young George Buck, of what Jane Wyatt is recalling for the benefit of her grandson, and also of what a dwindling generation of men and women up and down the land are telling—or perhaps choosing not to tell—about the different world into which they were born. The play's deep engagement with memory and its transmission is key to its own immediate and enduring dominion over all subsequent efforts to remember Richard III. Accounting for the play's extraordinary hold on collective memory would be the work of another book.[86] Yet I submit that much of the play's power

---

[85] For two persuasive versions of this argument, see Goodland, *Female Mourning*, 135–54; Marche, "Mocking Dead Bones."

[86] Its hold on the imagination has something to do with the brevity and dramatic structure of Richard's reign, which permits Shakespeare for once to cover the whole movement from coronation to death in a single play. On the play's afterlife, see M. G. Aune, "The Uses of Richard III: From Robert Cecil to Richard Nixon," *Shakespeare Bulletin* 24 (2006): 23–47; Andreas Höfele, "Making History Memorable: More, Shakespeare and *Richard III*," in *Literature, Literary History and Cultural Memory* ed. Herbert Grabes, *REAL: Yearbook of Research in English and American Literature* 21 (Tubingen: Gunter Narr Verlag, 2005), 187–204.

stems from the historical timing which allowed Shakespeare to seize hold of the image of Richard III just a moment before its passage beyond active memory—and at a moment, moreover, when his society was powerfully if almost silently engaged in pondering the extinction of a different sort of memory, and what that might mean for those left behind.

Though the impact of *Richard III* was instantaneous and ubiquitous, we should not think of it as monolithic. Later memories were not simply stamped with the image of Shakespeare's play, but rather refracted through it. This is clearly the case with those two small gems of Jacobean prose, Bacon's "lees in the bottome of mens hearts" and Scott's "moonshine in the water." Both are refractions of *Richard III*'s panoply of images of watery burial. Bacon and Scott are both writing about memory, and specifically about loyalty to a defeated cause (the loyalty of the north to the dead Richard, of Sir Henry Wyatt to the fugitive Henry Tudor). Yet the images are in every other sense opposed, with very different implications for the role of memory in the present. Bacon's lees lie deep, Scott's moonshine is on the surface. The lees are real and solid, the moonshine illusory and a reflection of something else. The lees retain the potential to rise up and transform conditions in the present; the moonshine will vanish the moment it is touched. Where one image insists that memory can provide genuine access to a genuine past, the other retorts that it can show us nothing but a reflection of the present, and the folly of our own desires. There are sources for both of these radically divergent perspectives in Shakespeare's play.

The conflicting claims of lees and moonshine require me to confront questions I have been skirting all along in regard to memories of Richard III, especially those from the mid-Tudor period and later. Is there *anything* at the bottom of the vessel? Do some of these memories have a real ("deep") origin in Richard's time? Might they retain some agency or authority of their own, independent of later contexts? Or are they so much moonshine, surface reflections of the cultural situation in which they were transmitted and recorded, with no real connection to the past at all? Such awkward questions attend studies of memory in every era. If research into flashbulb memory and survivors' testimony has demonstrated one thing, it is that even the most vivid personal recollections can prove profoundly unreliable as guides to historical truth. Yet some would argue that the value and indeed the truth of memory consist not (or not only) in the remembered details, but in the embodied and ethical relationship to the past experienced by the remembering individual or group.[87] Even demonstrably inac-

---

[87] Hodgkin and Radstone, "Introduction"; Robert Eaglestone, *The Holocaust and the Postmodern* (Oxford: Oxford University Press, 2004), 173–93.

curate memories, it has been argued, can convey the real significance of historical events more profoundly and authentically than historical discourses.[88]

The memories examined in this chapter do not speak for the experience of a single group, nor do they reflect a common political or religious perspective. If anything unites them it is a certain spirit of resistance or dissent, sometimes encoded in their content, sometimes evident in the context of transmission. Passed on in private speech or committed to writing, they register their resistance variously to official history, to the arbitrary exercise of royal power, to the desecration of the Eucharist, to the weakening of old social bonds, to intolerable price inflation. Those early modern men and women who responded to contemporary cultural crises by reaching for memories of the late fifteenth century and Richard III need not be convicted of nostalgia or denial. We can seek to understand them rather in terms of Walter Benjamin's injunction "to seize hold of a memory as it flashes up in a moment of danger"—that is, to interpret and potentially intervene in the present moment by aligning it with a specific moment in the past.[89] Benjamin's oft-quoted phrase accomplishes a remarkable fusion of the opposing images of lees and moonshine (which are themselves refractions of Shakespeare's play). In Benjamin's formulation, memory is imagined as flashing in the reflected light of the present circumstance, but also as rising "up" from the depths of the past. The two metaphors for memory are not entirely incompatible, after all. In diving after moonshine, though we may never catch the moon, we at least stand a chance of stirring up the sediment.

[88] Perhaps the most powerful version of this argument consists in Dori Laub's response to the inaccurate recollections of a survivor of the Auschwitz uprising, who vividly recalled four chimneys exploding in flames, rather than only one. "The woman was testifying . . . not to the number of the chimneys blown up, but to something more radical, more crucial: the reality of an unimaginable occurrence. . . . She testified to the breakage of a framework. That was historical truth." Shoshana Felman and Dori Laub, *Testimony: Crises of Witnessing in Literature, Psychoanalysis and History* (London: Routledge, 1992), 60.

[89] Walter Benjamin, "Theses on the Philosophy of History," in *Illuminations*, ed. Hannah Arendt, trans. Harry Zorn (London: Pimlico, 1999), 247.

3

Trophies, Relics, and Props
The Life Histories of Objects

Thomas Wilson was a man of many talents: jurist, rhetorician, diplomat, traveller, translator of Greek. His one foray into the field of interior decoration is, however, rather alarming. "In the bedsteade I will set Richard the thirde kinge of England, or some like notable murtherer."[1] There is something at once comical and a little nightmarish about the idea of Richard III being literally "in the bedstead"—not just lying on the bed, nor figured in the ornate woodwork, but apparently inhabiting the object itself. Wilson's weird image points us to the way that objects can seem to be haunted by the past: by memories, by untold secrets, by times that are gone forever yet seem almost tangibly immanent in an antique or an artifact. Buildings, books, and bedsteads participate in the present, sharing and shaping our *now*, but they are never wholly of the present. Witnesses to a time when we were not, whispering of a time when we will not be, even the most mundane household things can present themselves as *memento mori*.[2] Wilson's murderer in the bedstead finds an echo in the lines of Auden:

> The glacier knocks in the cupboard,
> The desert sighs in the bed,
> And the crack in the teacup opens
> A lane to the land of the dead.[3]

---

[1] Thomas Wilson, *The Arte of Rhetorique for the Use of all Suche as are Studious of Eloquence* (London, 1553), 115.

[2] Arguably, the capacity of objects to remind us of our mortality has been curtailed in modernity, where the anticipated lifespan of most household objects has drastically diminished, even as human longevity has increased. Younger people in industrialized societies today can be confident of outliving most of the material articles that surround them, a circumstance which certainly did not pertain in early modern England. Yet it may well be the fact of materiality itself that reminds us most insistently of death. Peter Schwenger's *The Tears of Things: Melancholy and Physical Objects* (Minneapolis: University of Minnesota Press, 2008) is devoted to the deep association between objects and human melancholy. Schwenger is attentive both to how human representation may entail "the death of the thing" (22) and, conversely, to how objects connote human mortality.

[3] W. H. Auden, "As I Walked Out One Evening," in *Selected Poems*, ed. Edward Mendelson (London: Faber and Faber, 1979), 62.

Wilson's real subject in the passage quoted above is not the art of interior design, but *The Arte of Rhetorique* (1553), and in particular that special branch of Renaissance learning known as the arts of memory. The orator wishing to enhance the power of his memory is advised to visualize a three-dimensional space (often a theatre, though in Wilson's case a bedroom) and in that space to invest different places or objects with specific memories or sets of associations.[4] "In the windowe I will place *Venus* . . . In the chimney I wil place the blacke Smythe, or some other notable traytoure."[5] Though the objects in the memory artist's chamber harbour the past within them—a multitude of pasts—the memories they contain have not been accumulated over the course of time, but artificially implanted by the memory artist. Moreover, the memories are not invested in real objects at all, but rather in mental images of things which may or may not have a real existence. The object in the memory chamber is thus at least twice removed from the historical event or person with which it is associated. Wilson is not suggesting that Richard III could inhabit his—or anyone's—actual bedstead.

Yet, unbeknownst to Wilson, even as he wrote his treatise in 1553, Richard III really was in a bedstead: a particular old-fashioned bedstead in an inn known as the Blue Boar in the city of Leicester. So we are assured by a tradition recorded only in the mid-seventeenth century, but which reflects local memories dating back much earlier. One Mrs Cumber, a native of Leicester born in the reign of Elizabeth, reported the remarkable history of this household article to Sir Roger Twysden in 1653. Having lodged at the Boar on the eve of his last battle, Richard had left behind "a great cumbersom wooddhen beadstead, in which hymself lay beefore the fight, guilded, and with planks or boords at the bottom." The bedstead remained at the inn, an object of no particular interest, it seems, until the late sixteenth century, when the landlord of the inn was one Mr. Clark:

> whose wife going one day to make up a bed they had placed in it,—in styrring of it, found a peece of gold to drop from it,—and then, upon search, perceived the Beadstead to have a double bottom, all which space between the two bottoms was fylled with gold and treasure, all coyned before Richard the 3ds time, or by him,—from whense this Clark reaped an incredyble masse of wealth . . .[6]

---

[4] On the Renaissance arts of memory and the memory theatre, see Frances Yates, *The Art of Memory* (London: Routledge & Kegan Paul, 1966), and, with specific reference to Shakespeare's stage, Lina Perkins Wilder, "Toward a Shakespearean Memory Theater: Romeo, the Apothecary, and the Performance of Memory," *Shakespeare Quarterly* 56 (2005): 156–75.

[5] Wilson, *The Arte of Rhetorique*, 115.

[6] Lambert B. Larking, "Richard III at Leicester," *Notes and Queries* 2nd series 84 (8/8/1857), 102.

The Clarks' fortune was made, and the landlord rose to become Mayor of the town. But the story has an unfortunate conclusion. In the early years of the seventeenth century, Mrs Clark, then widowed, was murdered by a maidservant, who "stopt her breath by thrusting her finger into her throat" in the course of an armed robbery. The thieves were said to have carried away "seven hors load of treasure, and yet left great storre scatterd about the howse of gold and silver."

We are free to wonder how such an astonishing trove could ever have been secreted within a single bedstead. Yet, for all its unlikelihood, at least part of the tale is true. A man was hanged and a woman burned for the murder of Mrs Clark in 1605.[7] And by this time or very shortly after, the bed had become a widely known tourist attraction. In 1611, Henry Peacham would list "King Richard's bed-sted i' Leyster" among sights that could be seen for a penny (alongside such "trifles, and toyes" as "Westminster monuments," the cave of Merlin, and a cassowary which ate hot coals).[8] The bedstead was but one of several Ricardian objects and artefacts which might be viewed on a tour of Leicester in the early seventeenth century, along with the trough at the Greyhound, the monument in Mr Herrick's garden, and the protruding stone of Bow Bridge. His body might have long since disappeared, but Richard's remains were the bedrock of a nascent civic tourist industry. Whether or not the Clarks ever profited from the fateful bedstead, their successors at the Blue Boar undoubtedly did.

This chapter will trace the afterlives of a range of objects associated with the reign and person of Richard III, including his crown, his dagger, his livery badges, his books, and his bed. To be sure, it is impossible to prove that all of the objects ascribed to Richard in the sixteenth and seventeenth century had really belonged to him, or even dated to his era. Some,

---

[7] James Thompson, "Richard III at Leicester," *Notes and Queries* 2nd series 86 (22/8/1857), 154. The woman's punishment took this horrible form because, as a maidservant, the murder of her mistress constituted "petty treason."

[8] Henry Peacham, prefatory verses in *Coryats Crudities* (London, 1611), k4ᵛ. Among the most valuable and visually impressive of early modern household items, it is not entirely surprising that bedsteads could become celebrated tourist attractions, as witnessed in the case of the Great Bed of Ware (now in the Victoria and Albert Museum), as well as Richard's bed at Leicester. On the economic and symbolic value of beds as items of inheritance, see Amy Louise Erickson, *Women and Property in Early Modern England* (London: Routledge, 1993), 65; Ann Rosalind Jones and Peter Stallybrass, *Renaissance Clothing and the Materials of Memory* (Cambridge: Cambridge University Press, 2000), 263. A great bed now at Donington le Heath Manor House in Leicestershire is purported to be "King Dick's Bed," having been purchased from the Blue Boar in the seventeenth century. Only the lower part of the frame is potentially fifteenth century, however, and it is clearly not the same bedstead described by Twysden, as it is strung with cords. See <http://www.leics.gov.uk/index/leisure_tourism/museums/museumcollections/revealed/revealed_objects/revealed_objects_kingdicksbed.htm>

including the bed at the Blue Boar, can be thought to have acquired the association at a later date, rather as the foundling in Wilde's play is advised to acquire a parent before the season is quite over. Yet, as will be seen, even objects with no original connection to Richard III became tied to him in the course of their careers to such an extent that the association with Richard determined their value, their significance, and their very survival (or otherwise). The divergent forms of value attached to Richard's putative possessions in the early modern period provide a context for interpreting the reemergence of many of these same items as theatrical props in *Richard III*. Stage properties such as Richard's prayer book, dagger, bedstead, and armour were objects with histories and complex associations, no less than those things in the world beyond the playhouse which were said to have belonged to the king himself. In its treatment of objects, I will suggest, *Richard III* invites us to consider how much and how little separates the dramatic property from the genuine article, and in doing so to gauge the proximity and the distance between Shakespeare's era and Richard's own.

As an essay in material biography, this chapter will draw on both modern and early modern understandings of what the "life history" of an object might involve. Although "object biography" has emerged as an academic buzzword only relatively recently, Shakespeare himself was an early and confirmed practitioner of the approach. Some of the most memorable passages in the plays involve the revelation of a material item's past. Shylock lends poignancy to his lament for the turquoise ring his daughter has stolen by recalling "I had it from Leah when I was a bachelor. I would not have given it for a wilderness of monkeys" (*The Merchant of Venice*, 3.1.101). The Ghost in *Hamlet* appears significantly in "the very armour he had on/When he th'ambitious Norway combated" (1.1.59–60), raising the question of why that armour, like the throne, escaped inheritance by his son.[9] Later, in Gertrude's chamber, the Ghost wears a nightshirt, leaving us to wonder what intimate stories the garment might be able to tell. Othello terrifies Desdemona by revealing the prehistory of the apparently normal handkerchief she has mislaid: "The worms were hallowed that did breed the silk,/And it was dyed in mummy, which the skilful/Conserved of maidens' hearts" (*Othello*, 3.4.71–73). For Othello, the "magic in the web of it" is the key to the object's enduring power and significance: origin is essence. Yet, with a previous career in English stage practice as well as within the dramatic narrative, the handkerchief has more than one

---

[9] On the Ghost's armour as a withheld material legacy, see Peter Stallybrass, "Worn Worlds: Clothes and Identity on the Renaissance Stage," in *Subject and Object in Renaissance Culture*, ed. Margreta de Grazia, Maureen Quilligan, and Peter Stallybrass (Cambridge: Cambridge University Press, 1996), 314–15.

history. As a type of charged theatrical property, it harks back to the bloody handkerchief of Kyd's *Spanish Tragedy*, and even to the holy handkerchief of Veronica seen on the pre-Reformation stage.[10] Whilst this too is a kind of sacred origin, the biography of the handkerchief *qua* prop does not testify to unchanging essence, but rather to ongoing processes of transformation, negotiation, de- and re-mystification.

Recent academic approaches to object biography continue to play out the tensions and contradictions implicit in the two histories of the handkerchief. In his seminal article "The Cultural Biography of Things" (1984), Igor Kopytoff argues that the life cycles of objects may involve repeated transitions between commodity status and other quite distinct forms of value (Leah's ring would be a case in point).[11] Archaeologists have drawn on this approach to material biography as a way of resisting their discipline's traditional fixation on origins; the archaeologist as object-biographer will not "privilege the moment of origin" but rather "interrogate the specific moments of crafting, forging, exchanging, installing, using and discarding."[12] Yet an approach to the lives of objects that privileges ceaseless transformation and recycling over origin and essence is not without its own pitfalls. Jonathan Gil Harris has criticized what he terms the "national sovereignty model of temporality," whereby things are understood to be citizens of the given moment, attaining meaning only in relation to the people and practices of that period.[13] In *Untimely Matter in the Time of Shakespeare*, Harris follows Michel Serres in identifying certain objects as "polychronic," material palimpsests in which past meanings and functions co-exist with those of the present.[14] Thus, a block of Roman masonry installed upside-down in the wall of a medieval cathedral

---

[10] On the handkerchief as prop and its links to objects of Catholic veneration, see Andrew Sofer, *The Stage Life of Props* (Ann Arbor: The University of Michigan Press, 2003), 61–88; Elizabeth Williamson, *The Materiality of Religion in Early Modern English Drama* (Farnham: Ashgate, 2009), 191–201; and Lina Perkins Wilder, *Shakespeare's Memory Theatre: Recollection, Properties, and Character* (Cambridge: Cambridge University Press, 2010), 141–43.

[11] Igor Kopytoff, "The Cultural Biography of Things: Commoditization as Process," in Arjun Appadurai, ed., *The Social Life of Things: Commodities in Cultural Perspective* (Cambridge: Cambridge University Press, 1984), 64–91.

[12] Lynn Meskell, *Object Worlds in Ancient Egypt: Material Biographies Past and Present* (Oxford: Berg, 2004), 4–5. See also Cornelius Holtorf, *Monumental Past: The Life-histories of Megalithic Monuments in Mecklenburg-Vorpommern (Germany)*. Electronic monograph. University of Toronto: Centre for Instructional Technology Development. (2000–08) <http://hdl.handle.net/1807/245>

[13] Jonathan Gil Harris, *Untimely Matter in the Time of Shakespeare* (Philadelphia, PA: University of Pennsylvania Press, 2009), 2.

[14] The idea of the polychronic object derives from Michel Serres's proposition that "an object, a circumstance, is . . . polychronic, multitemporal, and reveals a time that is gathered together, with multiple pleats." Michel Serres with Bruno Latour, *Conversations on Science, Culture, and Time*, trans. Roxanne Lepidus (Ann Arbor, MI: University of Michigan Press,

testifies to the supersession of one era by another, but does so, paradoxically, by preserving the past it claims to have vanquished; a medieval Hebrew
inscription emerges out of the paving of Elizabethan London to disrupt
new Protestant narratives of civic history.[15]

What light can these discrepant approaches to object biography shed on
the matter of Richard III (and, indeed, of *Richard III*)? It is fair to say that the
vast majority of objects from the world of 1483–85 passed into the succeeding era without carrying more than a flicker of untimeliness. Pots, pikes, and
paving stones were employed or destroyed on the basis of their usefulness in
the present, not for what they had been in the reign of Richard III. Yet a particular range of objects survived into the sixteenth and seventeenth centuries
as witnesses to lost world, their use value bound inextricably to their past.
Many of the objects with which this chapter is specifically concerned were
preserved precisely so that they might reassure their owners that Richard and
his age were no more—a tricky if not paradoxical function inasmuch as their
very survival was one means whereby that supposedly vanished past lived
on. Thus, whilst this chapter begins in a vein not unlike that of Kopytoffian
object-biography, it charts an inevitable resistance to this mode, in the
untimeliness of objects such as the Leicester bedstead, Richard's prayer book,
and the dagger with which he was said to have slain Henry VI. Shakespeare's
Richard III, I will suggest, marks the point at which the assumptions of object
biography begin to crumble in the face of uncannily memorious matter.

3.1 "HUNG UP FOR MONUMENTS"

In the years after 1485, chroniclers and others sought to grasp and encap-
sulate the meaning of Richard's fall with reference to objects that fell with
him. Wild rumours seem to have circulated almost immediately that Richard
had brought the whole royal treasury of England with him to the battlefield,
and that it had been lost there.[16] The implausible tale of lost treasure served
to highlight the drama of the tyrant's fall; like the Herod of contemporary
mystery plays, Richard was to be imagined in the midst of worldly comforts
when he met his sudden end. "For having with him the crown itself," wrote

---

1995), 60. Serres's image of time as a crumpled handkerchief underlies Harris's reading of
the handkerchief in *Othello* as both agent and palimpsest (*Untimely Matter*, 169–87).

[15] Both examples are drawn from Harris, *Untimely Matter*, 28–30, 95–118.

[16] As Diego de Valera reported in a letter of 1 March 1486 to Isabella and Ferdinand of
Castile and Aragon, "there was lost all the king's treasure, which he brought with him into
the field." Letter translated in Pamela Tudor-Craig, *Richard III* (Ipswich: The Boydell Press,
1973), 67–8.

John Rous, "together with great quantities of treasure, he was unexpectedly destroyed in the midst of his army . . . like a wretched creature."[17] The idea that the treasure of England had been unhappily trodden into Leicestershire mud may also have provided a way of accounting for the unprecedented levels of taxation experienced under Richard's successor. The archaeological survey of 2006–09, which has purportedly identified the actual location of the battle for the first time, has not turned up much in the way of treasure. What has been found instead is a scattering of pieces of bronze horse tack, and an unanticipated amount of heavy lead shot, demonstrating that the day involved a clash of artillery unprecedented on English soil.[18] This would seem to confirm the battle's status in marking the transition from one age to another, but in a way that quite undercuts traditional images of Bosworth, which centre on the armoured and mounted Richard leading the last charge of medieval chivalry.

Although we can be sure that Richard III did not bring the treasure of England to Bosworth or lose it there, some treasured items did indeed disappear on or near the day of the battle—hastily concealed by the vanquished in their flight, or buried beforehand by careful owners who never returned to retrieve them. A spectacular representative of these is the Bosworth Crucifix, a fifteenth-century gilt bronze processional cross unearthed on or near the reputed field of battle in the late eighteenth century (Fig. 3.1). The sun emblems on the rear of the device may be Yorkist emblems, suggesting an association with the losing side; a likely hypothesis is that the crucifix belonged to the travelling chapel royal (the same which so notoriously failed to muster the elements required for communion before the battle), and that it was lost and abandoned in the chaos of the battle or subsequent looting of the king's camp.[19] No less evocative is the silver gilt livery badge in the shape of a boar discovered in the recent archaeological survey of the battlefield. Its location near Fenn Hole probably indicates where one of the King's trusted knights fell, perhaps not far from his master.

---

[17] John Rous, *Historia Johannis Rossi de Regibus Anglie*, translated in Hanham, *Richard III*, 123.

[18] "The archaeological survey of Bosworth battlefield has so far produced twenty-two lead roundshot fired from artillery and bullets fired from early hand-guns—more than all the lead roundshot from all the other battlefields of the fifteenth and sixteenth century in Europe put together. They range in size up to 93 mm—so the train of artillery at Bosworth already contained some guns as large as saker, the largest mobile field pieces normally deployed on battlefields in succeeding centuries." Glenn Foard, "Update on the Bosworth Project: Autumn 2009," Bosworth Battlefield Survey, UK Battlefields Resource Centre, created by the UK Battlefields Trust: <http://www.battlefieldstrust.com/resource-centre/warsoftheroses/battlepageview.asp?pageid=824#>.

[19] See John Ashdown-Hill, "The Bosworth Crucifix," *Transactions of the Leicestershire Arcaeological and Historical Society* 78 (2004): 83–96; the cross is now in the possession of the Society of Antiquaries, and featured prominently in its 2008–09 exhibition, "Making History."

Fig. 3.1. The Bosworth Cross. Bronze, fifteenth century. Found on Bosworth Field around 1778. By permission of the Society of the Antiquaries of London.

Fig. 3.2. The Chiddingly Boar. Silver, late fifteenth century. Found at Chiddingly, East Sussex, 1999. ©The Trustees of the British Museum.

Such badges have been found at other locations across England; the silver Chiddingly Boar (Fig. 3.2), unearthed by a metal detectorist in East Sussex in 1999, would once have graced the hat of an elite adherent of the king.[20] Cheaper badges of pewter or copper alloy were distributed in their thousands in 1483 to celebrate Richard's coronation and the investiture of his son as Prince of Wales; one of this sort was found in the moat of Middleham Castle, Richard's Yorkshire stronghold, in 1930.[21] Whether pewter or silver, such badges after 22 August 1485 became traitors to their owners, no longer signaling steadfast loyalty but rather stubborn dissidence. It is hard to resist the idea that the Chiddingly and Middleham boars—and many like them—were hastily cast away by anxious bearers on receiving the news from Bosworth Field.[22]

Found objects like these, whose life histories we can only guess at, offer little evidence on their own as to the wider fate of Richard's signs and symbols following his death. Yet they resonate with the claims of chroniclers such as Edward Hall that the vengeance upon the tyrant's emblems was no less violent than that taken upon his person. Hall records that the "proude braggyng white bore (whiche was his badge) was violently rased and plucked doune from every signe and place where it myght be espied, so yll was his lyfe that men wished the memorie of hym to be buried with his carren corps."[23] If anything approaching such a concerted campaign of destruction took place in 1485, it was an event almost without cultural precedent. Although Yorkists had previously taken measures against the veneration of images of Henry VI, removing his statue from York Minster in the 1470s, there would seem to be no prior example of such a widescale and violent assault on the symbols of a fallen monarch.[24] It may be significant that the first reference to anti-Ricardian iconoclasm occurs only in

---

[20] Department for Culture, Media, and Sport, *Treasure Annual Report 2000*, Medieval Artefacts, Figure 155. Online at <http://www.culture.gov.uk/reference_library/publications/4817.aspx/>

[21] Tudor-Craig, *Richard III*, no. 139 on p. 60, and pl. 50.

[22] Such an option was not available to Richard's faithful adherent Ralph Fitzherbert; dying in the first year of Richard's reign, his effigy at Norbury in Derbyshire is unique among surviving examples in featuring a boar pendant, at the end of a collar of Yorkist suns and roses. A similar boar which once featured on the effigy of Ralph Neville (*d.*1484) at Brancepeth in Durham has since disappeared. Tudor-Craig, *Richard III*, no. 45 on pp. 24–5 and pl. 66.

[23] Hall, Richard III, lix[r].

[24] On Yorkist attitudes to royal images and the controversy over the York Minster statue, see Wendy Scase, "Writing and the 'Poetics of Spectacle': Political Epiphanies in *The Arrivall of Edward IV* and Some Contemporary Lancastrian and Yorkist Texts," in *Images, Idolatry, and Iconoclasm in Late Medieval England: Textuality and the Visual Image*, ed. Jeremy Dimmick, James Simpson, and Nicolette Zeeman (Oxford: Oxford University Press, 2002), 172–84.

the 1540s, in the wake of widespread assaults on images associated with popery and the cult of saints. Hall, in his imagining of how one regime gives way to another, may well have been influenced by the experience of more recent years, where the desecration of images was indeed central to marking the end of one dispensation and the commencement of another.

Whatever its origins, the idea of anti-Ricardian iconoclasm would be accepted by later historians. John Speed expands on Hall's clue to declare that "the white Bore his cognizance was torne downe from every Signe, that his monument might perish, as did the monies of Caligula, which were all melted by the decree of the Senate."[25] Though Speed stops short of saying that Richard's coinage was destroyed in a similar manner, the suggestion would not have been out of place, as coins from his brief reign were notoriously rare.[26] Whatever effort there was—organized or, more likely, spontaneous and self-interested—to erase emblems recalling Richard's reign, its success was inevitably partial. The Leicester inn which housed the notorious bedstead provides a case in point. Known simply as the Boar or possibly the White Boar before Bosworth, there is some indication that the inn subsequently changed its sign to the unincriminating Blue Bell. After a period of time, the name was altered by partial reversion to the Blue Boar, like an original trace peeping through a palimpsest.[27]

Narratives of supersession can be inscribed upon objects not only by destroying or defacing them, but equally by preserving and drawing attention to them, displaying them precisely as pieces of the past in a context that emphasizes their obsolescence and defeat. One example may be seen in Richard's tent-hangings, captured on the field by the Stanleys and displayed at Knowsley Hall for up to two centuries. In a list of family pictures and other heirlooms dated 1695, the second earl of Strafford noted "The fflat Capp Hangings old ones I found here the same with a suite at Knowsley taken in Richard 3.ds Tent in Bosworth field."[28]

[25] John Speed, *The History of Great Britain* (London, 1611), 725.
[26] Later in the seventeenth century, John Evelyn observed that, though he owned or had seen coins from the reign of every king "from Edward Confessor, to our present times," he had not lighted on a coin of Richard III: "and 'tis probable the Mint might not be much imploy'd during the short Reign of that Usurper, which render them so rarely found." Evelyn, *Numismata, a discourse of medals, ancient and modern* (London, 1697), 21–2.
[27] John Throsby, *The History and Antiquities of the Ancient Town of Leicester* (Leicester: J. Brown, 1791), 61. Charles Billson, *Medieval Leicester* (Leicester: Edgar Backus, 1920) found no evidence for the inn's reputed interim as the Blue Bell, which was the name of another Leicester inn well-known in the eighteenth century (179); Throsby, however, reported having seen a piece of glass from one of the inn's old windows decorated with a blue bell (61).
[28] Item 58 of "A schedule of such goods as shall be left at Woodhouse for heir loomes to be Continued with the House and the Estate," printed in Oliver Millar, "Strafford and Van Dyck," in *For Veronica Wedgwood These: Studies in Seventeenth-Century History*, ed. Richard

There is little reason to doubt the provenance. The appropriation of Richard's hangings as trophies attested to his defeat and to the place of the Stanleys on the right side of history. Well into the Tudor era, the deeds of the Stanleys at Bosworth were central to the family's self-aggrandizing narrative, even as they grew to be increasingly at odds with Henry VII and his heirs. One can imagine a rendition of the Stanley-favouring ballad *Bosworth Feilde* (composed before 1495) taking place at Knowsley with the hangings displayed prominently in the background.[29] Yet the lack of reference to the Knowsley hangings over a period of two centuries suggests that, after the initial phase of triumphal installation and display, they were not much noticed.

Comparable objects, fetched home from the field by an honored ancestor, were probably to be seen in many elite households at any point in the sixteenth century. Perhaps some in Shakespeare's audience thought of objects gathering dust in their own homes when they heard Richard refer in his opening soliloquy to "bruisèd arms hung up for monuments" (1.1.6), a line I will return to later in this chapter. By "monuments," Richard seems to mean objects which have lost their foothold in the present, except in the delimited and protected context of their display. Stripped of whatever agency or use-value they once possessed, monuments refer us to a past which, we are reassured, has no other or more potent means of erupting into the present. Perhaps this is why, as Robert Musil wrote, "the remarkable thing about monuments is precisely that one doesn't notice them. There is nothing in the world as invisible as a monument."[30]

3.2 PRETTY RELICS

Not all traces of Richard's reign were so inert and so innocuous as the Knowsley hangings. Some items associated with Richard III, such as his dagger, entered the early modern era under different auspices. This notorious

---

Ollard and Pamela Tudor-Craig (London: Collins, 1986), 133. Item 58 includes what is apparently a separate set of hangings depicting the life of Samson "given by my Lady Derby" at her daughter's marriage to the second earl of Strafford. The Derby connection would explain the passage of Stanley heirlooms to the Wentworths. It is not entirely clear whether the old hangings "found here" at Wentworth Woodhouse estate were part of the same suite as the Knowsley hangings taken from Richard's tent, or simply resembled them. In the fifteenth and sixteenth centuries, Knowsley was not yet the main seat of the Stanleys, but a hunting lodge in the grounds of Lathom Hall.

[29] See Chapter 5 on the various Stanley songs and poems celebrating their role at Bosworth.

[30] Robert Musil, "Denkmale," in *Nachlass zu Lebzeiten* (Zurich: Humanitas Verlag, 1936), 87. I am grateful to Naomi Howell for the translation.

weapon appears just once in the historical record, at what may have been the point of its destruction. In September 1538 the commissioner John London wrote to Thomas Cromwell that he had suppressed the small shrine of the Blessed Virgin at Caversham, near Reading. The warden of the shrine, he reported, "wasse acostomyd to shew many prety relykes, among the wiche wer (as he made reportt) the holy dager that kylled kinge Henry; and the holy knyfe that kylled seynt Edwarde."[31] London confirmed that he was sending these relics to Cromwell.

London does not mention Richard III by name, but that Richard had killed Henry VI with just such a weapon was a matter of common report. As Robert Fabyan noted in his chronicle, "the moost common fame wente that he was stykked with a Dagger by the handes of the Duke of Glouceter."[32] Admittedly, not every report specified the use of a dagger. Polydore Vergil recorded "the contynuall report . . . that Richerd duke of Glocester killyd him with a swoord."[33] Nonetheless, Polydore concurred in the tradition which made the dagger not just a potential implement of murder, but Richard III's emblem, his signature object or totem. According to Polydore, "he was woont to be ever with his right hand pulling out of the sheath to the myddest, and putting in agane, the dagger which he did alway were."[34] Thomas More presents an even more frenetic and unstable figure: "Where he went abrode, his eyen whirled about, his body privily fenced, his hand ever on his dager, his countenance and maner like one alway ready to strike againe."[35]

London, his pen dripping with sarcasm, calls the weapon confiscated at Caversham a "holy dagger" and a "pretty relic." The dagger certainly did not owe its imputed sanctity to Richard III, but rather to having touched the body of Henry VI, as the instrument of his martyrdom. The cult of the last Lancastrian king had been remarkable in the early sixteenth century, though he was never formally canonized.[36] There were other such relics scattered around the country. Henry's own sword and gilt spurs were in the keeping of a cell of Syon Abbey in Cornwall; another pair of spurs and a royal hat were on display at Henry's burial place at

---

[31] Thomas Wright, ed., *Three Chapters of Letters Relating to the Suppression of Monasteries* (London: Camden Society, 1843), 222.

[32] Fabyan, ccxxiii[r].

[33] Vergil, *Three Books*, 156. Thomas More also refers to the widespread report, without specifying a weapon: "He slewe with his owne handes king Henry the sixt, being prisoner in the Tower, as menne constantly saye." More, *History*, 8.

[34] Vergil, *Three Books*, 227.   [35] More, *History*, 87.

[36] John W. McKenna, "Piety and Propaganda: The Cult of Henry VI," in B. Rowland, ed., *Chaucer and Middle English Studies in Honor of Rossell Hope Robbins* (Kent, OH: Kent State University Press, 1974), 72–88.

Windsor.[37] Nor was Henry the only one of Richard's reputed victims to furnish Tudor religious houses with objects of reverence. At the Shrine of Our Lady at Doncaster, the hair shirt supposedly discovered on the body of Anthony Woodville, the 2nd Earl Rivers, was displayed before the image of the Blessed Virgin.[38] Shrines like Caversham and Doncaster were clearly keen to keep their collections of relics up to date, and were quick to seize on the sort of items which might draw interest and offerings from visitors motivated by a mixture of reverence and fascination with the celebrated personalities of the recent past.

Were objects like Richard's dagger and Rivers' shirt genuine relics? What distinguishes the relic from the trophy or the souvenir? As Alexandra Walsham has observed, the membrane dividing these categories is "shifting and porous"; what seems to divide relics most clearly from other objects "is their capacity to operate as a locus and conduit of power."[39] That power invariably has its sources in the past. A relic can be thought of as an object imprinted so strongly by an event that it carries the potent essence of that moment forward in time—an object for which the crucifixion of Christ or the stabbing of Henry VI is not only a part of its history but of its material essence for all time to come. Relics are thus paradigmatic participants in what Harris calls the temporality of explosion, in which "the traces of the past acquire a living agency within, and against, the present."[40]

John London was clearly rather fascinated by the pretty relics of Caversham, even as he wrote of them with scorn. He mentions the dagger that killed Henry and the knife that slew Saint Edward (Edward the martyr, a tenth-century English king) in three successive letters from

---

[37] John P. D. Cooper, *Propaganda and the Tudor State: Political Culture in the Westcountry* (Oxford: Clarendon Press, 2003), 38.

[38] Rous, *Historia*, in Hanham, *Richard III*, 120.

[39] Alexandra Walsham, "Introduction," in *Relics and Remains*, ed. Walsham (Oxford: Oxford University Press, 2010), 13. Regarding the nature and source of the power of relics, there have always been conflicting opinions. Orthodox opinion, as expressed by Thomas Aquinas, held relics to be deserving of honor because of their past association with a body which had served as a temple of the Holy Spirit: "It is for this reason that God himself grants honour to their relics by performing miracles when they are present"; *Summa Theologiae, Volume 50: The One Mediator (3a. 16–26)*, ed. and trans. Colman O'Neill (London: Blackfriars, 1965), 3a. 25, 6 (203). While Aquinas is careful to avoid the suggestion of any power or efficacy residing in the object itself, popular belief was undoubtedly closer to the position of St. Cyril of Jerusalem, who held that the bodies of saints, and also their garments, retained a powerful virtue because of the righteousness of the soul which had once been housed within them. See *The Catechetical Lectures of St. Cyril, Archbishop of Jerusalem* (Oxford: Parker, 1838), Lecture 18: 16, 248.

[40] Whether or not one is thinking of actual relics, it seems impossible to think about this category of object without drawing on religious terminology—Harris here references both the breaking of the seals in the book of Revelation and the "weak messianism" of Walter Benjamin (*Untimely Matter*, 91, 92–4).

Reading (two addressed to Cromwell, and one, probably, to Richard Rich). In the second letter he describes the instrument of Henry's death as including "schethe and all," as if he were remembering that passage in Polydore Vergil which has Richard constantly drawing the dagger in and out of the sheath.[41] Caversham does seem to have specialized in sacralized instruments of destruction. Along with the daggers, London says in his third letter, he is sending "the principall relik of idolytrie within thys realme, an aungell with oon wyng that brow3t to Caversham the spere hedde that percyd our Saviour is syde upon the crosse." To Rich he acknowledges having missed, however, "a peece of the holy halter Judas wasse hangyd withall."[42]

By London's account, the shrine at Caversham seems to have housed a veritable armoury of blood-shedding weapons under the name of relics. In itself, this was nothing out of the ordinary. The Holy Cross, the chief instrument of Christ's death, was a prolific source of relics across all Christendom. Nearby Reading Abbey possessed two pieces of the Cross.[43] But Caversham's specialization in a certain definite type of relic was open to misconstruction. It is likely enough that in displaying these items to London, the warden of the shrine was seeking to persuade the royal commissioner that Caversham was a place where kings were held in special reverence. In the context of the Act of Supremacy, the warden may have been taking the line: "the church has always looked to the king for spiritual leadership, and nowhere more so than at this shrine." London, however, seems intent on twisting this to suggest that the shrine has made a habit of collecting and venerating instruments of treason and regicide. When the "the holy dager that kylled kinge Henry; and the holy knyfe that kylled seynt Edwarde" are exhibited alongside "the holy halter Judas wasse hangyd withal," one is left to question whether the weapon is being venerated for its connection with martyrdom, or simply for having dispatched a villain. The contested meaning of this relic, then, can be summed up in the question: is it the instrument that martyred holy king Henry, or is it the perversely venerated dagger of Richard III?

London reported that he was sending the dagger to Cromwell by the next available barge, together with other relics of the shrine. What happened when the dagger reached its destination? In a season when monasteries and shrines were falling up and down the country, and their most

[41] Wright, ed, *Three Chapters of Letters*, 224.
[42] Wright, ed, *Three Chapters of Letters*, 225, 224.
[43] Other than this, Reading's copious relic collection centred around bones—possibly a sign that the abbey had completed its collection by the end of the twelfth century. See Peter Marshall, *Religious Identities in Henry VIII's England* (Aldershot: Ashgate, 2006), 140.

treasured items being confiscated by the crown, a flood of miscellaneous items would have been trundling by road and river into London. Different kinds of holy objects were dealt with in different ways. Highly venerated objects, especially images of saints and the Blessed Virgin, could be subjected to public humiliation and burning to demonstrate their lack of efficacy.[44] Things of genuine value—in terms of their metal or jewel content—were seized upon for the uses of the royal treasury. As for the great mass of disarticulated bones, pieces of the cross, stones and earth from the Holy Land, coagulated blood and milk, these were generally thrown away as so much rubbish.[45] We know too little of the Caversham dagger to say to which of these classes it was deemed to belong. Perhaps it was still attractive and serviceable, even if seventy years old—in which case Cromwell may have given it into the hands of some relatively junior servitor. At which point the holy dagger that killed King Henry disappears from history.

3.3 REUSE AND REINSCRIPTION

Trophies and relics are both examples of objects whose strong association with a particular past sets them apart from daily life. They are screened from the present, as it were, under glass, and generally owe their survival (and in some cases destruction) to that separation. Yet most objects from the past survive not because they are preserved as such, but because they continue to be useful in the present day. Such was the case with the great bedstead at the Blue Boar, at least up until the fateful day when Mrs Clark went to change the linen. The continuing use of an object, or its adaptation for a new purpose, does not require that its past should be erased or forgotten. Instead, objects may become a link or bridge between past and present users, the means whereby the living and the dead touch hands through a material medium.[46]

---

[44] Eamon Duffy, *The Stripping of the Altars: Traditional Religion in England, c.1400–c.1580* (New Haven: Yale University Press, 1992), 404.

[45] Thus Thomas Wriothesley, writing from St Swithin's shrine in Winchester in 1538, declared his intention "to sweep away all the rotten bones that be called relics; which we may not omit lest it should be thought we came more for the treasure than for avoiding of the abomination of idolatry." *Letters and Papers, Foreign and Domestic, Henry VIII, Volume 13, Part 2,* (London, 1893), 155. On Protestant responses to relics, see also Alexandra Walsham, "Skeletons in the Cupboard: Relics after the English Reformation": in *Relics and Remains,* ed. Walsham, 121–43.

[46] Harris describes this as the "temporality of conjunction." Whereas the temporalities of supersession and explosion both involve an antagonistic relationship between the present and the past—with one or the other triumphing respectively—the temporality of conjunction is marked by "a distribution of agency within the palimpsested object." *Untimely Matter*, 143.

A paradigmatic example of an object—or array of objects—which serves as a link between past and present would be the English crown. Richard, according to an array of sources, had actually worn his crown into battle on Bosworth field, an act which receives particular emphasis in the ballad *Bosworth Feilde*:

> he said, 'give me my battell axe in my hand,
> sett the crown of England on my head soe hye!
> ffor by him that shope both sea and Land,
> King of England this day I will dye!'[47]

After the fray, in the words of *The Great Chronicle of London*, "Incontynently . . . sir wylliam Stanley whych wan the possescion of kyng Rychardys helmett wyth the Croune beyng upon It, cam streygth to kyng henry and sett It upon his heed sayyng, sir here I make yow kyng of Engeland."[48] That particular battered headpiece may long since have disappeared, but elements of it are likely to survive to this day among the crown jewels of England. To take one example, Richard's crown probably featured a large red spinel known as the Black Prince's Ruby. Given to Edward the Black Prince by Pedro the Cruel of Castile in the 1360s, not long after Pedro's murder of the previous owner, Abu Said of Granada, the gem was subsequently worn by Henry V at Agincourt and, according to later tradition, by Richard at Bosworth. In 1649, the jewel, described as "a pierced balas ruby wrapt in paper by itself," was sold off to a private citizen by the commonwealth government for a mere £4 10s, only to be reacquired by the crown at the Restoration.[49] That jewel—blood red and slightly misshapen as if in token of its violent history—still features in the Imperial State Crown. On display in the Tower of London, where visitors glide past on a ceaselessly moving walkway, it participates in a heavily mystified narrative of continuity and legitimacy, yet its actual history arguably cuts a different way, bringing such narratives into sharp question.

Like the crown itself, many of the dead king's things were and would have remained royal property, passing into the keeping of Henry VII and his successors. It is likely that Richard's armour—his ceremonial suits, if not the battle gear worn at Bosworth—joined the armoury in the

---

[47] "Bosworth Feilde," in *Bishop Percy's Folio Manuscript: Ballads and Romances*, ed. John W. Hales (London: N. Trübner, 1868), vol. 3, p. 257, ll. 593–6.

[48] *GCL*, 238. In Diego de Valera's report, "he placed over his head-armour the crown-royal, which they declare to be worth one hundred and twenty thousand crowns" (in Tudor-Craig, *Richard III*, p. 68); also Rous, *Historia*, in Hanham, *Richard III*, 123; Polydore Vergil, *Three Books*, 225–6.

[49] See Lord Twining, *A History of the Crown Jewels of Europe* (London: B. T. Batsford, 1960), 175–82.

Tower of London. Richard's personal library was also, for the most part, subsumed in the royal collection. Fortunately for later researchers bent on reconstructing royal reading habits, Richard liked to write his name in his books. His signature as "R[ichard] Gloucestre" or "Ricardus rex" appears in volumes including the *Booke of Gostlye Grace*, the *Grandes Chroniques de France*, and the Prose *Tristan*.[50] James I and Charles I would later inscribe their own names on back leaves of some of the same volumes; rather remarkably, Oliver Cromwell chose to inscribe his name—with the date, 1657—directly beside or above Richard's on the front pages of Guido delle Colonne's *Historia destructionis Troiae* and Geoffrey of Monmouth's *Historia regum Britanniae*. These are volumes that bear directly on the theme of royal lineage and British History; it is as if Cromwell were recognizing his inevitable absorption into the very tradition and genealogy he had sought to disrupt, at a point when he was just a step or two from royalty, and a few months from death.

A still more complex history of reuse and reinscription is found in the case of Richard's personal prayer book. Unlike the dagger and the bedstead, this is an object we can say with certainty did belong to Richard and was used by him, thus enrolling him in a lineage with owners both anterior and posterior. The book was made around 1420, probably for a clerical user (Fig. 3.3). It is an ornate but not exactly sumptuous example of its kind. Richard seems to have adopted it around the time he came to the throne, inscribing in his own sprawling hand his name and birthday in the calendar: *hac die natus erat Ricardus Rex Anglie tertius Apud Foderingay Anno domini mlcccliio* [on this day was born at Fotheringhay Richard III King of England AD 1452] (Fig. 3.4).[51] He also had various prayers added to it, including a long prayer for help against besetting foes and tribulations, calling on God 'to make and keep concord between me and my enemies, to show me and pour over me your grace and glory, and deign to assuage, turn aside, destroy, and bring to nothing the hatred they bear towards to me. . . . '[52] Often referred to as the "prayer of Richard III," the prayer was in fact widely disseminated around Europe, being used by Maximilian I and Frederick of Aragon among others; yet the fact that it is conventional does not preclude the possibility that it offers us a glimpse of his personal

---

[50] Anne F. Sutton and Livia Visser-Fuchs, *Richard III's Books: Ideals and Reality in the Life and Library of a Medieval Prince* (Stroud: Alan Sutton, 1997).

[51] Lambeth Ms. 474, f.7ᵛ. See Anne. F. Sutton and Livia Visser-Fuchs, *The Hours of Richard III* (Stroud: Alan Sutton, 1990), 44–6.

[52] ". . . dignare inter me et inimicos meos stabilire et firmare concordiam, graciam et gloriam tuam super me ostendere et effundere, ac omne illorum odium quod contra me habent digneris mitigare declinare extinguere et ad ni chilare." Lambeth Ms 474, f. 181ʳ·ᵛ; Sutton and Visser-Fuchs, *The Hours of Richard III*, p. 76, with the translation on p. 77.

Fig. 3.3. The Office of the Dead, from the prayer book of Richard III. Lambeth Palace MS 474, 72ʳ. By permission of the Trustees of the Lambeth Palace Library.

psychology.[53] Perhaps a more illuminating addition to the prayer book is the prayer to St Ninian, "who has converted the peoples of the Britons and the Picts"; usually considered a Scottish saint, Ninian's presence in Richard's book suggests a royal outlook less Anglocentric than Shakespeare among others would suggest.

[53] See Jonathan Hughes, *The Religious Life of Richard III* (Stroud: Sutton, 1997); cf. Eamon Duffy, *Marking the Hours: English People and their Prayers 1240-1570* (New Haven: Yale University Press, 2006), 100–2.

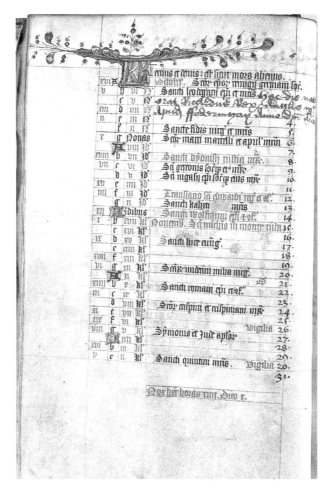

Fig. 3.4. Calendar page noting the King's birthday, from the prayer book of Richard III. Lambeth Palace MS 474, 7ᵛ. By permission of the Trustees of the Lambeth Palace Library.

Like the hangings in his tent, Richard's prayer book seems to have formed part of the spoils of Bosworth, where the new king's mother Margaret Beaufort laid claim to it.[54] Eamon Duffy has suggested that

[54] Michael K. Jones, Malcolm G. Underwood, *The King's Mother: Lady Margaret Beaufort, Countess of Richmond and Derby* (Cambridge: Cambridge University Press, 1992), 68.

Margaret acquired it "as a trophy rather than a devotional aid," though she did inscribe her name in the back when presenting it as a gift, requesting the unknown recipient to pray for her "in the honour of God and Sainte Edmonde." Duffy observes that Margaret "did not bother to scratch out Richard's name very thoroughly" where it appeared in the prayers—something a reader intent on adapting the book for their own devotional use would have done as a matter of course.[55] It is an intriguing reversal of the logic of supersession witnessed elsewhere; whereas other sources tell us that Richard's reign was consigned to history by the tearing down of his insignia, in this case the preservation of Richard's name relegates the prayer book to the past, a curiosity rather than a thing of use.

Yet the story of this object does not end with Margaret Beaufort. Richard's book of hours was still in regular devotional use as late as the 1540s. One Reformation-era user carefully crossed out every reference to the Pope in the calendar, but either that hand or another continued to mark the death dates of individuals—Thomas Harward, who died *contingenter* (accidentally, or unnecessarily) on 28 March 1542, "AF" who died 25 August 1548.[56] It is in the nature of such books to conjure relationships between successive users; perhaps this was especially true in the case of Richard's book. The failure to cross out Richard's name does not demonstrate that later owners did not use it themselves or read the prayers; but it does suggest a complex kind of use, where the reader might at once be using the book for genuine prayer, and as a means of self-consciously inhabiting Richard's vacated space, ghosting the dead reader. In two places in the long added prayer, Richard's name has been rubbed out of the phrase "*me famulum tuum Regem Ricardum*" (me, your servant, King Richard), but the word *Regem* remains.[57] Later users were thus enabled to insert their own names into the prayer and, even as they humbled themselves before God, imagine themselves as kings.

3.4 HAUNTED PROPERTIES

By the beginning of the seventeenth century, Richard's book of prayer was probably in the possession of Richard Bancroft, Bishop of London and subsequently Archbishop of Canterbury (1604–10), becoming after his death part of the Lambeth Palace Library, where it remains today.

---

[55] Duffy, *Marking the Hours*, 33.
[56] Sutton and Visser-Fuchs, *The Hours of Richard III*, 46.
[57] Sutton and Visser-Fuchs, *The Hours of Richard III*, 62, with reference to ff. 182, 183 of Lambeth Ms. 474.

Yet from the early 1590s the book was also to be found somewhere else: on Shakespeare's stage, and in the text of his play. Richard holds a prayer book in his hand when he enters "aloft between two bishops" (3.7.94 s.d) to hear the citizens of London entreat him to accept the crown. Buckingham draws attention to the object and its significance: "see, a book of prayer in his hand—/True ornaments to know a holy man" (3.7.98–99). Of course, Richard's book is not what it seems. It is a theatrical prop, and is understood as such by the characters within the drama, as well as by the actors who play them. Buckingham is both the deviser of the tableau—advising Richard to "get a prayer book in your hand/And stand between two churchmen" (3.7.47–48)—and its subsequent interpreter, drawing attention to Richard's brace of bishops as "Two props of virtue for a Christian prince" (3.7.96). Although it is arguable that the modern sense of "prop" as an object in a theatrical performance did not come into use before the nineteenth century, the resonance between these "props" and stage properties seems hard to ignore. As Elizabeth Williamson observes, the attention given to the prayer book creates "a moment in which the spectators, the actor, and the character are all simultaneously aware of the similarity between the object within the drama and the property used in the theatrical production."[58]

The volume that appeared on the Elizabethan stage and in subsequent performances was not, to be sure, the same volume that had once belonged to Richard III—indeed, the players may well have thought it safest not to use a religious text of any sort.[59] That the scene attracted controversy is perhaps witnessed by the omission of the lines referring to the prayer book from the Quarto version of the play. As John Jowett suggests, the prominence given to the book may have been read to suggest a satirical reference to the Protestant Book of Common Prayer.[60] Although the historical context of the play would indicate a Catholic book of hours, the manipulation of the property is eloquently suggestive of how the book, which Protestant discourse persistently privileged over the image, could itself function as a misleading outward sign.

The object with which Richard is associated most powerfully, in the dramatic as in the historical tradition, is of course his dagger. Shakespeare does

---

[58] Williamson, *Materiality of Religion,* 161.

[59] There is opportunity for a visual joke if the book in Richard's hand is obviously inappropriate. In Richard Loncraine's 1995 film, Buckingham hands Richard what appears to be a vulgar thriller; when Richard gives it a dubious look, Buckingham whips off the paper cover, leaving a black-bound volume which can pass for a book of prayer. For similar examples, see Williamson, *Materiality of Religion,* 161.

[60] See William Shakespeare, *Richard III,* ed. John Jowett (Oxford: Oxford University Press, 2000), n. to 3.7.93-94 on 272–3.

not take every available opportunity to portray Richard with the dagger made famous by Polydore Vergil and Thomas More. His murder of Henry VI—the event that sanctified the "holy dagger" of Caversham—is committed in *3 Henry VI* with a weapon of indeterminate nature. (Though Henry refers to Richard's dagger [5.6.27], Richard himself terms the fatal instrument a sword [5.6.63].) It is Richard's sword that he proffers to Anne when he woos her over Henry's corpse, urging her to drive it into his breast if she rejects his love. But the dagger does seem to have achieved a memorable prominence in early stagings of the play. Samuel Rowlands was probably thinking of Burbage's performance in the part when, in 1600, he satirized those who "like Richard, the usurper, swagger, that had his hand continual on his dagger."[61]

The notorious dagger does feature centrally in at least one scene, that in which Richard welcomes his nephews to London. Newly taken from his mother's side in sanctuary, the little Duke of York is pert in his requests.

> YORK: I pray you, uncle, render me this dagger.
> RICHARD: My dagger, little cousin? With all my heart.
> PRINCE EDWARD: A beggar, brother?
> YORK: Of my kind uncle that I know will give,
>   It being but a toy which is no grief to give.
>   (3.1.110–14)

In terming his uncle's far-from-harmless dagger a "toy," the young prince perhaps means only that it is a thing of little worth or significance—a common sense of "toy" in the sixteenth century. Yet the fact that the speaker is a child inevitably suggests the other sense of the term, familiar in the modern era and already emergent in Shakespeare's time: that is, a toy as a plaything, and more especially an object which represents another ("real") object.[62] The teasing phrase thus draws attention to the double nature of the actual object displayed upon the stage. The dagger used in early performances was in all likelihood a real weapon (possibly the personal possession of Richard Burbage). Yet in calling it a "toy," York seems wilfully to draw attention to the way its use as a prop creates a kind of split in its status an object—driving a wedge between the thing itself and its function

---

[61] That Rowlands is thinking of Shakespeare's Richard is probable. As James R. Siemon points out, though prior chronicle and dramatic versions of Richard also bear a dagger, they do not swagger. Siemon, ed., *King Richard III*, Arden Shakespeare (Methuen Drama: London, 2009), 84.

[62] *The Oxford English Dictionary* notes the occurrence in 1586 of "toy" in the familiar modern sense of "A material object for children or others to play with (often an imitation of some familiar object)."

as a dramatic sign.[63] His use of the word derives some of its force from its contemptuous application by Protestant reformers to Catholic relics—such as Richard's "real" dagger, last heard of at Caversham in 1538. For the Protestant polemicist John Bale, "ymages, rellyckes, [and] roodes" were mere "Popysh toyes"; describing such venerated objects as "outwarde shaddowes and toyes," Bale sought to expose them as material signs lacking in inner truth or substance, as blasphemous props.[64] As with the foregrounding of the prayer book later in the play, the exchange involving Richard's dagger draws on debates and discourses of the Reformation era to highlight the dubious ontological status of the stage property.

The properties of Elizabethan playing companies were not limited to small, portable items like books and weapons. The 1597 inventory of properties belonging to the Admiral's Men lists such substantial pieces as a Hell-mouth, various tombs, and "a bedsteade."[65] Although a bed is not specified in the original stage directions for *Richard III*, the king is required to sleep on stage and be awakened by ghosts in the scene covering the night before the battle. It seems probable that a bed was used for this scene when it was presented on the London stage, whilst a chair was employed in the more cramped conditions of touring. (This appears to have been the case earlier in the play where Clarence is seen asleep in the Tower; "There lies the Duke asleep" (1.4.91), says Brakenbury in the Folio, whilst in the touring text of the Quarto the line reads "There sits the Duke asleep."[66]) Later theatrical tradition would insist on giving the king a great curtained bed, as depicted in Hogarth's famous portrait of Garrick's

---

[63] On the stage property's "double life as sign and thing," see Sofer, *The Stage Life of Props,* esp. Chapter One, which traces the vexed semiotic status of the prop to late medieval and reformist debates over the nature of the Eucharistic host.

[64] John Bale, *An Expostulation or Complaynte agaynste the Blasphemyes of a Franticke Papyst of Hamshyre* (London, 1552), A2ᵛ; and John Bale, *Yet a Course at the Romyshe Foxe* (Zurich, 1543), E1ᵛ. In passages such as these, we witness the old sense of "toy" as "a light thing as opposed to serious matter" shading into the emergent sense of "a light or mock version of a genuine or serious thing." The English translation of Erasmus's *Peregrinatio religionis ergo,* published in 1537, similarly mocks the veneration of "bones, heades, jawes, armes, cotes, cappes, hattes, shoes . . . toyes" (quoted in Marshall, *Religious Identities*, 138). More broadly, Henry Peacham would dismiss as "trifles and toys" a whole range of wrongly venerated or simply overvalued objects, including everything from royal tombs at Westminster to Richard's own bedstead at Leicester (see n. 8 above). See also Williamson, *Materiality of Religion,* 193.

[65] "The Enventary tacken of all the properties for my Lord Admeralles men, the 10 of Marche 1598," in *Staged Properties in Early Modern English Drama*, ed. Jonathan Gil Harris and Natasha Korda (Cambridge: Cambridge University Press, 2002), 335

[66] Frances Teague, *Shakespeare's Speaking Properties* (Cranbury, NJ: Associated University Presses, 1991), 47.

Fig. 3.5. William Hogarth, "David Garrick as Richard III," painted about 1745. Courtesy of National Museums Liverpool.

Richard starting up aghast from hellish dreams (Fig. 3.5).[67] It thus seems likely that, just as visitors to Leicester might pay a penny to see the bed in which Richard spent the last night of his life, London audiences were being treated to the same sight—at much the same price.

Richard's book of prayer, his dagger, his bed, and, of course, his crown: the very objects which, as real or supposedly real remnants of the historical king's reign, this chapter has dwelt upon turn out to have a second afterlife as properties in Shakespeare's play.[68] Not only are these objects

[67] Hogarth's painting is crowded with objects that can be recognized as typical theatrical properties, including the bed, pieces of armour, a crown, a sword or dagger, and a devotional image (a pictorially legible substitution for Richard's prayer book). Carefully positioned, almost excessive in their emblematic weight, these things are there in place of what we might expect to see, in place of what Richard sees or has just awakened from seeing—a chorus of vengeful ghosts. The objects in the painting both displace the ghosts and stand in for them, for they too are vessels and remembrances of the past.

[68] The royal crown is visually and verbally prominent in the play, especially from 4.2, in which Richard enters crowned, to the final scene, where it is presented to Richmond, fresh "From the dead temples of this bloody wretch" (5.8.5). Richard's coinage—or at any rate his coins—also appear, as when he presents his purse in recompense to a messenger he has over-

present on the stage but attention is drawn to them, and in some cases specifically to their status as props. Is this pure accident? There is no reason to believe that Shakespeare knew about the "holy dagger" of Caversham, the bed at the Blue Boar, or the peregrinations of the king's prayer book. Yet neither the survival of these particular objects nor the appearance of their material echoes on the stage is a matter of random chance. The items in question are all "personal," in the sense that, at any given time, they will be the intimate belongings of one individual (or a small family group). At the same time, they are durable objects which may be expected to survive and retain their usefulness for several generations. Such objects define our identities, yet they are apt to outlive us, going on to enjoy equally intimate association with our chosen or unchosen successors. Shakespeare, famously, bequeathed a bed—the second best—to his wife in his will. Sometimes, of course, instead of being passed on, such belongings were sold off: because they were outmoded, or because the owners were in need of ready money, or because they had no heirs, or none who would care for the thing in question. Among the reliable purchasers of such belongings, especially but not only where clothing was concerned, were theatrical companies.[69] The objects on the Elizabethan stage had their own histories, which might be as haunting and tragic as those attributed to them in the drama.

The dagger, book, bed, and most of Richard's clothing in the play would have been secondhand or appropriated properties with past lives and uses in the outside world; other prominent objects, including the crown, the throne, and Hasting's severed head, would probably have been constructed as props, either for this play or past productions. The stores of theatrical companies were well-stocked with both kinds of object, and the property list of the Admiral's Men, with its "i bedsteade . . . i golden scepter...ii rackets . . . owld Mahemetes head" does not seem to distinguish or discriminate between them.[70] Of course, even a "born" prop is, in material terms, a real thing, and thus capable of acquiring a history or biography of its own. Antony Sher's memoir of his experience playing Richard III for the Royal Shakespeare Company in the 1980s records an uncanny encounter with the material vestiges of past performances. Rehearsals took place in a room "full of old things from old productions: a goblet, a sceptre, a throne. Theatre props age faster than their real counterparts. The cardboard

---

hastily struck (4.4.445). Seeking a murderer, he asks "Know'st thou not any whom corrupting gold/Will tempt unto a close exploit of death?" (4.2.35–36)—a question which reminds us, queasily, of the secret in the Clark's bedstead, and that story's violent denouement.

[69] Jones and Stallybrass, *Renaissance Clothing and the Materials of Memory*, 175–206.
[70] "The Enventary," 335.

shows, the plaster shows, they look crude and childish, reminding you of school productions."[71] Though Sher assumes a clear and obvious distinction between theatre properties and real things, the spectacle of the aging prop undercuts and almost inverts this distinction. The failure of the prop's illusionistic potential highlights its sheer materiality. Marked by their histories, the props seem if anything more real than their "real counterparts" which, concealing their age, readily subordinating the past to the needs of the present, begin to seem almost tawdrily theatrical.

Sher goes on to describes the storeroom as "full of ghosts—one of them sits on an upper level looking down, a white polystyrene figure from some long-forgotten show, sitting intently forward, elbows on knees, keeping a watchful eye on this latest production. The Ghost of RSC Past."[72] The image of the ghost-as-property/property-as-ghost serves as a reminder that dramatic properties could and did develop their own biographies.[73] *Richard III* has been particularly haunted by past performances, past actors, and past stage properties. Not only Garrick's performance but his pantaloons and ermine robe were faithfully copied by subsequent Richards for a century or more. Richard's clothing—unspecified in Shakespeare's text—became one of his most immediately recognizable features. The sword worn by Edmund Kean in his celebrated performance in the role in 1813 was handed down from one actor to another throughout the nineteenth century, becoming a sort of emblem of pre-eminence. Henry Irving used it for the part of Richard; at length it came to John Gielgud, who presented it to Laurence Olivier in recognition of his definitive performance of the part. With Olivier, the sword's remarkable lifecycle seems to have come to an end, or at least a temporary halt.[74]

Fetishized theatrical objects like Kean's sword differ from normal theatrical properties in that their display on stage refers us not only to the past event involving their real counterpart (the sword Richard wore at Bosworth, for example), but, at least for those in the know, to the series of past occasions on which this object has graced the stage.[75] If we accept Elizabeth Williamson's provocative designation of such props as theatrical "relics," this would be the second time in history that Richard's notorious

---

[71] Antony Sher, *Year of the King* (London: Nick Hern, 2004), 158.

[72] Sher, *Year of the King*, 158–9.

[73] On "ghosting" in the theatre—Marvin Carlson's term for the way aspects of performance including sets, actor's bodies, and props can refer to or draw links with past performances—see Carlson, *The Haunted Stage: The Theater as Memory Machine* (Ann Arbor: University of Michigan Press, 2001).

[74] Barbara Hodgdon, "Shopping in the Archives: Material Memories," in *Shakespeare, Memory and Performance*, ed. Peter Holland (Cambridge: Cambridge University Press, 2006), 165.

[75] On the fetishized prop, see Sofer, *The Stage Life of Props*, 26–7.

blade attained the status of a relic.[76] Arguably, the full cultural history of this object would have to be traced through a series of distinct but homologous material forms—Kean's sword, the blade wielded by Burbage in the first productions, the Caversham dagger, the weapon of the real King Richard. From this point of view, Richard's blade would belong to that special category of objects and artworks which Alexander Nagel and Christopher S. Wood have described as "anachronic." As they argue, early modern minds were especially prone to recognize and ponder the principle of substitution whereby a work of art or craft might "retain its identity despite alteration, repair, renovation, and even outright replacement," and whereby "a material sample of the past could somehow be both an especially powerful testimony to a distant world *and* at the same time an ersatz for another, now absent artifact."[77]

If stage properties associated with *Richard III* have proven particularly prone to fetishization and anachronic substitution, the sources of this phenomenon seem to lie in the play itself. It is not that it features an unusual number of props, or objects of an unusual kind; rather, of all Shakespeare's plays, it has been said to contain the most typical assemblage of items, in terms of their number and variety.[78] What is less typical about the play is the double and almost contradictory focus it places on certain of its properties, thematizing them at once as theatrical props ("toys") and as objects with histories. This peculiar way of looking at things has everything to do with the specific span of time between Richard's era and Shakespeare's, and the capacity of objects to both bridge and testify to the temporal gap. The period of time between 1485 and 1592, though beyond any normal human lifespan, did not exceed the use-life of some ordinary objects, potentially including beds, books, weapons, and items of personal adornment. From its first moments, the play is deeply engaged with the problem of things that have outlived their time, yet linger on both to bear witness to the past and to offer themselves for use in the present.

Richard's opening soliloquy turns partly on the melancholy fate of things that have survived the era of their usefulness. "Now are our brows bound with victorious wreaths,/Our bruisèd arms hung up for monuments"

---

[76] Williamson, *Materiality of Religion*, 204–10.

[77] Alexander Nagel and Christopher S. Wood, *Anachronic Renaissance* (New York: Zone Books, 2010), 8, 31.

[78] Douglas Bruster, drawing on Frances Teague's tabulation of Shakespearean properties, notes that "were a typical Shakespeare play to exist, it might contain at least one light (eg, a torch, a candle), three rewards (money bags, coins), six documents (letters, proclamations) five tokens of identity (crowns, gloves, rings, scepters), six weapons, and nine "other" or miscellaneous objects." No play comes closer to fitting this bill than *Richard III*. Douglas Bruster, "The Dramatic Life of Objects," in *Staged Properties*, ed. Harris and Korda, 78 and 95n.36.

(1.1.5–6). The supersession of an era of war by an age of peace is indicated in the differing fortunes of two kinds of object. Yet the proverbial impermanence and fragility of wreaths, in contrast to the durability of (even dented) arms and armour, conveys a warning—or, from Richard's point of view, a hope—that the change may not be as lasting as it seems. The phrase "our bruisèd arms" creates an association between battered and outmoded weapons and armour from the civil wars and Richard's own body—not least because his arm is misshapen, "like a blasted sapling withered up" (3.4.69).[79] Richard thus figures himself as an object out of time, relegated to the trophy cabinet because he is not shaped for the sportive tricks of the new era. He interprets the celebration of peace as a rejection of the past, and therefore of himself. In displaying their arms as monuments, the victors are not only celebrating the victory of their house over that of Lancaster, but also the victory of the present era over the immediately preceding one, of a time of peace and pleasure over a time of war and risk and fear. Richard, by contrast, is aiming for a victory of the past over the present. What he wants is for the exhausted energy in those bruised arms to reassert itself, like the sinister secret in Mrs Clark's bedstead suddenly spilling forth.

The arms and armour which Richard summons down from the walls in his first soliloquy go on to feature prominently in the play, above all of course in the final act devoted to the field of Bosworth. Francis Teague has noted how references to Richard's armour are used to convey the passage of time in the scenes devoted to the night before the battle (a period of some twelve hours covered in just over 350 lines).[80] Richard initially enters "in arms" (5.3.0 s.d.) but fifty lines later, after an exit and re-entrance, he is asking Catesby if his armour is all laid up in his tent (5.5.5); he tells Ratcliffe to come to his tent and help him don his armour "about the mid of night" (5.5.30) and later in the same scene, after the king's awful encounter with the ghosts, Ratcliffe duly enters to say that the cock has crowed, "your friends are up, and buckle on their armour" (5.5.165). A timely object indeed, Richard's armour in Act 5 functions almost as a clock to mark the passage of the hours.

The armour which Richard is seen wearing earlier in the play has a more complex relationship to the passage of time. At the beginning of Act 3, scene 5, where Richard has just accomplished the death of Hastings and must now convince the mayor and people of London that the baron posed an immediate danger to the state, the opening stage direction

---

[79] The effect can be compared to the line in Shakespeare's Sonnet 73 in which the autumnal "boughs which shake against the cold" (l. 3) seem weirdly close to human limbs.
[80] Teague, *Shakespeare's Speaking Properties*, 20–1.

reads "Enter Richard and Buckingham in rotten armour, marvellous ill-favoured." This remarkable phrase—second only to "Exit pursued by a bear" amongst the handful of genuinely memorable Shakespearean stage directions—is a transmutation of a line in Thomas More's *History*, where it is explained that Richard and Buckingham dressed themselves in "old il faring briginders, such as no man shold wene that thei would vouchsafe to have put upon their backes, except that some sodaine necessitie had constrained them."[81] This is an almost unique instance of a stage direction which is indisputably authorial, drawn directly from the playwright's chronicle sources.[82]

The type of armour specified by More, a brigander or brigandine, is in essence a leather or canvas vest with metal rings or studs sewn or riveted into it (Fig. 3.6). Comparatively lightweight and inexpensive, the brigander was widely worn by footsoldiers in the fifteenth and early sixteenth centuries (though there are also examples of more ornate court armour in this style). By the late Elizabethan period, the brigander was outmoded; as the old soldier Humfrey Barwick noted in a treatise on firearms contemporary with Shakespeare's play, "as for the armours, the best is the Brigandine . . . [yet] for shot all men doth know that the like armours will not defend the force therof. . . . Why then should such meane armors be allowed, with men of understanding and knowledge? it were most fit that our enemies were so armed. . . . "[83] Yet the brigander remained a useful theatrical property, because it could be donned and removed comparatively easily. Though the stage direction in *Richard III* does not specify that the men are wearing briganders, the description of the armour as "rotten" strongly suggests it. The adjective is appropriate to leather that is decaying, crumbling to pieces—not, as is sometimes assumed, to rusty plate.[84]

---

[81] More, *History*, 52.

[82] The line is in fact a conflation of the slightly divergent passages in Holinshed ("old ill faring briganders," 724), and Hall ("olde evill fauoured briganders," Edward V, 15ᵛ). See the discussion in Dominique Goy-Blanquet, *Shakespeare's Early History Plays: From Chronicle to Stage* (Oxford: Oxford University Press, 2003), 219–20. There may also be an echo of Holinshed's contemptuous description of Richard's northern troops, who arrived in time for the coronation "evill apparelled, and worse harnessed, in rustie harnesse, neither defensible, nor scowred to the sale" (732).

[83] Humfrey Barwick, *A breefe discourse, concerning the force and effect of all manuall weapons of fire and the disability of the long bowe or archery, in respect of others of greater force now in vse* (London, 1592), 21–2. Most references to briganders in the literature of this period appear to refer to biblical warfare or chivalric romance, not contemporary military practice.

[84] See *Richard III*, ed. Jowett, note to 3.5.02. Cf. F. P. Barnard: "Not *rusty*, as is usually explained, for the metal of the brigandines would not show, since it was sewn or riveted inside the material (velvet, leather, or quilted) of which the brigandine was made"; *New Variorum Edition of Shakespeare: King Richard III*, ed. H. H. Furness (London: J. B. Lippincott, 1908), 242. Speed, *History of Great Britaine*, has Richard and Buckingham "harnessed in olde rusty briganders" (704), and the *Mirror of Magistrates*, a source for Shakespeare,

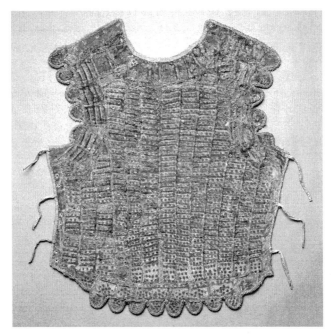

Fig. 3.6. Body Guard (Brigandine), c.1500–25. Italy (?), early sixteenth century. Linen; gold velvet; steel; brass, 56.5 x 47.6 cm. The Cleveland Museum of Art, gift of Mr and Mrs John L. Severance, 1921.1250.

Shakespeare's adaptation of More's phrase is both careful and pointed. Whereas More describes the briganders as both "old" and "ill-faring"— implying that the armour is not only antiquated but badly knocked about—the stage direction puts much stronger emphasis on the fact that the armour is *old*, with its poor condition resulting from sheer antiquity rather than mistreatment. The impression of having been roughed up is transferred from the armour itself to the men who wear it, who are, if not ill-faring, "marvelous ill-favoured." The stage direction's emphasis on the age and rottenness of the armour is likely to be an accurate reflection of the sort of properties employed in early performances of this scene. There is little reason to doubt that the Elizabethan actors were wearing precisely "rotten armour," that is, old briganders which were falling to

has the plotters appear in unspecified "rousty armure" (ed. Lily B. Campbell (Cambridge: Cambridge University Press, 1938), 294, l. 689). What seems safest to say is that any kind of armour can be rusty, but only certain kinds, such as briganders, can also be rotten.

pieces. Unlike the gilt crowns and wooden shields which feature prominently in the property list of the Admiral's Men, rotten armour would
have been quite difficult to mock up out of available materials—sewing
rusty rings onto disintegrating leather cannot be imagined as an easy job.
Stage armour in good condition would of course have been too valuable
to wreck for the purpose.

The two rotten briganders would, I propose, constitute examples of
theatrical props that were also the genuine article—genuine armour, that
is, which was genuinely old and rotten. The suits might easily have been
half a century old, made for service in the French or Scottish campaigns
of the 1540s; they could conceivably have been a good deal older still.
Imagination alone is capable of providing a link between the armour in
the play and the two pairs of brigandines listed in an inventory of the possessions of William Catesby, Richard III's Chancellor of the Exchequer, in
1484.[85] What is beyond doubt is that if Catesby's fine court armour—one
pair covered in "blewe & talbuy saten," the other "covered with clothe of
gold"—had survived the intervening century to present itself for use in
Shakespeare's play, it would have been most appropriately "rotten."

An alternative imagined history for Richard's rotten armour would
make it the very coat worn by Shakespeare's own great-grandfather when
he fought on Henry's side at Bosworth.[86] However improbable such specific scenarios may seem, it is probable enough that the old briganders
employed in early productions were something of the sort—that is, that
they were someone's family heirlooms. Armour was often passed down
from generation to generation as a memorial of past achievement, even
when wear and changing fashion had rendered it long past service, a practice exemplified in Anne Clifford's bequest to her grandchildren of "the
remainder of the two rich armors which were my noble father's, to remaine
to them and their posterity (if they soe please) as a remembrance of him."[87]

---

[85] "William Catesby's Inventory," 10 December 1484 (PRO E/154/2/4), in Tudor-Craig,
ed. *Richard III*, 97–98. An inventory of Sir John Fastolf's possessions at his death in 1469
also includes two pairs of brigandines. See Malcolm Mercer, *The Medieval Gentry: Power,
Leadership and Choice in the Wars of the Roses* (London: Continuum, 2010), 59.

[86] Cf. M. C. Bradbrook's speculation that the deeds of Shakespeare's ancestor had
remained a matter of family pride and tradition; *Shakespeare, The Poet in His World* (London, 1978), 58. The emergence of the shadowy Shakespeare "grandfather" in documents of
the College of Arms is discussed in Chapter 4 of this book.

[87] Quoted in Jones and Stallybrass, *Renaissance Clothing and the Materials of Memory*,
203. Brigandines both humble and ornate appear fairly regularly in late-fifteenth and
early-sixteenth-century wills. The merchant William Maryon left a pair of brigandines to
"William Clerk my child" in his will, drawn up in 1493; William Pakeman of Suffolk
(*d.*1504) left John Mellor "my brekandenes . . . or elles my grett spone." See Alison
Hanham, *The Celys and their World: An English Merchant Family of the Fifteenth Century*
(Cambridge: Cambridge University Press, 1985), 424; A. G. Dickens, *Late Monasticism and the*

The place for such antiquated equipment was on a gentleman's wall rather than a soldier's back. Reviewing the readiness of the Elizabethan militia, the Earl of Essex complained of its being supplied with "furniture only fitt to hang over the skreene in a halle the whole age of a man ere yt be taken downe."[88] Familiar with such displays, early audiences would have understood that Richard and Buckingham were now wearing the very objects invoked in the play's opening soliloquy, bruised arms taken down from walls where they had been hung up for monuments.[89]

To be sure, the moldering briganders worn by Richard and Buckingham would not have been the only garments on the Elizabethan stage whose histories stretched back a good many decades, having already "lived" rather longer than the actors who wore them. In Henry Peacham's sketch of a scene from *Titus Andronicus*, the soldier adjacent to Titus wears what appears to be "a real Gothic cuirass of about 1480, that had found its way eventually to a theatrical wardrobe."[90] In early performances of *Richard III*, the vestments that graced the body of the Bishop of Ely may well have been made for a Catholic churchman of the 1530s or earlier.[91] Playing companies invested in old clothes, both for their economic and their symbolic value. Old clothes in good condition lent more than visual

---

Reformation (London, Hambledon, 1994), 77. For the statistical prevalence of brigandines in a sample of wills of early-sixteenth century knights and urban officials, where they appear to outnumber other kinds of defensive clothing, see Maria Hayward, *Rich Apparel: Clothing and the Law in Henry VIII's England* (Farnham: Ashgate, 2008), 130, 198, 324. The long-serving Master of the Revels Thomas Cawarden (*d.*1559) left brigandines and similar pieces of armour to various gentlemen of Kent in his will; see E. A. J. Honigmann and Susan Brock, *Playhouse Wills 1558-1642* (Manchester: Manchester University Press, 1993), 39.

[88] Quoted in L. W. Henry, "The Earl of Essex as Strategist and Military Organizer," *English Historical Review* 68 (1953), 370. The age and condition of the arms and armour in parish stores was a matter of perennial concern for the Privy Council. See Lindsay Boynton, *The Elizabethan Militia* (London: Routledge and Kegan Paul, 1967), 22–5, 61–2, 74–5, 195.

[89] Martin Holmes speculated that the Chamberlain's men possessed a particular old suit of armour that inspired Shakespeare's imagination, resulting in both the rotten armour of *Richard III* and the "rusty armor" featured in *Pericles*. The distance between the plays and, more crucially, the difference in the type of armour implied makes this unlikely, but Holmes' general point that there was "old armour available in or about the property room" is surely right; *Shakespeare and his Players* (London: John Murray, 1972), 154.

[90] Holmes, *Shakespeare and his Players*, 152.

[91] See Jones and Stallybrass, *Renaissance Clothing and the Materials of Memory*, 192; Stephen Greenblatt, "Resonance and Wonder," in *Learning to Curse: Essays in Early Modern Culture* (New York: Routledge, 1990), 161–2. We may never know if the actor playing Thomas Wolsey in Shakespeare's *Henry VIII* wore the cardinal's own hat, but there is a good likelihood that his costume included genuine Catholic vestments made before the Reformation, contributing to a sense of direct contact with Wolsey and his world. The implied parallel between the actors and the original wearers of the clothing could cut both ways; when Elizabethan players donned old Catholic vestments, they both appropriated some of the mystery and authority of the old rites for dramatic purposes, and implied that Catholic rites and liturgy had always been a kind of performance, or indeed a deception.

glamour to a performance; in historical drama, the presence of such garments contributed to the blurring of the boundary between the present and the past, and hence between the players and the persons they presented. Such effects would naturally depend on the clothes being kept in the best possible state of repair, looking as they might have done when worn for the first time. The unusual thing about the rotten armour as a stage property is thus not that it is old but that, like the props witnessed by Sher in the Royal Shakespeare Company storeroom, it shows its age. Beyond repair, it bears ironic witness to the irreversible passage of time and to the irrecoverability of origins, in a manner that would seem to undermine the basic project of historical drama. Rather than allowing the audience to believe that they are seeing the past as it really was, the armour reminds us of the way the past generally survives in the present—as remnant, as residue, as rubbish.

The use of the armour as a prop creates a tension between two kinds of authenticity. In historical terms the armour is authentic—more than any other property on the stage, it might plausibly have its origins in the era of Richard III. Yet, by reminding the Elizabethan audience of the distance between the present time and 1483, the armour undermines the authenticity of the historical performance. In the context of Act 3, scene 5, the armour becomes an emblem of theatricality and deceit, somehow impelling the two men who wear it—men whom the audience has been instructed to recognize as "Richard" and "Buckingham"—to acknowledge that they are only players after all:

> Tut, I can counterfeit the deep tragedian,
> Tremble and start at wagging of a straw,
> Speak, and look back, and pry on every side,
> Intending deep suspicion. . . . (3.5.5–8)

The rotten briganders of Act 3 are thus the chiastic double and opposite of the armour that features so prominently in Act 5. The Bosworth armour would have been shiny and new in appearance, very probably gilt copper or wood, and therefore within the terms of the play-world it is real; the rotten armour, by contrast, is genuinely from the past, and therefore within the terms of the play-world it is false.

To employ the terms which Brian Walsh has applied to the play, this is a moment in which the "repertoire" directly confronts the "archive."[92]

[92] Brian Walsh, *Shakespeare, the Queen's Men, and the Elizabethan Performance of History* (Cambridge: Cambridge University Press, 2009), 144–5, 164–5. The categories of the *archive*, consisting of the textual and material evidence of the past, and the *repertoire*, consisting of embodied practices usually regarded as ephemeral, are drawn from Diana Taylor, *The Archive and the Repertoire: Performing Cultural History in the Americas* (Durham, NC: Duke University Press, 2003). For Walsh, *Richard III* is distinguished by the dynamic

.

The encounter is fraught with risks for both. On the one hand, as I have suggested, the decaying briganders have the potential to expose the falsity of the historical performance. On the other, the staging of the timeworn armour can be read as a deliberate humiliation of the material remains of the past, whose veracity the play contrives to discredit in favor of its performative truth. Yet the manner in which *Richard III* so persistently interrogates its objects, drawing attention both to their status as props and to their histories beyond the theatre doors, suggests a more complex interaction between performance and the material archive. By highlighting its struggle to contain those objects whose untimeliness threatens to disrupt the time of performance, the play discloses a parallel between its own operations and those of its protagonist, who also struggles to keep alternative temporalities at bay. The tensions between the actor playing Richard and the properties he wields and wears are mirrored in the tensions between the character Richard and the past he seeks at various points to revive, deny, and outrun. The time of objects cuts across the performance as the past embodied in the ghosts cuts across the present on the night before battle.

The rotten armour-as-prop has a story of its own to tell—one that is neither Richard's story (about resistance to Hastings' supposed *coup*), nor Shakespeare's story (about Richard and Buckingham's sinister theatricality). The full story of what peregrinations led from its first manufacture to its tattered last hurrah on the Elizabethan stage was no doubt as unknown to Shakespeare's audience as it is to us. The case of the crumbling briganders suggests how it is in part the very fragility of material things, their susceptibility to being marked by the passage of time, that keeps them from being subsumed entirely into our current systems of significance, and perhaps even grants them a kind of extra-human agency. This chapter has drawn pragmatic distinctions between different kinds of old objects— trophies, relics, palimpsests—which bear the imprint of the past in different ways. In reality, of course, these categories blend into one another. Objects transform themselves unevenly over time, neither preserving the untarnished essence of the past, nor altering their natures entirely to serve the demands of the present. Shakespeare's play is aware of this. Even as it registers the powerful fantasy of separating objects from their histories—a fantasy common to the tyrant who crows "all the world to nothing!" (1.2.225), and to a certain strain of object biography—*Richard III* acknowledges the impossibility of ever fully controlling its properties, or containing the pasts they carry with them into the theatre.

interaction of the repertoire with the archive: "the events of the past . . . become inextricably tied to their theatrical embodiments" (145–6).

4

"He Lived Wickedly, Yet Made Good Laws"

Institutions and Practices

Several early accounts of Bosworth Field describe the battlefield coronation of Henry Tudor—an event which in Shakespeare's play takes place quite literally over Richard III's dead body. Most versions suggest that the battered crown was presented to Henry by the Lord Stanley, having been found amid the debris of the engagement; a well-known if late tradition insists that it was discovered in a hawthorn bush.[1] Early Tudor ballads such as *Bosworth Feilde* and *Ladye Bessiye* take care to record the physical separation of the crown from Richard's head prior to that head's becoming the target of fatal violence:

> besides his head the[y] hewed the crowne,
> & dange on him as they were wood;
> the[y] stroke his Basnett to his head
> untill his braines came out with blood.[2]

The rough sundering of Richard from his crown before his death accomplishes some useful ideological work. It suggests that the man slain on the battlefield had already ceased to be king, thereby neatly evading the problem of regicide.[3] Further, the serendipitous discovery of the crown in the field—thorn bush or no thorn bush—implies that it came to Henry not

---

[1] Polydore Vergil states that the crown was found "among the spoyle in the feilde"; *Three Books,* 226. The tradition involving the hawthorn bush, unattested before the seventeenth century, seems to arise from Henry VII's device of a crown encircling a rose-tree. See Virginia K. Henderson, "Retrieving the 'Crown in the Hawthorn Bush': The Origins of the Badges of Henry VII," in *Traditions and Transformations in Late Medieval England*, ed. Douglas Biggs, Sharon D. Michalove, A. Compton Reeves (Brill: Leiden, 2002), 237–60. Whilst Vergil and the Stanley ballads are among the sources crediting Lord Thomas Stanley with the coronation, *GCL* attributes the deed rather to Sir William Stanley, who would be executed under Henry VII some ten years later.

[2] *Ladye Bessiye*, in *Bishop Percy's Folio Manuscript: Ballads and Romances*, ed. John W. Hales (London: N. Trübner, 1868), 3.362, ll. 1051–4. This description seems to accord with the profound cranial injuries found on the body discovered in Leicester in 2012.

[3] This is also the thrust of the Act of Attainder which declared that Henry had become king the day before the battle.

in succession from a wicked king but rather from nature itself; the scarred plain functions as a *tabula rasa*, hovered over by more than a hint of divine providence.

In Shakespeare's play, by contrast, the crown's route from one possessor to another is different and more immediate. Delivering it up, Stanley declares that he has "plucked" the crown "From the dead temples of this bloody wretch" (5.8.5–6). There is no escaping the direct transmission of crown and authority from Richard to Richmond. Stanley's frank phrase is perhaps subtler than it first appears. In what is arguably an example of the trope *hypallage,* the adjectives seem intent on pulling towards each other's positions; the more obvious and literal reference, after all, would be to "the bloody temples of this dead wretch."[4] Thus, although "bloody" in Stanley's phrase applies to Richard's character as much as to his corpse, it contributes to a sense that the crown on Henry's head bears Richard's most intimate physical trace. Later, at Westminster, Henry will be anointed with holy oil; here on the battlefield he is anointed with Richard's blood.

The bloody crown draws attention to the paradox inherent in every act of succession, and above all in the rite of coronation. However much the ceremonial crowning of a new king may seek to signal a new beginning, it derives its meaning from its position in a sequence. Every coronation affirms the relationship—even, in a special sense, the identity—of the new king with his predecessor. *Le roi est mort—vive le roi!* Thus, though Richmond may aspire to be the very antithesis of the tyrant he has defeated, to rule as King Not-Richard, he cannot rid himself of Richard's trace. Rather, he can affirm his success and his succession only by taking Richard's place, wearing Richard's crown, partaking in his blood. (The striking similarity in their names, varying only in the first part of the second syllable, enhances this powerful sense of metonymic linkage.)

Henry's formal coronation took place at Westminster on 20 October 1485, some ten weeks after Bosworth. Though Richard's body lay securely in its Leicester grave, the proceedings could not escape his trace. The ceremony was modelled closely on Richard's coronation, even to the extent of recycling some of the same documents. One extant manuscript of "the little Device" detailing the order of ceremonies was clearly the same document produced for Richard's coronation; rather than copying it over, the herald or scribe has simply struck out Richard's name and inserted Henry's.[5] As Alice Hunt

---

[4] Hypallage is found "when by change of propertie a thing is delivered, as to saie, *Darkesome wandring by the solitary night*"; Angel Day, *The English Secretary* (London, 1599), 83.

[5] BL Egerton MS 985, printed in Leopold G. Wickham Legg, *English Coronation Records* (Westminster: A. Constable, 1901), 220–39. See Richard C. McCoy, "'The Wonderful Spectacle': The Civic Progress of Elizabeth I and the Troublesome Coronation,"

observes, "the legitimacy of Henry VII's coronation derives in part from its likeness to Richard's—hence the deposed king's name can be struck out and replaced by the new, legitimate one."[6] The substitution of one name for another could be interpreted as the correction of a mistake— this is the name that should have been there all along—but it also risks collapsing the distinction between the detested usurper and the legitimate saviour of the realm into a quibble over Christian names.

The point drawn from the coronation device can be applied more broadly to the politics and culture of Tudor England. In spite of all efforts either to forget the preceding reign or to demonize it, scraps and traces of Richard's period of rule clung to Tudor institutions, practices, and habits. Sometimes studiously ignored, sometimes blandly accepted, this phenomenon could also be acknowledged on occasion as a paradox or a scandal. An incident from the 1520s, recorded by Hall, is suggestive in this regard. When Cardinal Wolsey proposed to examine the Mayor and aldermen of London, so as to wrest benevolences from them, he was answered "by a counsailer of the citee, that by the lawe there might no suche benevolence be asked, nor men so examined, for it was contrary to the statute made the first yere of kyng Richarde the thirde . . ." The Cardinal declared himself astonished by this argument:

> Sir I marvell that you speake of Richard the third, whiche was a usurper and a murtherer of his awne nephewes: then of so evill a man, how can the actes be good, make no suche allegacions, his actes be not honorable. And it please your grace said the counsailer, although he did evill, yet in his tyme wer many good actes made not by hym onely, but by the consent of the body of the whole realme, whiche is the parliament.[7]

Here Richard's rule in Parliament serves as a foil to Tudor over-reaching.

By the turn of the century, Richard's paradoxical excellence as a law-giving and law-abiding monarch had evolved into a byword, at least for some learned freethinkers. William Camden noted that "albeit hee lived wickedly, yet [he] made good Lawes," and that "by the common consent of all that are wise, he was reckoned in the ranke of bad men, but

---

in *Coronations: Medieval and Early Modern Monarchic Ritual*, ed. János M. Bak (Berkeley: University of California Press, 1990), 217. Records of Richard's coronation ceremony are printed in Anne F. Sutton and P. W. Hammond, *The Coronation of Richard III: The Extant Documents* (Gloucester: Alan Sutton, 1983).

[6] Alice Hunt, *The Drama of Coronation: Medieval Ceremony in Early Modern England* (Cambridge: Cambridge University Press, 2008), 21–2.

[7] Hall, Henry VIII, Cxlᵛ.

of good Princes."[8] William Cornwallis, in a paradoxical defence of the vilified monarch, declared that "some, accompted both good Lawyers, and good Statists affirme, that in those three yeares of his goverment, there were more good statutes for the weale publique enacted, then in 30tie yeares before."[9] Richard's respect for and reliance upon the Parliament that in 1484 confirmed his title to the throne through the Act of Settlement made for a pointed contrast with James I's prickly and domineering relationship with the commons.[10] Viewed from a different angle, the paradigmatic tyrant and usurper emerged as an unlikely champion of the English constitution.

Nor was it in the sphere of law and precedent alone that Camden could credit Richard with a positive legacy. The town of Poole in Dorset, he noted, had special cause to look back with nostalgia on Richard's reign. Poole had grown into a prosperous port in the fifteenth century and been granted various privileges, including that of a wall. Work on the defences "was begun at the haven, by King Richard III, a prince who deserved to be rancked among the worst men and the best Kings."[11] Yet Poole's felicity had lasted no longer than Richard's brief reign: "ever since that time, by what fatall destinie I know not, or rather through the idlenesse and sloth of the townesmen, it is decaied: in so much as for want of inhabitation, the very houses at this day, runne to ruine."[12] Although it is left open to the reader to locate the seed of the town's "fatal destiny" in the personal wickedness of Richard III, the emphasis on the failings of the townspeople implies that the Tudor era has seen a decline in public spirit and care for the commonweal. From the imagined perspective of Poole's impoverished and improvident citizens, scratching out a living amidst the ruins of Richard's good works, the late fifteenth century looks rather like a golden age.

This chapter will consider the extent to which the some of the central institutions, customs and practices of the Tudor era were constructed, paradoxically, on Ricardian foundations. The examples explored here range from institutions founded in Richard's reign, to buildings on which he left his physical or memorial mark, to the traces of late fifteenth century

---

[8] William Camden, *Remaines of a Greater Worke, Concerning Britaine* (London, 1605), 216; Camden, *Britain,* trans. Philemon Holland (London, 1610), 371. For the argument that Shakespeare was among those who looked back to Richard III as a model of consensual and constitutional government, see Erica Sheen, *Shakespeare and the Institution of Theatre: "The Best in this Kind"* (London: Palgrave, 2009), 52–5.

[9] William Cornwallis, *The Encomium of Richard III,* ed. A. N. Kincaid (London: Turner & Devereaux, 1977), 14.

[10] David Weil Baker, "Jacobean Historiography and the Election of Richard III," *Huntington Library Quarterly* 70 (2007): 311–42.

[11] Camden, *Britain,* 211–12.   [12] Camden, *Britain,* 212.

trajectories and traditions still evident in the palimpsest of everyday urban life in the Elizabethan period. Shakespeare's world—the world into which he launched his *Richard III*—was Richard's as well: a world whose administrative and cultural contours the last Plantagenet would have recognized, and which he had in certain respects helped to bring into being.

4.1 INSTITUTIONS (COLLEGE OF ARMS, WAX CHANDLERS)

Although some historians have followed Camden in highlighting Richard's achievements as a champion of constitutional rule, there is no question that his reign was too brief and its military distractions too pressing to allow for much in the way of institutional reform or innovation. Suggestive as they may be of grander ambitions, Richard's accomplishments were necessarily few. His Parliament of 1484 passed a clutch of important reforms, including the prohibition of the notorious benevolences exacted under Edward IV. A less creditable piece of legislation restricted the activities of foreign merchants within the realm, albeit with an exemption for those involved in the printing and sale of books.[13] Richard's foundations included a college of canons at All Hallows by the Tower, which probably did not survive his fall, and another at Middleham, which lasted against the odds into the nineteenth century.[14] His Council in the North, companion to the Council in the Marches of Wales founded by his brother, became an important instrument of Tudor statecraft, especially in the aftermath of the Pilgrimage of Grace.[15] In September 1483 Richard granted a charter of incorporation to Gloucester, seat of his old dukedom, shaping the city's administrative destiny for centuries to come.[16] In the first year of his reign he also granted charters to two institutions: the

---

[13] See Charles Ross, *Richard III* (London: Methuen, 1981), 187–90; Paul Murray Kendall, *Richard III* (New York: W. W. Norton, 1996), 338–43. Richard has occasionally been credited with a foundational role in the history of press freedom; see, eg, Fred S. Siebert, *Freedom of the Press in England, 1476–1776: The Rise and Decline of Government Control* (Urbana: University of Illinois Press, 1965), 14, 32; Kendall, 343. Given that what Siebert describes an "Act to encourage foreign printers" (14) is in fact merely an exemption for printers from new xenophobic legislation, this seems like an over-statement.

[14] Rosemary Horrox, "Richard III and Allhallows Barking by the Tower," *Ricardian* 6 (1982), 38–40: J. Melhuish, *The College of Richard III, Middleham* (London: Richard III Society, n.d); Richard Barrie Dobson, *Church and Society in the Medieval North of England* (London: Hambledon, 1996), 242–3.

[15] R. R. Reid, *The King's Council in the North* (London: Longman, 1921). F. W. Brooks, *York and the Council of the North* (London: St. Anthony's Press, 1954); Rosemary Horrox, *Richard III: A Study in Service* (Cambridge: Cambridge University Press, 1989), 215–16.

[16] N. M. Herbert, R. A. Griffiths, Susan Reynolds, Peter Clark, *The 1483 Gloucester Charter in History* (Gloucester: Alan Sutton, 1983).

College of Arms and the Worshipful Company of Wax Chandlers. Both of these foundations seem to reflect, in different ways, Richard's preoccupations in his brief term on the throne; both, having survived a series of crises in the Tudor era, have endured down to the present day.

For centuries before their incorporation in the College of Arms, heralds had played a central role in English aristocratic and military culture, serving as the custodians of pedigrees and crests and as ambassadors between armies; they were also frequently the devisers and chroniclers of royal pageants and ceremonies. Over the course of the fifteenth century, the heralds of England had functioned increasingly as a corporate body, holding their first chapter in 1420.[17] They had their own established hierarchy surmounted by the Kings of Arms, beneath whom stood the heralds and the pursuivants of arms. As Constable of England in his brother's reign, Richard of Gloucester had issued a series of ordinances designed to reform the internal government of the heralds and increase their capacity for cooperation.[18] As King of England, he crowned this work with a charter granted to the heralds on 2 March 1484:

> constituting them and their successors in office a body corporate, with perpetual succession and a common seal, and in order that they might have a fitting place wherein to meet and communicate for the advancement of their faculty giving them and their successors forever a messuage in the parish of All Saints the little called Colde Erber . . .[19]

The gift of Coldharbour was a boon indeed. One of the great mansions of late medieval London, the house had been the dwelling of a string of noblemen, kings, and royal mistresses. The charter further granted lands for the maintenance of a chantry priest to pray for the souls of Richard, his wife and his son, as well as for other benefactors of the College of Arms.

At least one biographer of Richard III has detected in this foundation a key to the antitheses of his character: "the movement toward organization and systematization pointing to the future, and the interest in crests, coats of arms, and ancestral lineage suggesting a love of the past."[20] Richard probably had several reasons for thus favouring the heralds. One motive may have sprung from his undoubted

[17] Jackson W. Armstrong, "The Development of the Office of Arms in England, *c.*1413–1485," in *The Herald in Late Medieval Europe*, ed. Katie Stevenson (Woodbridge: Boydell, 2009), 26.

[18] Adrian Ailes, "Ancient Precedent or Tudor Fiction? Garter King of Arms and the Pronouncements of Thomas, Duke of Clarence," in Stevenson, ed., *Herald in Late Medieval Europe*, 32–4.

[19] Anthony Wagner, *Heralds of England: A History of the Office and College of Arms* (London: H.M. Stationery Office, 1967), 130.

[20] Kendall, *Richard III*, 386.

concern with purity of descent, as seen in the desperate assertion of June 1483 that the Queen and her allies were intent on destroying "the old royall blode of this realme," and in his determination to demonstrate the bastardy of his nephews.[21] Yet the officers of arms had the potential to lend Richard's reign a legitimacy that was more than merely lineal. In the Yorkist era, heralds had become more than ever the overseers and guarantors of the grand ceremonies of royal state, from birth to death. Twenty-four officers of arms attended the churching of Queen Elizabeth in 1466, following the birth of her first child; fifteen heralds partook in the king's funeral in 1483.[22] The eighteen officers of arms who participated in Richard's coronation received a largess of £100.[23] In September 1483, Richard brought five heralds north to York for the elaborate festivities attending his son's investiture as Prince of Wales.[24] The heralds were useful to Richard in demonstrating his right to the throne, but perhaps even more so for the éclat they lent to the ceremonies of his tottering state. They made things look official.

As the heralds presided over Richard's efforts to present a convincing spectacle on the royal stage, so they presided over his grim exit. Naked and bloody, Richard's body was borne from the field on the back of a horse managed by a pursuivant of arms. Whilst the *Great Chronicle of London* names the pursuivant as "Norrey" (suggesting a confusion with Norroy, King of Arms), Hall and Holinshed identify him rather as Richard's personal herald, Blanche Sanglier (White Boar).[25] The pursuivant's attitude in this incident is left unspecified. Was he forced into this role as a humiliation, or did he undertake it willingly as a last service to his master—or even in a desperate bid to signal his allegiance to the new order? If Richard's pursuivant faced an uncertain future under the new regime, so too did the late King's creation, the College of Arms.

Henry VII certainly had no less need of heralds than his predecessors; arguably, given his somewhat dubious descent, he needed them rather

---

[21] Letter to the City of York, June 10, 1483, in *York Civic Records, vol. 1,* ed. Angelo Raine (Leeds: Yorkshire Archaeological Society, 1939), 73–4.
[22] Ailes, "Ancient Precedent," 33; the deeds of the heralds at the funeral of Edward IV are recorded in College of Arms MS I.7, printed in Anne F. Sutton and Livia Visser-Fuchs with R. A. Griffiths, *The Royal Funerals of the House of York at Windsor* (Bury St. Edmunds: Richard III Society, 2005).
[23] Sutton and Hammond, *The Coronation of Richard III*, 26; for the role of the heralds at Richard's coronation, see Holinshed, 734.
[24] Mark Noble, *A History of the College of Arms* (London: Debrett, 1804), 51.
[25] *GCL*, 238; Hall, Richard III, Lviii'.

more. Yet this did not guarantee the safety of the College of Arms, nor of its members, in the new order. Garter King of Arms John Writhe was initially held in suspicion, his salary going unpaid for a number of months, but was eventually restored to favour, with arrears. Coldharbour, however, was lost to the heralds for good, consequent of the act revoking all of Richard III's grants; in 1487, Henry VII gave the house to his mother.[26] It is not clear whether the collegiate status of the heralds was also cancelled, or if the chaplain bound to pray for Richard's soul was relieved of his duties. When the heralds Thomas Wriothesley and Thomas Hawley recorded Richard's epitaph in their books, at some point in the early Tudor era, they did so in the knowledge that, whatever his faults, Richard had shown more concrete favour to their profession than either Henry VII or his son. Only in the reign of Mary was the status of the College of Arms confirmed by a new royal charter, and a new residence granted to them at Derby House, once the seat of Lord Stanley.

From the beginning to the end of the sixteenth century, the officers of arms were pestered with accusations that they dispensed pedigrees and coats of arms to unworthy persons for private gain. These charges came, more often than not, from their own colleagues. In 1530 an exceptionally bitter quarrel erupted between Thomas Wriothesley, Garter King of Arms, and Thomas Benolt, Clarenceaux King of Arms. Benolt declared that Wriothesley had brought the College into disrepute by granting arms "to bound men, to vile persons not able to uphold the honour of nobleness." Wriothesley retorted tartly that "he knoweth no person to be more unworthy nor of less reputation to whom at any time he hath given patent of arms than is the said Benolt Clarenceaux."[27] In his own support, Wriothesley invoked the ordinances delivered to the heralds under Edward IV by Richard of Gloucester. However—whether to lend the ordinances a greater air of antiquity, or to avoid the Ricardian taint, or both—he identified them instead as ordinances of Thomas Duke of Clarence, made in the reign of Henry V.[28]

By Benolt's own self-serving account, the venality and back-biting of the heralds had reached such a pitch that Henry VIII was on the verge of depriving them of the right to grant arms, which he proposed to retain for himself. Such a blow would certainly have spelled the end of the College as a relevant institution. Instead, Clarenceaux prevailed upon the King to charge the heralds with the duty of touring the provinces in order to inspect the claims to gentility of the local elite. The heralds were authorized

[26] Wagner, *Heralds of England*, 134–6.
[27] Quoted in Wagner, *Heralds of England*, 163, 165.
[28] Ailes, "Ancient Precedent," 29–38, esp. 38.

to grant arms where appropriate and also to deprive those who laid claim to them without desert. They were specifically empowered to efface and destroy unmerited coats of arms wherever they appeared, be it on plate, in windows, or on tombs. So began the custom of regular Visitations which would persist into the later seventeenth century.[29]

One of these Visitations, conducted in Warwickshire in 1563, would prove specially significant for the future author of *Richard III*, born in the following year. It was probably on this occasion that John Shakespeare of Stratford began to contemplate the possibility of obtaining a coat of arms, thereby elevating himself and his family to a position of equality with his wife's family, the admired Ardens. By the early 1570s, Shakespeare was in correspondence about the matter with Clarenceaux Cooke, who had conducted the Warwickshire visitation. Cooke went so far as to provide a pattern of the proposed Shakespeare arms, the shield bearing the image of a spear in a diagonal band, surmounted by a spear-bearing falcon; the accompanying motto was to be "non sanz droict" (not without right). Yet for reasons unknown, possibly connected to John Shakespeare's declining fortunes, the application was unsuccessful or at least inconclusive at this time.[30]

In the mid-1590s, John's application was renewed, almost certainly with the assistance of his London-based son, who would have been able to deal directly with Garter King of Arms William Dethicke at his office in Derby Place. The name of William Shakespeare does not appear in any of the documents relating to his father's application, which focus rather on the deeds of his ancestors at the dawn of the Tudor era. One draft grant of arms declares that John Shakespeare's "parentes and late antecessors were for theyre valeant & faithefull service advaunced & rewarded by the most prudent prince King Henry the seventh of famous memorie" (Fig. 4.1).[31] A subsequent draft affirms with a little more precision that the applicant's "grand-father" received the gratitude of the first Tudor king.[32] Three years later, a draft exemplification of the Shakespeare arms alongside those of Arden adds further detail regarding the "parent great Grandfather

---

[29] See D. R. Woolf, *The Social Circulation of the Past: English Historical Culture 1500–1730* (Oxford: Oxford University Press, 2003), 105–13.

[30] See Samuel Schoenbaum, *William Shakespeare: A Compact Documentary Life*, revised edition (Oxford: Oxford University Press, 1987), 38–9.

[31] College of Arms MS Vincent 157, Art. 23. Reproduced in Samuel Schoenbaum, *William Shakespeare: A Documentary Life* (Oxford: Clarendon Press in association with Scolar Press, 1975), fig. 128.

[32] College of Arms MS Vincent 157, Art. 24, where the word "grandfather" is added above the word "antecessor." Reproduced in Schoenbaum, *William Shakespeare: A Documentary Life*, fig. 129.

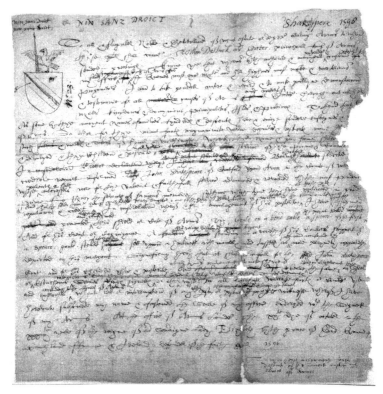

Fig. 4.1. Draft of the Shakespeare grant of arms, 1596. College of Arms MS Vincent 157, Art. 23. By kind permission of the College of Arms.

and late Antecessor [who] for his faithefull & approved service to the late most prudent king H 7 of famous memorie, was advaunced & rewarded with Landes & Tenementes geven to him in those partes of Warwikeshere where they have continewed bie some descentes in good reputacon. . . ."[33] From one draft to another, a figure emerges as if out of the mist and takes on definite form, the figure of a grandfather or great-grandfather who fought with valour on an early Tudor field. To what extent this figure had any basis in history, and to what extent he was simply cooked up between William Shakespeare and William Dethicke, is unknown. What we can say is that a few years

---

[33] College of Arms MS R21. Reproduced in Schoenbaum, *William Shakespeare: A Documentary Life*, fig. 130.

after the first composition of *Richard III*, Shakespeare seems to have found a way of writing himself into the story of Richard's downfall. He did so, moreover, in collaboration with Richard III's own creation, the College of Arms.

William Shakespeare's dealings with the College must have heightened his awareness of the similarities between the heralds' profession and his own double occupation as playwright and player. The resemblance went far beyond the occasional collaboration between playing companies and officers of arms in the production of great public spectacles, such as royal entries. The heralds were accomplished storytellers, weaving historical figures and the odd invented character into genealogical narratives that brought the past into living contact with the present. They were the makers and (in their authority to raze escutcheons) unmakers of men. Yet if they were like playwrights the heralds were also players, serving as stand-ins, representations, or even embodiments of noble persons. This function was especially apparent in the role of those private heralds who served in aristocratic households, and took their titles from their master or his badge.[34] Thus, Richard III had his Blanche Sanglier, whilst Hastings had Hastings Pursuivant. With his master's arms emblazoned on his tabard, the private pursuivant was not only the servant of his lord but his emblematic embodiment, his other and in some respects truer self. As Shakespeare knew well from the chronicles, this doubling of selves could lead to powerful ironies, above all at the point of the master's death.

We have already noted the role of Blanche Sanglier in bearing the corpse of Richard III away from Bosworth Field. Whether this act be construed as one of loyalty or of betrayal is in a sense beside the point. There is in either case an unsettling irony in the spectacle of the dead man being carried off by his own double or doppelganger—the Boar borne away by the Boar.[35] No less sinister in implication is the meeting between Lord Hastings and the "pursevant of his own name" in More's account of Hastings' final hours.[36] Here the encounter with the other

---

[34] This practice was still common in the reign of Henry VIII, though it seems to have been on the wane later in the sixteenth century.

[35] As Daniel Kinney has remarked, Richard in this account "is finally no more than his own heraldic token"; see "The Tyrant Being Slain: Afterlives of More's *History of King Richard III*," in *English Renaissance Prose: History, Language and Politics*, ed. Neil Rhodes (Tempe, AZ: Medieval & Renaissance Texts & Studies, 1997), 41, n. 19.

[36] More, *History*, 51. In Hall and Holinshed, the herald is described as "a pursyvaunt of his awne called Hastynges" (Hall, Edward V, fol. xvʳ). Editors of Shakespeare's play sometimes conclude that Hastings is a pursuivant in the humbler sense—a server of warrants—making the similarity of names a mere coincidence. Yet in the Latin text of More's history he is identified as a *caduceator*—the Roman bearer of the caduceus, or in other words, a herald.

self heralds the imminent erasure of life and identity. The irony is deepened by the knowledge that the historical Hastings Pursuivant, one John Walsh, seems to have moved quickly and without compunction into the service of Richard III, whom he served as Falcon Herald.[37] In a further twist, More goes on to state that after Hastings' execution Richard sent "one herode of armes" to declare his treason to the people.[38] Remembering the duty imposed on Blanche Sanglier, we must acknowledge the possibility that John Walsh's last service as Hastings Pursuivant—or his first as Falcon Herald—was to proclaim the abhorrent crimes and deserved death of his erstwhile master.

If Shakespeare took inspiration from the heralds and pursuivants who weave their sinister way through Richard's story, he did not always incorporate them directly into his play. Indeed, he omitted some of the more striking references to officers of arms. Blanche Sanglier does not appear, and the herald dispatched to trumpet Hastings' treachery is transformed into the Scrivener (a more direct figure of the author). In the Folio, the pursuivant who speaks with Hastings has no name, and there is no indication that Shakespeare understands him to be a genuine herald, rather than the humbler server of warrants that went by the same title. Hastings seems to know him only vaguely, calls him "sirrah," and concludes the encounter by throwing him his purse with the instruction "drink that for me." In the Quarto text, on the other hand, the pursuivant is identified as Hastings, and the nobleman addresses him twice by this title; though the substance of their brief conversation remains the same, Lord Hastings is more respectful, greeting him with "well met, Hastings" (3.1.92) rather than "how now, sirrah," and in conclusion giving him his purse to "spend" rather than tossing him money to "drink" (3.1.102). There are smaller alterations too, with the Folio's "when thou met'st me last," becoming "when I met thee last" (3.1.95). The pursuivant in the Quarto is both more clearly a herald and more clearly a doppelganger, with the identity of names and interchangeability of pronouns foreshadowing Hastings' imminent loss of self.

---

[37] Hastings Pursuivant, who undertook several missions to France in the latter years of Edward IV's reign and in 1480 supplied cloth and ostrich feathers to the court, has been identified with John Walsh, who served under the name of Falcon Herald in the court of Richard III and was subsequently attainted in the reign of Henry VII under the name of "John Walsh, alias Hastings." See Walter H. Godfrey with Sir Anthony Wagner, *College of Arms, Queen Victoria Street* (London: Committee for the Survey of the Memorials of Greater London, 1963), 265–6; Hanham, *Richard III*, 173, n. 1.

[38] More, *History*, 53.

Both texts include one unequivocal reference to an officer of arms.[39] On the eve of Bosworth, Richard instructs Catesby to "send out a pursuivant-at-arms/To Stanley's regiment" (5.5.12–13), threatening Stanley with the execution of his son George if he fails to bring his power. There is a glimmer of dark wit involved in sending a herald, normally a guarantor of correct lineage, to threaten a nobleman with the elimination of his heir. The irony is deepened significantly by recollection of Stanley's prophetic dream that "the boar had razed his helm" (or, in F, "razed off his helm"; 3.2.8). Here the threat posed by Richard, the heraldic Boar, is directed against Stanley's own heraldic emblem, the helm that in his coat of arms surmounts the shield and bears his crest.[40] This dream is different from that reported in Holinshed and Hall, where the nightmare that the boar "rased them both by the heads, that the bloud ran about both their shoulders" foreshadows a literal assault on the heads of both Hastings and Stanley in the Tower.[41] In the play, the dream is less prophetic of physical violence ("racing," or goring) than of a heraldic dishonouring (razing, or erasure, of the helm). The potential for just such razing of the family crest must have struck fear into many gentry families who were required to present their arms and pedigrees to the heralds on their regular visitations. The officer of arms was empowered to "deface at his discrecon" all unmerited coats of arms, "as well in coote armors, helmes, standard, pennons, and hatchmets of tents and pavilions as also in plate, jewells, pap[er], parchement, wyndowes, gravestones, and monuments."[42] To gore a man in the head is a threat to his life and personal future; to raze his crest or his helm is to deface the past and future of his line as well. Stanley's dream figures Richard as a malign herald embarking on a destructive Visitation

---

[39] There are two figurative references to heralds: Clarence's derision of "night-walking heralds/That trudge between the King and Mrs Shore" (72–3) and Richard's invocation of "Jove's Mercury" as "herald for a king" (4.3.55). The latter phrase is followed by lines rhyming on the words "shield" and "field," two words with heraldic connotations.

[40] As Eve Sanders notes, "The phrase suggests the erasure of the emblem of Stanley's helmet, a key component of his heraldic symbology." Sanders goes on to suggest that "Stanley and Hasting's use of the term 'raze' alludes to Richard's scribal mastery, his ability to obliterate them symbolically as well as physically, to leave them without any mark to show the world they are gentlemen." Eve Rachele Sanders, *Gender and Literacy on Stage in Early Modern England* (Cambridge: Cambridge University Press, 1998), 148–9. The heraldic reading is supported by Siemon in his Arden 3 edition of the play, but disputed by Jowett in the Oxford edition.

[41] Holinshed, 723. Stanley is said to have received a wound to the head in the scuffle, escaping a worse fate only by ducking under a table.

[42] Elizabeth's injunctions to the Kings of Arms, quoted in Arthur Charles Fox-Davies, *A Complete Guide to Heraldry* (London: T. C. & E. C. Jack, 1909), 61. On the authority granted to the heralds to raze false funerary escutcheons, see Clare Gittings, *Death, Burial and the Individual in Early Modern England* (London: Croom Helm, 1984), 93.

of the English nobility. (In light of this, the fact that the College of Arms should have taken up quarters in Stanley's former London residence takes on a certain irony.)

In *Richard III*, Shakespeare seems to identify and probe a sinister association between heraldry and loss of identity or self-estrangement. The association is arguably particularly prominent in the Quarto; if, as most scholars agree, this text is slightly later in date than the Folio, it is likely to be closely contemporary with the procurement of the Shakespeare arms.[43] Yet the passages colored by heraldry do more than shed light on Shakespeare's possible preoccupations in the mid-1590s. They bring into fresh relief anxieties associated with doubling and loss of identity already pervasive in the play: in Richard's preoccupation with his own reflection, in his seeking out and attempted destruction of "other selves" in Buckingham and Richmond, in his radical divorce from himself in the tent on Bosworth Field. The heralds Shakespeare encountered in his sources, and perhaps in Derby House as well, participate in one the play's most pervasive and haunting motifs, serving—alongside shadows and mirrors—as figures for the externalized, inimical self.

Shakespeare's coat of arms did not fail to provoke scepticism both within and beyond the College of Arms.[44] The most memorable remark on the matter belongs to Ben Jonson, who in *Every Man Out of His Humour* (1599) baldly satirized the Shakespeare motto *non sanz droict* by letting the social-climbing fool Sogliardo be advised to choose the phrase "not without mustard."[45] Yet the grotesque coat of arms which this motto accompanies in the play (described in a passage whose comedy is fully accessible only to those with a detailed grasp of heraldry) does not resemble Shakespeare's so much as a parodic version of the arms of Richard III, featuring "a boar's head *proper*" and, for the crest, a "boar without a head, rampant."[46] As one of Sogliardo's interlocutors dryly remarks: "A

---

[43] See Peter Davison, "Commerce and Patronage: The Lord Chamberlain's Men's Tour of 1597" in *Shakespeare Performed: Essays in Honour of R. A. Foakes*, ed. Grace Ioppolo (Cranbury, NJ: Associated University Presses), 56–71.

[44] Even the herald who drew up the draft award of arms in 1596 could not resist twice miswriting the Shakespeare motto as "non, sanz droict" ("no, without right"). In 1602, Dethicke was forced to respond to the accusations of York Herald Ralph Brooke that "Shakespear the Player" was unworthy of arms, and also that the arms in question were too similar to those of Lord Mauley. See Schoenbaum, *William Shakespeare: A Compact Documentary Life*, 230–2.

[45] Ben Jonson, *Every Man Out of His Humour*, ed. Helen Ostovich (Manchester: Manchester University Press, 2001), 3.1.244.

[46] Jonson, *Every Man Out of His Humour*, 3.1.239–40, 220. The complex heraldic humour of the passage is deciphered in Arthur Huntington Nason, *Heralds and Heraldry in Ben Jonson's Plays, Masques and Entertainments* (New York: Gordian Press, 1998), 89–98.

boar without a head. That's very rare."[47] Boars of any sort—let alone headless ones—were comparatively rare in Tudor heraldry, probably owing to
the overwhelming association of the device with Richard III, who took
the boar as his badge, and whose royal arms were supported by two boars
rampant.[48] (Among those to abandon the boar device in the sixteenth century were the Wyatts, for whereas the arms of Sir Henry Wyatt had featured three boars' heads, in the arms of his descendants these were dropped
or de-emphasized in favour of the barnacles, the implement with which
Sir Henry was supposed to have been tortured in Richard's dungeons.[49])
Sogliardo is lampooned as a debased version of Richard III, with the same
desperate thirst to rise in status, but without the wit to achieve it.

If Sogliardo's boar refers us to Richard III, its headlessness refers
more specifically to *Richard III*, and to Stanley's dream that "the boar
razed off his helm." Read reflexively, the phrase suggests a boar who has
rubbed away his own head. In the technical language of heraldry, an
"erased" head refers not to a headless body but to a head represented
on its own, generally with a jagged edge. Sogliardo's crest is thus the
product of an amateurish misunderstanding of heraldry, a misunderstanding which Jonson attributes to Shakespeare not only through the
parody of his motto but by reference to *Richard III*. The criticism of
Shakespeare in this scene, arguably, is not only of a buffoonish social
climber, but of a Ricardian over-reacher, wounding himself in his
heedless drive for mastery.

One document upon which the rampant boars of Richard's royal arms
may still be seen today is the charter granted to the Honourable Company of
Wax Chandlers on 16 February 1484 (Fig. 4.2). The main initiative behind
this royal foundation would presumably have come from the company rather than the King. The charter signalled the importance of a craft which in
the late fifteenth century was thriving as never before, or indeed since. It is
difficult to exaggerate the centrality of wax to the rites and customs of the
late medieval church. Sweeter and slower burning than common tallow, wax
lent itself to thoughts of purity and timelessness. On the festival of Candle-

[47] Jonson, *Every Man Out of His Humour*, 3.1.221. In other editions this line is given to
Sogliardo himself.
[48] Though found in continental and Irish coats of arms, "a boar rampant is almost
unknown in British heraldry"; see Arthur Charles Fox-Davies, *The Art of Heraldry: An
Encylopedia of Armory* (London: T. C. & E. C. Jack, 1904), 38.
[49] As Thomas Scott recorded, "afterwards because of certaine prophesies of the boars head
(which untill then was the armes of that house) . . . the true armes of the Wyat's was laid
aside, and the three barnicles chosen"; *Some Passages taken out of an old manuscript by Thomas
Scott of Egreston*, BL Add MS 62135, fol. 467ʳ. See also Clare Stuart Wortley, "Holbein's
Sketch of the Wyat Coat of Arms," *The Burlington Magazine for Connoisseurs* 56 (1930):
211–13.

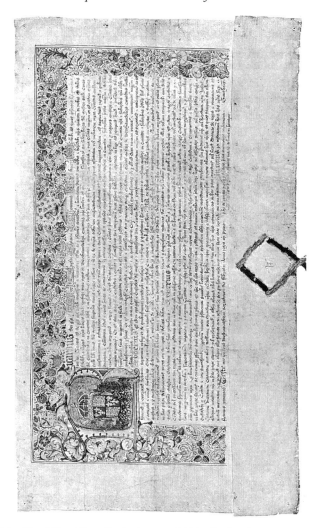

Fig. 4.2. The Wax Chandlers' charter, 1484. By kind permission of the Worshipful Company of Wax Chandlers.

mas, every parishioner in every church across the land bore a wax candle in honour of the Virgin.[50] Among the most common bequests in fifteenth cen-

---

[50] Eamon Duffy, *The Stripping of the Altars: Traditional Religion in England 1400–1580* (New Haven: Yale University Press, 1992), 14–22.

tury wills are a few pence for the keeping of a wax light before a holy image.[51] As a hermit remarks in Malory's *Morte Arthur* (printed by Caxton a year after the Wax Chandlers' incorporation), "the candell which sheweth clerenesse and syghte sygnefyeth the ryyt way of Jhesu Cryst."[52] Richard, who seems to have been a genuinely pious man as well as a somewhat sanctimonious one, may have been particularly willing to support a craft so powerfully associated with sanctity and the rites of the late medieval church. Whereas his carnally-given elder brother had incorporated the Company of Tallow Chandlers, Richard would find his emblem in pious, sombre wax.

As with the foundation of the College of Arms, the Wax Chandlers' charter included provision for a chantry priest to pray for the King in life and for his soul after death, as well as for the souls of his ancestors.[53] Though such provisions were standard, they were peculiarly appropriate to the wax chandlers, for whom a major source of income arose from the rites and offices of the dead. Wax tapers and torches were among the chief expenses associated with high-status funerals; to take an extreme case, the funeral procession of Henry V in 1422 called for 1,400 wax tapers borne by the clergy and a still greater number of torches carried by the citizens of London.[54] The candles in the hands of hired mourners were, Eamon Duffy has suggested, "a prayer in themselves."[55] Long after the mourners had departed, slow-burning candles supplied their place as suppliants. Though the candles were not, of course, everlasting, they conveyed intimations of eternity whilst contesting the finality of death.[56] In their very different ways, Richard's two foundations, the Wax Chandlers and the College of Arms, both dealt in technologies for bridging time; like crests and devices, wax candles symbolized and maintained links between the living and the dead. It is difficult to avoid the intuition that in favouring such institutions, Richard was providing for his own posthumous future.

Besides the church itself, few institutions felt the impact of the Reformation more heavily than did the Wax Chandlers. From the 1530s

---

[51] Such lights, Kathleen Kamerick notes, "represented the donor before the representation of the saint," and allowed the dead parishioner a still active role in the life of the church, at least while the candles they had paid for lasted. See *Popular Piety and Art in the Late Middle Ages: Image Worship and Idolatry in England 1350–1500* (London: Palgrave, 2002), 98.

[52] Thomas Malory, *Le Morte Darthur* (London, 1485), Book 16, ch. 4.

[53] See John Dummelow, *The Wax Chandlers of London* (London: Phillimore, 1973), 132. I have relied on Dummelow for details regarding the history of the company in the Tudor era.

[54] One wax chandler alone was paid just over £300 for his contribution to the ceremonies, and many others must have profited as well. See Dummelow, *Wax Chandlers,* 16.

[55] Duffy, *The Stripping of the Altars,* 362.

[56] One of the marvellous tombs in Malory features twelve "tapyr[s] of wax that brent day and nyyt" without diminishment (*Morte Darthur*, Book 2, ch. 11). The candles in this case are not strictly eternal, as they will be extinguished when their maker, Merlin, finally dies.

onwards, a string of injunctions forbade many of the ecclesiastical rites and ceremonies in which light had played a central part, whilst the use of candles was discouraged as tending to superstition. In 1538, orders were issued to the clergy to preach a quarterly sermon against the superstitious offering of lights, and to permit "no candles, tapers, or images of wax to be set afore any image or picture but only the light that commonly goeth across the church by the rood-loft."[57] The membership of the Company fell precipitously in the early years of Reformation, from 54 members paying quarterage in 1531 to 34 in 1538.[58] Although the restoration of traditional religion in the reign of Mary brought some relief to the troubled trade—including the requisition of a three hundred pound Paschal Candle in 1558—Elizabeth proved staunchly unsympathetic. When the monks of Westminster greeted her at the opening of her first Parliament with lights, incense, and holy water, the Queen ordered "Away with those torches, for we see very well."[59] (It was a different matter in private for, unbeknownst to most of her subjects, the Queen retained candles on her own altar.) The Worshipful Company of Wax Chandlers survived in a reformed England, and even found some new markets for its products including, in the early seventeenth century, private indoor theatres such as the Blackfriars.[60] Never again, however, would they play such a prominent and lucrative role in the life of the national community as they had in the reign of Richard III, and for half a century after.

Although some of Shakespeare's later plays may have been lit by candle-light, the uses the playwright found for wax in his early works were mostly metaphorical.[61] In striking contrast to the associations with timelessness that wax enjoyed before the Reformation, wax in Shakespeare's works

---

[57] Duffy, *Stripping of the Altars*, 407. Among the lights extinguished in this year was that of the "great candle" which Henry VIII had paid to be kept burning at the shrine of Our Lady of Walsingham every year since 1509. See William Page, ed, *A History of the County of Norfolk: Volume 2* (London: A. Constable, 1906), 394–401.

[58] Dummelow, *Wax Chandlers*, 56.

[59] McCoy, "Wonderful Spectacle," 219; Dummelow, *Wax Chandlers*, 40.

[60] On the use of wax candles for indoor and court performances, see Robert B. Graves, *Lighting the Shakespearean Stage, 1567–1642* (Carbondale: Southern Illinois University Press, 1999.) The use of wax candles inevitably enhanced the already potent parallel between the new theatres and the old church, nowhere more inescapably than in the closing tableaux of John Ford's *The Broken Heart*, another Blackfriars play: "An altar covered with white; two lights of virgin wax . . . Soft music. CALANTHA and the rest rise, doing obeisance to the altar"; *The Selected Plays of John Ford*, ed. Colin Gibson (Cambridge: Cambridge University Press, 1986), 5.3 s.d. See Elizabeth Williamson, *The Materiality of Religion in Early Modern English Drama* (Farnham: Ashgate, 2009).

[61] When Iachimo in *Cymbeline*, a play written for the Blackfriars, speaks of "an eye/Base and illustrous as the smoky light/That's fed with stinking tallow" (1.6.109–11), he seems bent on reminding the audience that the clear light in which they behold him comes from wax.

stands mainly for mutability, impermanence, and evanescence. Henry VI, Hermia, and Adonis are all compared to wax forms that are infinitely malleable when subjected to heat and pressure, surrendering their identities to the will of others.[62] In *King John*, Melun's life "bleeds away, even as a form of wax/Resolveth from his figure' gainst the fire" (5.4.24–25); Hamlet, raging at his mother, cries "let virtue be as wax/And melt in her own fire" (3.4.74–75). For Shakespeare, it seems, the most significant thing about wax was not that it burned longer than tallow but that it left no residue, making it an ideal figure for physical and psychological dissolution.

With an echo of Shakespeare, wax is the substance implicitly troped in Marx and Engels' description of the historical process: "all that is solid melts into air." For Marx and Engels, medieval institutions and industries were so much wax in the face of the bourgeois fire. "All fixed, fast-frozen relations, with their train of ancient and venerable prejudices and opinions, are swept away . . . All old-established national industries have been destroyed or are daily being destroyed."[63] Among the old industries and venerable customs which have fallen in this way we may surely count both the craft of the wax chandlers and the science of heraldry. In light of this, it must seem remarkable that Richard III's two foundations, the College of Arms and the Wax Chandlers, survive into the present day. Indeed, though their halls have been rebuilt as a consequence of the Fire of London, neither institution has changed its address since the sixteenth century. The improbable persistence of these organizations, so apparently out of step with modern priorities, is testimony to the power of institutionalization—to the power, that is, of those fifteenth-century charters that brought them into being and made them "one body and one comonaltie forevermore."

It is tempting to dismiss institutions such as these as archaic, and to ascribe their survival into the present largely to mere inertia.[64] Yet this is perhaps to sidestep too easily the small but subversive threat they pose to our understanding of the present as a coherent and homogenous temporal

---

[62] *3 Henry VI*, 2.1.71; *Midsummer Night's Dream*, 1.1.49; *Venus and Adonis*, l. 565.

[63] Karl Marx and Friedrich Engels, *The Communist Manifesto* (New York: International Publishers, 1948), 12.

[64] On the distinction between the merely residual and the outright archaic ("that which is wholly recognized as an element of the past"), see Raymond Williams, *Marxism and Literature* (Oxford: Oxford University Press, 1977), 121–7. An alternative perspective is propounded by Karl Polanyi: "The theory of 'survivals' [is] sometimes adduced as an explanation, according to which functionless institutions or traits may continue to exist by virtue of inertia. Yet it would be truer to say that no institution ever survives its function—when it appears to do so, it is because it serves in some other function, or functions, which *need not include the original one*"; *The Great Transformation* (Boston: Beacon Press, 1944), 183. It is perhaps possible to square this circle by suggesting that if the institutions in question are not completely archaic, it is because they have taken on the new function of serving as icons of unapologetic archaism.

terrain, as a moment entirely contemporary with itself. It would be naive to describe the College of Arms as a "piece of the past," or to suppose that within the walls of Wax Chandlers' Hall it is not the same year as it is outside. Yet these institutions persist in lively, sustaining contact with a historical epoch whose character and concerns otherwise seem drastically remote from those of contemporary society.[65] They challenge our understanding of the present not because they are not part of it, but because they inhabit a region of it in which the twenty-first century still borders on the fifteenth, as in a pleated handkerchief (to borrow a now-familiar image from Michel Serres).[66] As I shall argue in more detail in the final chapter, it is with such disruptions of temporality that Shakespeare's *Richard III* is centrally engaged.

4.2 BUILDINGS (TOWER OF LONDON, CROSBY PLACE)

In the midst of his remarkable excoriation of the late Richard III's character, physique, motives, and actions, John Rous paused for a short enumeration of his positive achievements. "The King Richard was praiseworthy for his building, as at Westminster, Nottingham, Warwick, York, and Middleham, and many other places, which can be viewed."[67] To these concrete and visible remnants of a brief reign may be added the wall at Poole and repairs made to Carlisle Castle, where Richard's arms were still to be seen inscribed in stone in Camden's time.[68] A good many of these projects, undertaken like the fortifications at Poole in the urgent need for defence against threats from abroad and within, must have been left unfinished at the time of Richard's death. When John Leland visited Warwick

---

[65] The conservative social theorist Arnold Gehlen coined the phrase "Transzendenz ins Diesseits" (transcendence into the here and now) for the manner in which long-lived institutions imbue the political present with what he regarded as a stabilizing supratemporality. See Gehlen, *Urmensch und Spätkultur* (Frankfurt: Athenäum, 2004), 16. For a further exploration of these themes with a critique of Gehlen, see Antje Gimmler, *Institutions and Time: A Critical Theory and Pragmatist Approach,* Sociologisk Arbejdspapir 13 (Aalborg: Aalborg Universitetsforlag, 2003).

[66] Michel Serres with Bruno Latour, *Conversations on Science, Culture, and Time*, trans. Roxanne Lepidus (Ann Arbor: University of Michigan Press, 1995), 60.

[67] John Rous, *Historia Johannis Rossi de Regibus Anglie*, translated in Hanham, *Richard III*, 121. Rous also notes a chantry foundation at York cathedral, the colleges at Middleham and St Mary of Barking, and an endowment granted to Queens College Cambridge. "The money that was offered him by the peoples of London, Gloucester, and Worcester he declined with thanks, affirming that he would rather have their love than their treasure" (121).

[68] Camden, *Britain*, 778.

castle more than fifty years later, he was able to observe that "K. Rich. 3. pullyd downe a pece of the waulle, and began and halfe finishid a mighty tower, or strengthe, for to shoute out gunns. This peace as he left it so it remaynethe onfinishid."[69] At Westminster, John Stow noted "a verie faire gate begun by Richard the third, in the year 1484, and was by him builded a great height, and many faire lodgings in it, but left unfinished."[70] In most places Richard's works have long since disappeared or been subsumed in later alterations, though his additions to York's Monk Bar gatehouse have survived, and today house the small Richard III Museum.

The building which most clearly bears Richard's imprint today is, without question, the Tower of London. This imprint is not, however, primarily physical. Early in his reign, Richard apparently commissioned one Thomas Daniel to draft as many masons and bricklayers as needed for what seems to have been planned as an extensive programme of alterations.[71] The nature and extent of these works can no longer be determined, and it is possible that they were never carried out. Yet Richard through his deeds, both real and reputed, left a mark upon the Tower more profound if less palpable than bricks and mortar. Richard lies very near the wellspring of the Tower's subsequent reputation as a site of fear, confinement and murder, a reputation already well-established in Shakespeare's time, and unshaken in our own.

The Tower had been employed as a prison many times before the reign of Richard III.[72] As early as 1100 a Norman bishop had been incarcerated there (though he escaped within a matter of months). In the first half of the fifteenth century, Charles Duke of Orleans had been kept in the Tower for some part of his twenty-six years of captivity, and a manuscript made for Edward IV shows Charles writing poetry within the White Tower (Fig. 4.3). Before Edward's reign, few prisoners had died in custody, among the notable exceptions being the Welsh prince Gruffydd ap Llywelyn Fawr, who died whilst attempting to escape in 1244. It was in the latter half of the fifteenth century that the Tower first emerged in the public imagination as a site not only of incarceration but of covert execution. Neither the deposed Henry VI nor the disgraced George, Duke of Clarence emerged alive from its confines, and lurid tales were soon in circulation regarding the manner and agent of their deaths. In addition to setting a grim precedent in the use of the Tower, Edward had strengthened its

---

[69] John Leland, *The Itinerary of John Leland, Parts IV and V*, ed. Lucy Toulmin Smith (London: George Bell and Sons, 1908), 40.
[70] Stow, *Survey*, 2.122.
[71] John Strype, *Survey of London* (London, 1720), I.i.79.
[72] See the summary in Kristen Deiter, *The Tower of London in English Renaissance Drama: Icon of Opposition* (London: Routledge, 2008), 27–53.

Fig. 4.3. Charles of Orleans in the Tower of London, from Royal MS. 16 F.ii, f73^r. ©British Library.

defences, enclosing part of Tower Hill within an outer bulwark of brick.[73] The irony was not lost on observers when, not many weeks after Edward's death, the Tower became the prison and probably the last resting place of his two sons. In the contemporary "Lament of the Soul of Edward IV," the dead king is made to complain "not being ware who should it occupy/I made the Tower strong I wist not why."[74]

The Bulwark built by Edward, to which Richard III appointed a captain in 1484, not only strengthened the Tower as a fortress, it increased

[73] Anna Keay, *The Elizabethan Tower of London: The Haiward and Gascoyne Plan of 1597* (London: London Topographical Society, 2001), 27.
[74] "Lament of the Soul of Edward IV," in Anne F. Sutton and Livia Visser-Fuchs with R. A. Griffiths, *The Royal Funerals of the House of York at Windsor* (Bury St. Edmunds: Richard III Society, 2005), 83.

its separation from the city of London, acting as a visual screen as well as a further barrier to physical access. As with lesser medieval castles, the plan of the Tower and its environs required the visitor to progress through a series of layers, with differences of visual scope and perceptual frame closely linked to gradations of access and prestige.[75] We get a sense of this in the reports regarding the confinement of Edward IV's sons in 1483 (as discussed in Chapter 1). Whereas initially the boys were "seen shooting and playing in the garden," later, according to Mancini, they were withdrawn into the Tower proper, "and day by day began to be seen more rarely behind the bars and windows."[76] The gardens where the boys were seen to play most likely lay to the east of the Lanthorn Tower, which housed the royal apartments. A wide variety of people whose posts or business gave them access beyond the Bulwark and the Lion's Gate would have been able to view, if not participate in, the games in the garden. Only a small fraction of these witnesses would have had access to those inner areas into which the princes were subsequently withdrawn (probably the central bulk of the White Tower, though a number of other towers in the complex have been proposed).[77]

Over the course of the sixteenth century, the gardens where the princes had played became increasingly subdivided. In 1506, Henry VII threw a gallery from the Lanthorn Tower to the Salt Tower, dividing the gardens into the southern Privy (or Queen's) Garden and the northern Wardrobe (or King's) Garden.[78] Under Henry VIII, the expansion of the wardrobe in a long building from the Wardrobe Tower to the Broad Arrow Tower created a further barrier to the north. In the general refurbishment of the royal quarters in 1532, probably for the festivities surrounding the coronation of Anne Boleyn, the gardens were decorated with ornamental bridges. Thereafter, however, they were less often used by royalty than by prisoners, including Anne Boleyn herself a few years later. In the reign of Mary the Privy Garden was permitted to privileged prisoners such as Jane Grey and Elizabeth. In the course of the century it seems to have become overgrown; a map made early in Elizabeth's reign shows a disorderly grouping of trees (Fig. 4.7, later). Beyond the gardens, the proliferation of screens and subdivisions around the heart of the Tower included the addition of a new wall along the wharf, the first part of which, extending from Edward IV's bulwark, was under construction in

---

[75] Matthew Johnson, *Behind the Castle Gate: Medieval to Renaissance* (London: Routledge, 2002), 144–54 and *passim*.

[76] *GCL*, 234; Mancini, *Usurpation*, 93.

[77] On the various theories regarding the place of the princes' lodging, see Helen Maurer, "Bones in the Tower: A Discussion of Time, Place and Circumstance," *Ricardian* 8 (1990): 474–93.

[78] Details in this paragraph are drawn from Keay, *Elizabethan Tower of London*.

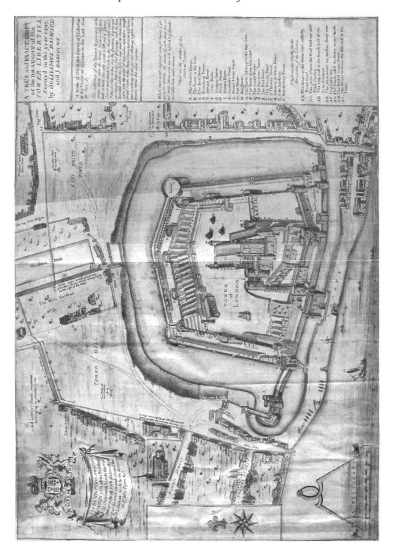

Fig. 4.4. Plan of the Tower of London in 1597 (1741 copy of the Haiward/ Gascoyne Plan). By permission of the Society of Antiquaries of London.

1592–94, as Shakespeare wrote his play. The plan of the Tower drawn up in 1597 (Fig. 4.4) shows this wall and also a "new brick wall" on Tower Hill. These walls were not designed primarily as fortifications. Rather, they added further layers to the onion, creating further potential distinctions of access both physical and visual.

As with a number of other English castles, alterations to the structure and appearance of the Tower of London in the Tudor era were undertaken with overt attention to symbolism and spectacle. Whereas, according to Matthew Johnson, the late medieval castle "was a living system, largely implicit," the sixteenth century castle embodied "a conscious attempt to invoke values seen as being under threat."[79] This is by no means to say that users and occupants of the Tower before the sixteenth century did not reflect on its long history and palimpsested layers of meaning; yet as the Tower's practical functions as a fortification and royal residence receded, its power and complexity as an icon inevitably grew. Already four hundred years old when Henry VII came to the throne, the Tower had the potential to signify continuity with the values and splendours of medieval monarchy. Henry, who made it his primary residence while in London, even staged a tournament there in 1501, watching the jousting from a seat in the ordnance house (a vantage-point suggestive of the gulf between old and new styles of warfare). The extensive renovations in 1532, including a decorative avenue of "crestes and coynes" on the approach to the Lion Gatehouse, prompt a vision of Henry VIII and Anne Boleyn self-consciously playing at being kings and queens of the old world.[80] The fact that, after Anne's coronation, the Tower never again served as a royal residence for any length of time suggests the limited viability of this kind of role-play. Instead, the Tower throughout the sixteenth century became ever more associated with the confinement and execution of enemies of the regime. This meaning, too, had roots in the past—specifically in the use made of the Tower by the Yorkist kings Edward IV and Richard III.[81]

Hundreds of prisoners were confined in the Tower over the course of the Tudor era, and dozens died there, by formal execution, malnourishment, or

[79] Johnson, *Behind the Castle Gate*, 133.
[80] Keay, *Elizabethan Tower of London*, 39, 28.
[81] The transformation in the Tower's reputation is complete in Thomas Heywood's *Second Part of Edward IV* (1599). Here the Tower is understood by all concerned to be nothing other than a prison, making Richard's proposal to house Edward V and his brother there obviously shocking. Brakenbury is made to state, with gross historical inaccuracy, that Edward IV never spent a night within its walls. Richard's attempt to insist that the Tower served as a "royal mansion" for "Caesar himself" hardly avails in the face of the fortress's fearsome reputation, a reputation which largely originates with the disappearance of the princes themselves. See Thomas Heywood, *The First and Second Parts of King Edward IV*, ed. Richard Rowland (Manchester: Manchester University Press, 2005), II.14.58, 62.

causes more mysterious. Over the same period, the reputation of the Tower as the site where Richard III had committed a series of murders by various ghastly means steadily grew. Even as the first two Tudor monarchs used the Tower to confine and destroy the last of their rivals to the throne (Edward, Earl of Warwick, in 1599; Edward, Duke of Buckingham, in 1521; Margaret, Countess of Salisbury, in 1537), historians and chroniclers wove increasingly gruesome and circumstantial accounts of the deaths of Clarence and the sons of Edward IV in the preceding era. It is a particularly grim irony that Thomas More and John Rastell, who between them wove the standard Tudor narrative of the death of the Princes in the Tower, would both die in the Tower themselves (More on the block in 1535, and Rastell of poverty in 1536). For some, perhaps including More, the recollection of Richard III's Tower crimes offered a means of obliquely condemning the deeds of the ruling dynasty; for others, probably a majority, the contrast with Richard III worked in the Tudors' favour, mitigating if not justifying the uses to which they put their royal fortress. In either case, the deeds attributed to Richard III were not only part of the Tower's history but materials out of which new meanings were assembled over the course of the sixteenth century.

The case of the "Bloody Tower" offers an apt illustration of this phenomenon. Well into the sixteenth century, this southern gatehouse went by the gentler name of the Garden Tower. Frequently used as a prison for particularly important detainees, its inmates in this period included Silken Thomas, the Earl of Kildare, John Dudley, Duke of Northumberland, and Thomas Cranmer.[82] It could have been with reference to any or all of these unfortunates that the gatehouse was rechristened the Bloody Tower—a name first recorded in the 1560s and by which it is designated on the 1597 plan. There is no reason to suppose that the new name involved a reference to Richard III, or that there was a pre-existing tradition of his nephews having been confined there. (The gardens in which they were seen playing in 1483 would have been those adjoining the royal lodgings rather than those by the Garden Tower, which were for the use of the Lieutenant.) Yet by the dawn of the seventeenth century and probably earlier, guides were pointing to the Bloody Tower as the site of the princes' confinement and death (a practice which continues to this day).[83] The Duke of Stettin-Pomerania recorded his 1602 visit to the "Bloody Tower,

---

[82] Keay, *Elizabethan Tower of London*, 38.
[83] See Deiter, *Tower of London*, 75–6. A century ago, however, a printed guide attributed the name not to the deaths of the princes but to the suicide of the Earl of Northumberland in 1585. This is impossible, as the name predates the Earl's death by at least two decades, but it is suggestive of how the name might shift in connotation and take on new associations over time. See W. J. Loftie, *Authorized Guide to the Tower of London* (London: HM Stationery Office, 1902), 7.

so named because of King Richardus having there most miserably put to death his two young cousins who were placed under his guardianship."[84] In 1604, the Tower Chaplain William Hubbocke welcomed the newly crowned James I, directing his attention to the structure which "our elders tearmed the bloody Tower, for the bloodshed, as they say, of those Infant Princes of Edward the fourth, whom Richard III of cursed memory (I shudder to mention it), savagely killed two togither at one time."[85]

How deeply Richard's sins seemed to have seeped into the very stones of the Tower can be gauged in another work of the early seventeenth century. Richard Niccols' *Sir Thomas Overburies Vision* (1616) records an imaginary visit to the Tower in the company of the ghost of Overbury, famously poisoned there in 1613. Entering by the gate in the Bloody Tower, the poet's thoughts turn immediately to the princes, and then to more recent deaths:

> as we entred in, the very sight
> Of that vast building, did my soule affright:
> There did I call to minde, how or'e that gate,
> The chamber was, where unremorsefull fate
> Did worke the falls of those two Princes dead,
> Who by their foes were smothered in their bed.
> And there I did behold that fatall greene,
> Where famous Essex woefull fall was seene:
> Where guiltie Suffolks guiltlesse daughter Jane
> The scaffold with her noble blood did staine:
> Where royall Anne her life to death resign'd,
> Whose wombe did beare the praise of women kind:
> And where the last Plantaginet did pore
> Her life out in her blood, where many more,
> Whom law did justly, or unjustly taxe,
> Past by the sentence of the bloody axe . . .[86]

Encountering the memory of the princes at the point of his entry into the Tower, Niccols makes their assassination the point of origin for a subsequent and ongoing legacy of violent death. Although the question of whether particular deaths were just or otherwise is one that Niccols declines to address, the primal crime of Richard III sets the tone and places all subsequent royal motives in doubt. Intriguingly, Richard is not named in this passage, only gestured to in the guise of "unremorsefull fate." This

---

[84] "Diary of the Journey of Philip Julius, Duke of Stettin-Pomerania, through England in the Year 1602," ed. Gottfried von Bülow and Wilfred Powell, *Transactions of the Royal Historical Society*, n.s. 6 (1892): 17.

[85] William Hubbocke, *An Oration Gratulatory to the High and Might James* (London, 1604), B1ᵛ.

[86] Richard Niccols, *Sir Thomas Overburies Vision* (London, 1616), 5–6.

piece of reticence increases the parallel between the fate of the princes and that of Overbury, whose death may or may not have had royal approval. The unnamed Richard III becomes a shadow for the unnameable James I. Later in the poem, Overbury's ghost broods obsessively over Richard's various royal victims, apostrophizing the Tower with a reminder of the horrors it has witnessed in times past:

> Those royall roses of Plantaginest,
> Which that white boare of Yorke, that bloody beast
> Hath rooted up, within those walls of thine,
> In death felt little paine compar'd to mine:
> Thou knowest that King, son to that kingly Knight,
> Beneath whose sword in Agincourts great fight,
> France fell upon her knees, thy flore did staine
> With his deare blood, by bloody Richard slaine:
> Thou didst looke on, when Clarence blood was shed,
> And didst behold, how hee poore Duke halfe dead,
> Yet bleeding fresh, in Malmesie-but was dround,
> Whose body sithence never could be found:
> Thou sawst when Tirrels bloody slaves did smother
> This kingdomes uncrownd King, and his young brother:
> Those princely babes of Yorke, thou heardst them crie,
> When they betwixt the sheets did strangled die . . .[87]

There is a certain sense of suffocation in the passage itself, which struggles to escape from the image of the murdered princes, only to stumble over more scenes of murder and then slip back into the strangling sheets. The fate of the "princely babes" spills out into other stories, leading to the surprising assertion that Clarence's body could never be found (in fact he is buried at Tewkesbury Abbey). The ghost goes on to recall the tradition that the Tower was built with a mortar of blood mingled with lime and sand: "Well may it be, thy walls with blood were built,/Where so much guiltlesse blood hath since bin spilt."[88] This deed is attributed to "the Conquerour," yet the reader would be forgiven for taking this is as yet another reference to Richard III. Imagined neither as a royal palace nor as a fortress, but simply as the site of endless unjust and agonizing deaths, the Tower in *Sir Thomas Overburies Vision* is the house that Richard built.

The passage quoted above contains several apparent echoes of Shakespeare's play, including the rooting boar (1.3.225), the sobriquet "bloody Richard" (3.4.103), and the precise manner of Clarence's death

---

[87] Niccols, *Sir Thomas Overburies Vision*, 13–14.
[88] Niccols, *Sir Thomas Overburies Vision*, 14.

(first stabbed then drowned).[89] More broadly, it draws its atmosphere from the group of dramas identified by Kristen Deiter as Tower plays, some two dozen works featuring the Tower as a site of violence, injustice and misrule.[90] Shakespeare's *Richard III* certainly merits inclusion in this category, with the Tower serving as setting for the crucial scenes in which Clarence and Hastings are dispatched; it provides the setting for the memorable entrance of Richard and Buckingham in rotten armour, and the backdrop for Elizabeth's foiled attempt to visit her sons. Throughout the play, characters orient themselves in physical and symbolic relation to the Tower.[91]

The Tower looms so large in *Richard III* in part because it is equally linked to two powerful and opposing tendencies in the play, one of which casts sharp doubt on the possibility of the past's survival, whilst the other insists on its inevitable resurgence. Both Prince Edward and his brother imagine the Tower as a site where the past lives on, be it in the form of angry ghosts (3.1.142–45) or of those oral traditions which, Edward imagines, would be capable of preserving the memory of Caesar's initial construction there for fifteen hundred years and more (3.1.75–78). Given that the princes depend for their very lives on the principles of continuity and orderly succession, it is not surprising that they should seek and find such meanings in the Tower. Yet, as Buckingham observes, if Caesar began the place, "succeeding ages have re-edified" (3.1.71) it, altering not only its appearance but its symbolism and its uses.[92] For the scheming Richard, the Tower is meaningful less as an icon of continuity than as a pragmatic site of rupture, where the links between the present and the past (in the form of potential heirs to the throne) can be "cut away" (3.7.146).

The most vivid and temporally complex evocation of the Tower in the play occurs as Elizabeth and her companions are turned back from their attempt to visit the princes there, a rebuff that coincides with the unwelcome news that Richard is to be crowned king. Elizabeth looks back and apostrophizes the Tower (just as the ghost of Overbury would in Niccols' poem, some years later):

> Stay: yet look back with me unto the Tower.—
> Pity, you ancient stones, those tender babes
> Whom envy hath immured within your walls.
> Rough cradle for such little pretty ones,
> Rude ragged nurse, old sullen playfellow

---

[89]   Hall, Holinshed and the *Mirror for Magistrates* all record drowning in a butt of malmsey as the sole cause of Clarence's death.
[90]   Deiter, *Tower of London*, 1–2.
[91]   See Sheen, *Shakespeare and the Institution of Theatre*, 67.
[92]   See Deiter, *Tower of London*, 150.

> For tender princes: use my babies well.
> So foolish sorrow bids your stones farewell.
> (4.1.96.1–96.7)

The curiosity of this short speech lies in its determined development and compulsive restatement of a single contrast, between the age and roughness of the Tower on the one hand and the youth and tenderness of the princes on the other (ancient stones/tender babes; rough cradle/little pretty ones; rude ragged nurse/tender princes; old sullen playfellow/babies). The Tower's battered antiquity, its very pastness, is represented here as an active force. The princes, imagined as newborn babies, may embody the present, but by that same measure they are understood to be utterly fragile and without agency. It is the Tower to whom the Queen attributes a vigorous and variable agency whereby it will "use" her babes for good or ill. For the powerless princes, it as if their present were already a kind of past, or as if they were dead. As the opposing images accumulate, rough antiquity seems on the verge of overwhelming and swallowing up the defenceless present. By the final line it has effectively done so, for although the Queen restates the contrast yet once more (stones/foolish sorrow), the princes have disappeared, their place supplied by their mother's despair.

This last of the Tower scenes is arguably the hinge of the play, marking the point at which Richard's fortunes have reached their height. (Even in the ensuing scene, following the coronation, his break with Buckingham hints at the ebbing of his power.) The scene also marks a pivotal point in the depiction of the Tower. Earlier in the play, the Tower has featured primarily as a destination and the site of violent action. Hereafter, it will be associated mainly with retrospection and regret, as in Tyrrell's account of the deaths of the princes, and in the appearance of the ghosts at Bosworth. Where Richard himself would make the Tower the emblem of his majesty—"The King's name is a tower of strength" (4.3.12)—the Ghost of Henry VI makes it rather the emblem of his crimes: "Think on the Tower and me" (5.5.80). The inescapable association of Richard with the Tower helps explain why he does not need to be present in the scene marking the highpoint of his success. When Elizabeth instructs Dorset to "Hie thee from this slaughterhouse" (4.1.43) and "live with Richmond from the reach of hell" (4.1.42), she conflates the Tower, the kingdom, and the King.

There are more than twenty-five references to the Tower in *Richard III*, not counting stage directions. Its dominance of the imagined urban landscape is almost entire. By contrast, there are two references to the Guildhall, two to St Paul's, and two to Baynard's Castle, the Yorkist base in the city. Slightly ahead of these, though hardly rivalling the Tower, is

Crosby Place, which Richard refers to on three occasions as his London residence. Both the Lady Anne and the murderers of Clarence are instructed to "repair to Crosby Place" (1.2.200, 1.3.343), and Richard makes clear that he and Buckingham will stay there on the eve of the council at the Tower, telling Catesby to seek them "at Crosby House" (3.1.187).[93] Always mentioned in conjunction with the development or fruition of one or another of Richard's vicious schemes, the place takes on a sinister significance, like the centre of a spider's web. The source for these lines is a short passage from More's *History*, as incorporated in Holinshed: "by little and little all folke withdrew from the Tower, and drew unto Crosbies in Bishops gates street, where the protector kept his houshold. The protector had the resort, the king in maner desolate."[94]

Crosby Place was among the newest and most fashionable mansions of late fifteenth-century London. Situated on Bishopsgate Street, facing the corner of Threadneedle Street, the building was constructed in the late 1460s on land leased from the nuns of the adjoining St Helen's Priory.[95] The great hall was distinguished by its magnificent arched roof, with a central boss adorned with the arms of the first owner, Sir John Crosby (Fig. 4.5). A prosperous wool tradesman and warden of the Grocers Company, Crosby had served as Sheriff in 1470 and was knighted by Edward IV for his service in repelling Thomas Neville's assault on London. Yet, as John Stow remarks, Crosby "deceased in the yeare 1475 so short a time enjoyed hee that his large and sumptuous building."[96] The building may have been occupied for a few years by his widow, but by the spring of 1483 it was in the possession of Richard of Gloucester, who made it his base in the months leading up to his coronation. Although a tradition of unknown date suggests that a civic deputation came to Crosby Place to offer the crown to the Protector, most early sources agree that this event took place rather at Baynard's Castle. There is no reason to believe that Richard's association with Crosby Place lasted more than a handful of months in the spring and early summer of 1483.

Like other London houses of similar standing, Crosby Place played host to a range of notables in the early Tudor era, usually for short periods. It was a palace more frequently used as a temporary base or for a grand occasion than as a permanent dwelling. On Candlemas Eve in 1496, an

[93] In F, the lines in 1.2 and 3.1 refer to "Crosby House"; Q in all instances has "Crosby Place."
[94] Holinshed, 721.
[95] This account of the history of Crosby Place in the fifteenth and sixteenth centuries is drawn primarily from Charles W. F. Goss, *Crosby Hall: A Chapter in the History of London* (London: Crowther & Goodman, 1908). See also Philip Norman and W. D. Caroe, *Crosby Place* (London: Committee for the Survey of the Memorials of Greater London, 1908).
[96] Stow, *Survey*, I.173.

GREAT HALL, CROSBY PLACE, BISHOPSGATE.[3]—From a drawing by J. W. Archer.

Fig. 4.5. Crosby Hall in the nineteenth century. © Look and Learn.

embassy from the Duke of Burgundy was lodged there, as was Casimir of Brandenburg when he arrived in 1502 to extend the Emperor Maximilian's sympathies on the death of the Queen. At that time the lease was held by Sir Bartholomew Reed, who celebrated his mayoralty with a memorable banquet for "more than 100 persons of great estate."[97] The leasehold came subsequently to another Lord Mayor, Sir John Rest, from whom it passed in 1519 to Sir Thomas More. In 1524, More in turn sold the lease to his friend Antonio Bonvisi for £200.

To us, there is an inescapable irony in the fact that the author of the *History of Richard III* should have lived in Richard's own house, even if he did not live there while writing it. The irony might not have struck contemporary observers quite so forcibly; there were, after all, a strictly limited number of suitably prestigious mansions in London, and they changed

[97] Stow, *Survey*, I.305. Stow puzzles over the tradition that the banquet was held at Goldsmiths' Hall, which could not have accommodated so many guests. As Norman and Caroe observe, the celebrated dinner is much more likely to have taken place at Crosby Place.

occupants frequently. Yet, having drawn attention to Crosby Place as the site where "the Protector had the resort," More might well have paused to reflect on the meaning of his own tenancy there. In the years around 1515, when he wrote his *History*, More had been near the outset of his career as a royal councillor and politician, with the anxieties recorded in *Utopia*. By the early 1520s he was fully enmeshed in the service of the king and Wolsey, who had recommended him to the speakership of the House of Commons. More now "had the resort" of courtiers and ambitious men seeking access and preferment. To take possession of the house of Richard III at such a moment might have been an irony to his taste. Yet his deeper identification is likely to have been with the loyal Sir John Crosby, whose arms stared down at him from the ceiling and the walls of the hall. Having served as undersheriff and played a role in quelling a small revolt, in the form of Ill May Day (1517), More may have looked on the valiant Crosby as a role model.

Crosby Place remained in the possession of Antonio Bonvisi for most of the next 35 years. The son of Italian merchants already established in England in the fifteenth century, Bonvisi now dwelt in the house of the king whose anti-immigrant legislation had likely caused his parents grief. Upon the dissolution of the Priory of St Helen's he became the outright owner. Bonvisi remained a traditionalist in religion, and for a period the house seems to have served as a centre for Catholics, as well as for the growing cult of Thomas More. In 1547, as Edward VI came to the throne, Bonvisi leased the house to William Roper, More's son-in-law and biographer, and William Rastell, More's nephew and first editor of his works. Yet Roper, Rastell, and Bonvisi himself were all soon to flee to the continent. Edward VI seized Crosby Place in 1550, and though under Mary the property was restored to Bonvisi, he seems to have died abroad. In the first decade of Elizabeth's reign Crosby Place was in the hands of Bonvisi's friend German Cioll, another merchant of foreign origin and Catholic sympathies; it then fell to the merchant adventurer William Bond and his heirs, who possessed it until 1594. Over these years it again played the role of host to various embassies, including the Duke of Alva in 1569, and the Danish ambassador Henry Ramelius, who arrived in 1586. The burial of the French ambassador's secretary at St Helen's Bishopsgate, now a parish church, in 1592, suggests that the French embassy was in residence around the time that Shakespeare wrote his play.[98]

What would Crosby Place have meant to Shakespeare in the early 1590s? The answer—either next to nothing or a good deal—rests on when he first took up residence in the little parish of St Helen's Bishop-

---

[98] Goss, *Crosby Hall*, 80.

sgate. Shakespeare was certainly there by 1596, when he was assessed for payment of a subsidy of 5s, a sum which a year later remained unpaid.[99] The location was ideal for an actor–dramatist, offering easy access to the clutch of playhouses beyond Bishopsgate on the northeastern side of the city. When the Chamberlain's Men moved their operations to the Globe Theatre on the south bank in 1599, Shakespeare too relocated to Southwark. Although the supposition that Shakespeare was already a denizen of St Helen's by *c.*1592 can only rest on the circumstantial evidence of the prominence given to Crosby Place in *Richard III*, there is no firm reason to think he was not dwelling in Bishopsgate by this date.[100] Living in sight of the sumptuous fifteenth-century hall, as well as worshipping in St Helen's amid the imposing monuments of former occupants of Crosby Place, would have confronted Shakespeare, as it does us, with several questions. To what extent does a sense of place serve as a bridge across time, creating a bond of common experience between the denizens of different centuries? To what extent was the London Shakespeare knew the same city it had been in 1483?

4.3 WALKING IN THE CITY

The historian who sets out to write the biography of a building like the Tower of London or an institution like the College of Arms has certain advantages. However elusive or scanty the source material, there is at least something there, a solid kernel around which the inquiry may centre. Whatever radical transformations they may have undergone in terms of social function and significance, it is possible to speak intelligibly of the College or the Tower in the fifteenth century, the sixteenth, and the twenty-first. But what of the history of urban experience, or of everyday life? To what extent are habits of movement and perception—favouring a particular route, associating a building or a meeting of roads with a funny or a tragic story, quickening one's pace when passing through a certain district—passed on from one generation to another? If Shakespeare's play, with its close attention to everyday social experience, forces this question upon us, it may also provide some ways of beginning to answer it.

---

[99] Schoenbaum, *William Shakespeare: A Compact Documentary Life*, 221–2.

[100] Most accounts of Shakespeare's life suggest that he moved to Bishopsgate from the poorer extramural district of Shoreditch at some point in the mid-1590s. In fact, there is no evidence for this earlier address beyond John Aubrey's statement that Shakespeare, at an unspecified point in his career, "lived in Shoreditch." Aubrey does not provide a date, and there is no reason to suppose that Shakespeare came to Bishopsgate later than 1592. See Park Honan, *Shakespeare: A Life* (Oxford: Oxford University Press, 1999), 121–2.

It might seem peculiar to think of *Richard III*, with its unparalleled focus on one highly atypical personality, as a play about everyday life. Yet in the long central movement of the play (from the death of Edward IV in Act 2, scene 2 to the coronation of Richard III in Act 4, scene 2), both the experience of the common citizens and the quotidian preoccupations of the nobility come under close scrutiny. Three scenes depict the response of the London populace to, successively, the death of Edward IV (2.3), the execution of Hastings (3.6), and Richard's usurpation of the throne (3.7)—a sequence that traces a repressive movement from dialogue to soliloquy to perfect silence. Other scenes in this central movement explore how members of the elite, Hastings chief among them, experience and articulate the pleasures of the everyday. Lords and commoners alike cling to a language rooted in common knowledge and shared norms, even as events take a form radically different from anything they have known.

The encounter of two citizens on a London street at the opening of Act 2, scene 3 signals a widening of the dramatic lens beyond the claustrophobic worlds of court and prison that have dominated up until this point. These are not the first commoners to feature in the play, as the murderers of Clarence certainly belong to that category, but unlike the murderers they are not discovered at the margins of the courtly world, but rather at the heart of a world they know, and in which they embody the norm. The scene begins with the First Citizen's commenting on a departure from custom seen in his neighbour's unusually hurried pace: "Whither away so fast?" (2.3.1) The Second Citizen's non-committal response, "I scarcely know myself," drives the First to a more direct prompt: "Hear you the news abroad?" Here it transpires that the Second has indeed heard the news: "the king is dead" (2.3.2–4).[101] The Second Citizen's initial evasiveness suggests that he does not want to broach the subject himself, without assurance that his neighbour has already been informed. Such reticence is understandable when we recall that to "compass or imagine" the death of the king was high treason; should the news prove false, the disseminators of such rumours could find themselves in serious peril.[102] The Third Citizen who soon enters to the other two shows fewer qualms, immediately raising the matter of "good King Edward's death" (2.3.8), though still in the form of a question about the news rather than as a statement of fact.

---

[101] Here I follow the assignment of lines in Q; in F, it is the Second Citizen who asks the First if he has heard the news. The difference is not greatly material, but Q seems best to capture the tensions surrounding the communication of this kind of news.

[102] See Rebecca Lemon, *Treason by Words: Literature, Law, and Rebellion in Shakespeare's England* (Ithaca: Cornell University Press, 2007), 5–10.

With the news of the king's death established, the citizens move to prognostications of the future, with the First and Second wavering between hope and gloom whilst the Third steadily foretells the worst. They draw on a range of available sources of knowledge, including historical precedent ("So stood the state when Henry the Sixth/Was crowned" [2.3.16–17]), insight into the personalities of the great ("O full of danger is the Duke of Gloucester" [2.3.25]) and above all a store of common proverbs and truisms: "When clouds are seen, wise men put on their cloaks;/When great leaves fall, then winter is at hand" (2.3.32–33). The question hanging over them is whether everyday understandings, rooted in common experiences and a grasp of shared norms, are sufficient to interpret a situation which fundamentally disrupts those norms. The final proverb invoked by the Third Citizen is somewhat different from those that precede it, in that it assigns a role to the supernatural.

> Before the days of change still is it so.
> By a divine instinct men's minds mistrust
> Ensuing danger, as by proof we see
> The water swell before a boist'rous storm. (2.3.41–44)

Here the citizen paraphrases Thomas More's comments on the unsettled mood of Londoners before Richard's seizure of power:

> began there here & there about, some maner of muttering amonge the people, as though al should not long be wel, though they neither wist what thei feared nor wherfore: were it that before such great thinges, mens hartes of a secret instinct of nature misgiveth them. As the sea without wind swelleth of himself somtime before a tempest . . .[103]

Putting this observation in the mouth of a member of the muttering populace introduces a slightly eerie reflexiveness; where More represents popular disquiet as a phenomenon that those learned in the ways of nature can interpret, the Third Citizen looks inward and foretells the worst on the basis of his own and his comrades' unaccountable anxiety. The scene ends with the citizens exiting together, upon learning that each of them has been called before the Justices. Though the nature of the summons is unclear, it adds to the sense of foreboding.

Did Londoners exchange intelligence and anxieties this way in 1483? Chance has in fact preserved a taste of the "news" circulating in the city in the wake of the death of Edward IV. The wool merchant George Cely

---

[103] More, *History*, 44.

recorded some of the rumours flying in the middle weeks of June, between the death of Hastings and the coronation of Richard III:

> There is great rumour [uproar] in the realm. The Scots has done great in England. Chamberlain [Lord Hastings] is deceased in trouble. The chancellor is disproved and not content. The Bishop of Ely is dead.
>
>   If the king, God save his life, were deceased, the Duke of Gloucester were in any peril, if my lord prince, wh[ich] God defend, were troubled, if my lord of Northumberland were dead or greatly troubled, if my lord Howard were slain.[104]

Although most of the rumours recorded by Cely were false, or at least premature, the care and caution with which he recorded them, even in obvious haste, is illuminating. The first items of news, some true and some not, are recorded as indicative statements. Cely feels no compunction in writing "the Bishop of Ely is dead" (though in fact John Morton, arrested alongside Hastings, had many years to live). Yet with much the same caution displayed by the Second Citizen in Shakespeare's play, Cely can record the rumoured death of Edward V only in the subjunctive mood, and with a loyal protest of "God save his life"; the rumour that young Richard of York is "troubled" likewise prompts a plea of "God defend." Cely's compulsion to record what he has just been told is clearly matched by anxiety about its being read. So much is evident in the peculiar phrase "Chamberlain is deceased in trouble." Hastings' treachery having been publicly proclaimed, there was certainly no mystery about the manner of his death, and rumours were undoubtedly rife about the Protector's real motives in ordering his execution. Shakespeare captured very much the same anxious reticence in his depiction of the Scrivener, who cannot say what he and all else know about the Chamberlain's downfall: "Bad is the world, and all will come to naught,/When such ill dealing must be seen in thought" (3.6.13–14).

   The central movement of the play also provides glimpses of the pleasures and obligations of everyday life for those at the top of the social order. The scene in which Lord Hastings embarks on his fatal journey to the Tower is particularly stuffed with observations about the quality of the day and the passage of time. Woken early by Stanley's messenger, Hastings asks "What is't o'clock?" and, on learning that it is "Upon the stroke of four," demands "Cannot my Lord Stanley sleep these tedious nights?" (3.2.2–3) Hastings' mild petulance at being woken is understandable, but

---

[104] Alison Hanham, *The Celys and their World: An English Merchant Family of the Fifteenth Century* (Cambridge: Cambridge University Press, 1985), 287. Cely attributes these reports to "Monsieur Saint Johns," that is, Sir John Weston, Prior of the Knights of St John.

also suggests that this is a man who enjoys the comforts of his bed. At what would have been the hour of sunrise in June, many of his fellow Londoners, including his own servants, would already have been awake.[105] (As the somewhat remorseless Thomas Tusser observed in *Five Hundreth Points of Good Husbandry*, "In winter at five a clock, servant arise,/in Sommer at fower, is ever the guise."[106]) Later in *Richard III*, Richmond will call himself a "tardy sluggard" (5.5.179) for rising only "upon the stroke of four" (5.5.189) when the village cock has already crowed twice.

Hastings also describes his next visitor, Catesby, as "early stirring" (3.2.33), but Catesby is nonetheless welcome for the news he bears of the deaths of Rivers and his kinsmen at Pomfret. Hastings' delight in the downfall of his enemies is heightened by the fact that their deaths are to occur "this same very day" (3.2.46). Their miserable deaths coincide with the day he is currently enjoying, and the contrast adds immeasurably to his enjoyment. He repeats the news incorrigibly to everyone he encounters. "Today the lords you talked of are beheaded" (3.2.87). "This day those enemies are put to death" (3.2.99). Hasting also interprets the pleasure he experiences in the moment as a token of happiness to come, declaring "I shall laugh at this a twelve month hence" (3.2.54) and be avenged on others "ere a fortnight make me older" (3.2.57). Here his logic mirrors that of the Third Citizen, who predicts future trouble for the realm on the basis of his own inner disquiet. It is left to Stanley to observe, fruitlessly, the obvious fallacy in such reasoning.

> The lords at Pomfret, when they rode from London,
> Were jocund, and supposed their states were sure,
> And they indeed had no cause to mistrust;
> But yet you see how soon the day o'ercast. (3.2.79–82)

Though Stanley detects in the fate of the Woodvilles an instance of the turning of Fortune's Wheel, Hastings fails to grasp how the lesson might apply to him. His happiness is not rooted simply in the fact of his good

---

[105] Whereas More has Stanley's messenger arrive at midnight, the play shifts the event to the early morning a few minutes after sunrise. Before the correction of the calendar, 13 June, the date given by More, would have been no more than one or two days from the summer solstice. According to J. D.'s *A triple almanacke for the yeere of our Lorde God 1591*, the sunrise in London took place on that date between 3:45 and 3:46 in the morning (B4ʳ). Today, of course, clocks in London are set ahead for British Summer Time, and sunrise in mid-June takes place a few minutes before 5am. Hastings' grumpiness is understandable if he is thought to have been called from the arms of Mistress Shore—but unlike sources including More, *The Mirror for Magistrates*, and *The True Tragedy of Richard III*, Shakespeare does not specify her presence in his bed.

[106] Thomas Tusser, *Five Hundreth Points of Good Husbandry* (London, 1573), 76ᵛ. See Craig Koslofsky, *Evening's Empire: A History of the Night in Early Modern Europe* (Cambridge: Cambridge University Press, 2011), 202.

fortune as contrasted with others' misery, but in the pleasing texture of everyday life, sprinkled with inconsequential encounters which provide an opportunity for gossip and small acts of self-promotion. It is a pleasure for him to let slip to Buckingham that he will not leave the Tower with him after the Council, "for I stay dinner there" (3.2.116). The anticipated enjoyment of the meal itself mingles with the satisfaction of being high in the Protector's favour. In this scene we are presented with one rather unattractive man's version of a perfect day—or, at least, a perfect morning.

Part of what makes the sudden arrest and execution of Hastings in the Tower scene so chilling is the way that horror blossoms out of the normal. On his first entrance, Richard dwells on the same pleasant themes that have preoccupied Hastings in the previous scene, namely sleeping and eating. He has been "long a sleeper" (3.4.23) at Crosby Place and has apparently missed his breakfast: "My Lord of Ely, when I was last in Holborn/I saw good strawberries in your garden there./I do beseech you send for some of them" (3.4.31–33). It is little wonder that Hastings concludes that the Lord Protector is in good spirits and "with no man here . . . offended" (3.4.56), for he evinces precisely those attitudes and appetites which for Hastings accompany a sense of bonhomie. The sudden closing of the trap, when Richard re-enters the chamber, constitutes not only the betrayal of an ally but a betrayal of the comradeship of the everyday. The Protector's insistence that he will not dine before Hastings dies perversely reinstates commensality as the handmaiden of violence rather than a refuge from it. "The Duke would be at dinner . . . he longs to see your head" (3.4.94–95).

Shakespeare's chief source for the events and atmosphere of Hastings' final day is Thomas More. Here as elsewhere in the *History*, More's narrative is peppered with apparently mundane events, chance remarks, and observations drawn from daily life. If these slices of the everyday lend verisimilitude, they can also serve—like the words exchanged between Potter and Mistlebrook, remembered by More's father—to shed light on the unfolding shape of events. In the Hall text of More's *History*, Hastings meets his pursuivant "upon the very tower wharfe so nere the place where his hed was of so sone after as a man might wel cast a balle," a comment that plays out in miniature the transition from everyday pleasure to fatal horror witnessed in Shakespeare's play.[107] More believes in portents, yet he is well aware of how difficult it is to sort out a true omen from the cluster of chance occurrences which make up ordinary experience. Thus he recounts the ominous stumbling of Hastings' horse on the journey to the Tower, commenting "which thing albeit eche man wote wel daily happeneth to

---

[107] Hall, Edward V, xv[r].

them to whom no such mischaunce is toward: yet hath it ben of an olde
rite & cutome, observed as a token often times notably foregoing some
great misfortune."[108]

Not only in the Hastings scenes but throughout the long central movement, Shakespeare emulates More's attentiveness to everyday life and the
common perspective. More's influence is felt well beyond those passages
adapted directly from the *History*. Shakespeare does not depict the conversations of the common citizens coming away from Baynard's Castle,
but the relevant passage in More—in which the citizens compare what
they have seen to "Kynges games, as it were stage playes, and for the more
part plaied upon scafoldes"—sheds light not only on *Richard III* but on
the spectacle of monarchy and power in Shakespeare's theatre generally.[109]
Yet there is some difference between their uses of the everyday. For More,
apparently mundane incidents typically offer an opportunity to draw
morals (in Hastings' case, that we are closer to death than we think), and
he has a fondness for placing some of his own more flippant or irreverent
observations in the mouths of commoners. In Shakespeare's version it is
Richard who displays the quickest and most incisive wit, and who likes
to pull the rug from under pompous ceremonials. It is Richard too who
knows best how to exploit assumptions grounded in ordinary experience
to achieve his extraordinary ends.

The setting of More's *History* is the London of his childhood, and he
writes of it with the familiarity of a native, noting not only major landmarks like the Tower and Crosby Place but obscure addresses in "reddecrosse strete without crepulgate." Where Polydore Vergil is content to
report that Buckingham addressed the citizens at the Guildhall, More tells
us that he did so "in the east ende of the hall where the maire kepeth the
hustinges."[110] Though Shakespeare's play rarely delivers the same degree
of detail, its urban topography is derived almost entirely from More.[111]
Writing some eighty years later, Shakespeare was following in More's
footsteps, and not only in a textual sense. In many respects, Shakespeare's
London was still the city More—and, indeed, Richard III—had known.
From Crosby Place to the Tower Wharf, from Baynard's Castle to Red
Cross Street, there is not a site or street mentioned in the *History* that
did not survive up to and beyond the turn of the century. Although

---

[108] More, *History*, 50. Hall's text, as elsewhere, is at once more definite and more awkward
on the subject of portents: "yet hath it bene as an olde evyll token observed as a goyng
toward mischiefe." Hall, Edward V, xv[r].
[109] More, *History*, 81.   [110] More, *History*, 9, 69.
[111] The only reference to a building or landmark which cannot be traced directly or indi-
rectly to More is the puzzling mention of "Whitefriars" as the destination of Henry VI's
corpse, discussed in Chapter 1.

population growth, demographic change, and religious upheaval had initiated sweeping transformations, walking in the city still brought the late Elizabethan Londoner into conscious or unconscious communion with a palimpsest of past lives.

We can explore the palimpsestic layers of London further by retracing in the imagination one of the routes suggested by More's *History* as it might have been experienced by a walker in the early 1590s.[112] Whether or not Shakespeare ever engaged in such a self-conscious exercise, he can hardly have avoided walking in the paths of the Protector during his residence in Bishopsgate. From Crosby Place to the Tower of London—passing along Bishopsgate Street, Gracechurch Street, Fenchurch Street, and Tower Street—is a short walk of fifteen or twenty minutes (see Fig. 4.6). This is a way Richard of Gloucester must have ridden or trod a good many times in the spring of 1483 (including on the morning of Hastings' execution), and which Thomas More must have travelled often enough during his residence at Crosby Place. There can be little doubt that Shakespeare made the same journey, in segments or in its entirety, both before and after the writing of *Richard III*. In the 1590s, as in the 1480s and 1520s, following this route meant traversing a densely symbolic and presignificant terrain. On their daily journeys down streets such as these, the inhabitants of London negotiated an intricate network of material, spiritual, and mnemonic petitions and prompts.[113]

Many of the spectacles, social practices, and shared memories that gave shape to urban experience in the late fifteenth century would have pressed themselves no less insistently on the Elizabethan traveller. Crosby Place itself remained a powerful symbol of the grandeur to which an assiduous

---

[112] Hastings' last journey to the Tower would be ideal for this purpose, except that More does not specify the starting point. In fact, from his dwelling at Beaumont Place on Paul's Wharf, Hastings is more likely to have travelled by river than on a "footcloth horse" (3.4.84). Going by land would have involved traversing the whole of Thames Street, the dockside thoroughfare devoted, as Mancini observed, to the sale of "distasteful goods" (*Usurpation*, 103). It is not clear whether either More or Shakespeare knew where Hastings was living in 1483.

[113] On walking in the late medieval city, see Paul Strohm, "Three London Itineraries: Aesthetic Purity and the Composing Process," in *Theory and the Premodern Text* (Minneapolis, MN: University of Minnesota Press, 2000), 3–19. In Strohm's argument, "the peculiarity of medieval space involves the extent to which it is already symbolically organized by the meaning-making activities of the many generations that have traversed it . . . [A]s a typical late medieval city, London incorporated a noticeably durable and complicated set of *pre-significations*" (4). Recent work by geographers and psychogeographers on the relationship between walking, memory, and identity cries out for historicization. My imagined walk through the streets of London is indebted to James Sidaway's analysis of a walk in contemporary Plymouth, which unravels "how the repercussions of war and death are folded into the textures of an everyday urban fabric"; Sidaway, "Shadows on the Path: Negotiating Geopolitics on an Urban Section of Britain's South West Coast Path," *Environment and Planning D: Society and Space* 27 (2009): 1091–16, esp. 1092.

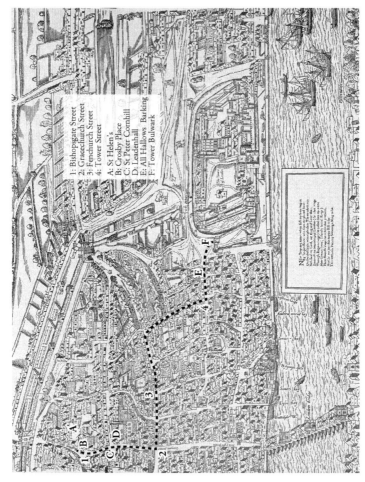

Fig. 4.6. "Agas" map of London, c.1561 (detail), showing the route from Crosby Place, Bishopsgate Street, to the Tower of London. © City of London.

tradesman could aspire; if no longer the tallest house in London, it was a predecessor and prototype for the "diverse faire and large builded houses for Marchants" which lined this part of Bishopsgate Street by the end of the sixteenth century.[114] The grandest of these, Gresham House, stood directly across the road. The tombs of the fifteenth-century merchant and mayor Sir John Crosby (*d.*1476) and the Elizabethan entrepreneur Sir Thomas Gresham (*d.*1579) lay similarly close to one another in St Helen's Bishopsgate, where Shakespeare is presumed to have worshipped.

Going south on Bishopsgate Street, towards the heart of the city, the traveller would soon reach the crossing with Cornhill Street, whose well-supplied shops had astounded Dominic Mancini in 1483: "they are not encumbered with merchandise only at the entrance; but in the inmost quarters there are spacious depositories, where the goods are heaped up, stowed and packed away as honey may be seen in cells."[115] Here stood the Leadenhall, the city's great granary and meat market, which had grown steadily in size and privileges since its foundation in the fourteenth century. Yet this district was not given over solely to Mammon. Facing Leadenhall across Bishopsgate Street stood an equally powerful symbol of London's heritage, St Peter Cornhill. Supposed to have been founded as early as the second century AD as the seat of Britain's first archbishop, the church had been largely rebuilt under Edward IV.[116] Its ceiling and walls were adorned with the coats of arms of citizens who had contributed to the rebuilding, including, unsurprisingly, Sir John Crosby. Here, in a manoeuvre familiar to Elizabethan Londoners, the late fifteenth century elided itself with British antiquity, inscribing itself into narratives of national and spiritual origin.

South of Cornhill, where Bishopsgate becomes Gracechurch Street, the steps of our traveller would begin to coincide with one of the city's great ceremonial routes—that of the coronation procession from the Tower to Westminster.[117] Shakespeare's older contemporaries would retain clear memories of Elizabeth I's progress along this route in 1559, and perhaps those of Edward and Mary some years before. Few indeed would be able to recall the coronation procession of Anne Boleyn, with its magnificent pageants and resentful lookers-on. Further back, the processions of Richard III and Anne Neville in 1483, Henry VII in 1485, and Elizabeth of York in 1487 had long since passed beyond living memory, yet they were nonetheless borne forward in time as part of the accumulated meaning of the ceremony, recalled and in a sense re-enacted each time a new monarch

---

[114] Stow, *Survey,* I.173.
[115] Mancini, *Usurpation,* 103.   [116] Stow, *Survey,* I.194.
[117] Lawrence Manley, *Literature and Culture in Early Modern London* (Cambridge: Cambridge University Press, 1995), 223–5.

walked the old way. When Elizabeth came to Gracechurch Street on her progress, the pageant featured figures representing her grandparents and her parents as well as herself; thus both the audience and the new queen were reminded of predecessors who had walked this way before her at intervals over the last seventy-four years.[118]

Turning left into Fenchurch Street, the sixteenth-century traveller was following a route saturated with memories of civic as well as royal ceremonies. This was a leg of the famous Midsummer Watch—an annual custom which had been growing in importance from the later fifteenth century, and which had reached a height of magnificence around the time that Thomas More was living at Crosby Place. On two nights in the month of June, many hundreds of armed Londoners would process with cresset lights and wax torches along the established route; the Watch also featured elaborate pageants (the trappings for which, Stow records, were kept in the Leadenhall).[119] The splendour of the Midsummer Watch had declined after the 1540s, giving way as the main event in the civic calendar to the Lord Mayor's Show, whose route lay further east.[120] Yet under Elizabeth a standing watch still took place along parts of the old route at midsummer, and on at least a few occasions a marching watch.[121]

A right turn along any one of several lanes would bring the traveller to Tower Street. It is here, with the great fortress already looming ahead in clear view, that More has Hastings pause to pass the time of day with a priest. At the end of Tower Street stood the church of All Hallows Barking and the adjoining chapel of St Mary, where the heart of Richard I was reputedly interred, and to which Richard III had shown distinct favour (possibly out of respect for his namesake, as well as for a thirteenth-century tradition promising victory over the Welsh and Scots to any king who supported the chapel).[122] Beyond lay the liberties of the Tower of London. The traveller might glance north to Tower Hill, whose permanent scaffold had done so much grim service since it was installed under Edward IV, before turning south to approach Edward's other innovation, the gun-topped Bulwark, through which lay the entrance to the Tower itself.

This short account of a short walk in the city has emphasized the continuities between the experience of late-fifteenth-century Londoners and

[118] Hunt, *Drama of Coronation*, 165. On coronation progresses before Elizabeth's, see also Anne Begor Lancashire, *London Civic Theatre: City Drama and Pageantry from Roman Times to 1558* (Cambridge: Cambridge University Press, 2002).

[119] Stow, *Survey*, I.159.   [120] Lancashire, *London Civic Theatre*, 153–70.

[121] See Ian Archer, "The Nostalgia of John Stow," in *The Theatrical City: Culture, Theatre and Politics in London, 1576–1649*, ed. David L. Smith, Richard Strier, and David Bevington (Cambridge: Cambridge University Press, 1995), 23.

[122] See Horrox, "Richard III and Allhallows Barking by the Tower"; Nigel Saul, *The Three Richards: Richard I, Richard II and Richard III* (London: Hambledon Continuum, 2005), 106–7.

their late-sixteenth-century successors. This is not to deny that there had been enormous changes as well; among the most immediately apparent of these were the architectural and social consequences of the Reformation. With the dissolution of the monasteries, the church of St Helen's Bishopsgate had lost the distinctive double nave which had allowed the nuns to worship apart from the parishioners, whilst the main priory buildings had been transformed into the Leatherseller's Hall. The chapel of St Mary at All Hallows Barking, where Richard III had endowed a college, had been pulled down under Edward VI, and in its place stood a newly constructed storehouse for the use of merchants. At St Peter Cornhill, John Stow noted that "monuments of the dead in this Church [are] defaced."[123] The same regretful phrase recurs throughout Stow's *Survey of London*. Whilst the assault on parish memorials—including the destruction of images, razing of inscriptions, and theft of memorial brasses—may look like an attempt to efface the past altogether, its effect on worshippers in churches like St Peter Cornhill was probably more complex.[124] Defaced monuments—even the pale shadows on the walls showing where brasses had been removed—might serve as memorials or mnemonic devices in themselves, commemorating the event of iconoclasm as well as the dead. We should not assume that Reformation-era vandalism created an insuperable gulf between the living and their late-medieval predecessors. In certain ways it may have brought them closer together, as the long dead became associated with comparatively recent events that remained fresh in collective memory.

The extraordinary growth in London's population over the sixteenth century had an equally profound impact on the experience of walking or dwelling in the city. The suburbs beyond the walls had greatly expanded, and offered a range of attractions; Shakespeare himself probably chose a home in Bishopsgate Ward because of the easy access it offered to playhouses such as The Theatre and The Curtain in the northern suburbs. Yet the growth of the suburbs did little or nothing to ease overcrowding within the walls, where many of the larger houses and monastic buildings had been divided into cramped tenements for the poor. Even Edward IV's Bulwark had become the backbone of an Elizabethan shanty town, its defensive capability much reduced by the shops and houses with which it was now entirely encrusted, some of them "inhabited by Strangers manie of them being very poore and disordred persons."[125]

---

[123] Stow, *Survey*, 1.195. Stow also notes the loss of the church's library, which had been visited and commended by John Leland (1.194).

[124] Robert Whiting, *The Reformation of the English Parish Church* (Cambridge: Cambridge University Press, 2010), 224–6.

[125] Sir John Peyton (Lieutenant of the Tower 1597–1603), quoted in Keay, *Elizabethan Tower of London*, 27.

Almost any route through late sixteenth-century London would expose the same overcrowding and the same improvisational use of the built heritage. Shakespeare's city was bursting at the seams, reinventing itself at a dizzying pace, and often apparently at war with its past. But it was still in a meaningful sense the city known to the fifteenth-century citizen.[126] As John Schofield observes, "In 1600, London was a medieval city on the edge of spectacular expansion in the century to come."[127] Although there were some genuinely novel constructions reflecting new customs and practices (the suburban theatres, the Royal Exchange), change in London was mostly driven by the adaptation and reuse of pre-existing buildings, institutions, and routes. The measure of how much the city had changed was thus also a measure of how much it had not. It was a city whose streets and rhythms Richard III would have recognized, and one which also remembered him in aspects of its everyday life—nowhere more so, perhaps, than in the involuntary shudder that many would have experienced on Little Eastcheap or Tower Street, as the Tower loomed up before them.

Under normal circumstances, Londoners remembered Richard III and his era largely through habitual behaviours and customary acts which either dated to the fifteenth century or were assumed to do so. On occasion, however, the palimpsested past could rise to the surface with a sudden relevance and urgency. One such moment came on a day in June 1595, when the master of Crosby Place came to the Tower of London with a drawn sword. The master in this case was Sir John Spencer, Lord Mayor of London, who had purchased and renovated the house to provide a suitably grand residence for his mayoralty. Spencer was widely despised in the city for his rumoured miserliness and corruption, his arrogance, and his autocratic habits. In the unruly early summer of 1595, rioters had even set up a gallows outside Crosby Place. Then, on the evening of 29 June, more than 1,000 apprentices rioted on Tower Hill.[128] The date was the feast of Sts Peter and Paul, on the eve of which it had once been customary to hold the Midsummer Watch. Some of the rioters, as well as the Lord Mayor who arrived with his sheriffs to restore order, might well have participated in a muster at Leadenhall and a standing watch the previous

[126] As Helen Cooper observes, imagining how Chaucer's contemporaries might respond if transported into Shakespeare's London: "They would have been shocked . . . But they would not have got lost." Cooper, *Shakespeare and the Medieval World* (London: Methuen Drama, 2010), 11–12.
[127] John Schofield, "The Topography and Buildings of London, ca. 1600," in Lena Cowen Orlin, ed., *Material London, ca. 1600* (Philadelphia: University of Pennsylvania Press, 2000), 319.
[128] See Ian W. Archer, *The Pursuit of Stability: Social Relations in Elizabethan London* (Cambridge: Cambridge University Press, 1991), 1–9; John Stow, *The Abridgement of the English Chronicle* (London, 1618), 400–1.

night, and some on both sides must have followed the traditional route of the marching watch to arrive at the Tower. The date may, in different ways, have seemed propitious for both sides, for the meaning of the Midsummer Watch had always hovered between a celebration of the Lord Mayor and a celebration of the armed urban citizenry.[129]

The Lord Mayor's entry with his sword of authority borne before him provoked an unanticipated response from the Lieutenant of the Tower. Though the Tower warders had done nothing to quell the riot, they now sallied forth in arms to confront the Mayor and condemn him for letting his sword be held aloft within the Tower Liberties. The Mayor's sword-bearer was, it was alleged, severely beaten, and Spencer was forced to withdraw whilst the Tower warders rescued certain of the rioters who had been taken into custody. It was a humiliation for the Mayor, but it proved no better for the Lieutenant, Sir Michael Blount. Complaints from the city authorities about his actions provoked an investigation which led in November to the discovery of Blount's participation in a bizarre plot to use the Tower to place the Earl of Hertford on the throne after the Queen's death.[130] Blount found himself stripped of office and imprisoned in the fortress which had previously been his domain. He escaped the harsher penalty meted out to five of the apprentices who had participated in the riot; convicted of treason, they were hanged, drawn, and quartered on Tower Hill in July.

For the second time in just over one hundred years, the tenant of Crosby Place had come to the Tower in June, and sudden violence had erupted between those who should have been allies in upholding order. There had been charges of treason, executions, and allegations of conspiracy to alter the succession to the throne. Though the events of 1595 were not in any obvious sense a repetition of the events of 1483, they were composed out of many of the same materials, with actors on every side of the conflict aiming to exploit presignificant landmarks, institutions, itineraries, and customs (as well as the memory of customs recently abrogated). This was a moment when Londoners of all classes and sympathies might, in Benjamin's phrase, seize hold of a memory flashing up in a moment of danger, turning to the story of Richard III to make narrative and moral

---

[129] See Sheila Lindenbaum, "Ceremony and Oligarchy: The London Midsummer Watch," in *City and Spectacle in Medieval Europe*, ed. Barbara A. Hanawalt and Kathryn L. Reyerson (Minneapolis, MN: University of Minnesota Press, 1994), 171–88.

[130] R. B. Manning, "The Prosecution of Sir Michael Blount, Lieutenant of the Tower of London, 1595," *Historical Research* 57(1984): 216–24; the article reproduces in an appendix Edward Coke's account of the events on Tower Hill, drawn up in the case against Blount.

sense of the occurrences on Tower Hill.[131] To some, Spencer might have seemed a type of Richard of Gloucester, the tyrannical tenant of Crosby Place contemptuous of the popular will. To others he may have looked more like the Lord Mayor of 1483, hopelessly overawed and outmanoeuvred by the power vested in the Tower, a power plotting its own treachery.

Whatever connections Londoners may have been tempted to draw between these two moments in time, they did not need to turn to the chronicles or remembered lore. The events, personalities, and places of 1483 were already vividly present in the imaginations of many, thanks in no small measure to Shakespeare's play. Here we catch a glimpse of the potential for reciprocity between the theatre and the urban landscape, each in their different ways serving as mnemonic devices, each capable of giving prompts to the other. Just as Londoners may have drawn on *Richard III* to interpret the events on Tower Hill, so audiences would inevitably bring to the theatre their associations with the Tower and Crosby Place—associations which only became more complex and arguably still more relevant to the matter of the play following the absurd and tragic occurrences of 1595.

---

[131] Walter Benjamin, "Theses on the Philosophy of History," in *Illuminations*, ed. Hannah Arendt, trans. Harry Zorn (London: Pimlico, 1999), 247.

5

"Every Tale Condemns me for a Villain"

Stories

Alone and in despair on the last night of his life, Shakespeare's Richard complains of how "every tongue brings in a several tale,/And every tale condemns me for a villain" (5.5.148–49). The tongues he speaks of belong to his own tormented conscience, yet his words could as well apply to the literary traditions that sprang up around the historical Richard III almost immediately after his death, gathering in variety and complexity over the ensuing century. Over the course of the Tudor era, Richard's reign and personality would be explored in ballads and beast fables, riddles and prophecies, chronicles and histories, verse complaints, paradoxes and plays in both Latin and English. It is quite true that practically every surviving text from this remarkable range of genres condemns Richard for a villain; yet they remain fascinatingly "several," both in their accounts of his character and career and in their understanding of the relationship between his era and the present in which they were composed. Before Shakespeare placed what would prove an all but indelible stamp on the character of Richard III, he was represented variously as a raving, animalistic tyrant and as a smoothly dissembling Machiavel, as a hell-spawned scourge and as a merely mediocre monarch who made the error of alienating the regional aristocracy. For some writers, the relevance of the Yorkist past consisted strictly in its capacity to furnish examples of misfortune and misrule; for others, late-fifteenth-century conflicts and their consequences still provided the key to understanding the Tudor present.

Like the bodies, memories, objects, and institutions explored in preceding chapters, the literary tradition I examine here can be tracked from the days immediately following Bosworth down to Shakespeare's era, and beyond. There is, of course, an important distinction. The songs, poems and plays considered in this chapter are not in any literal sense remains of the period 1483–85. They are (at best) the vehicles whereby certain traces of that experience were borne into the future. As a consequence, they are not prey to the continual winnowing suffered by other species of historical trace across the course of the sixteenth century. Instead, from decade to decade, the literary works dealing with the reign of Richard III grow in number, complexity, generic variety, and length. As objects, monuments, and memories disappear, stories rush in to take their place. This should not necessarily lead to the conclusion that, with the passage of the years, the grain of Ricardian time surviving in the tradition becomes an ever smaller proportion of the whole. Up until at least the end of the sixteenth century, the expansion of the literary tradition was not the result of fiction-making alone, still less of "Tudor propaganda," but of an ever more urgent dialogue with the surviving remnants of a receding epoch.

Much of the earliest poetry about Richard III is quite literally beastly. The last Plantagenet enters the literary tradition not as a malevolent hunchback but as a marauding boar. The derogatory identification of the King with his crest was a tradition already established in his reign, as witnessed in the couplet attributed to the rebel William Collingbourne: "The Catte, the Ratte, and Lovell our dogge/Rulyth all Englande under a hogge."[1] In Dafydd Llwyd's *cywydd* on the outcome of Bosworth, Richard is referred to by a wide range of animal names, including the heraldic "little boar" (*trymyniad bach*) the prophetic "mole" (*gwadd*) and the more straightforwardly derogatory "caterpillar," "ape," and "dog" (the last, as seen in Chapter 1, described as dying in a ditch).[2] Bernard Andre dwells on the significance of Richard's crest in *Les Douze Triomphes de Henry VII*, in which the deeds of the first Tudor king are compared to the twelve labours of Hercules (indeed, the source of the far-fetched conceit probably lies in Henry's triumph over a boar). Andre wonders why Richard should have chosen to associate himself with such a low animal:

> Now he had taken for his device
> The great hog [*le grant pourreau*], which is a very foul animal;
> And I know not why he took it,
> Unless it be God who prompts the heart.[3]

Beyond identifying Richard as a particularly vile beast, Andre finds it difficult to say anything of substance about the late king or the manner

---

[1] Fabyan, ccxxix[v]. On the historical Collingbourne and the verses attributed to him, see Kenneth Hillier, "William Colyngbourne," in *Richard III: Crown and People,* ed. J. Petre (London: Richard III Society, 1985), 103–6; Kenneth Hillier, Peter Normark, Peter W. Hammond, "Colyngbourne's Rhyme," in the same volume, 107–8. The poem is discussed further below, in relation to the *Mirror for Magistrates.*

[2] Andrew Breeze, "A Welsh Poem of 1485 on Richard III," *Ricardian* 18 (2008): 46–53.

[3] Bernard Andre, *Les Douze Triomphes de Henry VII*, in James Gairdner, ed., *Memorials of Henry VII* (London: Longman, 1858), 312 (with the original French on 138).

whereby he first gained and subsequently lost the crown; tellingly, although he mentions the killing of the nephews as an example of Richard's "blunted feelings," he avoids the question of whether Edward V was a true heir to the throne. We find less reticence—and more sympathy for the claims of the house of York—in the poem *Tres sunt Ricardi,* where Richard again features as a bloody boar. Probably composed in the later 1480s, the poem develops the thesis that the three Richards who had reigned in medieval England had led dissimilar lives but suffered similar (violent) deaths.

> The third, after exhausting the ample mines of wealth that Edward had accumulated, was not content until he suppressed his brother's offspring, and outlawed their supporters; at last, two years after taking violent possession of the kingdom, he met these same supporters in battle and now has lost his savage life and his crown. In the year 1485 [*Anno milleno C. quarter quarter atque viceno/ Adiuncto quinto*], on the 22nd day of *sextilis* (that is, August), the teeth of the boar were blunted, and the red rose, the avenger of the white [*vindex albe rosa rubra*], shines upon the world.[4]

With its invocation of the feuding roses and its slightly fiddly fascination with dates, the poem bears comparison with the epitaph for Richard III recorded by Thomas Wriothesley and others (as discussed in Chapter 1). Unlike the epitaph, however, *Tres sunt Ricardi* does not hesitate to identify Richard III as a legitimate king with a place in the timeline of monarchical history: "There were three Richards, Kings of England." This opening gesture undercuts contemporary efforts to deny the legitimacy of his reign. A stronger indication of Yorkist sympathy is the surprising insistence that the proscribed partisans (*auxiliaries*) of the murdered princes (Yorkists, not Lancastrians, in other words) defeated the usurper at Bosworth. The Red Rose, which in the epitaph is said to have reclaimed its honours from the White, is here subservient even in victory, in that its blossoming is reimagined as a service to its erstwhile enemy.

Though they deal with the immediate past rather than the future, these early Latin, French, and Welsh verses on the fall of Richard III bear many similarities to the prophetic poetry of the period. Prophecy was indeed Dafydd Llwyd's most accustomed mode, and he had been predicting the victory of the "dragon" Harri Tudur and his kin (and with it, the restoration of the lineage of Cadwaladr) long before the possibility had crossed more than a very few English minds.[5] Yet in England, too, prophecies

---

[4] Julian M. Luxford, "*Tres sunt Ricardi* and the Crowland Chronicle," *Ricardian* 18 (2008): [21–30], 25. As Luxford notes, the poem, long known only through the Crowland Chronicle, is also found in an independent version in Eton College MS 213.

[5] See See Gruffydd Aled Williams, "The Bardic Road to Bosworth," *Transactions of the Honourable Society of Cymmrodorion* (1986): 7–31; Philip Schwyzer, *Literature, Nationalism*

revolving around beasts, numbers, names and initials were rife in this era. The infamous forecast that a certain "G" would seize the throne from the sons of "E," first recorded by John Rous in 1486, is representative of the type. Another which seems to have circulated in the spring of 1483 declares that in that year the "Bull" (Edward IV) shall depart and "E" will be crowned by "trew R" (an initial that, conveniently, permitted retailers of the prophecy to hedge their bets between Richard and Rivers).[6] Yet another prophecy—apparently from the same period—hinges, like *Tres sunt Ricardi*, on the identity of names:

> Then rise up, Richard, son of Richard,
> And bless the happy reign
> Thrice happy who sees this time to come
> When England shall know rest and peace again.[7]

Although each of these prophecies purports to foretell the future from the vantage point of the period before Richard's usurpation, in each case the earliest surviving text dates from after his death. Prophecies and obituaries, then, circulated alongside one another and drew upon many of the same conventions, in spite of their different temporal bearings.

5.1 THE STANLEY TRADITION

A familiar parade of beasts and flowers spills across the stanzas of *The Rose of Englande*—the first substantial poem in English on the subject of Richard's overthrow, and the first in a remarkable series of works on this theme written to advance the glory of the Stanley family. The poem imagines England as a rose garden invaded by "a beast men call a bore."[8] The boar's attempt to bury the branches of the rose "under a clodd of clay" (19) are foiled by the Eagle (Lord Stanley) who bears one branch away and helps it to escape over the seas. The rescued rose subsequently re-enters the land at Milford Haven and with the assistance of the Eagle and other heraldic animals the white boar is slain. Fairly brief at 128 lines, the poem is nonetheless long enough to expose the incapacity of the pro-

---

and Memory in Early Modern England and Wales (Cambridge: Cambridge University Press, 2004), 16–20.

  [6] Lesley Coote and Tim Thornton, "Richard, Son of Richard: Richard III and Political Prophecy," *Historical Research* 71 (2000): 323. The prophecy occurs in BL MS Lansdowne 762, datable to the later 1520s.

  [7] Coote and Thornton, "Richard, Son of Richard," 326.

  [8] *The Rose of Englande* in *Bishop Percy's Folio Manuscript: Ballads and Romances*, ed. John W. Hales (London: N. Trübner, 1868), 3.187–94, l. 13. Further line references in text.

phetic lexicon of beasts and flowers to deal with events of any complexity. Although it is easy and poignant to describe a boar uprooting defenceless roses, it is harder to see how a rose can defeat a boar in a pitched fight. The inevitable consequence (possibly not unwelcome to the Stanley-favouring poet) is that Henry Tudor is reduced to the status of a wall-flower on Bosworth Field. In a central section, the poet drops the cumbersome floral imagery altogether in order to recount the magnanimity shown by "Erle Richmond" to the bailiff of Shrewsbury.

Written within a decade of the events it describes, *The Rose of Englande* seems determined to predict if not preempt the content of the historical record. Twice the poet insists that "the Chronicles of this will not Lye" (66, 88). Yet the poem's allegorical truisms are not easily translated into conventional historical narrative. Difficulties are posed from the outset by the motif of the national garden, over which a "rose soe redd" (7) presides as "crowned King" (11) until the entrance of the predatory boar. Whereas the chronology of succession would indicate Edward IV if not the uncrowned Edward V, the colour of the rose points rather to the last Lancastrian, Henry VI. The burying of the rose's branches would, in that case, refer primarily to the death of Henry's son Edward at Tewkesbury as well as to the exile of Henry Tudor (and not to the Princes in the Tower, as modern readers of the poem are apt to infer). Edward IV and his sons are effectively expunged from the poem's version of history (if they are not understood to be subsumed within the criminal person of the boar). Such unlikely allegorical manoeuvres call to mind Ernest Renan's dictum that nations are united as much by what their populations forget as by what they remember.[9] In commemorating the boar's assault on the true Lancastrian lineage, *The Rose of Englande* invites us to forget both the many years of civil conflict and the period of mostly peaceful Yorkist rule that preceded the usurpation of Richard III.

Bosworth Feilde—another poem composed in the Stanley milieu within ten years of the event—adopts a strikingly different attitude to national memory. In its opening stanzas the ballad refers to Henry VII's victory as a very recent event, calling upon its auditors to join in saying "welcome Henery, right-wise king!"[10] Yet the writer is troubled by the possibility that the new king's subjects are already beginning to take the comparative

---

[9] On Renan and remembering to forget, see Benedict Anderson, *Imagined Communities*, new edition (London: Verso, 2006), 203–7.

[10] *Bosworth Feilde*, in *Bishop Percy's Folio Manuscript*, 3.236, ll. 8, 16, 24. Further line references in text.

peace of his reign for granted, forgetting the horrors from which he has delivered them:

> how had wee need to remember, & to our minds call
> how England is transported miraculouslye
> to see the great Mischeefe that hath befall
> sith the Martyrdome of the holy King Henery!
> how many young lords have been deemed to dye
> young innocents that never did sinn! (17–22)

Although the last line above might just be read as an allusion to the death of the princes, the poem offers no account of Richard's seizure of the throne, nor is he condemned as a usurper. His sole error—one that will prove fatal—is to hearken to "wicked councell" (77) advising him to destroy the overmighty Lord Stanley. By the same token, Henry Tudor's chief virtue is his availability to abet the Stanleys in their feud with the king.[11]

Bosworth Feilde marks the first attempt after 1485 to portray the fallen Richard as a real—if bloody-minded—human personality, and the poem appears to draw on first-hand recollections of the monarch and his mannerisms. To those who had known him, the observation that "King Richard smiled small" (193) when he heard of Stanley's defiance may have rung true. The King's subsequent vaunt may also have jogged memories: "I wold I had the great turke against me to ffight/or Prester John in his armor bright/the Sowdan of Surrey with them to bringe!" (196–98) Richard had said as much to the German visitor Nikolas von Poppelau in 1484: "I wish my kingdom lay upon the confines of Turkey; with my own people alone and without the help of other princes I should like to drive away not only the Turks, but all my foes."[12]

Like Thomas More's *History*, written some two decades later, *Bosworth Feilde* insists that its sources lie in the oral testimony of those who were there: "with tounge I have heard it told" (33); "men said that day that dyd him see" (471). The account of the battle itself contains a good deal of specific detail apparently based on eye-witness reports, and modern scholarship has recognized the poem as a valuable if problematic source for the events of 1485.[13] Even the poem's insistence on Richard's massive firepower ("7 scores Sarpendines" and "as many bombards" [489–91]), which once seemed wholly fanciful, has been partly borne out by the recent archaeological survey of the field. Yet this circumstantial detail supports and is subordinated to an ideological fiction, whereby the victory is due entirely to the Stanley

---

[11] See Robert W. Barrett, Jr., *Against All England: Regional Identity and Cheshire Writing, 1195–1656* (Notre Dame, IN: University of Notre Dame Press, 2009), 177–80.
[12] Quoted in Paul Murray Kendall, *Richard III* (New York: W. W. Norton, 1996), 388
[13] Charles Ross, *Richard III* (Berkeley, CA: University of California Press, 1983), 235–7.

affinity, and Henry is crowned on the field largely owing to the generous impulse of Lord Stanley, to whom the crown is initially "delivered":

> the crowne of gold that was bright,
> to the Lord stanley delivered itt bee.
> anon to King Henery delivered it hee,
> the crowne that was soe delivered to him,
> & said, "methinke ye are best worthye
> to weare the crowne and be our King." (635–40)[14]

Both *The Rose of Englande* and *Bosworth Feilde* can be assigned with relative confidence to a date before 1495, for although both poems emphasize the role of Sir William Stanley in bringing Henry VII to the throne, they show no awareness of Sir William's execution for treason ten years later. This might be taken as a tactful (or pointed) omission, but there is a clear contrast between these poems and works produced in the Stanley *milieu* in the early sixteenth century, which tend to offer a more positive portrait of Richard III whilst highlighting the tensions between the Stanleys and his successors. In *Scotish Feilde*, composed in the wake of the battle of Flodden, Richard is remembered as "a king noble" and a "riche lorde, in his bright armour," fighting (in implicit contrast to Henry Tudor) "full fuerslye his formen amonge."[15] The point of this recollection is brought home forcefully in *Flodden Feilde*, a ballad on the same theme, in which the Earl Stanley answers a rebuke from Henry VIII with the blunt retort "whoe brought in your father at Melforde haven?"[16]

The reconsideration of Richard's reign and its end is taken a step or two further in *Ladye Bessiye*, a long poem emphasizing the perspective and personal initiative of Elizabeth of York. Richard's reputed sins are by no means glossed over. As Bessy complains, she has good reasons to wish to be "wroken" on her uncle:

> "he did my brethren to the death on a day
> in their bedd where they did lye";

> "he drowned them both in a pipe of wine;
> itt was dole to heare and see!
> & he wold have put away his Queene
> for to have lyen by my bodye!"[17]

---

[14] See Barrett, *Against All England*, 178.

[15] *Scotish Feilde*, in *Scotish Feilde and Flodden Feilde: Two Flodden Poems*, ed. Ian F. Baird (New York: Garland, 1982), 1–2, ll. 28–30.

[16] *Flodden Feilde*, in *Scotish Feilde and Flodden Feilde*, ed. Baird (New York: Garland, 1982), 23, l. 33.

[17] *Ladye Bessiye*, in *Bishop Percy's Folio Manuscript*, 3.322, ll. 27–32. Further line references in text.

Bessy wins the initially reluctant Lord Stanley to her cause by reminding him of another of Richard's misdeeds, the execution of the good Duke of Buckingham, who "crowned King Richard of England free" (39), and "was as great with King Richard as now are yee" (36). Yet for all his manifest faults as a relative and a ruler, Richard comes across in his first appearance in the poem as a surprisingly affable and conscientious king. Unaware of the conspiracy being spun around him, he spontaneously proposes to Stanley that they divide England and rule together as "2 ffellowes" (488), and goes on to stress his care for the poor.

> Whilest I am King & weare the Crowne,
> I will be cheeffe of the poore Comynaltye.
> Tax nay mise I will make none,
> in no Cuntry ffar nor neare;
> ffor if by their goods I shold plucke them downe,
> for me they will ffaight ffull ffainteouslye.
> There is no riches to me soe rich
> as is the pore Comynaltye. (491–98)

Whether sincere or not, the King's promise of good rule comes too late to save him from retribution for his past crimes (and for the additional offence of holding young George Stanley hostage before Bosworth, a piece of wickedness emphasized in all the Stanley poems). Richard has his brains knocked out on the battlefield, and Bessy greets his naked corpse with "merry cheere" (1057): "how likest thou they slaying of my brethren twaine?/ . . . /welcome, gentle unckle home!" (1059, 1062) Yet the poem does not conclude on this note. Instead it goes on to relate how, after helping to "sett the crowne" (1073) upon the heads of the new King and Queen, Sir William Stanley "came under a cloud" (1075) and was seen no more. The irony of Bessy's original warning regarding the fate of Buckingham—that a man who begins by crowning a monarch may end up being beheaded by him—is brought home. The fault of ingratitude turns out not to be Richard's alone. Even the concluding prayer for "the poore cominaltye" (1082) is double-edged, reminding the reader or auditor of Richard's concern for the commons and his determination to refrain from harsh taxation—a policy certainly not shared by his immediate successors. Without diminishing the valour of the Stanleys, *Ladye Bessiye* manages to suggest that both they and the commons have paid a high price for the glory reaped on Bosworth Field.

Although Bessy's surprising literacy is a source of wonder in the poem, the goodhearted Lord Stanley has no truck with pen and paper.[18] The

---

[18] In a scene of intended or unintended comedy, Stanley arranges a private meeting with Bessy where pen and paper are to be provided, only to fall into despair when he realizes that

poem seems to be written in his spirit, for it does not admit reliance on any kind of textual source. There is no hint of influence from More or Rastell, with their various elaborate theories as to the manner of the princes' deaths. Rather, Bessy's assertion that Richard drowned her brothers "in a pipe of wine" reflects popular (oral) tradition.[19] In the early sixteenth century the Stanleys and their dependents did not require written histories to help them recall the events of 1483–85; a good many of the participants were still living, and trophies like Richard's tent hangings at Knowsley bore material witness to Stanley prowess on the battlefield. Yet, even at Lathom and Knowsley, the past could not be kept indefinitely fresh. The death of Edward Stanley, Baron Monteagle (*c.*1460–1523), the last surviving son of Thomas Stanley, first Earl of Derby, may have marked a turning point in the family's ability to access direct recollections of the Yorkist era. When Edward Stanley's own son Thomas, Bishop of Sodor and Man, came to write the family's history in verse in the early 1560s, he had no choice but to consult the chronicles, however distasteful he sometimes found their matter.[20] Not unlike Bishop Stanley's shorter poem on the death of the princes (discussed in Chapter 1), *The Stanley Poem* both grounds itself upon and kicks against the textual tradition.

Whatever faults are attributed to Richard in the earlier Stanley ballads and songs, none of them makes him a figure of supernatural wickedness, and none includes mention of any physical deformity. In *The Stanley Poem*, however, the influence of Thomas More's twisted tyrant is clearly evident:

> Thus lo! Richard the usurper was made king
> A mercilesse manne and a monstrous thinge,
> A wretched body and a tyrante in harte,
> A devill in his deedes, deformed in ech parte . . .[21]

The revelation at the point of his coronation of the King's surpassing monstrosity comes as a surprise to the reader of the poem, for Richard has already featured prominently for several hundred lines as the Lord

---

no clerk is available to write for them. Bessy saves the day by revealing herself to be "a clarke ffull good" (96).

[19] As *GCL* records, "some said they were drownyd in malvesy, and some said they were stykkid with a venymous pocion" (236–7).

[20] The *Stanley Poem* has for centuries been attributed to Bishop Stanley, along with the briefer verses on the death of the princes discussed in Chapter 1. Stanley's authorship has recently been questioned by Andrew Taylor, who argues that the obsequious tone of certain passages would be more appropriate to a humbler personage, such as the minstrel Richard Sheale; see Taylor, *The Songs and Travels of a Tudor Minstrel: Richard Sheale of Tamworth* (Woodbridge: York Medieval Press, 2012), 66–8.

[21] *The Stanley Poem*, in *Palatine Anthology: A Collection of Ancient Poems Relating to Lancashire and Cheshire*, ed. J. O. Halliwell-Phillipps (London: C & J Adlard, 1850), 248.

Stanley's chief rival in the north country. Richard Duke of Gloucester is an unpleasant character to be sure, "a man of greate ire and of litle grace" who earns his brother's sharp reproofs for his repeated attempts to undermine the noble Stanley. At this stage, however, he is a second-rate and mildly comic villain, whose personal cowardice ("He never bod field ne fray but when he was slayne") and that of his men (running "dickduckfarte for feare") make him no match for his adversary.[22] The sudden transition from mockery of a bungling rascal to excoriation of a hellish usurper is thus a little awkward.

Intriguingly, the chronicle-derived blazon of Richard's monstrosity comes immediately on the heels of a passage denouncing the chronicles for their errors and omissions.

> I think ould true chronicles be gone there wayes,
> Stollen or purloyned from suppressed abbayes;
> Croniclers to flattery have such respecte,
> They set in trifles, and noble actes neglecte.[23]

This outburst against the chronicles results from their failure to give Lord Stanley full due for the capture of Berwick in 1482. In the poem's account, Richard promises to join Stanley in laying siege to Berwick, only to abandon him spitefully without doing battle. Stanley and his followers then singlehandedly march on Edinburgh, receive the submission of the King of Scots, and subjugate Berwick on their way home. "Thus Barwicke became Englishe by therle Standelay,/There is no true man that thereto dare say nay."[24] Unfortunately, as Bishop Stanley knew, Hall's chronicle contradicted this account, recording rather that Richard had left Stanley at Berwick in order to march on Edinburgh. Having forced terms of peace upon the Scots, he required them to give up the town of Berwick to Stanley without a fight. According to Hall, "kyng Edward hys brother … muche commended bothe hys valiaunt manhode, and also hys prudent pollicie, in conveyng hys busines, bothe to hys awne purpose, and also to the profit of the Realme."[25] There is thus a direct and inescapable conflict between Stanley family tradition and the content of the chronicle.[26]

Bishop Stanley sees Hall's error as symptomatic of a more general failure of historians to praise the deeds of the regional aristocracy, whilst wasting time on the trifling affairs of Londoners. When he looks to the chronicles for evidence of the deeds of Lancashire and Cheshire men, he finds

---

[22] *Stanley Poem*, 239, 234.   [23] *Stanley Poem*, 246.
[24] *Stanley Poem*, 246.   [25] Hall, Edward IV, CCxlvi^v.
[26] For an overview of the representation of the Stanleys and their deeds in Tudor chronicles, see Catherine Grace Canino, *Shakespeare and the Nobility: The Negotiation of Lineage* (Cambridge: Cambridge University Press, 2007), 180–6.

instead matter such as this: "such time William Horne was maior of London,/Sheriffes William Fynkle and John Rymyngton./A bushel of wheat
vi.ᵈ, iii.ᵈ bay-salt/ . . . These be high matters to put in memory!"[27] The
specific target of the poet's derision is Robert Fabyan's chronicle, which
indeed records that William Horne was mayor in 1487–88, with John
Fenkyll and William Remyngton sheriffs; the prices for wheat and bay-salt
are those for 1493–94, when Fabyan himself served as sheriff.[28] Citing
passages from Fabyan whilst pursuing an argument with Hall, *The Stanley
Poem* lumps the Tudor chroniclers together as uniformly biased, blinkered,
pedestrian, and Protestant. Yet for all this, it is no longer possible to do
without them. Even though the poet can occasionally cite oral testimony
regarding events of the later fifteenth century (as when he quotes from
witnesses to the entertainment of Henry VII at Lathom Hall in 1495),
such traditions no longer bear sufficient authority to stand alone.[29] Even
as he fulminates against the chronicles, Bishop Stanley acknowledges that
his and all other accounts of the reign of Richard III must henceforth be
written in their shadow.

5.2 SPECTRAL COMPLAINTS

The composition of *The Stanley Poem* is almost exactly contemporary with
the publication of a much more influential verse history of late medieval
England, *A Mirror for Magistrates*. In the pages of the *Mirror*, a succession of deceased monarchs, lords, and rebels rise as if from the grave to
recount their untimely falls and give warning to the living. The first edition, suppressed by the Marian authorities and eventually published under
Elizabeth in 1559, covers the period from the reign of Richard II to that
of Edward IV, concluding with the laments of George, Duke of Clarence
and Edward himself.[30] (The latter poem was not a new work, but rather a
version of the "Lament of the Soul of Edward IV," dating from the 1480s
and attributed, almost certainly wrongly, to John Skelton). In 1563 a sec-

---

[27] *Stanley Poem*, 246–7. Some seventy years later, John Taylor would mock the same
homely concern with commodity prices in the recollections of old Tom Parr (see Chapter 2).
Unlike *Ladye Bessiye,* the *Stanley Poem* has little interest in the doings or needs of "the poore
cominaltye."

[28] *Fabyan's Cronycle* (London, 1533), ccxxxʳ⁻ᵛ.

[29] "I hard men say that were of his trayne/They thought they should never se such faire
again"; *Stanley Poem*, 266.

[30] On the murky prehistory of the *Mirror*, from the suppressed *Memorial of suche Princes*
of 1554 to the printed text of 1559, see Scott Lucas, *A Mirror for Magistrates and the Politics
of the English Reformation* (Amherst: University of Massachusetts Press, 2009), 18–66.

ond edition appeared, carrying the spectral story forward into the reigns of Edward V and Richard III. *The Seconde Parte of the Mirrour for Magistrates* includes poems by a range of authors dealing with the sad fates of Rivers, Hastings, Buckingham, William Collingbourne, Richard III, and Jane Shore. Apart from a couple of stray tragedies tacked on at the end of the volume, the *Seconde Parte* is entirely devoted to the deeds of Richard, his rivals, and his victims in the years 1483–85.

Most of the authors associated with the *Mirror* and *The Seconde Parte*—including William Baldwin, George Ferrers, Thomas Chaloner, and Thomas Churchyard—had been born in the first quarter of the sixteenth century, at a time when many of the older generation retained memories of the reigns of Edward IV and Richard III. It is thus hardly surprising that several of the ghosts in the *Mirror* observe that their lives remain a matter of memory and oral tradition (or "brute"). As Mistress Shore, who died around the time her author Thomas Churchyard was born, asks: "who can forget a thing thus done so late?"[31] Yet it is difficult to pinpoint passages in which the authors rely on inherited memory or oral testimony. Rather, in the prose passages that link the verse laments, the reader is repeatedly reminded that the matter of the poems derives from reputable historians, including Fabyan, Hall, and More.[32]

Reliance on the chronicles is, however, no guarantee against controversy. So much becomes clear when, in the narrative frame, Baldwin and his collaborators meet to hear and judge the poems slated for inclusion in *The Seconde Parte*. As soon as the first of these, that of Rivers, has been read out, one of the assembly expresses alarm at the differences between the sources. Fabyan terms the Marquess of Dorset the Queen's brother, and has him escorting Edward V from Ludlow, whilst More and Hall call him the Queen's son, and have him take sanctuary with his mother.

> This disagreynge of wryters is a great hinderaunce of the truthe, & no small cumbrauns to such as be diligent readers, besides the harme that may happen in succession of herytages. It were therefore a wurthye and a good dede for the nobilytie, to cause al the recordes to be sought, & a true and perfecte chronicle thereout to be written. (267)

This looks like a nod to the great Elizabethan project that would eventually bear fruit in the form of Holinshed's *Chronicles*, which the printer Reginald Wolfe was probably already promoting in the early

---

[31] *The Mirror for Magistrates*, ed. Lily B. Campbell (Cambridge: Cambridge University Press, 1938), 373. Further page references in text.

[32] See *Mirror for Magistrates*, 110, 219, 267. The reference to More as an authority distinct and potentially discrepant from Hall suggests that the poets made use of Rastell's 1557 edition of *The History*.

1560s. In the absence of such a definitive chronicle, Baldwin makes the pragmatic choice to follow Hall, yet he also reserves the right to deviate from this and all sources: "and where we seme to swarve from his reasons and causes of dyvers doynges, there we gather upon conjecture such thinges as seeme most probable, or at the least most convenient for the furderaunce of our purpose" (267). This is close to a bald admission that the *Mirror* authors will alter and invent where necessary; yet after all, Baldwin reminds us, the *Mirror* is not a history, "for the only thing which is purposed herin, is by example of others miseries, to diswade all men from all sinnes and vices" (267).

The portrayal of Richard of Gloucester, who features as a villain in no fewer than eight complaints, is illustrative of how the *Mirror* authors both adapt the matter of chronicle and swerve beyond it. The first edition charges Richard unambiguously with the murder of his brother Clarence as well as that of Henry VI; these accusations are of course recorded in the chronicles, but generally as persistent rumours rather than facts.[33] Moreover, Clarence's lament states with an assuredness absent in any previous source that Richard was plotting to seize the throne long before the death of Edward IV, and for this reason used the "G" prophecy to poison the King's mind against Clarence. "For he endevoured to attayne the crowne/From which my life must nedes have held him downe" (232). The *Mirror's* depiction of Richard as a single-minded villain determined from his late adolescence to murder his way to the throne may reflect the influence of precisely those oral traditions to which the chronicles refer; more probably, though, the authors "swerve" from the textual sources on this point in order to further the didactic purpose of their work.

Recalling some of the earliest poems written after Bosworth, many of the tragedies in which Richard features lay stress on his inhuman and specifically bestial qualities. For Clarence he is a "wulfe," a "tirant," and a "butcher" (233); for Rivers he is an "incarned devyll" and a "cruell wolfe" (259), and for Shore's wife a "raging wolfe" (384). Hastings in the Tower's council chamber gazes with horror on the boar personified:

> Lowring on me with the goggle eye,
> The whetted tuske, and furrowed forhead hye,
> His Crooked shoulder bristellyke set up,
> With frothy Jawes, whose foame he chawed and suppd . . . (289)

---

[33] Hall goes further than More or Polydore Vergil in reporting Richard's killing of Henry VI in one place as fact, though in another as rumour; for Hall as for his predecessors, Richard's complicity in Clarence's death remains only a strong presumption. See Hall, *Edward IV*, CCxxiii[r], *Edward V*, 2[r]. See also David Womersley, *Divinity and State* (Oxford: Oxford University Press, 2010), 53; A. R. Myers, "Richard III and the Historical Tradition," *History* 53 (1968), 183.

Here the "crooked shoulder" derived from chronicle accounts merges seamlessly into the beast-fable figure of the boar.

Although the ostensible purpose of the *Mirror* is to dissuade readers from vice, Richard's victims generally owe their downfalls less to their moral failings than to their failure to interpret signs correctly, especially with regard to the animal imagery that pervades their tragedies. Clarence, victim of a twisted prophecy, offers a lengthy disquisition on how true prophecies can be distinguished from false. The true, he insists, "in writing though obscure/Are playne in sence" (191–2)—that is, though difficult to interpret, they are ultimately unambiguous. Moreover, where a prophecy indicates a particular man, it will not refer to him by contingent factors such as his initials or the beast he uses for a badge, but by indications of his essential character: "Truth is no Harold [herald] nor no Sophist sure:/She noteth not mens names, their shildes nor creastes,/Though she compare them unto birdes or beastes" (227). Yet while this should surely lead to the conclusion that Richard's crest has no particular significance, Clarence goes on to affirm the truth of a prophecy that "my brother Richard was the Bore,/Whose tuskes should teare my brothers boyes & me" (230). In this case, it appears, the contingent heraldic badge is also totemic essence of the man. The puzzle Clarence ponders here is the same encountered early in the reign of Henry VII by Bernard Andre, who wondered how Richard came to choose such an appropriately loathsome creature as his device, unless guided by God's hand.

Issues of interpretation and animal imagery come to the fore again in the lament of William Collingbourne, who appears with his heart smoking in his hand to complain of his unjust execution in Richard's reign. The historical Collingbourne was executed in 1484 for collusion with Henry Tudor, yet the *Mirror* follows Hall in claiming that Collingbourne was executed for no other crime than his verses: "not . . . contented with the deathe of diverse gentlemen suspected of treason, [Richard] muste extende his bloudy furye agaynste a poore gentleman called Collyngborne for makynge a small ryme."[34] That rhyme, of course, was the famous couplet "The Cat, the Rat, and Lovel our Dog/Do rule al England, under a Hog."[35] Collingbourne's lament emerges as both a plea for the liberty of poetry and a more pragmatic warning to poets to avoid stirring the wrath of the

---

[34] Hall, *Richard III*, xlii[r].

[35] *Mirror for Magistrates*, 349. The *Mirror* takes the wording of Collingbourne's rhyme from Fabyan, who does not fail to note Collingbourne's activities on behalf of Richmond. Lucas argues that Baldwin is responsible for reshaping Fabyan's account to make Collingbourne guilty of no other crime than poetry (210), yet it seems unlikely that Baldwin did not take inspiration from the relevant passage in Hall.

great.[36] Yet what Collingbourne purports to find most puzzling is how his rhyme could ever have been construed as treasonous. As he points out, the mere observation that Cat[esby], Rat[cliffe], and Lovell had highest authority under Richard was hardly controversial. "They ruled all, none could denye the same" (356). Nor, he insists, can it be treason to abbreviate a name for the sake of meter, nor to allude to someone by his heraldic badge. His argument, in other words, is that the connection between the animal names and the rulers of the realm is strictly metonymic, serving as a means of indicating the true subjects of his verse. Yet both Richard's counsellors and common readers have no trouble grasping that the relationship is also metaphoric, urging a comparison as well as acting as a pointer. As Collingbourne is forced to admit, "both sence and names do note them very nere" (357). Andre's dilemma rears its head again: by what is either pure coincidence or divine providence, the arbitrary badges and labels of the leaders of the regime correspond precisely with their essential natures.

Other speakers in *The Seconde Parte* show a similar puzzlement in the face of ambiguous—or all too transparent—signs. Rivers recalls how Richard, Buckingham, and Hastings met him on the road and trapped him with a false show of friendship. What startles him most is the perfection of their dissembling, "For commonly all that do counterfayte/In any thing, exceed the natural mean" (260), laughing or weeping with tell-tale immoderation. Rivers wonders how anyone should be able to keep so perfectly to the mean whilst departing so radically from the truth. The only answer can be that for Richard and his associates dissimulation is second nature, and hence not a departure from their true selves.[37] In the following tragedy, Hastings ponders the nature of signs and omens and comes to similar conclusions on the relationship between fate and contingency. Under normal circumstances, he acknowledges, the stumbling of a horse might mean nothing at all; most so-called signs "are but happs" (287), and it is both foolish and impious to imagine that one's fate can be disclosed by such events. Yet, he acknowledges, his own death at the Tower was the ordained punishment for his sins, and under these circumstances "happs" are indeed significant: "yf with sygnes thy synnes once joyne, beware" (287). In an atmosphere so suffused with providence as England in the

---

[36] On the contradictions of Collingbourne's lament, which appears to argue at once for freedom of speech and rigorous self-censorship, see Andrew Hadfield, *Literature, Politics and National Identity* (Cambridge: Cambridge University Press, 1994), 102–7; Lucas, *Mirror for Magistrates*, 210–20.

[37] Richard and his co-conspirators are not quite natural-born liars; Rivers blames the lawyer Catesby for corrupting their nobility, making "the boare a Hog, the Bul [Hastings] an oxe./The Swan [Buckingham] a Goose . . ." (261). They are nonetheless liars to the core.

days leading up to Richard's seizure of the throne, there are no chance events. Contingency and necessity go cheek by jowl.

These seeming paradoxes have a theological dimension. Following Aquinas, both Catholic and reformed theologians employed the term *convenientia,* or fittingness, to describe the coincidence of the necessary and the contingent. The term denotes God's capacity to order events (such as the Incarnation) in ways that are not only marvelous and just but aesthetically satisfying; it could also be used to describe the fitting correspondence between signs and their referents.[38] *Convenientia* is not a term one would expect to find associated with Richard of Gloucester who, as Baldwin remarks, "never kept measure in any of his doings" (371). Yet the *Mirror* authors would have found grounds for this perception of the man and his deeds in their primary source, Hall's chronicle, where the circumstantial and ironic history of Thomas More is overlaid with a resolutely providential vision of history. In Hall, Richard is not only a moral monster but a diabolical scourge "apoincted" to punish England before the land's redemption through the accession of the Tudors.[39] Minor additions and alterations to More's text underscore this implicit argument. Where More dismisses as a string of conjectures the theory that Richard connived in Clarence's death in order to smooth his path to the throne, Hall's version adds, somewhat incoherently "but this conjecture afterwarde took place."[40] In Hall, and still more in the *Mirror*, Richard resembles a penny that always comes up heads. He is (as a later adapter of the chronicle would observe) determined to prove a villain.

Richard's peculiar brand of determined evil makes him a splendid villain in the background of other men's and women's tragedies, but poses problems when the time comes for the tyrant to pronounce his own lament. In the introduction to Richard's tragedy, Baldwin transgresses the conventions of the *Mirror,* and indeed those of Christian charity, by affirming that Richard is damned: "imagine that you see him tormented with Dives in the diepe pit of Hell, and thence howling this that foloweth" (359). Even Hall had not gone so far, preferring to leave the fate of Richard's soul to "God whiche knewe his interior cogitacions at the hower of his deathe."[41] Baldwin

[38] See John Milbank and Catherine Pickstock, *Truth in Aquinas* (London: Routledge, 2001), 52–3; Michel Foucault, *The Order of Things* (London: Routledge, 1989), 20–1. On *convenientia* or "correspondence" in reformed theology, see Ann Kibbey, *The Interpretation of Material Shapes in Puritanism: A Study of Rhetoric, Prejudice and Violence* (Cambridge: Cambridge University Press, 1986), 78.

[39] Hall, Edward V, iʳ.; see Womersley, *Divinity and State,* 55 6.

[40] Hall, Edward V, iiʳ. See Myers, "Richard III and the Historical Tradition," 183.

[41] Hall, Richard III, lixʳ. Baldwin had earlier indulged a taste for imagining the horrors of the damned in his translated text, *Wonderfull Newes of the Death of Paule the III* (London, 1552?).

concludes that Richard must be damned because a penitent Richard cannot be imagined—such a Richard simply would not be Richard, at least not on the terms established by the preceding tragedies in the *Mirror*. Yet when the tyrant himself speaks, in a lament authored by Francis Segar, his tone is not so different from those mournful ghosts who have preceded him as might be expected. Richard is made to regret his overreaching and his sins, and even to extol Brakenbury's "constant minde" in refusing to be party to the murder of the princes: "Thee may I prayse, and my selfe discommend" (363). His adherence to the model of the penitent sinner provokes some consternation in the prose passage that follows the poem, with some of those assembled deeming it "not vehement ynough for so violent a man as kyng Rychard had bene." Baldwin admits that it is "to good for so yll a person" (371–2). Some are also troubled by the tragedy's irregular meter, but Baldwin makes this fault a virtue, saying "it is not meete that so disorderly and unnatural a man as kyng Rychard was, shuld observe any metrical order in his talke" (371). The dissatisfaction prompted by Segar's poem amongst the *Mirror* collaborators—who want a worse man, speaking better verse—is suggestive of the difficulties involved in giving such an overdetermined figure as Richard a plausible personal voice.

"Order"—the virtue which Richard III could observe neither in his life nor in Segar's poem—is something of a loaded term in *A Mirror for Magistrates*. As Baldwin acknowledges, the work was suppressed under Mary because "some of the counsayle would not suffer the booke to be printed in suche order as we had agreed and determined" (297). Though "order" here could mean simply manner or style, it is highly probable that the council's objections also bore on the book's order in the modern sense, that is, its sequence and scope. Why this period of English history, they must have wanted to know, and why these people? What sort of relevance to England's present state was being implied—and how near to the present did the authors intend to draw?[42] Baldwin works hard to soothe such anxieties with his repeated insistence that the sequence of the *Mirror* tragedies is derived directly from the chronicles. Thus, when he and his collaborators gather to hear and collate the tragedies of the *Seconde Parte*, their first action is to appoint one of their number to read aloud from the chronicle, so that they can note the "places" of their tragic subjects "& as they cum, so wil we orderly read them al" (244–5). By locking their historical subjects into this orderly sequence, the authors guard against the possibility that some of these dead men and women might get out of place and impinge upon the present in ways other than those prescribed by the *Mirror* format. The

---

[42] See Lucas, *Mirror for Magistrates,* 245.

apparent aim is to shut down all avenues of interaction between the past and the present except the approved mode of exemplarity.[43]

Yet Baldwin's determination to exclude any hint of untimeliness from the *Seconde Parte* by adhering to the correct sequence of deaths runs into difficulties almost at once. Following the tragedy of Rivers, the appointed reader takes up Hall's book in order to read further, but "whan the reader would have proceded in the chronicle which straight entreateth of the vilannous destruction of the lord Hastynges, I wylled him to surcease, because I had there his tragedye very learnedly penned" (267). Baldwin here seems to be referring us to a specific passage in Hall in which the downfall of Rivers is immediately followed by the destruction of Hastings—but any reader who turns to the chronicle for illumination will experience some perplexity. The passage in question is clearly not that which in Rivers is arrested *en route* from Ludlow to London, for though his eventual execution is foreshadowed there, it has not yet taken place within the chronology of the narrative, nor is there any mention of Hastings. The next reference to Rivers' fate occurs in a fairly complicated passage in the midst of the council chamber scene, when Hastings hears Richard accuse the widowed Queen of sorcery:

> the lorde Hastynges was better content in hys mynde that it was moved by her then by any other that he l[o]ved better, albeit hys hart grudged that he was not afore made of counsail of this matter as well as he was of the takyng of her kynred and of their puttyng to death, whiche were by hys assent before devysed to be beheaded at Pomfrete, this selfe same daye, in the whiche he was not ware that it was by other devised that he hym selfe should the same daye be beheaded at London: then sayed the protectour in what wyse that sorceresse and other of her counsayle, as Shores wyfe with her affinitie have by their sorcery and witchecrafte thus wasted my body . . .[44]

The closing of the snare on Hastings follows immediately after the reference to the sentence passed on Rivers and his fellows. Even here, both executions are described as things "devised" rather than done. It is only after the narration of Hastings' execution, and in the course of a retrospective account of his final morning, that the death of Rivers is reported as an accomplished fact. In conversation with his pursuivant, Hastings refers to a piece of knowledge "whiche few knowe yet, & mo shall shortly, that meant he that therle Ryvers and the lord Richard & sir Thomas Vaughan should that day be beheaded at Pomfrete, as thei were in dede, which acte

---

[43] One has only to recall the prominence in the politics of the 1550s of Cardinal Pole—grandson of the Duke of Clarence and last male heir of the Yorkist line—to grasp the necessity for caution in this regard.

[44] Hall, Edward V, xiii[r].

he wist wel should be done, but nothyng ware that the axe hong so nere his awne head."[45]

The question confronting Baldwin and his companions is apparently straightforward. Did Rivers meet his death before or after Hastings met his? What makes the question difficult to answer is not only the fact that their deaths occurred close together in time but almost two hundred miles apart; the greater difficulty is posed by the nested temporalities of More's narrative. First, the deaths of Rivers and his fellows are foreshadowed in the passage in which Hastings' death is reported as fact. Two pages later, the death of Hastings is foreshadowed in a passage in which the death of Rivers is reported as fact (a retrospective passage which also enfolds a flashback to the still earlier event of Hastings' imprisonment). It is not difficult to grasp the anxiety and occasional bafflement of Baldwin and his collaborators in the face of such narrative labyrinths. The project of the *Mirror* depends fundamentally on lives stopping at a definite point, whereafter the ghost may be imagined as returning to narrate its tragedy in full. As Segar's Richard III is made to say, "See here the fine and fatall fall of me . . . /Whych to all prynces a mu{}rour nowe may be" (370). Yet the chronicles, especially where Thomas More has left his mark, often fail to provide such timely satisfactions; instead, the order of chronicle time is always prone to be disrupted by shadows of future events, as well as by characters returning to influence events after their apparent deaths. As I shall argue in the final chapter, Shakespeare's creative encounter with this same aspect of chronicle time is crucial to what happens in *Richard III*.

By an unintended irony, the same sort of fluid temporality which perturbs Baldwin when he encounters it in the chronicles turns out to be profoundly characteristic of *The Seconde Parte of the Mirror for Magistrates*. The authors' concern with chronology breaks down entirely before the end of the volume, when the tragedies of Edmund, Duke of Somerset (*d.*1455) and the Blacksmith (Michael an Gof, *d.*1497) are inserted with the excuse that, though they fall out of sequence, the reading of them will "occupy the tyme while we be nowe together" (387). The "tyme" in which the company is supposed to be gathered is a still more vexed temporal question. In the opening address to the reader, Baldwin claims that the company met for a second time "according to our former appoyntment" (243), that is "seven nightes hence" (235) after their first meeting. Although this first meeting must be understood to have taken place in 1554–55, before the suppression of the first edition, the prose links early in *The Seconde Parte* suggest a date much closer to that of publication in 1563. Baldwin arrives bearing tragedies of

---

[45] Hall, Edward V, xv^r-v.

Hastings and Richard III delivered to him by the printer Thomas Marsh, who printed the first edition of the *Mirror* in 1559 and the second in 1563.[46] The collaborators express anxiety that one poem will be seen to endorse the Catholic doctrine of Purgatory, a concern that would hardly be necessary or appropriate under Mary. In the prose passage that precedes Hastings' tragedy, Baldwin implies that the company has access to William Rastell's edition of Thomas More, published in 1557; yet in the next prose link, he declares himself uncertain whether Lord Vaux, who died in 1556, has completed his poem on the Princes in the Tower. Some of the later prose passages are clearly set in the reign of Mary and Philip, with Baldwin expressing the wish to extend the *Mirror* "to the end of this king & Queenes raigne (if god so long will graunte us lyfe)" (387) and launching into a stern condemnation of those "frantyke heads whiche disable our Queene, because she is a woman, and our kynge, because he is a straunger" (420). The practical cause of this temporal incoherence is likely to have been Baldwin's death in 1563, which left the printer to publish a mixture of revised and unrevised material. The upshot is that the untimeliness of the *Seconde Parte* is easily a match for that of the chronicles it struggles to pin down in time.

Over the next half century and more, the *Mirror for Magistrates* gave rise to a host of additions, supplements, and imitations, peaking in the early 1590s with poems such as Samuel Daniel's *Complaint of Rosamund* (1592) and Drayton's *Matilda* (1594). These female complaints look back to and often explicitly refer to Churchyard's *Shore's Wife* as a precedent (and as a rival to be outdone). Yet in addition to seeking new tragic subjects from British history, English poets also returned to the Ricardian characters of the *Seconde Parte*. The single year 1593 saw a small flurry of such publications, including Giles Fletcher's "The rising to the crowne of Richard the third," Antony Chute's *Beawtie Dishonoured, Written Under the Title of Shore's Wife*, and Churchyard's own poem on Shore's wife reissued with augmentations by the author.

Like Francis Segar's earlier effort, Fletcher's poem on Richard III seeks to reproduce the voice of its dead subject; yet Fletcher's poem departs from the *Mirror* tradition when it asserts that it is not only narrated by Richard's ghost but "Written by him selfe."[47] Richard is driven to this autobiographical expedient by the fact that "the poets of this age" have become effeminate both in their subjects and their style, being willing only "to write of

[46] As Lucas notes (248), Marshe had printed a translation by John Dolman, the author of Hastings' tragedy, in 1561.
[47] Giles Fletcher, *Licia* (London, 1593), L1ʳ. (This interior title page is omitted from the volume's through-pagination.)

women and of womens falles/Who are too light for to be fortunes balles."[48]
Released from the *Mirror* framework, Richard is not required to repent
his misdeeds or offer himself up as a lesson in overreaching. Although he
acknowledges that following his rise to the throne he descended into the
misery of paranoia and self-doubt, he insists that he has no regrets. After
all, he argues, men have lost their lives and wits for lesser objects than the
crown that he attained, if only briefly. In his own eyes, that achievement
excuses all faults, moral and indeed metrical: "My verse is harsh, yet (reader)
doe not frowne,/I wore no garland but a golden Crowne."[49]

Richard's ability to avoid repentance is enabled in part by the fact that
the poem never arrives at Bosworth, though his fall is foreshadowed. The
narrative of Richard's "rising" embraces the period from the death of
Edward IV to Richard's usurpation and the murder of the princes, precisely the scope of time covered in More's *History*. Fletcher's strict adherence to the limits of More's text suggests that he was using Rastell's edition,
rather than the version embedded in longer chronicles, as does the fact
that he retains a degree of ambiguity (found in Rastell, but not in Hall) as
to Richard's culpability in the deaths of Henry VI and Clarence.

> *Henrie* the sixt deprived of his crowne,
> Fame doeth report I put him to the death,
> Thus fortune smyl'd, though after she did frowne,
> A daggers stab men say, did stop his breath.
> I carelesse was both how, and who were slaine,
> So that thereby a kingdome I could gaine.[50]

Though Richard leaves no doubt that he was capable of such deeds, he
neither admits nor denies having committed these murders in particular,
which are both described as matters of report. We are left with a tyrant
who glories in his crimes, but has only More's often ambiguous word as to
what they were.

Although Fletcher never departs from More's account, he does attribute
to Richard (or lets Richard attribute to himself) a more singular role in his
rise to power. Buckingham features in the poem only as an obstacle to be
overcome, and Catesby does not appear at all. Richard appears to rely less
on a circle of co-conspirators than on the support of the urban populace.
"I rais'd my friendes, my foes I cast them downe./This made the subjectes
flocke to me in swarmes."[51] This declaration seems to derive from More's

---

[48] Fletcher, *Licia,* 70. The image of "Fortunes balles" pursues an earlier conceit in which
Richard is at once Fortune's tennis partner and the ball in the match, but the gendered pun
is probably intended.
[49] Fletcher, *Licia*, 85.   [50] Fletcher, *Licia*, 72.
[51] Fletcher, *Licia*, 76.

report of how Edward V's erstwhile courtiers abandoned him to attend the Protector at Crosby Place; Fletcher, however, attributes the change in allegiance not to a small group of courtiers and politicians, but to the general public. Whereas in More the citizenry are never more than lukewarm in their embrace of the usurper, here they respond with enthusiasm to a political strongman who can demonstrate his power to reward and punish.[52]

Intriguingly, another poem published in the same year, Churchyard's augmented "Tragedy of Shores Wife," also draws attention to the role of popular and aristocratic support in Richard's rise to power:

> Woe worth the day, the time the howre and all,
> When subiects clapt the crowne on *Richards* head,
> Woe worth the Lordes, that sat in sumptuous hall,
> To honour him, that Princes blood so shead . . .[53]

Although the dissident Jacobean image of Richard III as a forerunner of constitutional monarchy (spurred by Camden's discovery of the "Titulus Regius") had yet to coalesce in the early 1590s, Fletcher and Churchyard both lay unprecedented stress on the role of the popular will in bringing Richard to the throne. There is some precedent for this in More's scornful description of Richard's "mockish election," but in all probability these writers were responding to growing public interest in elective monarchy in the context of the looming succession crisis of the 1590s. A similar interest would be shown on stage in *The True Tragedy of Richard III,* though in that play it is Henry VII, not Richard III, who benefits from election.

A more traditional image of Richard is found in Anthony Chute's *Beawtie Dishonoured.* "A true-borne-infant-bloud-spilling murtherer," Chute's Richard is no subtle Machiavel but an incontinent, ravening beast, "like to an yrefull bore" or "an angerie Bull."[54]

> Beare hence quoth he (and there withall reflected
> Fire sparkling furie from incensed eyes,
> Whose madding threat his lunacie detected,
> And told me he was taught to tyrannize)
> And then agayne in more incensed rage
> He cryes, beare hence this monster of her age.[55]

---

[52] Fletcher's vision of how a strong man might seize and wield power may owe something to his recent experience as ambassador to Russia. In *Of the Russe Common Wealth* (London, 1591), Fletcher declares that "the State and forme of their government is plaine tyrannicall" (20ʳ), describing a society in which everyone bullies those weaker than themselves whilst grovelling before their superiors.

[53] *Churchyard's Challenge* (London, 1593), 142.

[54] Antony Chute, *Beawtie Dishonoured, Written Under the Title of Shore's Wife* (London, 1593), 46, 48, 49.

[55] Chute, *Beawtie Dishonoured,* 47.

With Richard raving and Mistress Shore retaining her composure even as she is publicly stripped, the confrontation comes to resemble that between a pagan persecutor and an early Christian martyr. The irony of the grotesque Richard denouncing the beautiful and demure Mistress Shore as a monster is redoubled in his insistence that "Posteritie shall know thine Acte." It is, of course, Richard whose crimes will be remembered by all posterity, whilst Mistress Shore's "fame," the poem concludes, will "live for ever."[56]

Whereas Chute's raving, bestial Richard belongs to a type that would have been familiar to readers of earlier poetic works like the *Mirror for Magistrates*, Fletcher's scheming, self-sufficient Machiavel betrays the influence of another genre. If Fletcher had seen Shakespeare's *Richard, Duke of York* (or *Henry VI Part 3*), he would have discovered a Richard more independent and more cunning than any yet encountered in the poetic tradition, one who declares "I am myself alone" (5.6.84) and promises to "set the murderous Machiavel to school" (3.2.193). Intriguingly, Fletcher's Richard commences his tale with a theatrical metaphor, declaring "The Stage is set, for Stately matter fitte/Three partes are past, which Prince-like acted were,/To play the fourth, requires a Kingly witte."[57] Whether or not this passage involves a reference to Shakespeare's *Richard III*—as a play already acted or one yet to come—it makes clear that by 1593, even as Richard became the subject of a fresh outpouring of poetic complaint, the stage had become his natural home.[58]

5.3 RICHARD III ON THE ELIZABETHAN STAGE

The history of literary representations of Richard III in the Tudor era is a journey through genres. In the late fifteenth and early sixteenth centuries, Richard features primarily in ballads and songs. In the mid-Tudor era and well into the reign of Elizabeth, his characteristic genre is *Mirror*-style spectral complaint. Before the end of the century, however, Richard finds a

---

[56] Chute, *Beawtie Dishonoured*, 48, 54.

[57] Fletcher, *Licia*, L2ʳ.

[58] Katherine Duncan-Jones has suggested that the "three partes" refer to the popularly successful trilogy of *Henry VI* plays, whilst the reference to the fourth as yet to come implies that *Richard III* had not yet been acted in London. Katherine Duncan-Jones, "Three Partes are Past: The Earliest Performances of Shakespeare's First Tetralogy," *Notes & Queries* 248 (March 2003): 20–1. Alternatively, the three parts might be the three plays by Shakespeare to feature Richard of Gloucester, namely *The First Part of the Contention, Richard Duke of York,* and *Richard III*. Perhaps the greater likelihood is that the reference is to Thomas Legge's three-part *Richardus Tertius*, performed at Cambridge in 1579 when Fletcher was a senior fellow of King's College.

new home on the stage. Richard features in six extant plays (three of them by Shakespeare) authored late in Elizabeth's reign, as well as in at least two lost works: Robert Wilson's *The Second Part of Henry Richmond* (1599), and Ben Jonson's *Richard Crookback* (1602).[59] With the probable exception of Julius Caesar and his contemporaries, Richard III appeared on the Elizabethan stage more often than any other historical or legendary figure.

The first play to feature Richard III as a character, Thomas Legge's *Richardus Tertius*, has some claim to be considered the first Elizabethan history play.[60] This lengthy Senecan tragedy (or rather trilogy) was staged over three successive nights at St John's College, Cambridge in 1579. The action of the first part begins immediately following the death of Edward IV, with the widowed Queen fretting over the well-being of her elder son on his journey from the Welsh marches; the last part concludes on Bosworth Field, with the victorious Richmond giving order for the burial of the dead and rejoicing in the deliverance of young George Stanley. The atmosphere and characterization are so heavily indebted to Seneca (the final part is introduced by a Fury, and references to Allecto and the Olympian deities are implausibly frequent) that it is easy to forget that the actions the play depicts took place in England less than a century before its performance. Yet a powerful link is drawn between the past and present in the epilogue, when Henry VII's mother is praised for having "by her endowment founded this distinguished College, consecrated to Christ."[61] Thus the fellows and students of St John's were reminded that their present happiness was a direct consequence of the deeds represented in the play. The past touches hands with the present in the continuity of institutions like Cambridge colleges. There is perhaps a note of delicate reproof to ungrateful posterity in the statement that Margaret Beaufort "has left behind her, for all centuries to see, many signs of her royal hand and her mind, which can never be praised sufficiently."[62]

---

[59] A third lost play, the *Buckingham* performed by Sussex's Men in 1593–94, probably dealt with that Buckingham who conspired with and rebelled against Richard III, though this is not certain. See Roslyn L. Knutson, *The Repertory of Shakespeare's Company, 1594–1613* (Fayetteville, AR: The University of Arkansas Press, 1991), 48, 70.

[60] More precisely, *Richardus Tertius* is the first play dealing with medieval English history both written and performed in the reign of Elizabeth. Alternative cases could be made for Sackville and Norton's *Gorboduc* (performed 1562), whose ancient British matter is derived from the chronicles, or for John Bale's *King Johan*, written in the 1530s but probably revised for performance in 1561.

[61] Thomas Legge, *The Complete Plays, Volume 1: Richardus Tertius*, ed. Dana F. Sutton (New York: Peter Lang, 1993), 323.

[62] Legge, *Richardus Tertius*, 323. Legge does not mention Richard's small clutch of successful foundations, but there is a possible reference to his abortive foundation of a chantry for one hundred priests at York Minster when the tyrant is made to vow that "walls will rise up, to the accompaniment of a hundred sacrifices" (*centum sacrificiis*) in order to appease

Richardus Tertius has been described as "slavishly dependent" on Hall and More, and it is true that almost all the matter of the play, as well as its sequence, derives from chronicle.[63] Yet Legge did not feel obliged to dramatize everything he found in his sources. There is no definite reference to Richard's congenital deformity, nor, though the play abounds with a Senecan swarm of Fates and Furies, is there any suggestion that Richard has been assigned by providence to be England's scourge.[64] Rather, he is a thuggish opportunist with a streak of cowardice to match his taste for violence. Richard owes his rise to the diabolical subtlety of his advisers, Catesby and Lovell, who suggest several of his most dastardly plots whilst restraining him from lashing out prematurely against his enemies. Both the usurper and his counsellors are fairly typical specimens of human evil, such as exist in every age. If the play's setting can be mistaken for classical Rome, it bears an equal and uncomfortable resemblance to contemporary England.

In a general sense, *Richardus Tertius* makes itself available for contemporary application in that it warns against ambition, treachery, and opportunism. Given its composition and performance in 1579, the year in which Elizabeth's courtship by the Duke of Anjou provoked widespread alarm, the play may well also have a more specific application. The third part devotes five successive scenes to Richard's effort to wed his niece Elizabeth, urged on by Catesby and Lovell (an interesting reversal of the Crowland chronicler's account, in which they force him to relinquish this same plan). Whilst Lovell urges the logic of the match on Elizabeth's mother, Richard himself unsuccessfully woos the princess, even offering her the opportunity to run him through in revenge for her brothers (a theatrical moment which may lie behind the similar offer made by Richard to Anne in Shakespeare's play).[65] Elizabeth rejects him with a vehement defence of her virginity and an echo of Cicero: "Oh, our morality, our evil times! [*O mores, nefanda o tempora!*] But a fierce bird will first pick at my entrails, you will first lay your cruel hands upon me, or send against me whatever baleful monster you nourish, before I, a chaste

the populace (255–7). See Richard Barrie Dobson, *Church and Society in the Medieval North of England* (London: Hambledon, 1996), 227n.7. If Legge did know of the York chantry project, it may well have been by report rather than from textual sources.

[63] Thomas Legge, *Richardus Tertius*, ed. Robert J. Lordi (New York: Garland, 1979), x.

[64] The only reference to Richard's deformity occurs in the scene of Hastings' arrest where Richard complains that "this bloodless arm of mine has grown withered and refuses to work" (121) due to witchcraft; there is no indication that he refers to a pre-existing condition. See Howard B. Norland, *Neoclassical Tragedy in Elizabethan England* (Cranbury, NJ: Associated University Presses, 2009), 132.

[65] See Hugh M. Richmond, *Richard III* (Manchester: Manchester University Press, 1989), 26–7.

virgin, will succumb to this unclean marriage."[66] In the end, the audience knows, Elizabeth of York will relinquish her virginity in marriage to Henry Tudor, but the play does not appear to urge such a course on the reigning queen. Rather, the epilogue's reference to her as "a virgin who overcomes the hoary locks of age" suggests that her maidenhood should be accepted as a permanent condition.[67] *Richardus Tertius* thus participates, if somewhat ungallantly, in the celebration of Elizabeth as Virgin Queen—a cult which was emerging at precisely this time in the context of opposition to the Anjou match.[68]

Although *Richardus Tertius* circulated widely in manuscript and prompted the admiring Francis Meres to describe its author as one of "the best for Tragedie," the play was not printed, nor is it known to have been revived on stage.[69] The first Ricardian play to reach a broad English-speaking audience both on stage and in print was the anonymous *True Tragedy of Richard III*, written for the Queen's Men in the late 1580s or very early 1590s, and printed in 1594.[70] Its antihero is more central to the action than the tyrant in Legge's play, and also a good deal craftier. As in Clarence's tragedy in *The Mirror*, this Richard has been plotting his rise to power for years before the death of Edward IV:

> To be baser then a King I disdaine,
> And to be more then Protector, the law deny,
> Why my father got the Crowne, my brother won the Crowne,
> And I will weare the Crowne,
> Or ile make them hop without their crownes that denies me:
> Have I removed such logs out of my sight, as my brother Clarence

[66] Legge, *Richardus Tertius*, 293.   [67] Legge, *Richardus Tertius*, 323.

[68] Susan Doran, *Monarchy and Matrimony: The Courtships of Elizabeth I* (London: Routledge, 1996), 11, 171–2. Unlike some vocal opponents of the French marriage, Legge was not a militant Protestant, but was in fact noted for his toleration of Catholic students. If his epilogue is tepid in its praise of the reigning Queen, it is still more lacking in enthusiasm for the achievements of her father, singling out Elizabeth as "by far the most outstanding" legacy of Henry VIII. (So much for the Reformation.)

[69] Francis Meres, *Palladis Tamia* (London, 1598), 283.

[70] On the play's date, Roslyn L. Knutson suggests that it was in repertory before 1588, helping establish the Queen's Men's reputation as specialists in historical drama; see "The Start of Something Big," in *Locating the Queen's Men, 1583–1603*, ed. Helen M. Ostovich, Holger Schott Syme, Andrew Griffin (Farnham: Ashgate, 2009), 102; Brian Walsh argues that the play, which lacks a clown, was probably written after Tarlton's death in 1588; see *Shakespeare, the Queen's Men, and the Elizabethan Performance of History* (Cambridge: Cambridge University Press, 2009), 76. Lawrence Manley suggests that a performance of the play at New Park in 1588 would have helped establish the subsequent warm relationship between the Queen's Men and the Stanley family; see "Motives for Patronage: The Queen's Men at New Park, October 1588," in *Locating the Queen's Men,* 62. Scott McMillin and Sally Beth MacLean hazard no guess beyond that "it was written before it was published"; *The Queen's Men and their Plays* (Cambridge: Cambridge University Press, 1998), 95.

And king Henry the sixt, to suffer a child to shadow me,
Nay more, my nephew to disinherit me,
Yet most of all, to be released from the yoke of my brother
As I terme it, to become subject to his sonne,
No death nor hell shal not withhold me, but as I rule I wil raign. . . . [71]

It is hard to resist the suspicion that this speech gave Shakespeare part of the hint for Richard's groundbreaking soliloquy in *Henry VI, Part 3*:

I'll make my heaven to dream upon the crown,
And whiles I live, t'account this world but hell,
Until my misshaped trunk that bears this head
Be round impalèd with a glorious crown. (3.2.168–71)[72]

What both soliloquies introduce is a Richard substantially different from any seen before on the stage or page—one distinguished not only by his diabolical ambition but by his self-conscious adherence to an idiosyncratic set of mores. The self-congratulatory "As I terme it" of the *True Tragedy's* Richard denotes a character capable of standing outside his society's most hallowed customs and values, viewing them only as quaint habits ripe for the breaking.

Although the *True Tragedy's* Richard has more capacity for plotting than does Legge's tyrant, and it is he who leads Catesby into crime rather than the reverse, he is also characterized, as in *Richardus Tertius*, by a delight in violence for its own sake. Indeed, violence for him is an aesthetic activity, and it is generally when contemplating the murder of a rival that his language rises above the prosaic: "what are the babes but a puffe of/Gun-pouder?"; "the singing of a bullet shal send him merily to his longest home."[73] Violence is not only Richard's music but his meat and drink: "this verie day, I hope with this lame hand of mine, to rake out that hatefull heart of Richmond, and when I have it, to eate it panting hote with salt, and drinke his blood luke warme, tho I be sure twil poyson me."[74] The *True Tragedy's* Richard is not lacking in dynamism and even a certain grotesque charisma; nonetheless, G. B. Churchill's observations that he is "not only central but dominating," and that "the play is not the chronicle-history of a reign, it is purely the history of a character" seem greatly overstated.[75] Alongside the tyrant, a number of minor characters vie for the sympathy or fascination of the audience,

---

[71] *The True Tragedie of Richard the Third* (London, 1594), B4ʳ.
[72] These lines do not appear in the quarto text of *The True Tragedie of Richard, Duke of York*.
[73] *True Tragedie*, B4ʳ, G2ʳ.　　[74] *True Tragedie*, H2ᵛ–H3ʳ.
[75] George Bosworth Churchill, *Richard III up to Shakespeare* (Berlin: Mayer and Muller, 1900), 399.

including Richard's Page (a choric figure), and Shore's wife. There is also a brief appearance for Humphrey Banaster, the treacherous servant of Buckingham who, according to historical tradition, betrayed him into Richard's hands for the reward of a thousand pounds.

Much is also made of the role of the Lord Stanley in securing Richmond's victory, and of the perils undergone by his son George. The scene in which Stanley places the crown on Henry's head bears echoes of the old ballad *Bosworth Feilde*, suggesting that the king's elevation is a matter of aristocratic choice more than inherited right: "my sonne, the Peeres by full consent, in that thou hast freed them from a tyrants yoke, have by election chosen thee as King."[76] *The Stanley Poem* also finds an echo in the play, when Rivers charges Richard with having "kept thy skin unscard, and let thine armor rust" in the Scottish campaigns (a charge, as we have seen, directly contradicted by the chronicles).[77] Although none of the Stanley ballads and poems dealing with Richard III had been printed at this time, the author of *The True Tragedy* might have had opportunity to read or hear these works, or others like them, on one of the Queen's Men's several visits to the Stanley estates in the late 1580s.[78] *The True Tragedy* would have been an ideal drama to present on one of the two occasions in 1589 when the company played at Knowsley, performing in a hall where Richard's tent hangings from Bosworth may have formed part of the backdrop.

Whether or not its sources include unpublished texts from the Stanley corpus, *The True Tragedy* is clearly based on a range of accounts. Like the *Mirror* poets, the author of the play is conscious of discrepancies between the textual sources, and can be ingenious in finding means of resolving these differences. When the appointed murderers of the princes meet to discuss their plans, they run through a range of possible methods of execution. Would it be best "suddenly to shoot them both through," to "take them by the heels and beat their brains against the walls," to "cut both their throats," or "between two feather beds smother them both"? Taken with Richard's own suggestion earlier in the play that the boys might serve as "food for fishes"—which, like the throat-cutting, is one of two versions offered in John Rastell's *Pastime of People*—this passage reflects consultation of a range of chronicles.[79] If the different methods cannot all be represented as historical fact, they can at least be staged as possibilities mooted at the time, thereby offering a kind of account of how these variants found

---

[76] *True Tragedie*, H4ᵛ. See Paulina Kewes, "History Plays and the Royal Succession," in *The Oxford Handbook of Holinshed's Chronicles*, ed. Paulina Kewes, Ian W. Archer, and Felicity Heal (Oxford: Oxford University Press, 2012), 507–10.
[77] *True Tragedie*, C3ᵛ.   [78] See Manley, "Motives for Patronage," 75.
[79] *True Tragedie*, E4ʳ⁻ᵛ, B4ʳ.   [80] Walsh, *Shakespeare, the Queen's Men*, 77.

their way into the historical record. There is a comparable effect near the end of the play, when Richard's Page gives his account of Bosworth Field to the allegorical character Report. The play not only stages the matter of the historical record, it stages the construction of that matter.

As Brian Walsh observes, "the 'thickness' of the *Richard III* discourse by the end of the sixteenth century, the result of the fact that it had been well told so many times already, was prominent in the minds of those who wrote and performed *The True Tragedy of Richard III*."[80] Indeed, the characters themselves seem to have a kind of foreknowledge of how they will be represented in that tradition. With an unmistakable nod to Thomas Churchyard, Shore's wife laments that she is fated to become "a mirrour and looking glasse,/To all her enemies."[81] The play even features a minor character, Lodowicke, who determines to author a poem on the fall of Mistress Shore, even as he denies her the aid for which she begs. In a comparable moment, Rivers appeals to his prospective reputation when he tells Richard "The Chronicles I record, talk of my fidelitie, & of my progeny/Wher, as in a glas you maist behold, thy ancestors & their trechery."[82] Yet the insight these characters seem to possess into their textual afterlives gives them little solace.[83] Rather, Lodowicke's choice to immortalize Mistress Shore in a poem rather than keep her alive with food in the present suggests how the textual "life" may be an uncanny other self—a doppelganger that thrives not only independently of but at the expense of the human individual. Much as in the *Mirror for Magistrates*, story-telling begins at the point where life ends.

Opening with a dialogue between the allegorical figures Truth and Poetrie, *The True Tragedy* promises its audience the spectacle of the past brought to life on the stage.

POETRIE: Truth well met.
TRUTH: Thankes Poetrie, what makes thou upon a stage?
POET: Shadowes.
TRUTH: Then will I adde bodies to the shadowes.
    Therefore depart and give Truth leave
    To shew her pageant.
POETRIE: Why will Truth be a Player?
TRUTH: No, but Tragedia like for to present
    A Tragedie in England done but late . . .[84]

---

[81] *True Tragedie*, B2ᵛ.   [82] *True Tragedie*, C3ᵛ.

[83] In this, the characters resemble the Richard of Shakespeare's play, whose uncanny "'sense' . . . of his prior textual existence" is explored by Linda Charnes, *Notorious Identity: Materializing the Subject in Shakespeare* (Cambridge, MA: Harvard University Press, 1993), 30.

[84] *True Tragedie*, A3ʳ.

Whereas Poetry alone can offer nothing but shadows of absent actualities, Truth claims the semi-miraculous ability to make the real past really present.[85] In common with other Elizabethan accounts of historical drama, the play asks us to understand performance as a kind of resurrection.[86] A fundamental premise of such a resurrective theatre is, of course, that the past is truly dead and gone. For the necromantic magic of the drama to be worth performing, the past must be understood as incapable of participating in the present by any other means. This is a point that *The True Tragedy* does not fail to stress in variety ways. Truth's description of the matter of the entertainment as "a Tragedie in England done but late" emphasizes not only that the events it represents are comparatively recent, but also that they are fully concluded, *done*. The epilogue, in which the actors turn to the audience to recount the history of the English monarchy from the reign of Henry VII down to the present, is similarly fixated on conclusions. Thus we are told that Mary "raigned five yeares, foure moneths, and some odde dayes, and is buried in Westminster. When she was dead, her sister did succeed." Of Edward VI, it is said that "he did restore the Gospell to his light, and finished that his father left undone."[87] This statement must surely be regarded as controversial, if not simply false; many in Elizabethan England would have disputed whether the Reformation was indeed finished. Yet the work of the epilogue, which is also the work of the play as a whole, is to draw a line, or a series of lines, under the lives and deeds of the dead. The final speech celebrates the reign of Elizabeth as one whose peace and happiness constitute a clean break

---

[85] Truth's attempt to claim primacy and self-sufficiency is at least partially undercut by the odd suggestion that one might "adde bodies to the shadowes"—as if the body were a supplement to its shadow rather than the reverse, or as if a shadow could cast a body. See Walsh, *Shakespeare, the Queen's Men*, 79–84.

[86] The *locus classicus* is Thomas Nashe's comment on *1 Henry VI*: "How it would have joyed brave Talbot (the terror of the French) to thinke that after he had lyne two hundred yeares in his Tombe, hee should triumphe againe on the Stage, and have his bones newe embalmed with the teares of ten thousand spectators (at severall times), who, in the Tragedian that represents his person, imagine they behold him fresh bleeding"; *Pierce Penilesse his Supplication to the Divell* in *The Works of Thomas Nashe*, ed. R. B. McKerrow, rev. F. P. Wilson (Oxford: Basil Blackwell, 1966), 1.212. See the discussions of this passage and its implications for the historical drama of Shakespeare and his contemporaries in Holger Schott Syme, *Theatre and Testimony in Shakespeare's England: A Culture of Mediation* (Cambridge: Cambridge University Press, 2012), 175–6; Brian Walsh, *Shakespeare, The Queen's Men*, 128–31; John J. Joughin, "Richard II and the Performance of Grief," in *Shakespeare's Histories and Counter-Histories*, ed. Dermot Cavanagh, Stuart Hampton-Reeves, and Stephen Longstaffe (Manchester: Manchester University Press, 2006), 15–31; Phyllis Rackin, *Stages of History: Shakespeare's English Chronicles* (Ithaca: Cornell University Press, 1990), 113–17.

[87] *True Tragedie*, I1ᵛ-I2ʳ.

with the troubles of the past, and beyond which no future either can or should be imagined:

> This is that Queene as writers truly say,
> That God had marked downe to live for aye. . . .
> For if her Graces dayes be brought to end,
> Your hope is gone, on whom did peace depend.[88]

The True Tragedy was printed in 1594, a year or two after Shakespeare's *Richard III* is generally thought to have been written, and possibly with the aim of capitalizing on the latter play's popularity. Though most scholars today regard *The True Tragedy* as the earlier work, probably by several years, some have granted precedence to Shakespeare's text.[89] There are few definite signs of borrowing in either direction, though both Richards are made to cry for "a horse, a horse" on Bosworth Field.[90] In light of the palpable influence of Shakespeare's play over almost every subsequent treatment of Richard III, it is difficult to imagine that the author of *True Tragedy* could have found nothing in Shakespeare's play worthy of emulation beyond this plea for equine assistance. On the other hand, as I shall argue in the concluding chapter, there are grounds for seeing Shakespeare's play as both meditating on and refuting the understanding of historical drama purveyed in *The True Tragedy*.

A full review of Shakespeare's use of his textual sources, a subject which has been explored in a number of excellent studies, lies beyond the scope of this chapter.[91] Nonetheless, it is worth pausing to note what Shakespeare's omissions, expansions and innovations, when read against his sources and the preceding tradition, suggest about his programme in the play. First of all, it is striking how thoroughly Shakespeare excises certain roles which previous treatments had caused to seem almost *de rigueur*. Neither Mistress Shore nor Dr Shaw (whose sermon on the bastardy of Edward's children is given prominent treatment by More and in Legge's play) is permitted even to appear on stage. The treacherous Banaster goes unmentioned. The role of Rivers, reliably prominent in

---

[88] *True Tragedie*, I2ʳ.

[89] For the latter view, see Richard Rowland's Introduction in Thomas Heywood, *The First and Second Parts of King Edward IV*, ed. Rowland (Manchester: Manchester University Press, 2005), 47.

[90] "A horse, a horse, a fresh horse"; *True Tragedie*, H3ʳ.

[91] There have been a number of excellent studies, from G. B. Churchill's *Richard III up to Shakespeare* at the dawn of the twentieth century to Dominique Goy-Blanquet's *Shakespeare's Early History Plays: From Chronicle to Stage* (Oxford: Oxford University Press, 2003) at the dawn of the twenty-first. James Siemon's recent Arden edition provides a useful survey: William Shakespeare, *Richard III*, ed. James Siemon (London: Methuen, 2009), 51–79.

chronicle, verse and drama, is fairly drastically reduced. Not only does Richard dominate the action to an extent not seen in any previous version, he takes a more exclusive role in initiating it. The corrupting role that the *Mirror* and *Richardus Tertius* assign to evil counselors belongs in Shakespeare to Richard alone.

As James Siemon has observed, Shakespeare's Richard differs from every previous incarnation in a number of respects.[92] No previous poetic or dramatic account lays such stress on his deformity, or grants it such weight in determining his character (though *The Stanley Poem* at least runs a close second to Shakespeare in this regard). No prior Richard competes with Shakespeare's in Machiavellian subtlety, dissimulation, and self-conscious theatricality; most strikingly of all, perhaps, no Richard before this has been funny. Yet whilst none of these qualities has been so prominently associated with Richard, not one of them is actually foreign to the tradition. As noted in the previous chapter, both Richard's wit and his theatricality can be traced back to More, but in *The History of Richard III* they are not associated with the tyrant; it is rather the citizens who make sly asides on the manner of his proceedings and liken his manoeuvres to stage plays. The figure of the protean dissembler is equally well-embedded in the tradition, but in the *Mirror for Magistrates* and *Richardus Tertius* it is embodied in Catesby, whilst in *Ladye Bessiye* similar qualities are associated with the poem's protagonists, not least Bessy herself. In short, the Richard of Shakespeare's play differs from his predecessors not because he departs from the tradition but because he distils, absorbs, and embodies it, including aspects previously associated with his critics and enemies. It is a little as if a history of the United States in the early 1970s should contrive to locate all the most memorable voices of the era—from the passion of the peace movement to the dark hedonism of the Velvet Underground and the gritty cool of blaxploitation cinema—in the person of Richard Milhous Nixon.

There is a clear and intriguing parallel between the way Richard (the dramatic character) rises to power at the expense of various enemies and obstacles, and the way Richard (as a dramatic function) comes to dominate the play at the expense of various counterpoints and subplots. There is also some reason to think that Shakespeare himself did not anticipate the extent to which his central character would eat up and crowd out the rest of the cast and story. The first scene's lewd banter between Richard and Clarence on the subject of Mistress Shore certainly raises the expectation that she will appear on the stage, yet she never does (though many directors feel obliged to correct Shakespeare's judgement on this point). An

---

[92] *Richard III*, ed. Siemon, 3–4, 39–44.

even stronger hint regarding a character who does not ultimately appear is given by Buckingham, who wishes upon himself a very specific punishment if he ever proves false to the Queen and her kin:

> When I have most need to employ a friend,
> And most assurèd that he is a friend,
> Deep, hollow, treacherous, and full of guile
> Be he unto me. (2.1.36–39)

For audiences who knew one of any number of previous treatments of the story, this ill-judged vow could only suggest his eventual betrayal by his servant Humphrey Banaster, to whom the Duke had shown great favour since his childhood. Sackville's Buckingham in the *Mirror for Magistrates* had denounced Banaster as a "caytief, that like a monster swarved,/From kynde and kyndenes" (652–53); in *The True Tragedy*, only the intervention of Richard's men prevents Buckingham from killing the servant who has sold him "for lucre."[93] A ballad on Banaster, printed in the early seventeenth century, may also be Elizabethan in origin.[94] Either Shakespeare at one point in the composition of the play intended to include Banaster as a character, or he knowingly set about raising an expectation that would be disappointed. In the event, the details of Buckingham's capture are neither staged nor reported, and both Buckingham and the audience are left to conclude that the false "friend" is Richard. Though the details of the curse do not square perfectly with the person of the king, Richard has so thoroughly monopolized false friendship by this late point in the play that there is no niche left in its economy for another, lesser traitor.

Shakespeare's success in making Richard the full embodiment of the broader historical tradition explains in part why his version became so instantly influential, indeed all but inescapable, for subsequent writers in the same tradition. The Richard who would next appear on the Elizabethan stage bears the Shakespearean imprint unmistakably. When Richard of Gloucester makes his first appearance in Thomas Heywood's *Edward IV Part Two* (1599), he is busily engineering the downfall of his brother Clarence by use of the "G" prophecy, even as he commiserates with his brother over the king's irrationality and their enemies in the court. He almost immediately begins to trade in asides lifted more or less directly from the Shakespearean text.

CLARENCE: God bless the king and those two sweet young princes!
GLOUCESTER: Amen, good brother Clarence.

---

[93] *True Tragedie*, F2ʳ.

[94] *A most sorrowfull Song, setting forth the miserable end of Banister, who betraied the Duke of Buckingham, his Lord and Master. To the tune of, Live with me and be my love* (1625). Banaster's treachery is recorded in *GCL*, 234–235, Fabyan, ccxxixʳ, and Hall, Richard III, xxxixᵛ–xlʳ.

DOCTOR SHAW: Amen.
GLOUCESTER: (*Aside*) And send them all to heaven, shortly, I beseech him.[95]

Richard's asides are so constant in this scene, and so heavy-handed, that the impression conveyed is less that of an ironic dissembler than of a compulsive self-accuser. Yet he is clearly meant to be a figure of Machiavellian subtlety and cunning. Alone, he briefly soliloquizes on his ambitions and the obstacles to be surmounted in a manner that hearkens unmistakably back to *3 Henry VI,* and perhaps to the *True Tragedy* as well:

> Ha! The mark thou aim'st at Richard, is a crown,
> And many stand betwixt thee and the same.
> What of all that? Doctor, play thou thy part:
> I'll climb up by degrees through many a heart. (II.11.109–12)

Richard's appearances are only infrequent for the rest of the play, which concludes with his coronation. The main focus is on a range of other characters, some of whom do not even appear in *Richard III.* Heywood is resourceful in seeking out those patches of ground not darkened by Shakespeare's shadow. The unctuous climber Dr Shaw crumbles with guilt after preaching on Richard's behalf and, haunted by a ghostly friar, resolves to starve himself to death in his study. The imprisoned princes are depicted in the most sentimental hues, comforting one another and reflecting on the likeness of their bed to the grave. But the chief focus is on the fate of Jane Shore and her long-suffering husband, whose story carries over from the play's *First Part.* Reconciled as husband and wife, the two share a kiss before dying in the streets as a result of Richard's cruel persecution. Whilst these characters all fall as a result of Richard's villainy and their own frailty, the usurper is seen thriving in the last scene, preparing to marry his queen and institute the Order of the Bath. When Buckingham storms out intent on raising rebellion for Richmond, Richard remarks placidly "He is displeased. Let him be pleased again/We have no time to think on angry men" (II.23.109–10).

One respect in which *Edward IV* both builds on and betters the example of *Richard III* is its engagement with the topography and atmosphere of late medieval London. Edward IV seeks out Mistress Shore at the Pelican in Lombard Street (I.17.28), whilst Richard condemns her to progress in a penitential sheet from Temple Bar to Aldgate (II.18.194–95). Crosby Place and St Helen's Bishopsgate feature prominently as well, with Sir John Crosby, a hero in *The First Part,* making them the keystones of his legacy:

> In Bishopsgate Street a poor house have I built,
> And, as my name, have called it Crosby House;

---

[95] Heywood, *First and Second Parts of Edward IV,* Part 2, scene 11, lines 7–9. Further scene and line references in the main text.

> And when as God shall take me from this life,
> In little St Helen's will I be buried. (I.16.28–31)

Crosby Place was, of course, neither "poor" in itself nor built for relief of the poor; yet the passage seems to invite comparison between Crosby's benevolence and the notorious miserliness of Sir John Spencer, who still occupied the house in the late 1590s.[96]

After *Edward IV*, no surviving play produced before the Restoration attempts to wrest the matter of Richard III away from Shakespeare.[97] Other playwrights did try their hands at the story, but their works, if ever completed, are lost. One such play, Robert Wilson's *Second Part of Henry Richmond*, is known only through Henslowe's diary and through a note to Henslowe from Robert Shaa.[98] Stating that he has heard the play and liked it, Shaa provides a breakdown of the characters involved in the first scenes, with Scene 5 featuring "K Rich: Catesb: Lovell. Norf. Northumb: Percye." The cast list includes a "Davye," suggestive perhaps of a rustic Welsh milieu, and also a number of minor characters familiar from ballad and folklore, such as Mitton (the bailiff of Shrewsbury to whom Richmond shows clemency in *The Rose of Englande*) and Banaster. It is possible that this is the play in which, as Robert Chamberlain would recall in the 1630s, an actor misspoke his lines so as to say "My Liege, the Duke of Banaster is tane,/and Buckingham is come for his reward."[99] If anything may be safely said of the content of *The Second Part of Henry Richmond*, it is that the play followed Heywood's lead in focusing on the poignant tales of commoners caught up in grand events, whilst confining Richard to a courtly, martial, and no doubt paranoid atmosphere.

Jonson's *Richard Crookback* is a still more shadowy ghost. The only record of its existence occurs in Henslowe's recording in June 1602 of a payment of £10 to the author in earnest of the play, along with his addi-

---

[96] See Rowland's Introduction to Heywood, *Edward IV*, 42.

[97] *The English Princess or the Death of Richard III* (1667) and *The Miseries of Civil War* (1680) both rework matter from *Richard III* for the tastes and politics of their era, as of course does Colley Cibber's enormously successful adaptation of 1700.

[98] *Henslowe Papers*, ed. W. W. Greg (London: A. H. Bullen, 1907), MS I.27, Art. 26, 49.There is no record of a first part of *Henry Richmond*, though both Heywood's *Edward IV* (which does not feature Richmond) and the lost play *Owen Tudor* have been suggested as candidates. See Roslyn L. Knutson, "Toe to Toe Across Maid Lane: Repertorial Competition at the Rose and Globe, 1599–1600," in *Acts of Criticism: Performance Matters in Shakespeare and His Contemporaries*, ed. June Schlueter and Paul Nelsen (Madison & Teaneck: Fairleigh Dickinson University Press, 2005), 23–4. Though Owen Tudor died in 1461 when his grandson was four, this does not preclude the possibility that Henry—and perhaps even Richard—featured somehow in that lost play.

[99] Robert Chamberlain, *A New Booke of Mistakes* (London, 1637), 50.

tions to Kyd's *Spanish Tragedy*.[100] It is not known whether the play was completed; if it was finished and performed, Jonson clearly chose not to include it among his *Works* published in 1616. The two words of the title are our only guide to Jonson's intentions, and they suggest a much sharper focus on the character of Richard than attempted by Heywood or Wilson. Where those playwrights sought mainly to lay claim to the territory Shakespeare had left untouched, Jonson was apparently determined to present a direct response and rebuttal to Shakespeare's play. How the two plays would have differed is open to conjecture. *Sejanus his Fall*, Jonson's tragedy of the following year, is notable for its self-conscious fidelity to its classical sources, with whole speeches translated out of Tacitus. Jonson's copy of More's Latin history of *Richard III*, which survives in the library of Canterbury Cathedral, is thick with pencilled flowers and pointing hands, suggesting a similarly close engagement with the source text.[101] A particularly large hand points to the anecdote involving Mistlebrook and Potter which More had heard from his own father; this may well indicate an intention to dramatize the scene, but is perhaps also suggestive of an interest in the texture and transmission of memory. Such concerns are, of course, already pervasive in Shakespeare's version. One can well imagine that Jonson's aim was to produce a genuinely historical history play, with an implicit rebuke to Shakespeare's frequently cavalier treatment of the chronicles. Yet, if so, *Richard III* was an odd choice, for the extent of Shakespeare's engagement with More is apparent to any reader of both texts. Jonson may have concluded, on reflection, that this was not the right field on which to challenge the more senior playwright, turning instead to classical history where he had little difficulty in proving his greater learning and fidelity.

5.4 AFTER SHAKESPEARE

From the late 1590s onward there is hardly a poetic or dramatic text dealing with Richard III that does not reflect the influence of Shakespeare on the level of characterization, plot, verbal detail, or—in most cases—all three.[102] This

---

[100] Philip Henslowe, *Henslowe's Diary*, ed. R. A. Foakes, second edition (Cambridge: Cambridge University Press, 2002), 223.

[101] Robert C. Evans, "More's *Richard III* and Jonson's *Richard Crookback* and *Sejanus*," *Comparative Drama* 24 (1990): 97–132.

[102] That influence is not confined to *Richard III* alone. The play that introduces Richard as a Machiavellian schemer, *Henry VI Part 3*, was printed earlier (as *The True Tragedie of Richard Duke of York*, 1595) and its influence can be detected earlier as well. In Michael Drayton's *Englands Heroicall Epistles* (1597), Margaret derides Richard as: "Hee that's so

influence can be detected not only in the drama but in the old genre of the historical complaint, which enjoyed a revival in the second decade of the seventeenth century. Richard Niccols, whose poem on Sir Thomas Overbury in the Tower was discussed in the preceding chapter, was also the author of an addition to the *Mirror for Magistrates*; the various complainants in *A Winter Night's Vision* include the long neglected princes in the Tower as well as a new version of Richard III, replacing the unmetrical effort of Francis Segar. Niccols' main source for both of these tragedies is Thomas More, and at many points he closely paraphrases More's history.[103] Yet when Niccols is faced with the challenge of giving Richard a voice of his own, it is Shakespeare who provides a model. Where Shakespeare's Gloucester begins the play by lamenting the end of civil conflict—"Our stern alarums changed to merry meetings,/Our dreadful marches to delightful measures" (1.1.7–8)—Niccols' speaker echoes the complaint:

> The battels fought in field before,
> Were turn'd to meetings of sweet amitie,
> The war-gods thundring cannons dreadfull rore,
> And ratling drum-sounds warlike harmonie,
> To sweet tun'd noise of pleasing minstralsie . . .[104]

Another Jacobean poet, Christopher Brooke, went further in attempting to apply the lessons of Yorkist history to the present. *The Ghost of Richard III* (1614) follows Segar, Fletcher, and Niccols in making Richard the spectral narrator of his own rise and fall; at the same time, it depicts the ascent of a smooth political operator more suited to the Jacobean court than to the fifteenth century.[105] As Richard's Ghost prepares to tell of his rise to power, he offers a remarkable paean to the playwright who brought him back from the dead.

> To him that impt my fame with Clio's quill,
> Whose magick rais'd me from oblivion's den,
> That writ my storie on the Muses' hill,

like his Dam, her youngest Dick,/That foule, ilfavored, crookback'd stigmatick" (49ᵛ.) The verse is unmistakably a reworking of Margaret's words to Richard in *Henry VI Part 3*: "thou art neither like thy sire nor dam;/But like a foul misshapen stigmatic" (2.2.135–36).
[103] Thus, where More offers his famous description of Richard's paranoid behaviour after the murder of the princes—"Where he went abrode, his eyen whirled about, his body privily fenced, his hand ever on his dager" (More, *History*, 87)—Niccols versifies: "My eyes I whirled round about/ . . . And to be out of dreadfull danger's doubt,/My body privily was fenc'd about:/Upon my dagger still I kept my hand . . ." More, *History*, 87; Niccols, *A Winter Nights Vision*, in *A Mirour for Magistrates* (London, 1610), 758.
[104] Niccols, *Winter Nights Vision*, 753
[105] On the politics of Brooke's poem, see Michelle O'Callaghan, "'Talking Politics': Tyranny, Parliament, and Christopher Brooke's *The Ghost of Richard III* (1614)," *Historical Journal* 41 (1998): 97–120.

> And with my actions dignifi'd his pen;
> He that from Helicon sends many a rill,
> Whose nectared veines are drunke by thirstie men;
> Crown'd be his stile with fame, his head with bayes,
> And none detract, but gratulate his praise.[106]

Ensuing references to the great author's "scænes . . . on stage" extend and confirm the reference to Shakespeare's play. The poem abounds with close paraphrases of the Shakespearean text, from Richard's acknowledgement of being "not shap't for love" to his sarcastic "George rid post."[107] Even as it testifies to the adaptability of the Richard III saga to fresh political circumstances, Brooke's *Ghost* testifies to the extraordinary difficulty of stepping out of the crooked shadow cast by Shakespeare's tyrant. Whilst Brooke attempts to depict this influence in a positive light, as a revivifying stream from Mount Helicon, an apter image might be Milton's slightly later description of Shakespeare as a monument capable of petrifying his admirers, "mak[ing] us marble with too much conceiving."[108]

A certain literary tradition which, from the 1490s to the 1590s, had explored the crimes and punishment of Richard III in many styles and from many perspectives was effectively at an end.[109] Yet this is not the end of the story—nor the end of the stories. While it is true that Shakespeare's play had a tremendous and in some respects stifling impact on fresh literary production, it by no means follows that his was the only version of Richard III available to be read or heard in the early seventeenth century. The image of the past was not received from new works alone. Rather, it is demonstrably the case that the large majority of the poems and plays discussed in this chapter remained in circulation for decades after the composition of Shakespeare's play. *The Mirror for Magistrates* was reprinted and expanded into the seventeenth century and, though Segar's Richard gave place to Niccols', the larger body of complaints involving Richard remained intact. Legge's *Richardus Tertius* undoubtedly continued to circulate in manuscript; of eleven known copies, at least four date to the seventeenth

---

[106] Christopher Brooke, *The Ghost of Richard III* (London, 1614), D2ʳ.

[107] Brooke, *Ghost*, D4ʳ, E1ʳ; cf., "Till George be pack'd with post-haste up to heaven" (1.1.146).

[108] John Milton, "On Shakespeare," in *Complete Shorter Poems*, ed. John Carey, second edition (London: Longman, 1997), l. 14.

[109] If one were seeking a substantial seventeenth-century work dealing with Richard's reign which bears little or no mark of Shakespeare's influence, John Beaumont's battle poem *Bosworth Field* (London, 1629) would be the likeliest candidate. (Even in this case, however, the poem's opening lines—"The Winter's storms of civil wars I sing/Whose end is crowned with our eternal spring"—bear what is probably more than an accidental resemblance to the opening of Richard's first soliloquy.)

century, one probably as late as 1640.[110] For many decades after Shakespeare wrote, the old prophecy regarding "Richard son of Richard" remained current in Chester, eventually being adapted in the eighteenth century into a new prophecy concerning "George son of George."[111] Though composed in the late fifteenth century, *Bosworth Feilde* is known only through a mid-seventeenth-century text, along with a late sixteenth-century prose digest of its content.[112] The ballad as we have it preserves an early seventeenth-century reading, concluding with a prayer that names "James of England that is our King!" (656)

Of all literary genres, ballads and songs seem most to resemble those artworks dubbed "anachronic" by Nagel and Wood—artworks "belonging to more than one historical moment simultaneously" through their participation in a chain of replications.[113] Reading *Bosworth Feilde* or *Ladye Bessiye*, we are often baffled to judge whether a particular word, line, or incident has its origins in the fifteenth century, the sixteenth, or the seventeenth. What we have are texts comprised of layers of readings from disparate periods, by readers who did not suppose that altering the linguistic web of the text changed its status either as a work of art or as a work of testimony. Precisely because they remained current over a long period, they have tended to elude or disappoint the attention of literary critics and historians bent on locating the work in a specific historical context. Most perplexing and intriguing of all is the case of *Ladye Bessiye*, transcribed in the reign of Elizabeth, in the reign of James (two of the surviving copies conclude with prayers for "our comely queene" and "our comely king" respectively), and under Charles II. The Restoration copy differs significantly from the other two, and though it is clearly "later" both in its date of transcription and in its lexicon and verse forms, it appears to preserve elements of the original matter not found elsewhere (including the names of certain local worthies and repeated invocations of "mild Mary").[114] It is all but impossible to say which version is "earlier" or closer to the "original," or to which era either belongs. What is clear is that the song remained in circulation for at least a century and a half after its composition, not only as an object of antiquarian curiosity but as a living text.

---

[110] Legge, *Richardus Tertius*, ed. Sutton, xxvii–xxix.

[111] Lesley Coote and Tim Thornton, "Richard, Son of Richard: Richard III and Political Prophecy," *Historical Research* 71 (2000): 325–30.

[112] The prose summary is contained in BL Harley MS 542.

[113] Alexander Nagel and Christopher S. Wood, *Anachronic Renaissance* (New York: Zone Books, 2010), 30.

[114] The Restoration copy also lacks the passages borrowed from *Bosworth Feilde* found in the others. See Helen Cooper, "Romance After 1400," in *The Cambridge History of Medieval Literature,* ed. David Wallace (Cambridge: Cambridge University Press, 1999), 708n.50.

The lively anachronism of *Lady Bessiye* may help us begin to grasp the still stranger temporality of Shakespeare's *Richard III*. Like *Lady Bessiye*, *Richard III* exists in more than one authoritative text, with the later of the printed versions (the Folio) probably reflecting an earlier state of composition. Beyond this, it contains verbal passages which are demonstrably much older than the putative date of composition—indeed, many decades older than its author. Phrases taken almost word for word from Thomas More, such as "the people were not used/To be spoke to but by the Recorder" (3.7.29–30), or "I saw good strawberries in your garden" (3.4.32) predate other parts of the dramatic text by close to eighty years. Arguably at least one line, "the dog is dead," is more than a century older than the play in which it appears. Similar things could be said, to a greater or lesser degree, of most of the works discussed in this chapter. What makes *Richard III* different is its awareness of its temporal paradoxes—an awareness that Richard will signal to the audience in the very first word he speaks on stage.

6

Now

"The time is out of joint" (*Hamlet*, 1.5.189). So Hamlet is forced to conclude, fresh from his encounter with his murdered father. By "the time," Hamlet seems to mean both the age in which he lives and the rhythm of things, the beat of events.[1] Cause and effect have lost touch; a murderer has not been punished, a son has failed to succeed his father, a dead man has not stayed in the ground. The past refuses to return, and no less stubbornly refuses to recede. Hamlet's grappling with the problem of disjointed time will eventually drive him to dabble in the art of historical re-enactment. As adapted by the prince of Denmark, the play called *The Murder of Gonzago* restages events which, Hamlet has learned from the Ghost, occurred in the castle garden not many months before. (Hamlet's inability to keep in mind just how much time has passed since his father's death is one of the play's most notorious instances of temporal disjunction.) By presenting these events on stage, Hamlet hopes to make the past unbearably present to the murderer Claudius, and at the same time to identify it as history—to put the past (back) in its place.

Impatient to witness the embodied fact of his father's death, Hamlet encourages or rather taunts the actor playing the killer Lucianus: "Begin, murderer. Pox, leave thy damnable faces, and begin. Come: 'the croaking raven doth bellow for revenge'" (3.2.230-32). The quotation is a version of a line spoken in an earlier play by Richard III, a role that Richard Burbage, the actor for whom Shakespeare wrote the part of Hamlet, had made famous, and with which he remained strongly associated.[2] But Burbage's Richard had never spoken these words, for they do not belong to Shakespeare's play but to its predecessor on the stage, *The True Tragedy*

---

[1] See Agnes Heller, *The Time is Out of Joint: Shakespeare as Philosopher of History* (Lanham, MD: Rowman & Littlefield, 2002).

[2] This is suggested by the anecdote recorded by John Manningham a year or two after *Hamlet* was first performed, in which Shakespeare plays "William the Conqueror" to Burbage's "Richard III"—yet another story centring on chronology and (missed) timing. See Shakespeare, *Richard III*, ed. James Siemon (London: Methuen, 2009), 83.

of Richard III. The lines assigned to the tyrant in the printed text of that play are only a little less silly than those recited by Hamlet:

> The screeking Raven sits croking for revenge.
> Whole hea[r]ds of beasts comes bellowing for revenge.[3]

Gaily misquoting *The True Tragedy*, Burbage–Hamlet is not only reminding the audience of his own prior performance as Richard III, but burlesquing a rival's performance in a still earlier play, which must have haunted Burbage's interpretation of the role. In an instance of what Marvin Carlson has described as theatrical "ghosting," the action on stage takes on an additional layer of meaning as the audience is prompted to recollect past performances.[4] Given how haunted the stage in *Hamlet* has become by this point, it is no great surprise to find that the burlesqued lines from *The True Tragedy* belong to a speech about ghosts.

> Meethinkes their ghoasts comes gaping for revenge,
> Whom I have slaine in reaching for a Crowne.
> Clarence complaines, and crieth for revenge.
> My Nephues bloods, Revenge, revenge, doth crie.
> The headlesse Peeres comes preasing for revenge.
> And every one cries, let the tyrant die.[5]

Commentators on this passage are generally content to conclude that Hamlet cites *The True Tragedy* as an example of the kind of melodramatic fustian that he (along with Shakespeare) despises.[6] Yet this explanation falls wide of the mark. Like other Queen's Men plays, *The True Tragedy* can more plausibly be charged with underwriting than with its opposite; even the lines above bear no comparison in terms of stylistic excess to Shakespeare's own early exploits in the *Henry VI* plays and *Titus Andronicus.* There is clearly something more at stake in the choice of this particular passage from this particular play.

The speech Hamlet cites is one in which a usurping king suffers torments of guilt for having murdered his brother and displaced his nephew in order to gain the crown. Quoting it as a prompt and parallel to the bloody acts represented in the play-within-a-play, Hamlet is effectively accusing his uncle of re-enacting the crimes of Richard III. Yet in addition to providing Hamlet with a mirror for Claudius's offences, *The True Tragedy* also provides

---

    [3] *The True Tragedie of Richard the Third* (London, 1594), H1ᵛ.
    [4] Marvin Carlson, *The Haunted Stage: The Theater as Memory Machine* (Ann Arbor: University of Michigan Press, 2001).
    [5] *True Tragedie*, H1ᵛ.
    [6] John Dover Wilson, *What Happens in Hamlet* (Cambridge: Cambridge University Press, 1951), 161; James C. Bulman, *The Heroic Idiom of Shakespearean Tragedy* (London: Associated University Presses, 1985), 76; Marjorie Garber, *Shakespeare's Ghost Writers: Literature as Uncanny Causality* (London: Methuen, 1987), 173–4.

him with a theory of historical drama that seems to underlie the staging of *The Murder of Gonzago*. His goal is precisely to "add bodies to the shadows," to supplement the shadowy Ghost who haunts the battlements with a fully present and embodied father capable of confronting Claudius with his sins. At the same time, the play offers Hamlet a means of exorcising the Ghost, replacing him with the more safely containable Player-King. If his stage is haunted, Hamlet hopes, he will not have to be. It is a wish very much in the spirit of *The True Tragedy*, as discussed in the previous chapter. For the Queen's Men, the insistence that the past can live again on stage is accompanied by—indeed, predicated upon—the confidence that it is for all other purposes dead and gone.

In *Hamlet*, Shakespeare resumes a conversation (if not an outright quarrel) with *The True Tragedy* which he had begun almost a decade earlier. The opening soliloquy of *Richard III* is, amongst other things, a virtuoso variation on the theme of bodies and shadows introduced in the opening dialogue of *The True Tragedy*. When Shakespeare's Richard speaks of his "deformed, unfinished" body, of the reflection he declines to court in "an amorous looking-glass," and of the scorn evoked by his "shadow in the sun," he describes the circumstances that have "determined" him "to be a villain." Whereas in *The True Tragedy* the union of bodies with shadows was associated with the promise of plenitude—the real past made really present on the stage—in the opening of *Richard III* their irreconcilable antagonism signals a time out of joint. Richard's argument with the shadows and reflections waiting to ambush him in the mirror and the street seems to signal the conflict between the historical person and the posthumous reputation that, as Linda Charnes suggests, "has always already preceded him."[7] The prospects for the revival of the past in the present become more complicated when the present seems to be running ahead of the past.

As discussed earlier in this book, Richard's opening soliloquy sets out to overturn the temporality of supersession, whereby one age is understood to have succeeded another. The soliloquy resists this temporal mode not only by introducing multitemporal motifs that will take on added resonance later in the play—"the deep bosom of the ocean" (1.1.4), "our bruisèd arms" (1.1.6)—but even in its syntax. "Now is the winter of our discontent" (1.1.1) is famously among the most commonly misunderstood phrases in Shakespeare. Appearing initially to announce that the winter of discontent coincides with the present moment, the unexpected appearance of a verb in the past tense at the start of the second

---

[7] Linda Charnes, *Notorious Identity: Materializing the Subject in Shakespeare* (Cambridge, MA: Harvard University Press, 1993), 28.

line shifts that presumed present into the past. "Now is the winter of our discontent/Made glorious summer by this son of York . . . ." What appeared to be a free-standing and intelligible sentence is metamorphosed, through an unanticipated enjambment, into part of an utterance with a very different meaning and relationship to time.

The momentary befuddlement imposed on the reader or auditor is undoubtedly intentional. No other play by Shakespeare begins like this— that is, with a pentameter line which appears to have a clear meaning but whose sense is retrospectively transformed as the sentence continues.[8] The effect is, on the other hand, not uncommon in Shakespeare's sonnets. Among the most striking instances are the openings of Sonnet 71 ("No longer mourn for me when I am dead/Than you shall hear the surly, sullen bell . . .") and Sonnet 15 ("When I consider everything that grows/Holds in perfection but a little moment . . ."). In each case, the initial word of the second line requires the reader to sharply revise if not overturn the initially obvious meaning of the first line.[9] Both sonnets begin by appearing to gesture to a definable moment in time (that in which the poet has died, or that in which he considers everything that grows) which, with the discovery of the unexpected enjambment, becomes unmoored and irretrievably elusive. This is precisely what happens in Richard's first soliloquy and (just as in the sonnets) the unsettling of temporality and tense correlates with the wider themes of the utterance.[10] Whereas celebrants of the new era are ever swift to affirm that

---

[8] Of Shakespeare's plays, about a dozen—almost all written in the first half of his career—begin with a pentameter line which can be understood as a complete sentence. In all of these cases except for *Richard III*, the first line either really is a complete sentence, or the next line does nothing to alter its sense and thrust. (The plays in question are *Comedy of Errors, 2 Henry IV, 1 Henry VI, 3 Henry VI, Julius Caesar, King John, Merchant of Venice, Troilus and Cressida, Twelfth Night,* and *Two Gentlemen of Verona*; three other plays, *Henry V, Othello* and *Henry VIII* constitute borderline cases, where the first line could just about make sense on its own, but the reader or auditor is unlikely to mistake it for a complete sentence. Other plays begin with prose, or with a line of verse which obviously requires a further line to complete the sense.)

[9] Although the first line of Sonnet 15 cannot be mistaken for a sentence in itself, it promises a sense and a sentence structure very different from what is heralded by the verb at the start of line 2. The reader is effectively required to revisit the first line and insert a silent "[that]" after "consider." As Stephen Booth remarks, "sonnets like number 15 . . . do not merely describe inconstancy but evoke a real sense of inconstancy from a real experience of it"; Booth, *An Essay on Shakespeare's Sonnets* (New Haven: Yale University Press, 1969), 181. On the shifting syntactical patterns of Sonnet 71, see also Sara Guyer, "Breath, Today: Celan's Translation of Shakespeare's Sonnet 71," *Comparative Literature* 57 (2005): 328–51.

[10] It is worth observing the structural similarity of the opening of the soliloquy to the opening of a sonnet, with lines 1–8 consisting of two sentences in the form of unrhymed quatrains, each beginning "Now" (1.1.1, 1.1.5). The sonnet pattern begins to break down after this, but elements of it crop up throughout the soliloquy. Lines 13–27 ("But I, that am not shaped for sportive tricks ... descant on my own deformity") concentrate all the soliloquy's references to Richard's misshapen body within a sonnet–like structure.

"that was then, this is now," the first two lines of the opening soliloquy stand that principle on its head. Richard is effectively declaring—"That was now, this is then."

Throughout this book I have pursued two linked theses regarding the relationship of Shakespeare's play to the historical era of Richard III. The first of these is that *Richard III* is the product of a world still thoroughly pervaded by traces and remnants of Ricardian time, ranging from inherited memories to serviceable domestic objects, and including both established institutions and unofficial practices. The second thesis, which has cropped up more sporadically, is that Shakespeare's play owes much of its power to its awareness of and interaction with these traces—an awareness we find registered in charged moments and passages which disrupt the normal temporality of historical drama. In this concluding chapter I would like to explore one further instance of untimeliness which I think sheds particular light on Shakespeare's way of working in this play.

The passage in question is the only one of any length to appear in the first Quarto of the play and not in the Folio. The longer Folio text is generally regarded by editors as closer to Shakespeare's original version of the play, whereas the Quarto is held to represent a shortened version more suitable for performance, and perhaps especially for touring the provinces. Yet in spite of whatever exigencies called for the trimming of the text, Shakespeare found occasion to insert a new passage of some twenty lines into the scene following Richard's coronation. Here is the passage in full, with lines paralleled in the Folio text in italics.

KING RICHARD: *As I remember, Henry the Sixth*
  Did prophesy that Richmond should be king,
  When Richmond was a little peevish boy.
  A king—perhaps, perhaps.
BUCKINGHAM: My lord?
KING RICHARD: How chance the prophet could not at that time
  Have told me, I being by, that I should kill him?
BUCKINGHAM: My lord, your promise for the earldom.
KING RICHARD: Richmond? When last I was at Exeter,
  The Mayor in courtesy showed me the castle,
  And called it "Rougemont," at which name I started,
  Because a bard of Ireland told me once
  I should not live long after I saw Richmond.
BUCKINGHAM: My Lord.
KING RICHARD: Ay? What's o'clock?
BUCKINGHAM: I am thus bold to put your grace in mind
  Of what you promised me.
KING RICHARD: Well, but what's o'clock?

BUCKINGHAM: Upon the stroke of ten.
KING RICHARD: Well, let it strike.
BUCKINGHAM: Why "let it strike"?
KING RICHARD: Because that like a jack thou keep'st the stroke
    Betwixt thy begging and my meditation.
    I am not in the giving vein today.
BUCKINGHAM: *Why then, resolve me whether you will or no.*
KING RICHARD: Tut, tut, *thou troublest me. I am not in the vein.*[11]

Both Buckingham and Richard bear witness in this passage to a rupturing of temporal norms.[12] For Buckingham, the perceived breakdown has to do with the time of promises; Richard has become king, yet Buckingham has not received the earldom of Hereford, which was to follow as a consequence.[13] From Richard's perspective, on the other hand, Buckingham now inhabits the temporality of the vexing "jack," the mechanical figure who struck the clock in many English churches. The comparison identifies Buckingham as at once over-punctual (the jack, an automaton, never waits for an appropriate moment to strike) and out of sync. The clocks of London churches famously failed to keep time with one another, and even the jacks of the Great Dial in St Paul's were, according to Thomas Dekker, noted for "quarrelling to strike eleven."[14] The image of the jack, then, permits Richard to accuse Buckingham not only of failing to know his time, but of being out of, or "betwixt," time. Buckingham, Richard's "other self" (2.2.121) who "so long held out with me untired" (4.2.45), has through his reluctance to participate in the murder of the princes put himself out

---

[11] William Shakespeare, *Richard III*, ed. John Jowett (Oxford: Oxford University Press, 2000), 4.2.96–120 (cf. ll. 98–121 in *Norton Shakespeare*). At the equivalent of l. 119 in F, Buckingham says "May it please you to resolve me in my suit?" The difference in tone is appropriate, as the much shorter exchange in F would not drive Buckingham to the same pitch of impatience.

[12] Although Richard's coronation is not shown on stage, it is worth noting that this scene seems to take place immediately following a ceremony which has its own complex sacramental temporality, being at once a unique event and a precise re-enactment of a prior event. There is a comparable concern with iteration and presence in the scene following King John's second coronation (*King John*, 4.2), on which see Janette Dillon, *Shakespeare and the Staging of English History* (Oxford: Oxford University Press, 2012), 55–6.

[13] As Mark Robson observes, "Buckingham is attempting to hold [Richard] to a predictable, ordered and measured sense of time, in which the period between the promise and its intended fulfilment has elapsed." See Robson, "Shakespeare's Words of the Future: Promising Richard III," *Textual Practice* 19 (2005): 23.

[14] Thomas Dekker, *The Guls Horne–Book* (London, 1609), 19. Dekker's phrase does not (necessarily) indicate that the jacks of St Paul's were unsynchronized, but it does evoke a distinctive "betwixt" time, when the jacks were obviously in motion but the hour had not yet definitively struck. I am grateful to Tiffany Stern for sharing with me her unpublished paper, "'Observe the Sawcinesse of the Jackes': Clock Jacks and the Complexity of Time in Early Modern England," given at the 2012 MLA conference in Seattle.

of favour and into a different temporal frame. The synchrony between the co-conspirators has given way to doubt-laden syncopation.

The lines preceding the direct confrontation between Richard and Buckingham, in which Richard muses on a pair of prophecies, are concerned with the shape of time on a grander scale. As Marjorie Garber has observed, dramatic prophecy, whose proper tense is the *futur antérieur* of what "will have occurred," presents us with the paradoxical temporality of historical drama in its most condensed form.[15] Recollection of the two prophecies places Richard in a similar position to that of the audience, for whom Richard's death and Richmond's accession belong both to the past and to the future. (The difference is that from Richard's point of view these are events that have been represented but not yet accomplished, whilst from the audience's perspective they have long since been accomplished but are yet to be represented.) The Rougemont prophecy, which belongs exclusively to the Quarto, is almost dizzyingly multitemporal, knitting together no fewer than five moments in time, including:

(1) the original prophecy by an Irish bard;

(2) the prophecy's false fulfilment at Rougemont Castle;

(3) the dramatic present, in which the newly crowned Richard ponders the two previous moments;

(4) the prophecy's actual fulfilment on Bosworth Field;

(5) the present time of the audience, for whom Bosworth is at once an accomplished historical fact and an anticipated future spectacle.

All of these moments seem to be looking backward and forward at one another simultaneously, and each can be seen as an iteration of the same event: Richard's downfall.

The temporality of this passage is further complicated by the fact that in recalling his visit to Rougemont, Richard is remembering an event that has not yet taken place. As Shakespeare's source for the anecdote makes clear, the King's visit to Exeter occurred some months after his coronation, in the aftermath of Buckingham's rebellion and execution. The story is recounted in a brief note by the Devonshire antiquary John Hooker inserted into the account of Richard's reign in the second edition of Holinshed's *Chronicles* (1587). Abraham Fleming, the general editor of the second edition, calls the reader's attention to the point at which Hooker's story is incorporated

---

[15] Marjorie Garber, "'What's Past Is Prologue': Temporality and Prophecy in Shakespeare's History Plays," in *Renaissance Genres: Essays on Theory, History, and Interpretation*, ed. Barbara Kiefer Lewalski (Cambridge: Harvard University Press, 1986), 306–7.

into the text, immediately following a report of Richard's reprisals against certain West Country worthies.

> Sir Thomas Sentleger which had married the duchesse of Excester the kings owne sister, and Thomas Rame, and diverse other were executed at Excester. Beside these persons, diverse of his houshold servants, whome either he suspected or doubted, were by great crueltie put to shamefull death. [By the observation of which mens names, the place, and the action here mentioned, with the computation of time, I find fit occasion to interlace a note (newlie received from the hands of one that is able to saie much by record) delivering a summarie (in more ample sort) of their names, whome king Richard did so tyrannicallie persecute and execute: as followeth.] King Richard (saith he) came this yeare to the citie, but in verie secret maner, whome the maior & his brethren in the best maner they could did receive, and then presented to him in a purse two hundred nobles; which he thankefullie accepted. And during his abode here he went about the citie, & viewed the seat of the same, & at length he came to the castell: and when he understood that it was called Rugemont, suddenlie he fell into a dumpe, and (as one astonied) said; Well, I see my daies not long. He spake this of a prophesie told him, that when he came once to Richmond, he should not long live after: which fell out in the end to be true, not in respect of this castle, but in respect of Henrie earle of Richmond, who the next yeare following met him at Bosworth field where he was slaine.[16]

It is not difficult to understand why this prophecy should have caught Shakespeare's eye, for it is of a piece with those which he had exploited to darkly ironic effect in the *Henry VI* plays, and which would feature no less prominently in the later histories.[17] Yet even more than the content of the anecdote, it is its relationship to the surrounding chronicle text that seems to have seized the playwright's attention and stimulated his thinking about temporality, synchrony and repetition. The manner whereby Fleming "interlaces" Hooker's note into the narrative is at once painstaking and oddly clumsy, becoming obtrusive precisely by seeking not to be. Fleming is moved to insert the note at this point because the Holinshed text

---

[16] Holinshed, 746.

[17] Superficially at least, the Rougemont prophecy resembles a number of other prophecies relating to individual doom in Shakespeare's histories: that the Duke of Suffolk should die by water, and the Duke of Somerset beside a castle (*2 Henry VI*); that Henry IV should die in Jerusalem (*2 Henry IV*). In each of these cases the prophecy is misleading, playing cruelly with sound and sense; Suffolk dies by the hand of a man named Walter, Somerset by an alehouse called the Castle, Henry at home in the Jerusalem Chamber. In this case, however, the most obvious reading of the prophecy is in fact the right one: Richard will meet his end by the hand of the man known throughout the play as Richmond, who is known to be Richard's mortal foe. How could Richard imagine that the prophecy might refer to anything else? It is tempting to see Richard here as an over-canny reader of prophesies (and history plays); it is because he *knows* that "Richmond" cannot *really* mean Richmond that he reacts with such dismay to the strained resemblance between "Richmond" and "Rougemont."

has just noted the executions of St Leger and Rame, whose names and deaths also feature in the information he had received from Hooker. Yet in the internal chronology of Hooker's note, these executions belong to an episode separate from and subsequent to Richard III's personal visit to Exeter and Rougemont. Hooker specifies that Richard learned of the local conspiracy against him only "after his departure"; Richard then issued orders for the apprehension and trial of those involved, so that ultimately "sir Thomas Sentleger, and one sir John Rame," having been indicted at Torrington, "were brought to Excester, and there at the Carefox were beheaded."[18]

The upshot of the botched grafting of narratives is that Richard's visit to Exeter appears to be prompted by what is in fact its consequence. The Rougemont incident takes place both before and after the deaths of Rame and St Leger, just as, in the temporality of prophecy, it takes place both before and after Richard's own death at Richmond's hands. Fleming's overstated concern to "interlace" Hooker's note at precisely the right moment, without disrupting the historical time-stream, results in a kind of temporal loop; on a certain page in the 1587 edition of Holinshed, Richard is forever coming to Exeter, starting at the name of Rougemont, leaving again and then ordering the deaths of St. Leger and Rame, whose names prompt a return to Exeter. . . . To adopt a metaphor closer to Shakespeare's imagination, Richard here resembles an actor in a long-running play, one for whom every action is a re-enactment and every entrance a return. Although for some (possibly including Hamlet) re-enactment holds open the promise of temporal fusion, making the past present, what Richard is forced to re-enact is precisely the failure of this promise, the moment in which the prophecy did not come to pass. At Rougemont he inhabits a "now" whose only burden is "not now."[19]

We have encountered such wrinkles in time previously in the course of this study. Similar slippages can be found elsewhere in Holinshed and Hall, as when these chroniclers attempt to weave the living memory of Mistress Shore's beauty into texts produced long after her death. *The Seconde Part*

[18] Holinshed, 746. On the somewhat murky chronology of Richard III's visit to Exeter in November 1483 and the indictment of the suspected rebels, see Rosemary Horrox, *Richard III: A Study in Service* (Cambridge: Cambridge University Press, 1989), 155–7. In *GCL*, St Leger and Rame are arrested "by the time of his thidyr cummyng or shortly afftyr" (235), and Richard has them executed before departing from Exeter.
[19] On the temporality of re-enactment, see Rebecca Schneider, *Performing Remains: Art and War in Times of Theatrical Reenactment* (London: Routledge, 2011). As Schneider shows, participants in re-enactment events (on Civil War battlefields and in performance art) may be animated by the desire to "trip the transitivity of time. . . . [I]f they repeat an event *just so*, getting the details as close as possible to fidelity, they will have touched time and time will have recurred" (10). Rather than dismissing such desires as mere fantasy, Schneider is interested in exploring precisely those performative conditions under which "something other than the discrete 'now' of everyday life can be said to occasionally occur—or recur" (14).

of the Mirror for Magistrates is no less susceptible to temporal paradoxes, as Baldwin and his collaborators prove incapable of ordering their dead subjects at a fixed distance from the present, or even of keeping the date of their meeting from slipping back and forth across several years. Comparison could also be made with the repeated discovery of the bodies of the princes in the seventeenth-century Tower, each discovery a re-enactment of the ones before, and each interrupting the bodies at a different "moment" in the course of the posthumous peregrinations described by Thomas More. Shakespeare, in other words, does not introduce a new element of untimeliness into the tradition, for untimely and anachronic effects are already intrinsic to the matter of Richard III. What distinguishes Shakespeare from the likes of Baldwin and Fleming is that we do not find him endeavouring to paper over the temporal cracks, but rather to prise them open still further.

The introduction of the Rougemont passage into the Quarto text exemplifies a mode of dramatic writing that characterizes the play as a whole. It may seem perverse to seek a clue to the composition of *Richard III* in a passage which is itself belated in relation to the rest of the text; yet, I would argue, no move could be more in the spirit of Shakespeare's project. Shakespeare happens upon a remnant, a memory—a story about what Richard III is supposed to have done and said in Exeter one afternoon—embedded in another setting, to which it most probably owes its preservation. He proceeds to work this remnant, together with traces of its former context, into his own text. Though Shakespeare's skill at interlacing greatly exceeds Fleming's, the effect is not one of perfect, seamless assimilation. Rather, in *Richard III* as in Holinshed, the operation creates warps, ruptures, and pleats in dramatic time. The Rougemont prophecy conveys into the text both its own dense cluster of prophetic temporalities and the untimeliness of its awkward placement in the chronicle. The latter sets up an immediate reverberation in Richard and Buckingham's dispute over clocks, time, and timing.

As the ripples from the Rougemont passage spread further through the play, they meet with others emanating from other loci of temporal instability: dead dogs and rotten armour, the Tower of London and the Black Deeps, not to mention the marvelous disjunctions of the opening soliloquy. The whole of the dramatic action is witnessed by the audience member or reader through a ceaselessly wavering temporal surface. There is no genuine possibility of saying whether what we are beholding is taking place "now" or "then," or of estimating the distance between these points. Like figures glimpsed through restless water, the play's characters and situations can seem remote and indistinct in one moment, and in the next unsettlingly near.

Now, almost close enough to touch.

Now, as distant as the ocean floor.

Bibliography

Ailes, Adrian, "Ancient Precedent or Tudor Fiction? Garter King of Arms and the Pronouncements of Thomas, Duke of Clarence," in Stevenson, ed., *Herald in Late Medieval Europe*, 29–40.

Anderson, Benedict, *Imagined Communities*, new edition (London: Verso, 2006).

Anderson, Thomas P., *Performing Early Modern Trauma from Shakespeare to Milton* (Aldershot: Ashgate, 2006).

Andre, Bernard, *Historia regis Henrici septimi*, in Memorials of King Henry the Seventh, ed. J. Gairdner (London: Rolls Series, 1858).

—— *Les Douze Triomphes de Henry VII*, in James Gairdner, ed., *Memorials of Henry VII* (London: Longman, 1858).

Anglo, Sydney, *Spectacle, Pageantry, and Early Tudor Policy* (Oxford: Clarendon Press, 1969).

Aquinas, Thomas, *Summa Theologiae, Volume 50: The One Mediator (3a. 16–26)*, ed. and trans. Colman O'Neill (London: Blackfriars, 1965).

Archer, Ian, *The Pursuit of Stability: Social Relations in Elizabethan London* (Cambridge: Cambridge University Press, 1991).

—— "The Nostalgia of John Stow," in *The Theatrical City: Culture, Theatre and Politics in London, 1576–1649*, ed. David L. Smith, Richard Strier, and David Bevington (Cambridge: Cambridge University Press, 1995), 17–34.

Armstrong, Jackson W., "The Development of the Office of Arms in England, *c.*1413–1485," in *The Herald in Late Medieval Europe*, ed. Stevenson, 9–28.

Ashdown-Hill, John, "The Bosworth Crucifix," *Transactions of the Leicestershire Archaeological and Historical Society* 78 (2004): 83–96.

—— "The Epitaph of King Richard III," *Ricardian* 18 (2008): 41–4.

—— *The Last Days of Richard III* (Stroud: The History Press, 2010).

Assmann, Jan, *Religion and Cultural Memory: Ten Studies*, trans. Rodney Livingstone (Stanford, CA: Stanford University Press, 2006).

Aubrey, John, *Miscellanies upon the Following Subjects* (London, 1696).

—— *The Natural History of Wiltshire*, ed. John Britton (London: Wiltshire Topographical Society, 1847).

—— *Brief Lives*, ed. Richard Barber (Woodbridge: Boydell Press, 1982).

Auden, W. H., *Selected Poems*, ed. Edward Mendelson (London: Faber and Faber, 1979).

Aune, M. G., "The Uses of Richard III: From Robert Cecil to Richard Nixon," *Shakespeare Bulletin* 24 (2006): 23–47.

Bacon, Francis, *The Historie of the Raigne of King Henry the Seventh* (London, 1622).

Baker, David Weil, "Jacobean Historiography and the Election of Richard III," *Huntington Library Quarterly* 70 (2007): 311–42.

Baldwin, David, "King Richard's Grave in Leicester," *Transactions of the Leicester Archaeological and Historical Society*, 60 (1986): 21–4.

Baldwin, William, *Wonderfull Newes of the Death of Paule the III* (London, 1552?).

—— *The Mirror for Magistrates*, ed. Lily B. Campbell (Cambridge: Cambridge University Press, 1938).

Bale, John, *Yet a Course at the Romyshe Foxe* (Zurich, 1543).

—— *An Expostulation or Complaynte agaynste the Blasphemyes of a Franticke Papyst of Hamshyre* (London, 1552).

Barrett, Robert W., Jr., *Against All England: Regional Identity and Cheshire Writing, 1195–1656* (Notre Dame, IN: University of Notre Dame Press, 2009).

Barwick, Humfrey, *A breefe discourse, concerning the force and effect of all manuall weapons of fire and the disability of the long bowe or archery, in respect of others of greater force now in use* (London, 1592).

Bate, Jonathan, and Dora Thornton, *Shakespeare: Staging the World* (London: British Museum Press, 2012).

Beaumont, John, *Bosworth Field* (London, 1629).

Beckwith, Sarah, and James Simpson, eds., *Premodern Shakespeare* (Special Issue), *Journal of Medieval and Early Modern Studies* 40.1 (2010).

Benjamin, Walter, *Illuminations*, ed. Hannah Arendt, trans. Harry Zorn (London: Pimlico, 1999).

Bennett, Michael John, *The Battle of Bosworth* (Stroud: Alan Sutton, 1985).

Billson, Charles James, *Medieval Leicester* (Leicester: Edgar Backus, 1920).

Binski, Paul, *Medieval Death: Ritual and Representation* (Ithaca, NY: Cornell University Press, 1996).

Bishop Percy's Folio Manuscript: Ballads and Romances, ed. John W. Hales, 3 vols. (London: N. Trübner, 1868).

Booth, Stephen, *An Essay on Shakespeare's Sonnets* (New Haven, CT: Yale University Press, 1969).

Borges, Jorge Luis, *Labyrinths*, ed. and trans. Donald A. Yates and James E. Irby (New York: New Directions, 1964).

Bosworth Feilde, in *Bishop Percy's Folio Manuscript: Ballads and Romances*, ed. John W. Hales (London: N. Trübner, 1868).

Botelho, Lynn, ed., *The History of Old Age in England, Volume 1: The Cultural Conception of Old Age in the Seventeenth Century* (London: Pickering and Chatto, 2008).

Boynton, Lindsay, *The Elizabethan Militia* (London: Routledge and Kegan Paul, 1967).

Bradbrook, M.C., *Shakespeare: The Poet in His World* (London: Weidenfeld and Nicolson, 1978).

Breeze, Andrew, "A Welsh Poem of 1485 on Richard III," *Ricardian* 18 (2008): 46–53.

Briggs, Katharine M., *A Dictionary of British Folk-Tales in the English Language, Part A: Folk Narratives* (London: Routledge and Kegan Paul, 1970).

Brooke, Christopher, *The Ghost of Richard III* (London, 1614).

Brooke, Nicholas, "Reflecting Gems and Dead Bones: Tragedy Versus History in *Richard III*," *Critical Quarterly* 7 (1965): 123–34.

Brooke, Ralph, *A Catalogue and Succession of the Kings, Princes, Dukes, Marquesses, Earles, and Viscounts of this Realme of England* (London, 1622).

Brooks, F. W., *York and the Council of the North* (London: St. Anthony's Press, 1954).

Broughton, Rowland, *A briefe discourse of the lyfe and death of . . . Sir William Pawlet* (London, 1572).

Bruster, Douglas, "The Dramatic Life of Objects," in *Staged Properties*, ed. Harris and Korda, 67–98.

Buck, George, *The History of King Richard III*, ed. Arthur Noel Kincaid (Gloucester: Alan Sutton, 1979).

Bulman, James C., *The Heroic Idiom of Shakespearean Tragedy* (London: Associated University Presses, 1985).

Burton, William, *The Description of Leicestershire* (London, 1622).

Camden, William, *Remaines of a Greater Worke, Concerning Britaine* (London, 1605).

—— *Britain*, trans. Philemon Holland (London: 1610).

Campbell, John, *The Lives of the Chief Justices of England* (London: John Murray, 1849)

Canino, Catherine Grace, *Shakespeare and the Nobility: The Negotiation of Lineage* (Cambridge: Cambridge University Press, 2007).

Carlson, Marvin, *The Haunted Stage: The Theater as Memory Machine* (Ann Arbor, MI: University of Michigan Press, 2001).

Cavendish, George, *The Life of Cardinal Wolsey*, ed. Samuel W. Singer (London: Harding and Lepard, 1827).

Chamberlain, Robert, *A New Booke of Mistakes* (London, 1637).

Charnes, Linda, *Notorious Identity: Materializing the Subject in Shakespeare* (Cambridge, MA: Harvard University Press, 1993).

Chaucer, Geoffrey, *Riverside Chaucer*, ed. L. D. Benson, third edition (Oxford: Oxford University Press, 1988).

Churchill, George Bosworth, *Richard III up to Shakespeare* (Berlin: Mayer and Muller, 1900).

Churchill, Winston, *Divi Britannici* (London, 1675).

Churchyard, Thomas, *Churchyard's Challenge* (London, 1593).

Chute, Anton, *Beawtie Dishonoured, Written Under the Title of Shore's Wife* (London, 1593).

Cooper, Helen, "Romance After 1400," in *The Cambridge History of Medieval Literature*, ed. David Wallace (Cambridge: Cambridge University Press, 1999), 690–719.

—— *Shakespeare and the Medieval World* (London: Methuen Drama, 2010).

Cooper, John P. D., *Propaganda and the Tudor State: Political Culture in the Westcountry* (Oxford: Clarendon Press, 2003).

Coote, Lesley, and Tim Thornton, "Richard, Son of Richard: Richard III and Political Prophecy," *Historical Research* 71 (2000): 321–30.

Corbett, Richard, *Certain Elegant Poems* (London, 1647).

Cornwallis, William, *The Encomium of Richard III*, ed. A. N. Kincaid (London: Turner and Devereaux, 1977).

Cowell, John, *The Interpreter* (London, 1607).

The Crowland Chronicle Continuations: 1459–1486, ed. Nicholas Pronay and John Cox (London: Richard III and Yorkist History Trust, 1986).

Cuttica, Cesare, "Thomas Scott of Canterbury (1566–1635): Patriot, Civic Radical, Puritan," *History of European Ideas* 34 (2008): 475–89.

Cyril of Jerusalem, St, *The Catechetical Lectures of St. Cyril, Archbishop of Jerusalem* (Oxford: Parker, 1838).

D., J., *A triple almanacke for the yeere of our Lorde God 1591* (London, 1591).

Danchev, Alex, "Like a Dog: Humiliation and Shame in the War on Terror," *Alternatives: Global, Local, Political* 31 (2006): 259–83.

Davies, C. S. L., "Tudor: What's in a Name?" *History* 97 (2012): 24–42.

Davies, Kathleen, *Periodization and Sovereignty: How Ideas of Feudalism and Secularization Govern the Politics of Time* (Philadelphia: University of Pennsylvania Press, 2008).

Davies, Robert, ed., *Extracts from the municipal records of the city of York, during the reigns of Edward IV, Edward V, and Richard III* (London: J. B. Nichols, 1843).

Davison, Peter, "Commerce and Patronage: The Lord Chamberlain's Men's Tour of 1597," in *Shakespeare Performed: Essays in Honour of R. A. Foakes*, ed. Grace Ioppolo (Cranbury, NJ: Associated University Presses), 56–71.

Day, Angel, *The English Secretary* (London, 1599).

Jacobus de Voragine, *Legenda aurea sanctorum* (London, 1483).

Deiter, Kristen, *The Tower of London in English Renaissance Drama: Icon of Opposition* (London: Routledge, 2008).

Dekker, Thomas, *The Guls Horne-Book* (London, 1609).

Dickens, A. G., *Late Monasticism and the Reformation* (London, Hambledon, 1994).

Dillon, Janette, *Shakespeare and the Staging of English History* (Oxford: Oxford University Press, 2012).

Dobson, Richard Barrie, *Church and Society in the Medieval North of England* (London: Hambledon, 1996).

Donno, Elizabeth Story, "Thomas More and Richard III," *Renaissance Quarterly* 35 (1982): 401–47.

Doran, Susan, *Monarchy and Matrimony: The Courtships of Elizabeth I* (London: Routledge, 1996).

Dragstra, Henk, "The Politics of Holiness: Royalty for the Masses in *The Wandring Jews Chronicle*," in *Transforming Holiness: Representations of Holiness in English and American Literary Texts*, ed. Irene Visser, Helen Wilcox (Leuven: Peeters, 2006): 61–80.

—— "'Before woomen were Readers': How John Aubrey Wrote Female Oral History," in *Oral Traditions and Gender in Early Modern Literary Texts*, ed. Mary Ellen Lamb and Karen Bamford (Aldershot: Ashgate, 2008).

Drayton, Michael, *Englands Heroicall Epistles* (London, 1597).

Duffy, Eamon, *The Stripping of the Altars: Traditional Religion in England, c.1400–c.1580* (New Haven: Yale University Press, 1992).

—— "Bare Ruined Choirs: Remembering Catholicism in Shakespeare's England," in *Theatre and Religion: Lancastrian Shakespeare*, ed. Richard Dutton, Alison

Findlay and Richard Wilson (Manchester: Manchester University Press, 2003), 40–57.

—— *Marking the Hours: English People and their Prayers 1240–1570* (New Haven: Yale University Press, 2006).

Duffy, Mark, *Royal Tombs of Medieval England* (Stroud: Tempus, 2003).

Dummelow, John, *The Wax Chandlers of London* (London: Phillimore, 1973).

Duncan-Jones, Katherine, "Three Partes are Past: The Earliest Performances of Shakespeare's First Tetralogy," *Notes and Queries* 248 (March 2003): 20–1.

Eaglestone, Robert, *The Holocaust and the Postmodern* (Oxford: Oxford University Press, 2004).

Erickson, Amy Louise, *Women and Property in Early Modern England* (London: Routledge, 1993).

Evans, Robert C., "More's *Richard III* and Jonson's *Richard Crookback* and *Sejanus*," *Comparative Drama* 24 (1990): 97–132.

Evelyn, John, *Numismata, a discourse of medals, ancient and modern* (London, 1697).

—— *The Diary of John Evelyn, Volume 1* (London: Routledge/Thoemmes Press, 1996).

Fabyan, Robert, *The New Chronicles of England and France* (London, 1516).

—— *Fabyan's Cronycle* (London, 1533).

Felman, Shoshana, and Dori Laub, *Testimony: Crises of Witnessing in Literature, Psychoanalysis and History* (London: Routledge, 1992).

Fiennes, Celia, *The Journeys of Celia Fiennes*, ed. John Hillaby (London: Macdonald, 1983).

Fletcher, Giles, *Of the Russe Common Wealth* (London, 1591).

—— *Licia* (London, 1593).

Foard, Glenn, "Update on the Bosworth Project: Autumn 2009," Bosworth Battlefield Survey, UK Battlefields Resource Centre, created by the UK Battlefields Trust: <http://www.battlefieldstrust.com/resource-centre/warsoftheroses/battlepageview.asp?pageid=824#>

Ford, John, *The Selected Plays of John Ford*, ed. Colin Gibson (Cambridge: Cambridge University Press, 1986).

Foucault, Michel, *The Order of Things* (London: Routledge, 1989).

Fox, Adam, *Oral and Literate Culture in England, 1500–1700* (Oxford: Oxford University Press, 2000).

Fox-Davies, Arthur Charles, *The Art of Heraldry: An Encylopedia of Armory* (London: T. C. and E. C. Jack, 1904).

—— *A Complete Guide to Heraldry* (London: T. C. and E. C. Jack, 1909).

Freeman, Thomas S., "'Ut Verus Christi Sequester': John Blacman and the Cult of Henry VI," in *The Fifteenth Century V: "Of Mice and Men": Image, Belief and Regulation in Late Medieval England*, ed. Linda Clark (Woodbridge: Boydell Press), 127–42.

Furness, H. H., ed., *New Variorum Edition of Shakespeare: King Richard III* (London: J. B. Lippincott, 1908).

Gairdner, J., ed., *Memorials of King Henry the Seventh* (London: Rolls Series, 1858).

Garber, Marjorie, " 'What's Past Is Prologue': Temporality and Prophecy in Shake-speare's History Plays," in *Renaissance Genres: Essays on Theory, History, and Interpretation*, ed. Barbara Kiefer Lewalski (Cambridge: Harvard University Press, 1986), 301–331.

—— *Shakespeare's Ghost Writers: Literature as Uncanny Causality* (London: Methuen, 1987).

Gasquet, Francis Aidan, *The Religious Life of King Henry VI* (London: G. Bell, 1923).

Gehlen, Arnold, *Urmensch und Spätkultur* (Frankfurt: Athenäum, 2004).

Geoffrey of Monmouth, *The History of the Kings of Britain*, trans. Lewis Thorpe (London: Penguin, 1966).

Gilchrist, Roberta, and Barry Sloane, *Requiem: The Medieval Monastic Cemetery in Britain* (London: Museum of London Archaeological Service, 2005).

Gimmler, Antje, *Institutions and Time: A Critical Theory and Pragmatist Approach*, Sociologisk Arbejdspapir 13 (Aalborg: Aalborg Universitetsforlag, 2003).

Gittings, Clare, *Death, Burial and the Individual in Early Modern England* (London: Croom Helm, 1984).

Godfrey, Walter H., with Sir Anthony Wagner, *College of Arms, Queen Victoria Street* (London: Committee for the Survey of the Memorials of Greater London, 1963).

Goodland, Katharine, *Female Mourning in Medieval and Renaissance English Drama* (Aldershot: Ashgate, 2005).

Goss, Charles W. F., *Crosby Hall: A Chapter in the History of London* (London: Crowther and Goodman, 1908).

Goy-Blanquet, Dominique, *Shakespeare's Early History Plays: From Chronicle to Stage* (Oxford: Oxford University Press, 2003).

Graves, Robert B., *Lighting the Shakespearean Stage, 1567–1642* (Carbondale: Southern Illinois University Press, 1999.)

The Great Chronicle of London, ed. A. H. Thomas and I. D. Thornley (London: George Thomas, 1938).

Greenblatt, Stephen, *Learning to Curse: Essays in Early Modern Culture* (New York: Routledge, 1990).

—— *Hamlet in Purgatory* (Princeton: Princeton University Press, 2000).

Griffiths, Ralph, "Succession and the Royal Dead in Later Medieval England," in *Making and Breaking the Rules: Succession in Medieval Europe, c.1000–c.1600/ Établir et abolir les normes: la succession dans l'Europe médiévale, vers 1000— vers 1600*, ed. Frédérique Lachaud and Michael Penman (Turnhout: Brepols), 97–109.

Gunn, Steven J., "Early Tudor Dates for the Death of Edward V," *Northern History* 28 (1992): 213–6.

Guyer, Sara, "Breath, Today: Celan's Translation of Shakespeare's Sonnet 71," *Comparative Literature* 57 (2005): 328–51.

Hackett, John, *Select and remarkable epitaphs on illustrious and other persons . . . with translations of such as are in Latin* (London, 1757).

Hadfield, Andrew, *Literature, Politics and National Identity* (Cambridge: Cambridge University Press, 1994).

Hall, Edward, *The Union of the Two Noble and Illustre Famelies of Lancastre & Yorke* (London, 1548).

Hammond, P. W., Anne F. Sutton, and Livia Visser-Fuchs, "The Reburial of Richard, Duke of York, July 21–30, 1476," *Ricardian* 10 (1994–96): 122–65.

Hanham, Alison, *Richard III and His Early Historians, 1483–1535* (Oxford: Clarendon Press, 1975).

—— *The Celys and their World: An English Merchant Family of the Fifteenth Century* (Cambridge: Cambridge University Press, 1985).

—— "Honing a History: Thomas More's Revisions of his *Richard III*," *Review of English Studies* 59 (2008): 197–218.

Harris, Jonathan Gil, *Untimely Matter in the Time of Shakespeare* (Philadelphia: University of Pennsylvania Press, 2009).

Harris, Jonathan Gil, and Natasha Korda, eds., *Staged Properties in Early Modern English Drama*, (Cambridge: Cambridge University Press, 2002).

Hay, Denys, *Polydore Vergil: Renaissance Historian and Man of Letters* (Oxford: Clarendon Press, 1952).

Hayward, Maria, *Rich Apparel: Clothing and the Law in Henry VIII's England* (Farnham: Ashgate, 2008).

Heller, Agnes, *The Time is Out of Joint: Shakespeare as Philosopher of History* (Lanham, MD: Rowman and Littlefield, 2002).

Henderson, Virginia K., "Retrieving the 'Crown in the Hawthorn Bush': The Origins of the Badges of Henry VII," in *Traditions and Transformations in Late Medieval England*, ed. Douglas Biggs, Sharon D. Michalove, A. Compton Reeves (Brill: Leiden, 2002), 237–60.

Henry, L. W., "The Earl of Essex as Strategist and Military Organizer," *English Historical Review* 68 (1953): 363–93.

Henslowe, Philip, *Henslowe Papers*, ed. W. W. Greg (London: A. H. Bullen, 1907).

—— *Henslowe's Diary*, ed. R. A. Foakes, second edition (Cambridge: Cambridge University Press, 2002).

Herbert, N. M., R. A. Griffiths, Susan Reynolds, Peter Clark, *The 1483 Gloucester Charter in History* (Gloucester: Alan Sutton, 1983).

Here begynneth the Cronycle of all the Kynges Names that have raygned in Englande syth the conquest of Willyam conquerour (London, 1530).

Heywood, Thomas, *The First and Second Parts of King Edward IV*, ed. Richard Rowland (Manchester: Manchester University Press, 2005).

Higgins, Alfred, "On the Work of Florentine Sculptors in England in the Early Part of the Sixteenth Century, with special reference to the tombs of Cardinal Wolsey and King Henry VIII," *Archaeological Journal* 51 (1894): 120–2.

Hillier, Kenneth, "William Colyngbourne," in *Richard III: Crown and People*, ed. Petre, 103–6.

Hillier, Kenneth, Peter Normark, Peter W. Hammond, "Colyngbourne's Rhyme," in *Richard III: Crown and People*, ed. Petre, 107–8.

Hipshon, David, *Richard III* (London: Routledge, 2011).

Hirsch, Marianne, *Family Frames: Photography, Narrative, and Postmemory* (Cambridge, MA: Harvard University Press, 1997).

—— "The Generation of Postmemory," *Poetics Today* 29 (2008): 108–11.

Historie of the Arrivall of Edward IV, ed. John Bruce (London: Camden Society, 1838).

Hodgdon, Barbara, "Shopping in the Archives: Material Memories," in *Shakespeare, Memory and Performance*, ed. Peter Holland (Cambridge: Cambridge University Press, 2006), 135–67.

Hodgkin, Katharine, and Susannah Radstone, eds., *Memory, History, Nation: Contested Pasts* (Piscataway, NJ: Transaction, 2005).

Höfele, Andreas, "Making History Memorable: More, Shakespeare and Richard III," in *Literature, Literary History and Cultural Memory* ed. Herbert Grabes, *REAL: Yearbook of Research in English and American Literature* 21 (Tubingen: Gunter Narr Verlag, 2005), 187–204.

Holinshed, Raphael, *Chronicles of England, Scotland, and Ireland*, 3 vols. (London, 1587).

Holmes, Martin, *Shakespeare and his Players* (London: John Murray, 1972).

Holtorf, Corneliu, *Monumental Past: The Life-histories of Megalithic Monuments in Mecklenburg-Vorpommern (Germany)*. Electronic monograph. University of Toronto: Centre for Instructional Technology Development. (2000–2008): http://hdl.handle.net/1807/245

Honan, Park, *Shakespeare: A Life* (Oxford: Oxford University Press, 1999).

Honigmann, E. A. J., and Susan Brock, *Playhouse Wills 1558–1642* (Manchester: Manchester University Press, 1993).

Hope, W. H. St. John, "The discovery of the remains of King Henry VI in St. George's chapel, Windsor Castle," *Archaeologia* 62 (1910/11): 533–42.

Horrox, Rosemary, "Richard III and Allhallows Barking by the Tower," *Ricardian* 6 (1982): 38–40.

—— *Richard III: A Study in Service* (Cambridge: Cambridge University Press, 1989).

Horrox, Rosemary, and P. W. Hammond, eds., *British Library Harleian Manuscript 433*, (Gloucester: Richard III Society, 1979).

Hoskins, W. G., *A History of the County of Leicestershire, Volume 2* (1954).

Houts, Elisabeth van, *Memory and Gender in Medieval Europe, 900–1200* (Toronto: University of Toronto Press, 1999).

Hubbocke, William, *An Oration Gratulatory to the High and Might James* (London, 1604).

Hughes, Jonathan, *The Religious Life of Richard III* (Stroud: Sutton, 1997).

Hunt, Alice, *The Drama of Coronation: Medieval Ceremony in Early Modern England* (Cambridge: Cambridge University Press, 2008).

Hutton, William, *The Battle of Bosworth Field*, second edition with additions by J. Nichols (London: Nichols, 1813).

Igartua, Juanjo, and Dario Paez, "Art and Remembering Traumatic Collective Events: The Case of the Spanish Civil War," in Pennebaker *et al.*, eds., *Collective Memory of Political Events*, 79–102.

Jackson, Ken, "'All the World to Nothing': Badiou, Zizek and Pauline Subjectivity in *Richard III*," *Shakespeare* 1 (2005): 29–52.

Johnson, Matthew, *Behind the Castle Gate: Medieval to Renaissance* (London: Routledge, 2002).

Johnston, Alexandra F. and Margaret Rogerson, eds., *Records of Early English Drama: York* (Toronto: University of Toronto Press, 1979).

Jones, Ann Rosalind, and Peter Stallybrass, *Renaissance Clothing and the Materials of Memory* (Cambridge: Cambridge University Press, 2000).

Jones, Michael K., and Malcolm G. Underwood, *The King's Mother: Lady Margaret Beaufort, Countess of Richmond and Derby* (Cambridge: Cambridge University Press, 1992).

Jonson, Ben, *Every Man Out of His Humour*, ed. Helen Ostovich (Manchester: Manchester University Press, 2001).

Joughin, John J., "Richard II and the Performance of Grief," in *Shakespeare's Histories and Counter-Histories*, ed. Dermot Cavanagh, Stuart Hampton-Reeves, and Stephen Longstaffe (Manchester: Manchester University Press, 2006), 15–31.

Julius, Philip, "Diary of the Journey of Philip Julius, Duke of Stettin-Pomerania, through England in the Year 1602," ed. Gottfried von Bülow and Wilfred Powell, *Transactions of the Royal Historical Society* New Series 6 (1892): 1–67.

Kafka, Franz, *The Trial*, trans. Willa and Edwin Muir (New York: Schocken Books, 1992).

Kamerick, Kathleen, *Popular Piety and Art in the Late Middle Ages: Image Worship and Idolatry in England 1350–1500* (London: Palgrave, 2002).

Kantorowicz, Ernst H., *The King's Two Bodies: A Study in Medieval Political Theology* (Princeton: Princeton University Press, 1957).

Keay, Anna, *The Elizabethan Tower of London: The Haiward and Gascoyne Plan of 1597* (London: London Topographical Society, 2001).

Kendall, Paul Murray, *Richard the Third* (New York: W. W. Norton, 1996).

Kewes, Paulina, "History Plays and the Royal Succession," in *The Oxford Handbook of Holinshed's Chronicles*, ed. Paulina Kewes, Ian W. Archer, and Felicity Heal (Oxford: Oxford University Press, 2012), 493–509.

Kibbey, Ann, *The Interpretation of Material Shapes in Puritanism: A Study of Rhetoric, Prejudice and Violence* (Cambridge: Cambridge University Press, 1986).

Kinney, Daniel, "The Tyrant Being Slain: Afterlives of More's *History of King Richard III*," in *English Renaissance Prose: History, Language and Politics*, ed. Neil Rhodes (Tempe, AZ: Medieval and Renaissance Texts and Studies, 1997), 35–56.

Knutson, Roslyn L., *The Repertory of Shakespeare's Company, 1594–1613* (Fayetteville, AR: University of Arkansas Press, 1991).

—— "Toe to Toe Across Maid Lane: Repertorial Competition at the Rose and Globe, 1599–1600," in *Acts of Criticism: Performance Matters in Shakespeare and His Contemporaries*, ed. June Schlueter and Paul Nelsen (Madison and Teaneck, NJ: Fairleigh Dickinson University Press, 2005), 21–37.

—— "The Start of Something Big," in *Locating the Queen's Men, 1583–1603*, ed. Ostovich, Syme, and Griffin, 99–108.

Kopytoff, Igor, "The Cultural Biography of Things: Commoditization as Process," in Arjun Appadurai, ed., *The Social Life of Things: Commodities in Culutral Perspective* (Cambridge: Cambridge University Press, 1984), 64–91.

Koslofsky, Craig, *Evening's Empire: A History of the Night in Early Modern Europe* (Cambridge: Cambridge University Press, 2011).

Ladye Bessiye, in *Bishop Percy's Folio Manuscript: Ballads and Romances*, ed. John W. Hales (London: N. Trübner, 1868).

Lancashire, Anne Begor, *London Civic Theatre: City Drama and Pageantry from Roman Times to 1558* (Cambridge: Cambridge University Press, 2002).

Larking, Lambert B., "Richard III at Leicester," *Notes and Queries* 2nd series 84 (8 August 1857): 102–3.

Laslett, Peter, "The Bewildering History of the History of Longevity," in *Validation of Exceptional Longevity*, ed. Bernard Jeune and James W. Vaupel (Odense: Odense University Press, 1999), 23–40.

Legg, Leopold G. Wickham, *English Coronation Records* (Westminster: A. Constable, 1901).

Leggatt, Alexander, *Shakespeare's Political Drama: The History Plays and the Roman Plays* (London: Routledge, 1988).

Legge, Thomas, *Richardus Tertius*, ed. Robert J. Lordi (New York: Garland, 1979).

—— *The Complete Plays, Volume 1: Richardus Tertius*, ed. Dana F. Sutton (New York: Peter Lang, 1993).

Leigh, Edward, *Choice Observations of all the Kings of England from the Saxons to the Death of King Charles the First* (London, 1661).

Leland, John, *The Itinerary of John Leland in or about the Years 1535–1543*, ed. Lucy Toulmin Smith, 5 vols (London: G. Bell, 1906–10).

Lemon, Rebecca, *Treason by Words: Literature, Law, and Rebellion in Shakespeare's England* (Ithaca, NY: Cornell University Press, 2007).

Lindenbaum, Sheila, "Ceremony and Oligarchy: The London Midsummer Watch," in *City and Spectacle in Medieval Europe*, ed. Barbara A. Hanawalt and Kathryn L. Reyerson (Minneapolis, MN: University of Minnesota Press, 1994), 171–88.

Lindley, Philip, *Tomb Destruction and Scholarship: Medieval Monuments in Early Modern England* (Donington: Shaun Tyas, 2007).

Llewellyn, Nigel, "The Royal Body: Monuments to the Dead, For the Living," in Lucy Gent and Nigel Llewellyn, eds., *The Renaissance Body: The Human Figure in English Culture, c. 1540–1660* (London: Reaktion, 1990), 218–40.

Lloyd, Lodowick, *The First Part of the Dial of Days* (London, 1590).

Llwyd, Dafydd, *Gwaith Dafydd Llwyd o Fathafarn*, ed. W. Leslie Richards (Cardiff: University of Wales Press, 1964).

Loades, D. M., *The Life and Career of William Paulet* (Aldershot: Ashgate, 2008).

Loftie, W. J., *Authorized Guide to the Tower of London* (London: HM Stationery Office, 1902).

Lucas, Scott, *A Mirror for Magistrates and the Politics of the English Reformation* (Amherst, MA: University of Massachusetts Press, 2009).

Luminet, Olivier, and Antonietta Curci, *Flashbulb Memories: New Issues and New Perspectives*, (Hove: Psychology Press, 2009).

Luxford, Julian M., "*Tres sunt Ricardi* and the Crowland Chronicle," *Ricardian* 18 (2008): 21–30.

McCoy, Richard C., "'The Wonderful Spectacle': The Civic Progress of Elizabeth I and the Troublesome Coronation," in *Coronations: Medieval and Early Modern Monarchic Ritual*, ed. János M. Bak (Berkeley, CA: University of California Press, 1990), 217–27.

McGee, C. E., "Politics and Platitudes: Sources of Civic Pageantry, 1486," *Renaissance Studies* 3 (1989): 29–34.

McKenna, John W., "Piety and Propaganda: The Cult of Henry VI," in *Chaucer and Middle English Studies in Honor of Rossell Hope Robbins*, ed. B. Rowland (Kent, OH: Kent State University Press, 1974), 72–88.

McMillin, Scott, and Sally Beth MacLean, *The Queen's Men and their Plays* (Cambridge: Cambridge University Press, 1998).

McMullan, Gordon, and David Matthews, eds., *Reading the Medieval in Early Modern England* (Cambridge: Cambridge University Press, 2007).

Malory, Thomas, *Le Morte d'Arthur* (London, 1485).

Mancini, Dominic, *The Usurpation of Richard III*, trans. C. A. J. Armstrong (Oxford: Clarendon Press, 1969).

Manley, Lawrence, *Literature and Culture in Early Modern London* (Cambridge: Cambridge University Press, 1995).

—— "Motives for Patronage: The Queen's Men at New Park, October 1588," in *Locating the Queen's Men*, ed. Ostovich, Syme, and Griffin, 51–64.

Manning, R. B., "The Prosecution of Sir Michael Blount, Lieutenant of the Tower of London, 1595," *Historical Research* 57 (1984): 216–24.

Marche, Stephen, "Mocking Dead Bones: Historical Memory and the Theater of the Dead in *Richard III*," *Comparative Drama* 37 (2003): 37–57.

Marshall, Peter, "Forgery and Miracles in the Reign of Henry VIII," *Past and Present* 178 (2003): 39–73.

—— *Religious Identities in Henry VIII's England* (Aldershot: Ashgate, 2006).

Marx, Karl, and Friedrich Engels, *The Communist Manifesto* (New York: International Publishers, 1948).

Maurer, Helen, "Bones in the Tower: A Discussion of Time, Place and Circumstance," *Ricardian* 8 (1990): 474–93; *Ricardian* 9 (1991): 2–22.

Mayer, Thomas F., "Becket's Bones Burnt! Cardinal Pole and the Invention and Dissemination of an Atrocity," in *Martyrs and Martyrdom in England, c.1400–1700*, ed. Thomas S. Freeman and Thomas F. Mayer (Woodbridge: Boydell, 2007), 126–43.

Melhuish, J., *The College of Richard III, Middleham* (London: Richard III Society, n.d).

Mentz, Steve, *At the Bottom of Shakespeare's Ocean* (London: Continuum, 2009).

Mercer, Malcolm, *The Medieval Gentry: Power, Leadership and Choice in the Wars of the Roses* (London: Continuum, 2010).

Meres, Francis, *Palladis Tamia* (London, 1598).

Meskell, Lynn, *Object Worlds in Ancient Egypt: Material Biographies Past and Present* (Oxford: Berg, 2004).

Michaels, Walter Benn, "'You who never was there': Slavery and the New Historicism, Deconstruction and the Holocaust," *Narrative* 4 (1996): 1–16.

Milbank, John, and Catherine Pickstock, *Truth in Aquinas* (London: Routledge, 2001).

Millar, Oliver, "Strafford and Van Dyck," in *For Veronica Wedgwood These: Studies in Seventeenth-Century History*, ed. Richard Ollard and Pamela Tudor-Craig (London: Collins, 1986), 124–33.

Milton, John, *Complete Shorter Poems*, ed. John Carey, second edition (London: Longman, 1997).

More, Thomas, *The History of King Richard III*, ed. R. S. Sylvester, vol. 2 in *The Complete Works of St. Thomas More* (New Haven, CT: Yale University Press, 1963).

Moryson, Fynes, *An Itinerary* (London, 1617).

Musil, Robert, "Denkmale," in *Nachlass zu Lebzeiten* (Zurich: Humanitas Verlag, 1936), 87–93.

Myers, A. R., "Richard III and the Historical Tradition," *History* 53 (1968): 181–202.

Nagel, Alexander, and Christopher S. Wood, *Anachronic Renaissance* (New York: Zone Books, 2010).

Nashe, Thomas, *The Works of Thomas Nashe*, ed. R. B. McKerrow, rev. F. P. Wilson, 5 vols. (Oxford: Basil Blackwell, 1966).

Nason, Arthur Huntington, *Heralds and Heraldry in Ben Jonson's Plays, Masques and Entertainments* (New York: Gordian Press, 1998).

Niccols, Richard, *A Winter Nights Vision*, in *A Mirour for Magistrates* (London, 1610).

—— *Sir Thomas Overburies Vision* (London, 1616).

Nichols, John Gough, "The Old Countess of Desmond," *Notes and Queries* vol. s3-I, 16 (1862): 302.

Noble, Mark, *History of the College of Arms* (London: Debrett, 1804).

Norman, Philip, and W. D. Caroe, *Crosby Place* (London: Committee for the Survey of the Memorials of Greater London, 1908).

O'Callaghan, Michelle, "'Talking Politics': Tyranny, Parliament, and Christopher Brooke's *The Ghost of Richard III* (1614)," *Historical Journal* 41 (1998): 97–120.

"The Old Countess of Desmond," *The Dublin Review* 51 (1862).

Old Meg of Hereford-shire, for a Mayd-Marian (London, 1609).

Ostovich, Helen M., Holger Schott Syme, Andrew Griffin, eds., *Locating the Queen's Men, 1583–1603* (Farnham: Ashgate, 2009).

Page, William, ed., *A History of the County of Norfolk: Volume 2* (London: Constable, 1906).

Parker, Henry, Lord Morley, *The exposition and declaration of the Psalme, Deus ultionum Dominus* (London, 1539).

—— "Account of Miracles Performed by the Holy Eucharist"(1554), BL Add. MS 12060.

Peck, Francis, *Memoirs of the Life and Actions of Oliver Cromwell* (London, 1740).

Pennebaker, James W., and Becky L. Banasik, "On the Creation and Maintenance of Collective Memories," in Pennebaker *et al.*, eds., *Collective Memory of Political Events*, 3–19.

Pennebaker, James W., *et al.*, eds., *Collective Memory of Political Events: Social Psychological Perspectives* (Mahwah, NJ: Lawrence Erlbaum Associates, 1997).

Perry, Curtis, and John Watkins, eds., *Shakespeare and the Middle Ages* (Oxford: Oxford University Press, 2009).

Petre, J., *Richard III: Crown and People* (London: Richard III Society, 1985).

Plato, *Plato's Dialogues*, trans. Benjamin Jowett, third edition (Oxford: Clarendon Press, 1892).

Polanyi, Karl, *The Great Transformation* (Boston: Beacon Press, 1944).

Pollard, A. F., "Tudor Gleanings I: The 'de facto' Act of Henry VII," *Bulletin of the Institute of Historical Research* 7 (1929): 1–12.

Purdy, Anthony, "The Bog Body as Mnemotope: Nationalist Archaeologies in Heaney and Tournier," *Style* 36 (2002): 93–110.

Rackin, Phyllis, *Stages of History: Shakespeare's English Chronicles* (Ithaca, NY: Cornell University Press, 1990).

Raleigh, Walter, *The History of the World* (London, 1614).

Rastell, John, *The Pastyme of People* (London, 1529).

Reed, Edwin, *Brief for Plaintiff: Bacon vs. Shakespeare* (New York: De Vinne Press, 1892).

Reid, R. R., *The King's Council in the North* (London: Longman, 1921).

Richmond, C. F., "The Death of Edward V," *Northern History* 25 (1989): 278–80.

Richmond, Hugh M., *Richard III* (Manchester: Manchester University Press, 1989).

Robson, Mark, "Shakespeare's Words of the Future: Promising Richard III," *Textual Practice* 19 (2005): 13–30.

Rogers, J.E. Thorold, *A History of Agricultural Prices in England* (Oxford: Clarendon Press, 1866–1902).

The Rose of Englande, in *Bishop Percy's Folio Manuscript: Ballads and Romances*, ed. John W. Hales (London: N. Trübner, 1868).

Ross, Charles, *Richard III* (London: Methuen, 1981).

Sanders, Eve Rachele, *Gender and Literacy on Stage in Early Modern England* (Cambridge: Cambridge University Press, 1998).

Sandford, Francis, *A Genealogical History of the Kings of England* (London, 1677).

Saul, Nigel, *The Three Richards: Richard I, Richard II and Richard III* (London: Hambledon Continuum, 2005).

Scase, Wendy, "Writing and the 'Poetics of Spectacle': Political Epiphanies in *The Arrivall of Edward IV* and Some Contemporary Lancastrian and Yorkist Texts," in *Images, Idolatry, and Iconoclasm in Late Medieval England: Textuality and the Visual Image*, ed. Jeremy Dimmick, James Simpson, and Nicolette Zeeman (Oxford: Oxford University Press, 2002), 172–84.

Schneider, Rebecca, *Performing Remains: Art and War in Times of Theatrical Reenactment* (London: Routledge, 2011).

Schoenbaum, Samuel, *William Shakespeare: A Documentary Life* (Oxford: Clarendon Press in association with Scolar Press, 1975).

—— *William Shakespeare: A Compact Documentary Life*, revised edition (Oxford: Oxford University Press, 1987).

Schofield, John, "The Topography and Buildings of London, ca. 1600," in *Material London, ca. 1600,* ed. Lena Cowen Orlin (Philadelphia: University of Pennsylvania Press, 2000), 296–321.

Schwenger, Peter, *The Tears of Things: Melancholy and Physical Objects* (Minneapolis, MN: University of Minnesota Press, 2008).

Schwyzer, Philip, *Literature, Nationalism and Memory in Early Modern England and Wales* (Cambridge: Cambridge University Press, 2004).

—— *Archaeologies of English Renaissance Literature* (Oxford: Oxford University Press, 2007).

Scotish Feilde and Flodden Feilde: Two Flodden Poems, ed. Ian F. Baird (New York: Garland, 1982).

Scott, Thomas, "Some passages taken out of an old manuscript written by Thomas Scott of Egreston," BL Add MS 62135.

Serres, Michel with Bruno Latour, *Conversations on Science, Culture, and Time,* trans. Roxanne Lepidus (Ann Arbor, MI: University of Michigan Press, 1995).

Shakespeare, William, *King Richard III*, ed. Janis Lull (Cambridge: Cambridge University Press, 1999), 70.

—— *Richard III*, ed. John Jowett (Oxford: Oxford University Press, 2000).

—— *The Norton Shakespeare*, ed. Stephen Greenblatt, Walter Cohen, Jean E. Howard, and Katherine Eisaman Maus, second edition (New York: W. W. Norton, 2008).

—— *King Richard III*, ed. James Siemon (London: Methuen, 2009).

Sheen, Erica, *Shakespeare and the Institution of Theatre: "The Best in this Kind"* (London: Palgrave, 2009).

Shell, Alison, *Oral Culture and Catholicism in Early Modern England* (Cambridge: Cambridge University Press, 2007).

Sher, Antony, *Year of the King* (London: Nick Hern, 2004).

Sherbrook, Michael, "The Fall of Religious Houses," in *Tudor Treatises*, ed. A. G. Dickens, YAS Rec. Ser. 125 (Wakefield: Yorkshire Archaeological Society, 1959).

Sidaway, James, "Shadows on the Path: Negotiating Geopolitics on an Urban Section of Britain's South West Coast Path," *Environment and Planning D: Society and Space* 27 (2009): 1091–116.

Siebert, Fred S., *Freedom of the Press in England, 1476–1776: The Rise and Decline of Government Control* (Urbana, IL: University of Illinois Press, 1965).

Siemon, James R., "Reconstructing the Past: History, Historicism, Histories," in *A Companion to English Renaissance Literature and Culture*, ed. Michael Hattaway (Oxford: Blackwell, 2002).

Simpson, James, *Reform and Cultural Revolution: 1350–1547* (Oxford: Oxford University Press, 2004).

Smyth, John, *The Lives of the Berkeleys, Vol. 2*, ed. John MacLean (Gloucester: Bristol and Gloucestershire Archaeological Society, 1883).

Sofer, Andrew, *The Stage Life of Props* (Ann Arbor, MI: University of Michigan Press, 2003).

Speed, John, *The History of Great Britain* (London, 1611).

Spitzenberger, Friederike, "Die Tierknochen aus der Babenbergergruft der Melker Stiftskirche," *Annalen des Naturhistorischen Museums Wien* 78 (1974): 481–3.

Stallybrass, Peter, "Worn Worlds: Clothes and Identity on the Renaissance Stage," in *Subject and Object in Renaissance Culture*, ed. Margreta de Grazia, Maureen Quilligan, and Peter Stallybrass (Cambridge: Cambridge University Press, 1996), 289–320.

Stanley, Thomas, *The Stanley Poem*, in *Palatine Anthology: A Collection of Ancient Poems Relating to Lancashire and Cheshire*, ed. J. O. Halliwell-Phillipps (London: C. and J. Adlard, 1850).

Steele, Richard, *A Discourse Concerning Old Age* (London, 1688).

Stevenson, Katie, ed., *The Herald in Late Medieval Europe* (Woodbridge: Boydell, 2009).

Stow, John, *Chronicles of England from Brute unto this Present Yeare of Christ* (London, 1580).

—— *The Abridgement of the English Chronicle* (London, 1618).

—— *A Survey of London: Reprinted from the Text of 1603*, ed. C. L. Kingsford (Oxford: Clarendon Press, 2000).

Strohm, Paul, *Theory and the Premodern Text* (Minneapolis, MN: University of Minnesota Press, 2000).

Strype, John, *Survey of London* (London, 1720).

Summit, Jennifer, and David Wallace, eds., *Medieval/Renaissance: After Periodization* (Special Issue), *Journal of Medieval and Early Modern Studies* 37.3 (2007).

Sutton, Anne F., and P. W. Hammond, *The Coronation of Richard III: The Extant Documents* (Gloucester: Alan Sutton, 1983).

Sutton, Anne F., and Livia Visser-Fuchs, *The Hours of Richard III* (Stroud: Alan Sutton, 1990).

—— *Richard III's Books: Ideals and Reality in the Life and Library of a Medieval Prince* (Stroud: Alan Sutton, 1997).

Sutton, Anne F. and Livia Visser-Fuchs with R. A. Griffiths, *The Royal Funerals of the House of York at Windsor* (Bury St Edmunds: Richard III Society, 2005).

Syme, Holger Schott, *Theatre and Testimony in Shakespeare's England: A Culture of Mediation* (Cambridge: Cambridge University Press, 2012).

Tanner, Lawrence E., and William Wright, "Recent Investigations Regarding the Fate of the Princes in the Tower," *Archaeologia* 84 (1935): 11–26.

Taylor, Andrew, *The Songs and Travels of a Tudor Minstrel: Richard Sheale of Tamworth* (Woodbridge: York Medieval Press, 2012).

Taylor, Diana, *The Archive and the Repertoire: Performing Cultural History in the Americas* (Durham, NC: Duke University Press, 2003).

John Taylor, *The old, old, very old man: or, The age and long life of Thomas Par . . . Whereunto is added a postscript, shewing the many remarkable accidents that hapned in the life of this old man* (London, 1635).

Teague, Frances, *Shakespeare's Speaking Properties* (Cranbury, NJ: Associated University Presses, 1991).

Terrell, Katherine H., "Rethinking the 'Corse in clot': Cleanness, Filth, and Bodily Decay in *Pearl*," *Studies in Philology* 105 (2008): 429–47.

Thompson, James, "Richard III at Leicester," *Notes and Queries* 2nd series 86 (22 August 1857): 153–4.

Thomson, Patricia, *Sir Thomas Wyatt and his Background* (Stanford: Stanford University Press, 1964).

The Three Wonders of the Age (London, 1636).

Throsby, John, *The History and Antiquities of the Ancient Town of Leicester* (Leicester: J. Brown, 1791).

The True Tragedie of Richard the Third (London, 1594).

Tudor-Craig, Pamela, *Richard III* (Ipswich: The Boydell Press, 1973).

Tusser, Thomas, *Five Hundreth Points of Good Husbandry* (London, 1573).

Twining, Lord [Edward], *A History of the Crown Jewels of Europe* (London: B. T. Batsford, 1960).

Vergil, Polydore, *Three Books of Polydore Vergil's English History, comprising the reigns of Henry VI, Edward IV, and Richard III*, ed. Sir Henry Ellis (London: Camden Society, 1844).

Wagner, Anthony, *Heralds of England: A History of the Office and College of Arms* (London: H. M. Stationery Office, 1967).

Walker, Greg, *Writing under Tyranny: English Literature and the Henrician Reformation* (Oxford: Oxford University Press, 2005).

Walpole, Horace, *Historic Doubts on the Life and Reign of King Richard III* (London: J. Dodsley, 1768).

Walsh, Brian, *Shakespeare, the Queen's Men, and the Elizabethan Performance of History* (Cambridge: Cambridge University Press, 2009).

Walsham, Alexandra, ed., *Relics and Remains* (Oxford: Oxford University Press, 2010).

—— "Skeletons in the Cupboard: Relics after the English Reformation": in *Relics and Remains*, ed. Walsham, 121–43.

—— "History, Memory, and the English Reformation," *The Historical Journal* 55 (2012): 899–938.

Walter Map, *De Nugis Curialum/Courtier's Trifles*, ed. and trans. M. R. James, rev. C. N. L. Brooke and R. A. B. Mynors (Oxford: Clarendon Press, 1983).

Warkworth, John, *A Chronicle of the First Thirteen Years of the Reign of King Edward the Fourth* (London: Camden Society, 1839).

Warnicke, Retha M., "Lord Morley's Statements about Richard III," *Albion* 15 (1983): 173–8.

—— "Sir Ralph Bigod: A Loyal Servant to King Richard III," *The Ricardian* 6 (1984): 299–301.

Weever, John, *Ancient Funerall Monuments* (London, 1631).

Weiss-Krejci, Estella, "Unusual Life, Unusual Death and the Fate of the Corpse: A Case Study from Dynastic Europe," in *Deviant Burial in the Archaeological Record*, ed. Eileen M. Murphy (Oxford: Oxbow Books, 2008), 169–90.

Whiting, Robert, *The Reformation of the English Parish Church* (Cambridge: Cambridge University Press, 2010).

Wilder, Lina Perkins, "Toward a Shakespearean Memory Theater: Romeo, the Apothecary, and the Performance of Memory," *Shakespeare Quarterly* 56 (2005): 156–75.

—— *Shakespeare's Memory Theatre: Recollection, Properties, and Character* (Cambridge: Cambridge University Press, 2010).

Williams, Gruffydd Aled, "The Bardic Road to Bosworth," *Transactions of the Honourable Society of Cymmrodorion* (1986): 7–31.

Williams, Raymond, *Marxism and Literature* (Oxford: Oxford University Press, 1977).

Williamson, Elizabeth, *The Materiality of Religion in Early Modern English Drama* (Farnham: Ashgate, 2009).

Wilson, John Dover, *What Happens in Hamlet* (Cambridge: Cambridge University Press, 1951).

Wilson, Thomas, *The Arte of Rhetorique for the Use of all Suche as are Studious of Eloquence* (London, 1553).

Womersley, David, *Divinity and State* (Oxford: Oxford University Press, 2010).

Wood, Andy, *The 1549 Rebellions and the Making of Early Modern England* (Cambridge: Cambridge University Press, 2007).

Woolf, D. R., *The Social Circulation of the Past: English Historical Culture 1500–1730* (Oxford: Oxford University Press, 2003).

Wortley, Clare Stuart, "Holbein's Sketch of the Wyat Coat of Arms," *The Burlington Magazine for Connoisseurs* 56 (1930): 211–13.

Wren, Christopher, *Parentalia: or, Memoirs of the Family of the Wrens* (London, 1750).

Wright, Thomas, ed., *Three Chapters of Letters Relating to the Suppression of Monasteries* (London: Camden Society, 1843).

Yates, Frances, *The Art of Memory* (London: Routledge and Kegan Paul, 1966).

Index

Printed and bound by CPI Group (UK) Ltd, Croydon, CR0 4YY